CONTRACT LAW AND PRACTICE

Contract Law and Practice

the English System and Continental Comparisons

by

Michael H. Whincup, LL.B., LL.M.

Barrister at Law
University of Keele

Third revised and enlarged edition
with a Foreword by Professor Bernard Rudden,
Professor of Comparative Law, University of Oxford

Kluwer Law International
The Hague · London · Boston

A C.I.P. Catalogue record for this book is available from the Library of Congress

ISBN 90 – 411– 0213 –2

Published by Kluwer Law International,
P.O. Box 85889, 2508 CN The Hague, The Netherlands.

Sold and distributed in the U.S.A. and Canada
by Kluwer Law International,
675 Massachusetts Avenue, Cambridge, MA 02139, U.S.A.

In all other countries, sold and distributed
by Kluwer Law International,
P.O. Box 85889, 2508 CN The Hague, The Netherlands.

Printed on acid-free paper

Cover Design: Boudewijn Betzema

Printed in The Nederlands

Contributors on the Law of Member States of the European Community

DANISH LAW

Professor Børge Dahl
Copenhagen Business School

DUTCH LAW

Professor Ewoud Hondius
University of Utrecht

FRENCH LAW

Jean-Paul Bertolas
Avocat, Paris
Professor Rémy Cabrillac
University of La Réunion

GERMAN LAW

Professor Klaus Tonner
University of Rostock

ITALIAN LAW

Professor Massimo Bianca
University of Rome
Professor Maria Costanza
University of Parma
Professor Bruno Inzitari
University of Pavia
Professor Salvatore Patti
University of Trieste

SPANISH LAW

Juan Antonio Ortega Diaz-Ambrona
General Secretary, Board of Directors, Repsol Petroleo SA
Enrique Helguera de la Villa
Director of International Legal Affairs, Repsol Petroleo SA

SWEDISH LAW

Dr Christina Hultmark
University of Gothenburg

Foreword

Once upon a time there were more markets than nations. Now there are more nations than markets. Europe is witnessing the rapid growth of an internal, and bustling, market in which goods, services, capital and people move and flourish with ever greater freedom. This market now covers the territories of 15 once-sovereign States and, to the East, another dozen are lining up to join it.

The new Europe can – indeed, ought to – tolerate large differences in family customs, inheritance law and the like. But it would seem that in the law of contract – the basis of a market economy – the persistence of distinct national systems of rules and techniques jostling each other within the same space causes unnecessary costs to producers and confusion to consumers. At least this is what is often assumed, although it is worth remembering that the USA seems to manage tolerably well with 50 different systems whose harmonisation (in such matters as the Uniform Commercial Code) is achieved not by federal fiat but by the attraction of the model, offered for adoption by each State of the Union. However that may be, the European Parliament has already resolved that there be a European Code of Private Law and has affirmed that 'unification can be carried out in branches of private law which are highly important for the development of a Single Market, such as contract law . . .' (OJEC C 158/401 26 June 1989). Indeed, under the expert aegis of Ole Lando and Hugh Beale, a draft Code of part of contract law has just seen the light of day (Nijhoff, 1995). It seems safe to say, however, that it will be decades ere such a Code becomes a legal reality. Meanwhile, the lawyers of the different traditions need to be able to understand and communicate with each other as they labour in the growing field of cross-border trade. That this book meets some such need is evident from the fact that a third edition is called for so soon.

Of the systems of Western Europe, it is those of England and Ireland that are hardest to grasp (Scotland would be no great trouble were it not for the English admixtures). The reasons are many, complex, and disputed, but (in relation to England) the following seem to stand out. First of all the general system is filled with secrets. There are many features that no one talks about: not because they are shameful matters but because, to an insider, they are so obvious that discussing them would be a waste of breath. Yet these are precisely the kind of things that outsiders have no reason to expect. For instance, it is taken for granted that the legislator rarely enacts anything important, in the sense of the basic rules of the system. In England the deliberate and unlawful killing of another person is murder, yet the Mother of Parliaments has never deigned to say so. Next, it is taken for granted that any legislation that looks as if it might enact such basic norms will in fact merely tinker about with fundamental rules that it never states. Open the Homicide Act 1957 – from its title, the outsider would expect to find the crime of murder defined and condemned; instead the Act assumes that murder is a crime, adjusts the punishment for it, and lists a number of cases where deliberate killing is a crime less than murder. Even more bewilderment awaits the rational reader who opens the lengthy Law of Property Act 1925, hoping to find therein a statement of the law of property; or the Supreme Court Acts expecting to find in them something about the system's highest court. And a similar point could be made about many important enactments in the field of general contract law, from the Law Reform (Frustrated Contracts) Act 1944 through the Misrepresentation Act 1967 to the Unfair Contract Terms Act 1977.

This feature is merely exasperating and time-wasting. But a second difficulty is more serious: it is that the foreign lawyer who looks at English law is confronted, not merely with occasional different rules but with an entirely different way of approaching and understanding the legal order: with, in modern terms, not just different programmes but an entirely different operating system. Hence, as Hans Goldschmidt pointed out in 1937, the more study devoted to the common law by foreign lawyers, the more discouraged they become. Certain technical areas (say, patents or merger regulation) are relatively approachable. But as soon as a question arises that calls for a sense of the legal order as a whole, the answer becomes far from easy, since even knowing where to begin is so often a mystery. Most native textbooks are written for insiders and so are hard to understand; and even worse are common-law statutes and cases.

But the pages which follow will go a long way towards easing the burden of the non-common-law lawyer, and will incidentally greatly enlighten the native. The outsider will find a lucid and concise description of the basic background of English law, followed by an account of the main stages in the birth, life and death of contractual obligations. The summaries of the other systems at the end of each section provide both enlightenment and ample material for reflection on the English law itself. We are given accounts from the standpoint of the great traditional civil-law models as well as that of the Nordic nations and of the very recently re-worked Dutch New Civil Code. Sometimes the brevity of these contributions makes their law look much easier than in practice it must be, but together they provide a set of perspectives on contract law in general and the common-law version in particular. For instance, the standard civil-law texts on contract are likely to begin with a sermon on the autonomy of the will and the sanctity of contractual freedom. Yet it is the common law which seems ready to respect the parties' intentions and allow them to bind themselves in honour only: that is, to keep at bay the entire State apparatus of laws, courts, and bailiffs. On the other hand, the reader will notice that this book's pages on the common law feel no great need to distinguish contracts involving public authorities and the public service from those of purely private interests; that complex commercial transactions between great companies are approached on the same footing as the everyday deals of ordinary people; and indeed that the argument will cross insouciantly all the lines well-known to civil-law systems, and will go straight from an international shipping contract to one involving a local authority's attempts to provide some service for the populace. The reader will also be struck – though this is partly a result of the relative space available – by the way in which (in the absence of enacted general principles) the common law is tied to particular cases: the book cites over 700 of them.

What emerges from a perusal of the whole volume is a confirmation of the major difficulty confronting the future development of a European private law. The great difference seems to lie between the common-law countries and the rest of Europe, and operates most strongly at the level of the legal order's operating system. Yet the tasks of the law of contract, and the problems facing lawyers, are much the same in all the countries featured. Many – probably most – of their solutions are very much alike. This should come as no surprise. 'Nearly all contracts – sale, hire, loan, deposit, partnership – are common to all people, they are *juris gentium*'. The first page of Justinian's first-year textbook told us that.

Bernard Rudden
21 September 1995

Preface

As a firm believer in the ideal of European unity, I would like to think that this book will make a small but useful contribution to the realisation of that ideal. The process of European integration brings with it the need for greater awareness and understanding of one another's ways of living and ways of thought. The need is perhaps most apparent in relation to Great Britain, insular and in a sense isolated, fundamentally different in much of its history and culture, yet bequeathing a system of law which for better or worse governs more than one-sixth of the world's population and which is the basis of much of the world's commerce.

As the European partnership develops, so English and Continental lawyers and students of law must learn more of each other's legal systems. My object in writing this book has been to try to meet that need with a straight-forward explanation of the basic principles of English commercial contract law, accessible to both English and Continental readers, and at the same time to provide for English students what may well be their first insight into Continental rules. Other comparative materials include references to Commonwealth and American practice, and to the United Nations Vienna Convention on Contracts for the International Sale of Goods which has been adopted in almost every country except Great Britain. I have tried to concentrate on matters of practical importance, and wherever possible have given examples of standard commercial usages and discussed their likely effects in law.

I am particularly grateful to my Continental colleagues who with the same philosophy have written commentaries or summaries at the end of each chapter on the relevant rules of seven other Member States of the Common Market. The commentaries are intended overall to illustrate the main points of comparison and contrast between the various systems, and thus to provide what I hope may be found interesting and instructive cross-references for practitioners and academics alike.

In this third edition I have attempted to state the law as at 1 January 1996.

Michael Whincup
Keele, February 1996

xi

Table of Contents

Table of UK Statutes

(References are to paragraph numbers.)

Table of UK Regulations

(References are to paragraph numbers.)

Table of Cases

(References are to paragraph numbers.)

Introduction

The English legal system

0.1   The profound differences in form and content between English law and the laws of other European countries may ultimately be traced – like so much else in our common history – to the fall of the Roman empire. England was part of that empire, but not for very long – from conquest in A.D. 43 to the beginning of the fifth century, when Roman forces gradually withdrew to meet enemies closer to home. From that time on the country suffered a series of barbarian invasions and disintegrated into warring tribes and kingdoms, until reunited by Anglo-Saxon kings in the ninth and tenth centuries. England was therefore beyond the Roman sphere of influence at the time when Roman law reached the highest stage of its development, and having developed its own legal system remained so when Roman or civil law (after the 'civilians' or citizens of Rome) was rediscovered in the Middle Ages, and even in the great era of Continental law reform in the nineteenth century. For good or ill, England was deprived accordingly of the Roman tradition and the inheritance of codified law.

A. Sources of law

i. The common law

0.2   The law of England today has three main sources or elements – the common law, statute law, and the law of the European Community. The common law is case law or judge-made law; at one time also known as customary or unwritten ('informal') law. It consists of the decisions given by English judges in tens of thousands of individual disputes, as set down in records and reports published over the past five hundred years. As a recognisable body of law it dates back to the first written records of decisions in the fourteenth century, which slowly came to replace trial by battle and other forms of solution by Divine intervention, and to commentaries by writers of the time such as Bracton and Glanvill. In fact its roots go back much further into history, because after his successful invasion of England in 1066 William of Normandy expressly confirmed existing Anglo-Saxon

1

laws and customs, and initially at least these must have been the influences which shaped the medieval judges' views of what was right and just.

0.3   The subject matter of a modern judgment may be either civil or criminal. It may involve the application of an Act of Parliament or provide an answer to a problem which Parliament has not yet attempted to resolve. The basic principles of civil liability under English law, contractual and non-contractual, are almost entirely the product of the common law. The principles themselves are extracted from rulings in individual cases and applied in subsequent similar cases. It is a process of reasoning by analogy from one set of facts to another – a notoriously imperfect method of reasoning. This way of making law is therefore the opposite of the deductive method of reasoning – applying a general principle to the facts of an individual case – required by a codified system. The English system is inevitably complex and prolix, lacking in any 'Grand Design'. In some respects it could be said to be adaptable and pragmatic, and yet in others it appears rigid and dogmatic.

0.4   A case decided in one of the higher courts (*see* below) which states a principle of law is called a precedent. In the nineteenth century the judges developed the doctrine of obligatory precedent, or *stare decisis*. This broadly requires that precedents must be followed by judges in similar cases in the same court and in the courts below it, whether or not they agree with them or think them just, and however old they may be. Theoretically the doctrine of precedent gives the continuity, cohesion and predictability which every legal system needs – and particularly a system without a Code. Under the doctrine of precedent the judge's task is seen as merely that of finding the law as it already exists in the law reports and applying it to the facts of the case before him – a process which in turn enables him to disclaim any personal responsibility for his decision. In practice the position is very different. Most cases have to be decided on their own facts and merits. New problems arise and new answers must be given. The law cannot stagnate, whatever the doctrine of precedent might suggest. In the end, it is and must be the judge's own decision as to which of the possible answers to the problem he or she should give. It is true nonetheless that the doctrine of precedent encourages the judge to follow the safest and most conservative course. But that may not be so very different from the position of the Continental judge, bound by a Code laid down many years earlier.

0.5   When seeking to discover whether or how a precedent might apply to the case in hand, the English lawyer must first find in the judgment the reason for the decision. This is the statement of legal principle applicable to the facts of the case, and is the crucial part of the judgment. It is known as the *ratio decidendi*; contrasting with *obiter dicta*. These are observations of the judge in the course of argument or example, and not part of his ruling. The ratio – the reasoning – can only apply if the significant facts of both past and present cases are essentially the same. English judgments may thus involve lengthy comparisons of the facts of different cases, rather than discussion of the merits of the case in hand. But which facts are significant, and how many of them must be repeated before the same rule applies? If facts or issues which appear similar are found in some way different, then the present case is 'distinguished' from the precedent and a different rule thus applicable. For good reason or bad many meaningless distinctions have at one time or another taken root in the law and made it still more complex.

Equity

0.6   The description above of the origins and operation of the common law was intended essentially to contrast case law with the law made by Parliament. But the phrase 'common law' can be used also in an entirely different sense – to define the rules laid down by the royal or common law courts as distinct from those laid down by the Court of Chancery. Here the contrast is between common law and equity.

0.7   For explanation we must go back to the earliest days of the common law. In the fourteenth and fifteenth centuries rights and remedies were few and it was extremely difficult and expensive to get justice done. The practice grew of appealing over the heads of the judges directly to the king. Special petitions for his mercy begged for rulings on individual grievances for which the common law had no sufficient answer. The king gave these petitions to his Lord Chancellor; at that time a bishop or archbishop, now a lawyer and head of the House of Lords. The Chancellor reached his decisions in his own domain, the Chancery.

0.8   In the beginning, then, each case was decided on its own merits, as each individual Chancellor saw them. But over the years, as one Chancellor gave way to another, inevitably the Chancellors' practices developed into a system, and eventually into a system of courts with rules and precedents which became even more complicated and cumbersome than the common law. Throughout the Middle Ages and for centuries after there were two rival systems in England – the common law courts, set up, as it was said, to give law, and the Chancery courts set up to stop them. The citizen derived little benefit from either. He could spend a fortune in one court, only to be told he should have gone to the other. But it was at least established in the seventeenth century that if the rules of the two systems contradicted each other, Chancery was to prevail.

0.9   The main purpose of the great legal reforms of the nineteenth century, and in particular the Judicature Act of 1873, was to bring together these two streams of law – to unite them within one system, in which all courts could apply whatever rule and give whatever remedy was appropriate. Chancery then became one of the Divisions of the High Court, doing the kind of work which we describe below, which is a reflection of its historical development.

0.10   The name given to all the remedies developed by the Court of Chancery, and now as we have said available to other civil courts at and above county court level, is 'equity'. But the word is deceptive in this context. It does *not* simply mean fairness or justice. It means those *rules* of fairness or justice developed by the Court of Chancery, applicable in the situations determined by that Court. In Continental systems equity is an inherent part of the judge's powers and responsibilities, but not so in England. When an English judge invokes his 'equitable jurisdiction' he does *not* mean that he can decide the case in whatever way seems fair. He is saying in effect that he has considered the relevant common law rules and found them unsatisfactory for one reason or another, and would prefer the different solution to the problem available to him under the rules of equity. In the limited areas in which it applies, equity represents, in other words, a second or alternative source of case law, whose principles are generally more flexible and adaptable than those of the common law – as we may see, for example, in the law of mistake; Chapter 10.

Law reports

0.11   A case law system depends on efficient reporting of judges' decisions (and correspondingly little on text books and academic writing). From the earliest reports in the Year Books in the fourteenth century until today law reporting has always been in private hands, with nothing remotely resembling a 'system' until 1865. After the Year Books came a wide variety of reports from the sixteenth to the mid-nineteenth century which are referred to by the initials of the reporter, e.g. Co. Rep. – the reports of Lord Coke – and are collected together in a series known as the *English Reports*, or ER. In 1865 the Incorporated Council of Law Reporting for England and Wales was established under professional control to ensure more systematic and economic reporting (and it was at about this time that the doctrine of obligatory precedent was developed). Each volume covers the work of a particular court, e.g. Chancery, and so a case reference might be, for instance, *Smith* v. *Jones* [1980] Ch. 456. The reference 'AC' signifies Appeal Cases, which are reports of House of Lords and Privy Council cases. Several other series are commonly used, such as the *All England Law Reports* (All ER) and *Weekly Law Reports* (WLR). Others again are in professional periodicals, notably the *Solicitors' Journal* (SJ) and *Estates Gazette* (EG).

ii. Statute law

0.12   Statute law is the law made by or by the authority of Parliament. Parliament consists of the House of Commons, House of Lords, and Monarch, who are all jointly responsible for any given measure. The law includes not only Acts of Parliament but statutory instruments. These are the detailed rules and regulations made by government ministers under the authority given to them by the various Acts, to fulfil the general principles they lay down. These forms of delegated legislation still require Parliament's approval, which may be given actively or passively according to the wording of the 'parent' Act. Either statute law or common law or both may apply to any given problem. If both apply but appear to contradict each other, the judges are bound to follow statute. When considering the effect of a statute, particular attention should be paid to the interpretation section and to any schedules at the end which give details of its application. We should emphasise finally that the distinction between common and statute law is not the same as that between civil and criminal law. Nearly all crimes and their punishments are laid down by Act of Parliament, but many Acts create purely civil rights and duties. Common law likewise may affect both civil and criminal issues.

iii. European Community law

0.13 The European Communities Act 1972 sets out the legal consequences of Britain's membership of the Common Market. The most important point is that the rules of the Treaty of Rome, the Directives issued under the Treaty, and the decisions thereon of the European Court of Justice take precedence over any rule of statute or common law to the contrary. An appeal may be made from any UK court to the European Court on issues involving the Treaty.

B. The English courts

0.14 We now describe briefly the system of courts in England and Wales – but not that of Scotland, which, though subject to many of the same Acts of Parliament and to the rulings of the House of Lords on matters of civil law, has its own legal system and its own completely different court structure. A knowledge of the hierarchy of English courts is necessary not only for the practical purposes of litigation but also in order fully to understand the working of the doctrine of precedent discussed above. The administration of this system may change considerably in the near future. Loss of business because of unacceptable levels of cost and delay has led lawyers to take a keen interest in reform. Radical changes in court management proposed by a committee under the chairmanship of Lord Woolf are currently under discussion.

C. Civil courts

i. Magistrates' courts

0.15   At the bottom of the structure are the locally organised magistrates' courts. The office of magistrate or justice of the peace dates back to 1361, and in earlier forms to 1195. Apart from the few stipendiary magistrates, below, magistrates are essentially unpaid amateurs. They are proposed for office from all walks of life on 'good citizenship' grounds by local advisory committees of senior magistrates, and if acceptable are appointed by the Lord Chancellor in the name of the Queen. There are currently about 30,000 of these 'citizens' representatives', playing a very important part in the system. On appointment they are required to attend periodic lectures and training sessions – to make them proficient in their duties, but not by any means to make them into lawyers. They must be prepared to give at least one day every two weeks to the work of the court, for which they receive expenses and a modest loss-of-earnings allowance. Their appointments normally continue until retirement at the age of 70. The court usually sits as a panel of three magistrates, advised on the law by a legally-qualified clerk. In contrast, stipendiary magistrates are professional judges. They are practising lawyers – barristers or solicitors – appointed by certain of the larger local authorities to serve on a full or part-time basis for a suitable payment or stipend. They sit alone but have the same powers as the lay justices. All magistrates are addressed as 'your worship', or 'sir' or 'ma'am', as the case may be.

0.16   While magistrates' courts are mainly concerned with criminal matters, below, they have a quite substantial civil jurisdiction. This is, however, largely confined to 'domestic' matters, such as the granting of separation and maintenance orders as between husband and wife, adoption, affiliation and guardianship orders. There are also administrative duties, notably granting licences for the sale and consumption of alcohol in public houses and places of entertainment.

ii. County courts

0.17   The system of county courts was established in 1846. The courts have no connection with the county as a unit of English local government, but are part of a national system operating with over 500 judges in some 300 districts or circuits. County courts can try nearly every kind of relatively minor civil dispute, and in particular claims for damages for breach of contract and tort up to £50,000, or more by agreement between the parties. The court consists of a single judge, a practising barrister or solicitor, addressed as 'your Honour'. Very occasionally he or she may be assisted by a jury.

0.18　　England has no small claims court as such, but in cases involving claims for up to £3,000 (£1,000 in personal injury claims) – typically, breach of contract cases – there is a small claims procedure available within the county court. These cases are decided by the registrar, the court's administrative officer, who is also a solicitor. For small claims purposes the registrar is called a 'district judge'. The proceedings are informal, as in an arbitration. The strict rules of evidence do not apply, and there are different rules as to costs. In other civil cases the general rule is that the loser pays both sides' costs. In small claims, however, each side pays its own costs of legal representation whether it wins or loses. The theory is that this discourages the use of lawyers in such cases. Some 2,250,000 actions are begun in the county courts every year, of which about two-thirds are small claims. Appeals on questions of law or fact are to the Court of Appeal.

iii. High Court

0.19　　The High Court tries all the most substantial civil cases. It has about 100 judges, formerly practising senior barristers known as Queen's Counsel, appointed by the Lord Chancellor to one or other of the three Divisions of the Court. The High Court is bound by the decisions of the Court of Appeal and House of Lords. The decision of one Division is not binding on another, but is of persuasive value.

Queen's Bench Division

0.20　　The Queen's Bench Division – so called because it was originally the court in which the Monarch sat – tries all major contract and tort actions. Its president is the Lord Chief Justice. It sits in London and periodically in provincial centres. About 225,000 claims are begun in the Q.B.D. every year, though only some 5,000 get as far as judgment. Most of the claims are for personal injuries. There are different lists or subdivisions of work, including those of the Commercial Court and Admiralty Court. The Commercial Court was set up especially to offer business people a service which was speedy, simple and efficient – but delays here between starting the action and beginning the trial are currently of two or three years' duration, as in the Division as a whole. Some of the Court's work is done by county court judges and Queen's Counsel appointed to try 'official referees' business' – cases involving lengthy and expert examination of documents and accounts, particularly concerning building disputes. Q.B.D. cases are heard by a single judge (whose title is, for example, Mr. Justice Smith – written as 'Smith J.' in the Law Reports – and who is addressed as 'my Lord' or 'your Lordship'). Juries are used only in libel and slander cases and certain other exceptional circumstances.

Chancery

0.21   The head of the Chancery Division is the Lord Chancellor, but since under the English theory of separation of powers he is also a political appointee and as such head of the party in power in the House of Lords, his place in court is taken by the Vice-Chancellor. The Court is largely concerned with administering the rules and remedies of equity, as described above, in cases concerning, among other matters, the administration of land, the proving or probate of wills, intestacies, trusts, mortgages, patents, company law, partnerships, tax and bankruptcy. As the Court of Protection it administers also the property and interests of mental patients and others under its guardianship. There is some overlap of function between Chancery and the Queen's Bench Division. The Court consists of a single High Court judge, sitting without a jury.

Family Division

0.22   This Court has jurisdiction over defended divorces and miscellaneous other matrimonial disputes, adoption, wardship and guardianship of children. Again it is constituted by a single judge.

Appeals

0.23   All three Divisions have certain limited powers to hear appeals from subordinate courts. By a procedure known as judicial review, the Queen's Bench Division in particular has powers to supervise inferior courts and tribunals by means of 'prerogative orders', representing the original authority of the king or queen. By judicial review the Court may also decide cases where the validity of ministerial and local government edicts is challenged. In their appellate or supervisory capacities the Divisional Courts usually comprise two or three judges.

iv. Restrictive Practices Court and Employment Appeal Tribunal

0.24   Two other courts should be noted which are divisions of the High Court in all but name. Both are presided over by a High Court judge, each sitting with lay members. The Restrictive Practices Court was established in 1956 to decide whether various kinds of commercial agreements restricting competition were in the public interest, and, if not, to declare them void. The two non-lawyers sitting with the judge are drawn from a panel of economists and other experts. The Employment Appeal Tribunal was set up in 1975 to hear appeals from industrial tribunals, which decide questions of individual rights in employment, notably on dismissal, discrimination and equal pay. E.A.T. lay members are nominated by management and labour organisations.

v. Court of Appeal

0.25   A High Court judge may be promoted to the position of Lord Justice of Appeal in the Court of Appeal. There are some 30 Lords Justices, under the presidency of the Master of the Rolls in civil cases and the Lord Chief Justice in criminal cases. The civil division of the Court of Appeal, which sits in London, hears appeals on questions of law or fact from the county court, High Court, Restrictive Practices Court and Employment Appeal Tribunal. Appeal is usually as of right, but leave is required in minor county court actions and appeals from the Divisional Court of the High Court. Appeals are usually heard by three judges; normally the Master of the Rolls and two Lords Justices or High Court judges. The Court does not see the witnesses again but reaches its decision on the basis of transcripts of their evidence. It has power to order a re-trial, but rarely does so. With very limited exceptions the Court is bound by its own previous decisions and by those of the House of Lords.

vi. House of Lords

0.26   The House of Lords is the highest civil appeal court in Great Britain. Somewhat confusingly, however, the title of Supreme Court of Judicature applies not to this court but collectively to the High Court, Crown Court (below) and Court of Appeal – a usage which dates back to a period of law reform in the nineteenth century when it was proposed to abolish rights of appeal to the House of Lords. In its capacity as the final court of appeal the House of Lords is quite distinct from the second House of Parliament. It consists of between seven and eleven 'Law Lords', more formally known as Lords of Appeal in Ordinary – i.e. 'by virtue of office' – under the presidency of the Lord Chancellor. They are chosen from among judges of the Court of Appeal, or, exceptionally, the High Court, and given life peerages and appropriately increased salaries. The Law Lords can take part in House of Lords debates but rarely do so. The other members of the House – the religious leaders, hereditary and life peers – cannot take part in the legal proceedings. Appeals are usually heard by a committee of five of their Lordships. Decisions are by majority. Each may give his own written opinion (not strictly a judgment) at great length, and even if all agree they may do so for different reasons. This practice has tended to complicate the law, and has led in turn to a recent preference for one opinion only to be given. Some fifteen or twenty cases a year are heard.

0.27   Appeals to the House of Lords are made from the Court of Appeal, or occasionally, by a so-called 'leap-frogging' procedure, directly from the High Court. This procedure is used where the trial judge certifies that a point of law of general public importance is involved concerning the interpretation of a statute or the application of a binding precedent, and subject to the House itself giving leave to appeal.

9

0.28   It will be seen that from most points in the system there is a right to two appeals – first to the Court of Appeal and then to the House of Lords. While in practice most litigants must accept the rulings of the Court of Appeal, many will remain dissatisfied. They would no doubt prefer a final ruling from the House of Lords, but after spending the three, four, five or more years necessary to get to the Court of Appeal are too exhausted, financially or emotionally, to go further. The problem is that under the doctrine of precedent no rule of common law can be considered settled until the House of Lords has pronounced upon it. It remains questionable therefore whether Britain does its citizens a favour by giving them the opportunity and incentive to spend so much time and money in pursuit of final judgment. One might suggest in passing that if there were three judges instead of one at trial level there would probably be many fewer unsatisfactory decisions and much less need to consider appealing.

D. Criminal courts

i. Magistrates' courts

0.29   The main work of the magistrates' courts, otherwise known as courts of summary jurisdiction or petty sessions, is in dealing with crime. Between them they try over 95 per cent of all the criminal cases in England and Wales. Magistrates can impose fines of up to £5,000 per offence and imprison for up to six months for any one offence, or up to twelve months for several offences. They have no preliminary investigative role equivalent to that of the *juge d'instruction* or Scottish procurator fiscal. The decision to prosecute is that of the lawyers in the Crown Prosecution Service, based on evidence put before them by the police.

ii. Crown Court

0.30   This court consists of a single professional judge and a jury of twelve persons over eighteen selected at random from the voters' list. The judge may be a High Court judge, or a circuit judge (serving also as county court judge), or, if part-time, a recorder. The court sits in about 90 centres, trying all the most serious ('indictable') crimes. It also hears appeals from magistrates' courts, on which occasions lay magistrates sit with the judge. Another form of appeal is that 'by way of case stated' to the Divisional Court of the Queen's Bench Division. This latter kind of appeal puts the onus on the magistrates to explain – through counsel – why they decided as they did, and thus involves questions of law.

iii. Court of Appeal

0.31   The criminal division of the Court hears appeals from the Crown Court against conviction or sentence. It normally comprises the Lord Chief Justice and two High Court judges. Its powers include that of increasing sentence or in appropriate cases ordering a retrial. It may also determine points of law referred to it by the Attorney General or Home Secretary.

iv. House of Lords

0.32   Five Law Lords hear appeals on questions of criminal law of general public importance only. Leave to appeal must first be obtained from the Court of Appeal or Appeals Committee of the House. Either side may appeal. The Attorney General may refer a point of law to the House after an acquittal.

E. Other courts and tribunals

0.33   The courts described above are the main components of the English legal system – but not the only ones. We should take account also, for instance, of the Judicial Committee of the Privy Council. In the Middle Ages the Privy Council was the executive and advisory body closest to the king or queen, but its power was gradually transferred to the Cabinet – the Ministers of State in Parliament. It remains as an advisory and honourary body, consisting largely of ministers. The Judicial Committee, however, is an assembly of eminent British and Commonwealth lawyers, including the Lord Chancellor and the Law Lords, whose main function is to hear appeals from those few Commonwealth countries which still allow their citizens this final right of appeal. In effect it is the Commonwealth Court of Appeal, and as such its judgments – given in the form of advice to the Queen – were and to some extent still are important unifying influences in the common law world. Since it does not form part of the English hierarchy of courts, however, its decisions, while of great persuasive value, are not binding on other English courts. It is convenient to note here that the decisions of the higher Scottish and Commonwealth courts are similarly persuasive. American cases are occasionally cited by way of illustration. It is rare to refer to Continental judgments, other than the overriding rulings of the European Court of Justice.

0.34   There is also within the English system a wide variety of administrative tribunals, established to decide rights and duties under particular statutes. They include tax tribunals, industrial tribunals, patent tribunals and national insurance tribunals. Rights of appeal vary – sometimes to appeal tribunals and sometimes to the High Court or Court of Appeal. The tribunals are not regarded as part of the hierarchy of courts.

0.35   We note finally the absence from the system of certain courts which one would normally find in Continental systems. England has no *droit administratif* or Constitutional Court. The simple explanation for this omission must be that we have no written constitution, and so there could be no place for a court to ensure obedience to it. But that is not to say that problems of abuse of executive power cannot or do not arise, or that no challenge can be made. The common law has in fact developed a (still very rudimentary) set of rules of reasonableness to limit abuse of power. These rules can be invoked by means of an application for judicial review in the Queen's Bench Division.

0.36   Another perhaps surprising absence from the scene is that of a Labour Court. The explanation reflects Britain's industrial history. In the nineteenth century legislation on trade unions was both repressive and unsuccessful. From the beginning of the twentieth century a different approach was tried – one of non-interventionism. Collective agreements were seen as matters for the parties themselves to decide upon without help or hindrance from the law. It is still true to say that so far as the law is concerned the parties may make and break such agreements as and when they think fit. There have been correspondingly few rules as to the legality or otherwise of strikes. In recent years Conservative governments have gone some considerable way to limit unions' previous freedom of action, but on a piecemeal basis. There is still no overall rational regulation of collective bargaining in Britain – and so no need for the kind of organisational framework one would find on the Continent, or indeed almost everywhere. Any legal action which might arise takes place accordingly along with other contract and tort actions in the High Court or county court. The situation is different as regards the employment protection rights of individual employees. These have been quite comprehensively developed, and the machinery of industrial tribunals and the Employment Appeal Tribunal provided to resolve disputes in this area.

Chapter 1

Intention and certainty

1.1   English contract law has developed over hundreds of years, and is today the basis of countless commercial dealings across the world. It is made up of thousands of cases and many Acts of Parliament – but we still have to begin our study of its rules and vocabulary by admitting that we cannot say exactly what a contract is or how it is made. Even the word 'contract' is used in different ways – to signify both the fact of agreement and any written record which may be made of it. Without even attempting any precise definition, however, we might suggest that English law will treat an agreement – or arrangement or understanding (to use neutral expressions) – as a contract, and so give it legal effect, if it fulfils four main and interlocking requirements.

1.2   These requirements are *the intention to be legally bound, certainty as to terms, offer and acceptance*, and *valuable consideration.* Apart perhaps from valuable consideration, these are largely matters of common sense - though their effects may differ greatly from case to case. If all these elements are present, the result will usually be a valid, binding contract. In this Chapter and the next we discuss the first three of these fundamental requirements, and in Chapter 3 the more complex rules of valuable consideration. In Chapter 4 we note exceptions to the general rule that contracts do not have to be made in writing, and will see there also that problems occasionally arise as to legal status or capacity to make a contract.

A. Intention

1.3   The judges' main concern in disputes over contracts is first to discover and then to try to give effect to the parties' intentions. They ask accordingly whether the parties intended to make a legally binding agreement, and if so, what they were trying to achieve thereby. We see immediately that both inquiries beg various fundamental 'free will' questions. In reaching their agreement the parties may have given no thought at all to its enforceability, but now one of them demands the law's support. Again, it is a basic truth of contract law that the terms of the contract inevitably reflect the will of the economically stronger party. Individuals dealing with big businesses or state agencies cannot really be said to 'intend' to contract on the one-sided and disadvantageous terms put before them. And how can intention be found, and how much weight attached to it, when a person is mistaken as to the meaning or outcome of his agreement, and so says one thing but intends another?

1.4   In any such situation the court may be unable to enforce the actual intentions of one or both parties. It can only look at the outward appearances of agreement and endorse what the parties *appear* to have intended – which may well be quite different from what one or both of them actually wanted. So in *New Hampshire Insurance* v. *M.G.N.*, 1995, for example, the Court of Appeal held that in interpreting a written contract, evidence that both parties had had the same undisclosed intention as to its effect was inadmissible. On this basis also the court may say that a contract exists even though neither party thought there was one. In *Upton R.D.C.* v. *Powell*, 1942, the services of a fire brigade were asked for and supplied without any thought by either side as to the contractual position, but since at that time such services were in fact chargeable the brigade was held entitled to charge. Commercial expediency may dictate the same conclusion. Again, Acts of Parliament may on occasion add terms to contracts which neither side has contemplated, or conversely may hold a party liable for not making a contract, on grounds of illegal discrimination, or even compel a party to make a contract regardless of his intentions, e.g. where insurance is required or compulsory purchase permitted.

1.5   As a matter of general principle, the common law holds that agreements made in domestic, family or social settings are not intended to be legally enforceable, and so refuses to lend its support. There may be difficult border-line cases. Would it be desirable to enforce pre-marriage contracts, for example, given the likely youth, inexperience and over-enthusiasm of the parties, and the probability of drastic changes in their outlooks and circumstances in later years? English law provides little answer, but a Canadian court enforced such an agreement in *Charles* v. *Charles*, 1991, on the basis of the parties' advanced years at the time they made the agreement and the fact that they had had full legal advice. Agreements between husbands and wives on household allowances and expenses are unenforceable, unless questions of separation or divorce have formalised the relationship. Lord Atkin explained the courts' basic attitude to domestic agreements in *Balfour* v. *Balfour*, 1919: 'They are not sued upon, not because the parties are reluctant to enforce their legal rights when the agreement is broken, but because the parties, in the inception of the arrangement, never intended that they should be sued upon. Agreements such as these are outside the realm of contracts altogether. The common law does not regulate the form of agreements between spouses. The consideration that really obtains for them is that natural love and affection which counts for so little in these cold

14

courts. The terms may be repudiated, varied or renewed as performance proceeds or as disagreements develop, and the principles of the common law as to exoneration and discharge and accord and satisfaction are such as to find no place in the domestic code'. In contrast, an agreement between relatives that one of them should give up her home and come to live with the other was held to give a right to remain in the other's property in *Parker* v. *Clark*, 1960, because of the economic significance of giving up one's home. On principle again, agreements between friends and neighbours, e.g., to help each other with transport to work, are probably unenforceable: *Albert* v. *Motor Insurers Bureau*, 1971. But there are always exceptions, depending largely on the value of the subject-matter of the agreement. So a joint enterprise between the landlady, her grand-daughter, and the lodger in entering a newspaper competition was held in *Simpkins* v. *Pays*, 1955, to give rise to an obligation to share a valuable prize.

1.6 Statements or promises made in a commercial context – which may include the conduct of family businesses, as in *Snelling* v. *Snelling*, 1972, and *Nunn* v. *Dalrymple*, 1989 – are, of course, much more likely to be enforced. But even here there may be difficulties. Many things may be said in the course of negotiations which are not in any way intended as contractual obligations. A distinction must be drawn between mere sales talk or 'puff', which has no legal effect, statements which induce or encourage another to enter into a contract but do not form part of the contract – called 'representations' – and the actual terms of the contract. Terms and representations are discussed in detail in Chapters 5 and 11. The question before us at this point is how to draw the line between puffs on the one hand and any kind of enforceable promise on the other. What, for instance, is the legal significance of advertisements and sales literature?

i. Advertisements

1.7 Most advertisements have no legal significance, simply because they offer only comparatives and superlatives – 'bigger', 'better', 'the most', 'the best', etc. – which cannot be proved right or wrong. Others again may be regarded only as 'invitations to treat', i.e. to enter into negotiations as to the terms on which a contract might later be made. But if a contract results from a factual assertion in an advertisement which can be proved untrue, or from a specific promise which has clearly been broken, the advertiser may well be liable for breach of contract (and/or be guilty of committing a criminal offence under the Trade Descriptions Act 1968).

1.8 The leading case in this area is *Carlill* v. *Carbolic Smoke Ball Co.*, 1893. The company advertised that it would pay £100 to anyone who used its product as prescribed but nonetheless caught influenza. Mrs. Carlill proved that she had fulfilled these terms, but the company refused to pay. The company argued that the advertisement was a puff, not seriously intended, or at most an invitation to treat. The judge found that it contained a clear and factual offer, whose acceptance had been proved, and so could not be mere sales talk. Alternatively the company said it was not possible to make a contract with someone unknown who had not formally accepted the offer. This also was rejected. The offer was like that of a reward for a lost dog. It was clearly not necessary for Mrs. Carlill to make herself known beforehand or write a letter accepting the company's offer. Her victory is no doubt one very good reason why modern advertisements do not contain such incentive schemes.

1.9   It follows that advertisements which merely make promises without proposing or requiring any reciprocal action by the reader are unenforceable. This is the position with advertisements of future events such as sales or meetings or travel schedules: *Harris* v. *Nickerson*, 1873 – auction advertised but then cancelled – would-be bidder had no claim for expenses incurred. But if an advertisement can be interpreted as containing an offer, anyone who accepts will have a claim, as did Mrs. Carlill. So an advertisement of an auction to be held 'without reserve' could be understood as saying: 'If you come to the auction we promise it will be held on these terms'. An advertisement in these terms was therefore held enforceable by a disappointed bidder in *Warlow* v. *Harrison*, 1859, as also was a 'first come, first served' notice in the American case of *Lefkowitz* v. *G.M.S. Store*, 1957. In *D'Mello* v. *Loughborough College*, 1970, a college prospectus was held to be part of the contract subsequently made between student and college, and in *Jarvis* v. *Swan Tours*, 1973, the promises in a holiday brochure were found sufficiently factual to have the same effect. We look at other aspects of advertising in Chapters 2, 3, 7 and 11. An important question discussed in Chapter 7 is whether a contracting party can lawfully exclude any liability for statements made in his advertising material.

ii. Honour clauses

1.10   The common law allows contracting parties, even in business, expressly to make their agreements binding in honour only – so-called 'gentleman's agreements' – and will refuse accordingly to enforce them. In the leading case of *Rose & Frank* v. *Crompton*, 1923, an Anglo-American agreement was worded as follows: 'This arrangement is not entered into nor is this memorandum written as a formal or legal agreement, and shall not be subject to legal jurisdiction in the law courts either of the United States or England, but it is only a definite expression and record of the purpose and intention of the parties concerned, to which they each honourably pledge themselves'. Unfortunately self-interest prevailed over moral obligation, and the English supplier ended the agreement without giving notice. The House of Lords held that no claim for breach of the agency agreement could be made against him. But specific orders from the American agent, which the supplier had already accepted without reference to the honour clause, had to be fulfilled or damages paid, because these were new and self-contained contracts. Any other conclusion would encourage fraud.

1.11 An honour clause must be unambiguous. The party relying on it will not be allowed to escape liability in a commercial or industrial setting by the use of 'tricky' wording. In *Edwards* v. *Skyways*, 1964, an employer's offer of 'ex gratia' redundancy payments was held to be an obligation to pay, once the employees had resigned on the strength of it. Mr Justice Megaw said that where an agreement concerned business relationships and not social or domestic matters, 'the onus is on the party who asserts that no legal effect was intended, and the onus is a heavy one.' An honour clause will not be effective if it imposes liabilities despite the absence of legal remedy, e.g. when it makes one side's decision 'final' or is enforceable by some means other than a court order: *Baker* v. *Jones*, 1954. *See also* para. 1.24. Agreements to submit to arbitration, however, are not caught by this rule.

1.12 We should take particular note of the legal status of collective agreements – those made between an employer or association of employers and one or more trade unions. Section 179 of the Trade Union and Labour Relations (Consolidation) Act 1992, re-enacting earlier legislation, makes such agreements enforceable only if they state in writing that they are intended to be legally binding – an unusual event in practice. Collective agreements are in other words classified by English law as binding in honour only – a position quite unlike that of most other countries, and an example perhaps of the legendary English sense of humour. But that does not mean they are wholly without legal effect. If the terms of a collective agreement are expressly or impliedly incorporated in an individual employee's contract of employment, they can be enforced by and against that individual. Since English law usually regards trade unions as independent parties, not as agents of their individual members, it is a question of fact in each case whether collectively agreed terms have been so incorporated in any particular employee's contract.

1.13 The normal forms of agreement with suppliers of public utility services such as electricity boards and the post office are also of doubtful effect as contracts under English law: *Norweb* v. *Dixon*, 1995. The powers and duties of these bodies are laid down by Acts of Parliament, which usually impose fines for breach of duty. The judges say that it is not for them to add other penalties, and so refuse to allow claims for damages for breach of contract against such suppliers or their agents: *Willmore* v. *S.E. Electricity Board*, 1957; *Treifus* v. *P.O.*, 1957. Liability in tort may also be excluded: *American Express* v. *British Airways*, 1983. But claims for breach of contract may be made where extra services are offered for extra cost, e.g. registered post.

iii. Other informal agreements

1.14   Many other circumstances may arise where assurances given in a commercial context have no legal effect. The difficulty is usually uncertainty over the precise terms of the alleged contract, as in the vague 'understandings' between the parties in *Milner* v. *Bilton*, 1966, and *Dickinson* v. *Abel*, 1969. Or the promise may be invalidated because it was made at a pre-contractual stage and without contractual intention, as in *Independent Broadcasting Authority* v. *E.M.I.*, 1980, or for such reasons as the absence of a formal written record in circumstances where one might expect one, e.g. in a contract with a government department, or in an undertaking given at a company boardroom meeting: *Meates* v. *Westpac Corp.*, 1990; *Licences Insurance* v. *Lawson*, 1986. *See also Compagnie de Commerce* v. *Parkinson*, 1953, below.

B. Certainty

1.15   Overlapping with the previous requirement of intention to be legally bound is the obvious need for certainty or clarity of expression. One might hazard the guess that most contractual disputes involve problems of interpretation of the wording of the contract. We consider here some typical examples of such problems and their possible legal consequences. It should be remembered that each case turns very largely on its own merits, and that no particular form of words can be guaranteed always to have the same meaning or result.

1.16   As a general proposition, doubt as to the meaning of a vital term in a contract will make that contract unenforceable. Prices, salaries, rents, quantities, dates, etc. are among such vital terms. So in *May and Butcher* v. *The King*, 1929, a contract to deliver goods 'at a price to be agreed' was held void, as was a contract 'on hire purchase terms' – *Scammell* v. *Ouston*, 1941 – and another to pay an actress a 'West-end salary' – *Loftus* v. *Roberts*, 1902. A term in a lease providing for renewal 'at a rental to be agreed' was held unenforceable in *Kings Motors* v. *Lax*, 1969, as was a contract 'subject to satisfactory mortgage' in *Lee-Parker* v. *Izett*, 1971, another 'subject to *force majeure* conditions' in *British Electrical Industries* v. *Patley*, 1953, and a promise to negotiate 'fair and reasonable sums' in *Courtney* v. *Tolaini*, 1975. In *Walford* v. *Miles*, 1992, the House of Lords, following *Tolaini*, ruled an 'agreement to negotiate' – whether or not 'in good faith' – unenforceable because of the difficulty of saying how long such an agreement might last and on what grounds it might justifiably be ended. Lord Ackner pointed out that each party was free to pursue his own interests in the course of negotiations, so long as he made no misrepresentations, and in order to advance those interests had to be able to withdraw or threaten to withdraw from negotiations in the hope that the opposite party would offer better terms. This basic freedom of action was incompatible with a duty to continue negotiating. The same view was taken by the Supreme Court of New South Wales in *Coal Cliff Collieries* v. *Sijehama*, 1991.

1.17   The 'contracts' in the cases just described failed because the obligations in them amounted only to 'agreements to agree'. On principle, such agreements are unenforceable. No-one can say when or whether the parties might finally reach agreement, or on what terms. But there are nonetheless many cases reaching different conclusions on very similar wording. It was recognised in *Walford* and in *Pitt* v. *P.H.H. Asset Management*, 1993, for example, that a party may in effect lock himself into continued negotiations by making a collateral or subsidiary contract not to negotiate with anyone else for a certain time. We bear in mind also that agreements may be made during negotiations, e.g. to maintain confidentiality, which remain binding even though negotiations are broken off. *Walford* accepted also that a promise to 'use one's best endeavours' for a particular purpose was enforceable – though in *Bower* v. *Bantam*, 1972, the court found this expression too vague to be enforced by means of an injunction to stop conduct which was said to be inconsistent with the promise.

1.18   Other contrasting cases include *Foley* v. *Classique Coaches*, 1934, where the court upheld a contract for the supply of petrol 'at a price to be agreed', and *Sykes* v. *Fine Fare*, 1966, where it enforced a five-year contract for the supply of chickens which specified only that in the first year between 30,000 and 50,000 should be supplied and in the following four years 'such numbers as may be agreed'. The vital distinction between these latter cases and others such as *May*, above, is that the agreements here were broken *after* they had been acted on and goods supplied under them, whereas in *May*, the agreement was rejected while it was still executory (i.e. not yet begun upon). When one side delivers goods to the other the judge cannot usually deny the existence of a contract and so must award damages based on what seems to him the 'reasonable' price for the goods. *Smith* v. *Morgan*, 1971, likewise contrasts with *Kings Motors*, above. In *Smith* a contract for the sale of land gave the buyer a first right of refusal of other land belonging to the seller if and when he decided to sell it. This was held to be an enforceable promise to make the buyer a reasonable offer in that event. Similar cases where the court found it possible to overcome problems of uncertainty include *Brown* v. *Gould*, 1972 – valid agreement to fix a rent 'having regard to the market value of the premises' – and *British Coal* v. *S. Scotland Electricity Board*, 1988 – injunction to prevent breach of informal understanding to buy coal, though no price was ever agreed. In *Whitehouse Properties* v. *Bond*, 1992 (Australia), even a promise to fulfil a contract 'within a reasonable time' was held enforceable.

1.19   What one might hope and believe to be the basic attitude of the English courts to uncertainty in business contracts in particular was expressed by Lord Tomlin in *Hillas* v. *Arcos*, 1932: 'The problem of a court of construction [i.e. interpretation] must always be so to balance matters that, without violation of essential principles, the dealings of men may so far as possible be treated as effective and the law may not incur the reproach of being the destroyer of bargains'. We find the same sentiments in the judgment of the Scottish Court of Session in the *British Coal* case above. 'If parties have apparently intended to bind themselves, the court should be slow to abort that intention on the basis that there is some inadequacy on a particular aspect.' But how far should the courts go in trying to resolve the difficulties? This question arose in *Harvey* v. *Pratt*, 1965. All the necessary terms of a lease were agreed, except for the starting date. The court held the lease void for uncertainty and made no attempt to try to discover what date the parties had in mind. In contrast is *Storer* v. *Manchester Corp.*, 1974, where the specific terms of an offer for sale were held to make it unnecessary to fix a date. In *Bushwall* v. *Vortex Properties*, 1976, there was an agreement to buy land at a price payable by annual instalments. After each instalment a 'proportionate part of the land' was to be transferred to the buyer. But since the contract did not say how the land was to be apportioned, the Court of Appeal refused to enforce the agreement.

1.20   The presence of one or two uncertain terms among others sufficiently clear and comprehensive to be enforceable as a contract will not invalidate that contract. In *Nicolene* v. *Simmonds*, 1953, a written contract containing all necessary detail included also the provision that it was subject to 'the usual conditions of acceptance'. Neither side knew what these conditions were. The court rejected the argument that the contract was therefore void, and simply struck out the proviso. 'It would be strange indeed', said the judge, 'if a party could escape from every one of his obligations by inserting a meaningless exception . . . You would find defaulters all scanning their contracts to find some meaningless clause on which to ride free'. Alternatively, of course, the court may accept that some element of doubt is unavoidable and unimportant, as in a contract for 'approximately' 1,000 tons or delivery 'on or about' a certain date. A contract is not necessarily too uncertain merely because it enables one side to change some of the details, e.g. a credit contract with the usual term enabling the lender to vary the rate of interest: *Lombard* v. *Paton*, 1988. *See also* para. 7.28.

i. Agreements in principle

1.21   Another aspect of the problem is that of the adequacy of 'agreements in principle', or, as regards contracts for the sale of land, 'open contracts' – which state only the names of the parties, the property and the price. The question in each case is whether the outline agreement is sufficiently clear to be enforced, as for example in *Perry* v. *Suffields*, 1916, and *Bigg* v. *Boyd-Gibbins*, 1971 – both open contract cases – or is vitiated by lack of detail. In theory, at least a contract may be enforced without agreement on every last detail, but in practice the judges may have misgivings – particularly as regards contracts affecting land. 'It is quite possible for persons on a half sheet of notepaper, in the most informal and unorthodox [i.e. non-legal] language, to contract to sell the most extensive and most complicated establishment that can be imagined . . . *but having regard to the habits of the people in this country it is very unlikely*': *Clifton* v. *Palumbo*, 1944. (Author's emphasis)

1.22 Business agreements in principle are not invalidated merely because both sides know that certain details will be settled later, and on that basis the details themselves become enforceable even though apparently added after the contract has been made. Two contrasting cases on publishing agreements illustrate the question. In *Malcolm* v. *Oxford University*, 1991, a 'firm commitment' to publish a book written in accordance with the publisher's requirements was held binding despite the lack of agreement on price, quantity, etc. These were seen as relatively minor matters, which could be decided afterwards. But in *Australian and New Zealand Banking* v. *Frost*, 1989 (Australia), such details were regarded as essentials of the contract, which therefore had to be decided beforehand if the contract were to be enforced. Both decisions could be said to be 'right' on their own facts, although the decision in *Malcolm* seems more in line with practice in this particular commercial context. In insurance practice, contracts are often effective immediately even though made 'at a premium to be arranged' – *Glicksten* v. *State Assurance*, 1922. Similarly in *British Crane Hire* v. *Ipswich Plant Hire*, 1974, an agreement made on the telephone to hire a crane was held to incorporate the owner's standard forms subsequently sent to the hirer, since the hirer knew that these transactions were regulated by standard forms. Conversely, someone not accustomed to business dealings of this kind, such as a tourist booking a holiday at a travel agency, would probably not be bound by such forms unless produced at the time of booking: *Hollingworth* v. *Southern Ferries*, 1977. It may be very important to be able to say exactly when a contract was made, so as to rule out subsequent alterations or additions by one side: para. 7.8.

ii. Conditional terms

1.23 Many agreements depend on suspensive or conditional terms such as 'subject to contract', 'letter of intent', 'letter of comfort', 'without prejudice', 'subject to satisfactory survey', and the like. The effects vary according to their contexts, and we must say again that no particular form of words can ever be guaranteed always to have the same result. As a general rule an agreement made subject to contract is unenforceable because

21

and insofar as the parties intend that there are further details to be settled and formally recorded. This is usually the position as regards contracts for interests in land: *Eccles* v. *Bryant*, 1947; *Regalian* v. *L.D.D.C.*, 1995. But if the terms are already sufficiently agreed by word of mouth, and all that is intended is that the agreement shall be written down, then changing the form of the agreement from spoken to written adds nothing, and so the original spoken or provisional agreement is enforceable: *Branca* v. *Cobarro*, 1947. Even in agreements about land, 'subject to contract' may not affect the validity of terms already clearly agreed, recorded and acted upon: *Alpenstow* v. *Regalian*, 1985; *Westway Homes* v. *Moore*, 1991.

1.24   Agreements made 'subject to satisfactory survey' or 'subject to planning permission', or other such suspensive terms, are clearly not fully effective until these 'conditions precedent' (Chapter 5) are fulfilled. They may nonetheless oblige one party to take the necessary preliminary steps to have the property surveyed or to apply for planning permission, as the case may be: *Ee* v. *Kakar*, 1979. If, as above, enforcement of the contract depends on one party being 'satisfied', then he must act reasonably and not arbitrarily or capriciously in deciding whether or not he is satisfied: *Gordon D.C.* v. *Wimpey*, 1988 (Scotland). Declaring oneself 'sole judge' of satisfactory performance of a contract would not stop a court inquiring into allegations of fraud or bad faith: *West of England Shipowners* v. *Cristal*, 1995. We note lastly that a condition in a contract which is for the benefit of one party only may be waived by that party: *Graham* v. *Pitkin*, 1992.

Letters of intent and letters of comfort

1.25   On the face of it, a letter of intent indicates a willingness to make a contract in the near future along the lines proposed in the letter, but because and insofar as it is only an expression of intention the letter is not itself a contractual document. That does not necessarily mean it has no effect at all in law. We bear in mind the purpose and likely consequences of the letter. The sender very probably intends that the recipient will rely on the letter and make preparations to carry out the contract as soon as agreement is reached. Normally when a business spends time and money in preparation for a contract, it does so at its own expense, but the situation here may be different. If in the end no agreement is reached it might sometimes be unfair not to let the recipient recover the costs he has incurred in acting on the letter – and particularly so where the sender has received some direct benefit as a result. *British Steel Corporation* v. *Cleveland Bridge Co.*, 1984, is a good example. In the course of negotiations between these two parties, the company sent B.S.C. a letter of intent as to the terms of the proposed contract, but also asking B.S.C. to begin work immediately producing the goods required by the company. B.S.C. did the work and delivered the goods, but the parties never agreed on the terms of the contract. Following a dispute over prices and delivery dates, the company refused to pay for the goods. B.S.C. sought to recover its costs from the company on a (non-contractual) restitutionary or *quantum meruit* – 'as much as it's worth' – basis. The claim was successful because the company had had the benefit of the faster delivery it had asked for in its letter of intent. The company's counter-claim for damages for late delivery failed, since that was necessarily a breach of contract claim and no contract had ever been made. If the sender of a letter of intent is at fault in breaking off negotiations, again the recipient might be able to recover expenses incurred in reasonable reliance upon it: *Sabemo* v. *N. Sydney Municipal Council*, 1977 (Australia). We note finally the possibility that if a letter of intent does result in a contract, the letter may then be interpreted as an offer. The contract will not be nullified merely because part of it was originally written as a letter of intent: *Wilson* v. *Bangladesh Co.*, 1986.

1.26   A 'letter of comfort' is evidently intended to reassure another party that he may safely act in a certain way, but it may not amount to a binding promise to that effect. If the sender is not too concerned with keeping his good name or his customers or clients, the letter might indeed be quite worthless. *Kleinwort Benson* v. *Malaysian Mining Corp.*, 1989, is an important case in this connection, concerning a holding company's refusal to repay a loan made to its subsidiary by a bank. When the subsidiary first approached the bank, the bank sought assurances from the holding company, M.M.C., as to its responsibility for its subsidiary's debts. M.M.C. replied in writing: 'It is our policy to ensure that [our subsidiary's] business is at all times in a position to meet its liabilities to you'. On this assurance the bank lent the subsidiary £5 million, and then a further £5 million following another similar letter from M.M.C. Some months later the subsidiary went into liquidation and the bank claimed repayment from M.M.C. What was the legal effect of M.M.C.'s 'letters of comfort'? Were they promises as to liability, or merely statements of fact as to company policy? The Court of Appeal held that they were only statements of fact and not contractual commitments. They gave rise accordingly, said the Court, to a moral responsibility for the subsidiary's debts, but not to legal liability. This decision is nothing if not debatable. If moral responsibility was clear, the letters must surely, in the absence of any express disclaimer of liability, have imported more than statements of fact. To the extent that M.M.C.'s assurances were evidently intended to have legal consequences and did in fact have them – in that the bank was persuaded to make the loans – the decision seems inconsistent with basic principles of English contract law. It would appear also to attach too much importance to forms of words, and thereby not only to invalidate letters of comfort but wilfully to encourage commercial immorality.

1.27   Two Australian cases are of especial interest here. The first, *Commonwealth Bank of Australia* v. *TLI Management*, 1990, endorses the Court of Appeal's view in *Kleinwort Benson*. The key passage in the letter in question said: 'We confirm that the company will complete takeover arrangements' – in return for which the bank provided credit facilities. The takeover was not in fact completed, but the court nonetheless held that because of the terms of the letter there was no breach of contract. 'It would have been very simple . . . to have used words of promise, such as "we agree", "we undertake", or even "we promise".' The judge thought that 'confirm' was ambiguous in its context, and merely a statement of intention. In contrast are the perhaps more agreeable words of Chief Justice Rogers in *Banque Bruxelles* v. *Australian National Industries*, 1989: 'There should be no room in the proper flow of commerce for some purgatory where statements made by businessmen, after hard bargaining and made to induce another business person to enter into a business transaction, would, without any express statement to that effect, reside in a twilight zone of merely honourable engagement. The whole thrust of the law today is to attempt to give proper effect to commercial transactions. It is for this reason that uncertainty, a concept so much loved by lawyers, has fallen into disfavour as a tool for striking down commercial bargains. If the statements are appropriately promissory in character, courts should enforce them when they are uttered in the course of business and there is no clear indication that they are not intended to be legally enforceable.'

Estimates and quotations

1.28   An estimate is usually regarded as an informed guess, and so without contractual effect. A quotation is more probably a final figure; the basis of any subsequent offer or acceptance. But neither result can be guaranteed. It is more a matter of what the parties intended and understood than of the use of particular words. The context may suggest that a so-called estimate should be understood as a quotation: *Croshaw* v. *Pritchard*, 1889. An estimated price much lower than that finally demanded may make the supplier liable for negligence or misrepresentation: *Nye* v. *Bristow*, 1987; *Kidd* v. *Mississauga Commission*, 1979 (Canada). A quotation cannot be final if a contract is subsequently made on suppliers' terms such as: 'All quotations are subject to confirmation and acceptance by us upon receipt of an order and will not be binding until or unless so confirmed by us in writing'. On the other hand, the terms of the invitation to quote may be such that the 'quotation' is in fact an acceptance of the employer's offer: *Northern Construction* v. *Gloge*, 1986 (Canada).

1.29   Suppliers commonly give both estimates and quotations free of charge in the hope of attracting business. *Lacey* v. *Davis*, 1957, is therefore a decision of some interest, holding that a supplier could charge for the extra work he did in providing exceptionally detailed figures at the request of a prospective customer, who then abandoned the project. Where a property developer told a building contractor he would be awarded the contract, but in the event did not go on with the development, he had to pay the contractor for the preparatory work he knew he had undertaken: *Marston* v. *Kigass*, 1990; *Regalian* v. *L.D.D.C.*, above.

iii. Arbitration clauses

1.30   We discuss arbitration clauses and their effects in more detail in Chapter 5. We note here, however, that such a clause may be a valuable means of resolving uncertainty in a contract. *'Id certum est quod certum reddi potest'*, as the maxim says – 'that is certain which can be made certain'. Even so, adding an arbitration clause will not save a contract which is otherwise completely obscure. The arbitrator must be given enough to go on. So in the Australian case of *Whitlock* v. *Brew*, 1969, an agreement to lease land 'upon such reasonable terms as commonly govern such a lease' was held void for uncertainty despite a provision for arbitration. An arbitrator here would have had to invent the terms of the contract rather than resolve ambiguities in them, which is his proper function. Where the contract requires each party to appoint an arbitrator, or to agree on the appointment, neither can frustrate the contract by unreasonably refusing to appoint or to agree. In *Sudbrooke* v. *Eggleton*, 1982, the House of Lords said that when a party refused to appoint an independent valuer as required by his contract the property should be sold at a price fixed by the court.

iv. Course of dealings; trade usages; implied terms

1.31   Previous dealings between the parties may explain apparent uncertainties in their agreement, as may the standard practices in their trade. Examples include *Hillas* v. *Arcos*, above, where a contract for timber of 'fair specification' was held to have a particular meaning in the timber trade, and *British Crane Hire*, above, where the court accepted that an outline agreement reached between business parties over the telephone was understood to be subject to the standard written terms which one would send the other at a later date. As we see in Chapter 5, the courts may also be able to interpret contracts by reference to terms added into them either by Act of Parliament or the common law. Section 8 of the Sale of Goods Act 1979, for example, says that if no price has been agreed, the buyer must pay a reasonable price for goods received. For their part, the judges will add terms into contracts only on the basis of presumed common intention or necessity, and not merely on the basis of what seems fair and reasonable in the circumstances: paras. 5.45–54.

v. Conclusion

1.32   These introductory cases are for the most part merely examples of the practical difficulties faced by judges in their day-to-day task of interpreting and enforcing contracts. We bear in mind again that the answers they have given depend very much on the facts of each particular case – but they may nonetheless provide helpful illustrations of judicial attitudes and statements of judicial policy.

1.33   We end this chapter with a note of caution. We have seen that the courts' willingness or otherwise to resolve problems of interpretation depends largely on how far the parties have gone with their contract. If it is still executory on both sides it may be declared void for uncertainty. But if one side has fulfilled his duties under the alleged contract the judge may have to acknowledge its existence and enforce it despite other uncertainties: *Sykes*, above. At the same time, however, we should note that what a person does in the belief that there is a contract does not of itself bring that contract into existence if it is otherwise wholly uncertain, or if terms as to the formation of the contract have not been fulfilled.

1.34   An important case on this latter point is *Compagnie de Commerce v. Parkinson*, 1953. The seller's order form said that no contract would be made unless the buyer signed and returned the seller's acceptance slip. But instead the buyer sent a letter indicating agreement, to which the seller raised no objections, and for a time both parties then acted as if there was a contract. The Court of Appeal held that the seller's subsequent refusal to supply was not a breach of contract, because under the terms of the order form no contract had been made. If the seller had stood by and let the buyer spend money in reliance on the alleged contract, then of course he would not have been able to deny its existence, or alternatively he might have been liable on a *quantum meruit* basis, as noted above.

Danish law

1.35   For the purposes of the commentaries on Danish contract law in this and following chapters, we should note first of all Danish law's position as representative of the Scandinavian or Nordic legal tradition. This tradition is shared with Sweden, Norway, Iceland and Finland. Over the past 100 years co-operation between these countries has led to the adoption of almost identical Sale of Goods Acts, Contract Acts, etc. Nordic law is essentially pragmatic in approach. It is not as conceptual and code-orientated as the rest of continental European law, and not as case-orientated as the common law.

1.36   As we see in Chapter 3, Danish law has no requirement of consideration, nor even of the continental European concept of *causa*. So a promise of a gift may be just as binding as an agreement to buy goods. But excuses for breach of promise may be more acceptable with regard to gifts than in the case of a sale. The differences between Danish and English law here may thus be more matters of theory than practice. This is particularly so as regards questions of intention to be legally bound, though many of the problems dealt with by English law under this heading would be considered in Denmark more as questions of what the promisee might reasonably expect in the given social or economic or commercial situation. Danish law thus provides a more flexible basis for deciding whether a contract exists and avoids rules which are not adapted to current economic life.

1.37 A Danish Supreme Court case in 1994 (UfR 479) concerned a document with the title 'letter of intent', which stated: 'In view of the fact that [the Bank] has placed credit facilities at the disposal of the [subsidiary company], the undersigned [parent company] hereby declares . . . that we shall if required transfer [to the subsidiary company] sufficient liquid funds to make sure that the subsidiary company will at all times be able to fulfil its obligations towards the bank. . .' The Supreme Court found that the parent company had made a clear and unconditional promise in accordance with the contents of the document. Regardless of the title of the letter, the parent company was bound accordingly unless it could prove the existence of circumstances justifying a contrary conclusion. The fact that during the advance negotiations with the bank, the parent company had refused to act as guarantor for the subsidiary company was not sufficient reason to establish that the bank had accepted that – in spite of the wording – the declaration was not to be considered legally binding. The Court noted that refusal to act as guarantor was (for accounting reasons) the typical reason for the use of a 'comfort letter' as in this case.

1.38 We should mention also these particular issues. First, collective agreements are binding without the need to say so expressly. Second, contracts with public utilities are governed by the same rules as other contracts unless there is specific statutory provision to the contrary. Finally, estimates have contractual effect in that the price stated cannot be substantially exceeded unless the work becomes more expensive for unforeseen reasons. The supplier must then inform the buyer as soon as possible and secure his agreement to proceed.

Dutch law

1.39 The basis of Dutch contract law is the New Civil Code or *Nieuw Burgerlijk Wetboek* which came into force in 1992, replacing the Civil Code of 1838. Revision of the whole system of civil law had been under consideration since 1947. The Code offers now 'a great number of new rules, designed to meet the needs of modern society' (*The New Netherlands Civil Code*: Haanappel & Mackaay). A contract is defined as a 'multilateral juridical act whereby one or more parties assume an obligation towards one

or more other parties'. It is 'formed by an offer and acceptance': Articles
6.213, 217. Case law under the old Code is still important, e.g., on questions
of interpretation of contract which are not explicitly covered by the new
Code.

1.40   Of the four main requirements for a contract in English law – para.
1.2 – only the consent of the parties is of fundamental importance in the
Dutch Code. Apparent intention, certainty and capacity are also requirements, but of less significance. There is no rule of consideration in Dutch
law.

1.41   In the absence of any provisions in the new Code directly relating
to interpretation of contracts, or of any very significant new cases on the
effects of the Code itself, previous case law remains of interest. The courts
saw it as their main aim to give effect to the meaning the parties could and
should have attributed to what they had agreed, and to what they could
reasonably expect from each other in this connection: *Ermes* v. *Havillex*, NJ
1981, 635. A similar approach is taken where there is an obvious omission
in a contract: *Bunde* v. *Erckens*, NJ 1977, 241. Article 3.35 of the Code
seeks generally to protect interests arising from reasonable reliance on
others' declarations or conduct.

1.42   Gentleman's agreements, even when expressly worded to be binding
in honour only, may sometimes be enforceable under Dutch law. Dutch law
holds collective agreements binding in the same way as contracts between
individuals. Public utility services are provided by private contract, although
some aspects of the relationship between the utility and consumer are
governed by public law. For most public utility services, such as the supply
of electricity, gas and water, mail and telephone, general conditions of
contract have been agreed between professional or trade organisations and
consumers' organisations.

French law

1.43   The basic rules of contract in French law are in the Civil Code, the
great Napoleonic Code of 1804, model of the Codes of Belgium, Holland,
Luxembourg, Switzerland, Italy, Spain, Portugal, Egypt, Louisiana, Quebec,
and the states of South America. The Code has been very substantially
developed and explained by case law (*la jurisprudence*), academic commentaries (*la doctrine*), and by later statutes. Judges' decisions are essentially
applications of the Code or a statute to particular facts, and are not precedents in the English sense. But statements of principle by the *Cour de
Cassation* are usually followed by the *Cour* itself and by the lower courts.

1.44   Expressing the principles of eighteenth century French philosophers on the fundamental importance of free will, a contract is defined in Article 1101 of the Code as 'an agreement by which one or more persons promise one or more others to give, to do or not to do something'. Article 1108 sets out the four essential conditions for the validity of a contract: consent of the party who undertakes to perform the obligation, his or her capacity to contract, a predetermined *objet* or obligation and lawful 'cause' (as to which, *see* paras. 3.73–6).

1.45   Contracts are always seen as bilateral agreements, even when they bind only one party. Contrary to the position under English law, unilateral promises – options, guarantees, etc. – are matters of contract: Article 1103. Their enforcement may depend on the extent of the promisee's reliance. In the absence of common contractual intention, remedies may be in quasi-contract or quasi-tort. Under Article 1371 *et seq.*, where one party has enriched another without contractual cause, as in *negotiorum gestio*, he can claim repayment or compensation. Under Article 1382 *et seq.*, a person injured by another's wrongdoing may claim compensation. It is most important to decide whether a relationship is contractual or not because contract and tort remedies are mutually exclusive. This is the '*non cumul*' rule (Civ. 11 January 1989). Rules of evidence and limitation differ accordingly.

1.46   It may be difficult to decide when or whether a contract has been made in the course of negotiations, or as a result of letters of intent or comfort. Under Article 1156 the judge's duty is to 'determine what was the common intent of the parties, rather than follow the literal meaning of the instrument' – an approach essentially different from that of English judges, seeking the objective meaning of the agreement. French judges are not bound by the parties' own assessment of their relationship, and may always 'recharacterise' it (Req. 11 November 1884). But they must respect the parties' intentions as to the substance of their obligations. Thus, depending on judicial interpretation of the parties' intentions, letters of intent are sometimes binding, sometimes not. And if a holding company undertakes that its subsidiary will always be in a position to repay a loan, this undertaking may be binding even though not construed as a guarantee by the holding company itself: Com. 21 December 1987.

1.47   The parties' agreement on the subject matter of the contract is essential. Article 1129 says: 'The obligation must have as its "object" a thing of a definite description. The amount thereof can be undetermined provided it is ascertainable'. In sales, Article 1591 says: 'The sale price must be determined and indicated by the parties'. It must therefore be either fixed or ascertainable. Where the price is defined only by reference to one side's tariff, variable at his discretion, the contract may be held void (Com. 5 November 1971; Com. 11 October 1978). This result is increasingly criticised, and may not now apply (Civ. 29 November 1994). *See* Cabrillac, *Droit des Obligations*, paras. 76 *et seq*.

German law

1.48   The German Civil Code, the *Bürgerliches Gesetzbuch* or BGB, was one of the last but most important expressions of the Napoleonic age of codification. The BGB expresses the influence both of German customary law and of Roman law. It came into force in 1900, to meet the needs of a newly united Germany. It was subsequently the basis of Swiss, Italian, Turkish and Japanese codes, and influential in Austria, Greece and elsewhere. In form the BGB consists of five Books, dealing with obligations, family law, succession, etc. The first Book is the General Part, stating principles of interpretation and application which underlie the whole Code. The Code is complex and conceptual in approach. Various amendments and later Acts are noted in our later paragraphs. We bear in mind also the important role of judge-made law.

1.49   But case law has not the same significance in German law as it has in England. Case law means that the court cites one of the general clauses of the Code – a provision with a broad wording – and develops rules on the basis of this provision. The courts never 'find' the rule, but always apply – at least *pro forma* – a provision of the Code. Precedents therefore cannot and do not play such an important part in the development of the law as they do in England.

1.50   An understanding of the so-called *Abstraktionsprinzip*, the separation between the law of obligations and the law of property, is essential for any study of the BGB. The making of a contract does not automatically mean, for example, that ownership of goods passes from the seller to the buyer. The passing of ownership is a separate legal act which follows the rules of the law of property: Articles 929 *et seq*.

1.51   So far as the Code is concerned, a contract is made as soon as the parties are agreed: Article 145. There is no requirement of consideration; only of a clear declaration of will – *Willenserklärung* – on each side, constituting offer and acceptance, and a common serious intention to be bound: Article 118. (We note that in BGH NJW 1974, 1705, the court found no enforceable agreement in a case like *Simpkins* v. *Pays*, para. 1.5.) While in theory the court is required under Article 133 to find what the parties really intended rather than to give effect to the literal meaning of what they said or wrote, in practice, much as in English law, their intentions tend to be judged objectively. Article 157, for example, says that contracts should be interpreted according to requirements of good faith and common usage.

So if a person drives into a car park where there is a notice charging a fee, he must pay that fee whether or not he agrees with, or even sees, the notice.

1.52   Advertisements do not usually have contractual effect, but if the terms of a contract are not clear a brochure or the like may be used to fill the gap. So *D'Mello* and *Jarvis*, para. 1.9, would be decided in the same way in the Federal Republic. 'Honour' clauses are not used in German law. As regards collective labour agreements, the Law on Collective Agreements – the *Tarifvertragsgesetz* of 1918 – not only makes such agreements binding but also enables employees who are not union members to claim benefits under them. Other special statutory provisions regulate public utilities.

1.53   The requirement of certainty seems less important in German law than in the English system. Several of the cases mentioned in para. 1.16, for instance, would probably have been regarded as valid in German courts, because Article 316 makes it unnecessary to state the 'counter-performance' (i.e. the consideration), notably the price. In such cases the party who has fulfilled his part of the contract can demand a reasonable counter-performance, e.g. a reasonable price, as determined by the court.

1.54   Standard forms cannot be incorporated in contracts as easily as they were in *British Crane Hire*, para. 1.22. Incorporation is only possible where one party expressly requires it or there are continuous business dealings between the parties. In consumer contracts, standard terms are incorporated only if the supplier expressly refers to or clearly displays them, and if the consumer has reasonable means of knowing what the terms are and agrees to their inclusion: Article 2 of the Standard Contract Terms Act 1976.

1.55   Letters of intent do not as such have any effect in German law. The so-called *Vorvertrag* or binding agreement to make a contract is, however, enforceable. Problems as to the legal effects of estimates and quotations have to be decided on the facts of the case. No charge can be made for either unless expressly agreed beforehand. In 1992 BGHZ 117, 227, a letter of comfort in terms very similar to those in *Kleinwort Benson*, para. 1.26, was held enforceable.

Italian law

1.56   While Italian law is the most direct descendant of the Roman system its present basis is the Civil Code of 1942. As with other more modern codes, the Italian Code regulates not only the rights of private citizens but also matters such as banking and insurance, which in many countries are the subject of separate commercial codes.

1.57   As regards questions of contracting parties' intentions, Article 1337 says that the parties must act in good faith in the conduct of negotiations and formation of the contract. There can be no contract without agreement and *causa* (as to which, *see* paras. 3.83–6): Article 1325. The object of the contract must be possible, lawful, and certain or ascertainable: Article 1346.

1.58   Articles 1362–7 lay down important rules on interpretation of agreements. They say that the court's primary duty is to find the common intention of the parties. It is not to be limited in this inquiry by the strict literal meaning of the words used, but can consider also the parties' overall conduct – including what they say and do *after* making the contract. This latter provision seems quite unacceptable under English law. The contract must if possible be interpreted to be effective rather than ineffective. Ambiguities should be interpreted according to relevant general practice, and in the sense most suitable to the nature and purpose of the contract and which 'equitably reconciles the interests of the parties'. The courts have not interpreted letters of intent as imposing contractual obligations on the senders. It is possible, however, that a sender might be liable in tort if he proves untrustworthy after having led the recipient to rely on him and so to suffer loss: Trib. Milano, 30 May 1983.

Spanish law

1.59   Spanish law distinguishes between civil contracts, regulated by the Civil Code of 1889, and commercial contracts, regulated by the Commercial Code of 1885. The basic rule on contractual intention is in Article 1254 of the Civil Code: 'A contract exists from the time when one or several persons consent to be bound in respect of another or other persons to give something or perform some service'. The essence of the contract is therefore an undertaking by a specific obligation, or the intention agreed between two or more parties to enter into an enforceable obligation: Article 1255.

1.60   Article 1261 says that a contract requires consent, a definite subject matter, and *causa* for the obligation. *Causa* may perhaps be defined as a legally acceptable objective. Consent may usually be expressed in any way agreeable to the parties: Article 1278 of the Civil Code. Commercial usages are important evidence of contractual intentions in business dealings: Article 1287; Articles 2 and 59 of the Commercial Code. Letters of intent and the like have no contractual force, strictly speaking, but carry an obligation to negotiate in good faith and may give rise to liability to repay another's pre-contractual expenses, as under English law: para. 1.25. In a judgment of 16 December 1995 the Supreme Court said that letters of comfort which merely affirmed facts or stated opinions gave rise only to moral obligations.

1.61   A clear and certain subject matter is another contractual requirement. But an uncertain quantity or sum is still acceptable if it can be
determined without the need for a new agreement: Article 1273. A Supreme
Court decision of 30 June 1972, illustrates the problem. One party contracted to pay a certain sum of money and the other to give a piece of land
of equivalent value – but which precise piece from among his various
holdings was left to be decided at a later date. The agreement was held void
for uncertainty.

Swedish law

1.62   Swedish contract law, not unlike English law, is a combination of
statute and case law. The Contract Act of 1915 mainly regulates offer and
acceptance, agency and void contracts. The interpretation of contracts has
been developed through case law. There are movements in Sweden towards
modernising the rules of offer and acceptance, but no immediate proposals
for reform. In general, Swedish contract law is very similar to Danish
contract law. Unless otherwise stated in the following chapters, the same
rules apply.

1.63   The main rule in the present context is that a contract does not have
to be in any particular form. There are some exceptions; for example, sales
of land must be in writing. Advertisements may have contractual effect.
Article 18 of the Swedish Sale of Goods Act 1990 says that if the goods do
not conform with information given in an advertisement or otherwise before
the contract is made, the seller is liable if the buyer relied on the information. Even if the information was not given by the seller himself but by the
producer, the seller is held liable if he was aware of the information.

1.64   Uncertainty does not necessarily make a contract void. The courts
try to fill in the gaps. It is not necessary, for example, to stipulate a certain
price (apart from sale of land, where the price must be specified in the
written contract). When the price is not specified, the buyer is obliged to
pay a fair price. It is quite common for the parties to a contract to agree
only on the main terms. The court may then add the details of the contract
with reference to the intentions of the parties, documentation, common trade
usages and non-mandatory rules such as those in the Sale of Goods Act. The
same method would be applied if the contract were to stipulate, e.g., that the
details should be decided 'upon such reasonable terms as commonly govern
such a lease' (*see* para. 1.29). But on the other hand, if the parties have not
agreed upon the main terms, such as the price or time of delivery, the court
may presume that there is no binding contract at all. This would not be
directly because of uncertainty, but because of a presumption that there is
not yet any basis for a mutual wish to be bound by a contract.

1.65   Letters of comfort (paras. 1.26–7) have attracted much interest in Scandinavian law recently. The effects of such letters depend partly on their precise wording, but also on the circumstances in which they were written. In NJA 1994 s.204 a letter of comfort was held enforceable. It was given to a seller by one of the main shareholders in the company buying the goods. Although the wording in the letter did not amount to a guarantee of payment, it was held that the shareholder should have disclosed that the company was about to enter into receivership, and so enabled the seller to stop the delivery. Since the shareholder failed to give this information, he was held liable to pay the seller.

1.66   Swedish law imposes no general obligation of good faith or disclosure during negotiations. One might, for example, negotiate with different parties at the same time without disclosing that fact, and there is no overall obligation to inform a person of the intention to stop negotiating with him or her. Letters of intent are not normally binding. Exceptionally, however, there may be a liability for *culpa in contrahendo;* i.e., a duty to pay damages for loss caused by an act that is against good faith during negotiations. This might occur when the negotiations have lasted for a long time and a party believes that it is only a matter of formalities to achieve the final agreement, and then suffers loss because the other party has not told him he is no longer interested in reaching agreement: NJA 1990 s.745; NJA 1978 s.147.

Chapter 2

Offer and acceptance

2.1   As we see in every legal system, an agreement requires a meeting of minds – a 'consensus'. The basic elements of that consensus are an offer by one party and an acceptance of the terms of the offer by the other party. English law does not require offer or acceptance to be expressly stated or described as such, and so either or both may be implied from the conduct of the parties. There may sometimes be considerable difficulty in saying who offered or who accepted, or exactly when or even whether acceptance took place. Commercial dealings are not always conducted on a precise and legalistic basis. It may be necessary, for example, to rely on a course of dealings between the parties to prove the existence of a contract between them: *Trentham* v. *Archital Luxfer*, 1993. Proving that a binding contract has been made in the course of social or domestic relationships may be still more difficult, as illustrated in *Simpkins* v. *Pays*, 1955; para. 1.5. Sometimes consensus is more apparent than real, as where the parties do not have equal bargaining power, but if they *seem* to be agreed that will usually suffice for legal purposes. Assuming that the parties intend legal consequences and express their intentions sufficiently clearly by their words or conduct, and that their agreement is not vitiated by fundamental mistake or fraud or other such difficulties discussed in Chapters 10 and 11, or by absence of writing in the few situations where English law requires writing (Chapter 4), acceptance of an offer makes an enforceable contract. But what do we mean by an offer, and how and when is it accepted? These are the questions we now examine.

A. Offer

2.2   An offer must be sufficiently precise to be capable of acceptance. A distinction must therefore be drawn between offers and 'invitations to treat'. An invitation to treat is only an expression of a general willingness to bargain and as such of no legal effect. We have seen that most advertisements are in that category – intended only to arouse the customer's interest so that he or she will make an offer, which the seller can then accept or refuse as he thinks fit. In English legal theory the same is true of statements of price *per se*, whether or not attached to the goods in question, and even if given in response to a specific inquiry: *Harvey* v. *Facey*, 1893; *Scancarriers* v. *Aotearoa*, 1985. Even when the buyer selects goods for himself or herself in a self-service store, the theory is that the buyer must still make an offer for them at the check-out point, where the offer could still be refused: *Pharmaceutical Society* v. *Boots*, 1953.

2.3   But circumstances alter cases, as usual. We have seen in *Carlill*, *Warlow* and *Lefkowitz*, in Chapter 1, situations where the advertisers were held to have made statements which amounted to offers because they proposed or required particular responses from their readers. Depending on the terms on which quotations or tenders are invited, the prices stated in them could be binding offers: *Butler* v. *Ex-Cell-O*, 1979; *Northern Construction* v. *Gloge*, 1986 (Canada). Again, a customer who puts petrol in his car at a self-service petrol station must be the one who accepts the offer to sell at the advertised price, because the situation is such that the proprietor cannot then change his mind and refuse to sell at that price.

2.4   It may sometimes be very difficult to decide which party has offered and which has accepted, and particularly so where contracts are made by conduct. When a person gets on a bus, for example, does he thereby accept the company's offer to carry him, or does he merely make an offer which the company may then accept by taking his money and giving him a ticket? Or is the ticket itself the offer? If the ticket is the basis of the contract, then at least in theory a passenger should have a reasonable opportunity to see and agree to its terms: *Baltic Shipping* v. *Dillon*, 1993 (Australia). English law has so far given no definite answer to this question (*see Wilkie* v. *L.P.T.B.*, 1947), though in this and many other situations it may be most important to decide when exactly a contract was made and what its terms were. It is clear at least that the parties' use of the words 'offer' or 'acceptance' is not conclusive. So when in *Clifton* v. *Palumbo*, 1974, the land owner said he was prepared to 'offer' his estate for £600,000, it was held that because of the high price and complexity of the estate, his words amounted only to an invitation to treat. This was the case also in *Bigg* v. *Boyd-Gibbins*, 1971, when the owner declared that for a quick sale he would 'accept' £26,000. That in turn meant that when the buyer replied: 'I accept your offer', he was himself only making an offer, which the seller was free to reject.

2.5   An offer must be communicated to the person purporting to accept it, either directly or by some more public announcement or notice, as in *Carlill*'s case. To put that another way, one cannot claim to accept an offer without at the time knowing of its existence. If I return a lost dog and then read of a reward for so doing, I cannot claim the reward.

36

2.6   An offer is essentially a proposal which can be freely accepted or rejected. If the 'offeree' is given no choice, there is no valid offer. Thus a builder who leaves a building half-completed cannot charge for the work he has done, nor can a contractor who does more than he is asked to do: *Sumpter* v. *Hedges*, 1898; *Forman* v. *Liddesdale*, 1900. (But partly performing a severable contract – one divisible into separate items – entitles the contractor to payment for those parts accepted by the offeree: Section 30, Sale of Goods Act 1979; *see also* Chapters 5 and 9.) For the same reason, when one person spends his own money to help another, without being asked to do so, English law will not usually compel that other to repay. Where, for example, A voluntarily paid B's insurance premium to stop the policy from lapsing, the judge said: 'The general principle is . . . that work and labour done or money expended by one man to preserve or benefit the property of another do not according to English law create any lien [right] upon the property saved or benefited, nor . . . create any obligation to repay the expenditure. Liabilities are not to be forced upon people behind their backs, any more than you can confer a benefit upon a man against his will': *Falcke* v. *Scottish Insurance*, 1886; *Owen* v. *Tate*, 1975.

2.7   This unsympathetic refusal to recompense a person who acts in good faith to help his neighbour – to recognise, that is, the Civil law principle of *negotiorum gestio* or 'management of affairs' – has been described as 'one of the most marked divergences . . . between the Civil law and the Common law' (Nicholas, *Introduction to Roman Law*). But inevitably there are exceptions. Money spent saving lives or property at sea must be repaid: *The Winson*, 1981. A railway company's claim for feeding and stabling a horse which was delivered to but not collected from the station was upheld in *G.N. Ry.* v. *Swaffield*, 1874, because of the necessity of the situation. A claim is perhaps more likely to be upheld if the plaintiff reasonably believes the property is his own. In *Greenwood* v. *Bennett*, 1972, an innocent buyer of a car from a thief spent money improving it. When the true owner reclaimed the car from the buyer he had to compensate him for the improvements – a principle confirmed by the Torts (Interference with Goods) Act 1977.

i. Duration of offer

2.8   An offer which is stated to be open for a specified time lapses if it is not accepted within that time. If no time is specified, it lapses within a reasonable time. What is reasonable must depend on the circumstances. An offer made by telegram or telex suggests that an equally prompt acceptance is called for: *Quenerduaine* v. *Cole*, 1883. When a company purported to accept an offer for shares six months after it had been made, the court held that the offer was already closed, and so no contract came into existence: *Ramsgate Hotel* v. *Montefiore*, 1866; similarly in *Hare* v. *Nicholl*, 1966. But negotiations following an offer for a valuable piece of land might be expected to take months before agreement could be reached: *Manchester Diocesan Council* v. *Commercial Investment*, 1969.

ii. Revocation of offer

2.9   An offer can be withdrawn at any time before it is accepted. That is still so even though the offeror has promised to keep it open for a specified period of time which has not yet expired. This latter rule may clearly cause injustice if the offeree has incurred expenditure in reliance on the promise, as in *Routledge* v. *Grant*, 1828. The difficulty arises because of English law's definition of 'acceptance', which we discuss below. An effect of the Uniform Laws on International Sales Act 1967 is to override the common law rule and hold offers open for the time promised – but the Act does not apply unless expressly adopted by the parties. If and when the 1980 Vienna Convention on Contracts for the International Sale of Goods is adopted by Britain, Article 6 would likewise override the common law, unless the contract in question expressly excludes the Convention. Such promises appear binding under Scots law – *Paterson* v. *Highland Ry.*, 1927 – as also under Section 2–205 of the American Uniform Commercial Code and Continental systems.

2.10   Revocation of an offer, other than by lapse of time, is not effective until the offeree learns of the offeror's intention to revoke. That will usually involve communication between the two, e.g. receipt of a letter from the offeror – *Byrne* v. *Van Tienhoven*, 1880 – or the offeree may be taken to know that the offeror has changed his mind if he has had reliable information to that effect from a third party: *Dickinson* v. *Dodds*, 1876. An offer of personal services is necessarily ended by the offeror's death, but otherwise his estate may be bound at least until the offeree learns of his death: *Bradbury* v. *Morgan*, 1862.

B. Acceptance

2.11   English law says that an offer has contractual significance only if it is conditional; that is to say, if it is more than a promise to give or do something for nothing. Expressly or by implication, an offer must require that something be done in return in order to make it binding. In effect it must say: 'I will do this for you, if you will do that for me'. Acceptance of an offer therefore involves the recipient, the offeree, expressly or impliedly agreeing to do what the offeror has asked of him – or, in certain circumstances, as illustrated below, para. 2.35, actually doing that thing.

2.12   It is for this reason that an offer said to be open for a given length of time can be withdrawn if not accepted within that time, as happened in *Routledge*, above. When an offeree is told, say, that he has three months in which to decide whether to buy the offeror's house, he does not accept the offer of three months 'thinking time' simply by agreeing to it, or even acting on it. Acceptance depends on his doing or promising to do something approved by the offeror in return for the offer. Such an offer can only be binding if in effect it says: 'I will hold this offer open for you for three months, *if in return* you will give me £5' – or one penny, or £1,000, or whatever else may be required by the offeror. This essential element of mutuality or reciprocity is known as valuable consideration, and is discussed at length in the next chapter.

i. Counter-offer

2.13   Where it is the acceptance itself which is conditional, not a straight-forward agreement with the offer as it stands, there may be no acceptance at all but only a counter-offer. The effect of a counter-offer is to nullify the original offer. In *Hyde* v. *Wrench*, 1840, for instance, A offered to sell his land to B for £1,000. B counter-offered £950, which A refused. B could not then hold A to his original offer, because that offer was no longer open.

2.14   A difficulty might sometimes arise in distinguishing between a counter-offer and a query or request for further information, which does not affect the validity of the offer. Contrasting cases include *Northland Airlines* v. *Ferranti*, 1970, and *Stevenson* v. *McLean*, 1880. In *Northland* a buyer sent a telegram purporting to accept the seller's offer of an aeroplane, but adding: 'Please confirm delivery to be made within 30 days'. This was regarded as a major new term not previously mentioned, still less agreed. Its effect was therefore of a counter-offer, requiring the whole agreement to be renegotiated. But in *Stevenson* the buyer's acceptance was held to be complete though coupled with an inquiry as to whether he could take delivery over four weeks.

ii. The battle of the forms

2.15   When buyer and seller seek to make a contract by sending each other copies of their own standard forms of purchase and supply – which may contradict each other in some significant respect – whose terms prevail? The possible answers to this common commercial problem were explored by Lord Denning in *Butler* v. *Ex-Cell-O*, 1979: 'In most cases where there is a battle of the forms there is a contract as soon as the last of the forms is sent and received without objection being taken to it . . . The difficulty is to decide which form, or which part of which form, is a term or condition of the contract. In some cases the battle is won by the man who fires the last shot. He is the man who puts forward the latest terms and conditions and, if they are not objected to by the other party, he may be taken to have agreed to them . . . In some cases, however, the battle is won by the man who gets the blow in first. If he offers to sell at a named price on the terms

39

stated on the back, and the buyer orders the goods purporting to accept the offer on an order form with his own different terms on the back, then, if the difference is so material that it would affect the price, the buyer ought not to be allowed to take advantage of the difference unless he draws it specifically to the attention of the seller. There are yet other cases where the battle depends on the shots fired on both sides. There is a concluded contract but the forms vary. The terms and conditions of both parties are to be construed together. If they can be reconciled so as to give a harmonious result, all well and good. If the differences are irreconcilable, so that they are mutually contradictory, then the offending terms may have to be scrapped and replaced by a reasonable implication.'

2.16   As a general rule, then, it is the 'last shot' which decides the battle – those terms which are the last or latest to be put forward without objection by the other side. But as his Lordship says, there are exceptions, up to and including the possibility that the conflicting terms will cancel each other out, or even, as he might have added, that there is no contract at all. The only weakness in his otherwise admirable summary is that it does not really tell us when or why any one of these totally different answers may be given. But there is a good reason for that, which is that the problem may arise at many different stages of negotiation between the parties and clearly there could not be one simple answer equally applicable to all. The facts of the cases themselves determine the outcome, as we shall now see.

2.17   In *British Road Services* v. *Crutchley*, 1967, B.R.S. delivered goods to Crutchley's warehouse. The driver handed over a delivery note stating that the goods were left on B.R.S.'s terms, which the warehouseman then overstamped to say that they were received on Crutchley's terms. The driver raised no objection; nor did B.R.S. Later a dispute arose between the parties. Again the question was: whose terms prevailed? The court held that B.R.S's delivery note was an offer and Crutchley's stamp a counter-offer. By its silence B.R.S. was deemed to have accepted the counter-offer and so Crutchley's terms carried the day. The case is therefore a straightforward example of victory for the party firing the last shot.

2.18   *Butler* v. *Ex-Cell-O*, above, was a more complicated case. The sellers quoted a price to the buyers. On the back of the quotation were various provisions including a price variation clause and the statement that 'these terms shall prevail over any terms in the buyer's order'. The buyers ordered the goods on their own standard form. This had no price variation clause but did include a tear-off acknowledgment form requiring the sellers to agree: 'We accept your order on the terms and conditions stated thereon'. The sellers signed and returned the form, but sent with it a letter saying they were fulfilling the order in accordance with their original quotation. Lengthy delays caused increased costs – which the sellers claimed to be entitled to recover under the price variation clause.

40

2.19 We see in this case that the sellers fired the first shot, in that they said the contract was to be made on their terms alone. Lord Denning seems to suggest that they should therefore win the battle – but what should be the effect of their returning the buyer's acknowledgment form? And against that in turn is the fact that by the letter accompanying the form the sellers seemed to reintroduce, if they had ever lost, the advantage of their own original terms.

2.20 At the trial the judge thought the sellers should win because they had made the price variation clause the basis of all subsequent dealings. The Court of Appeal reversed his decision. Apart from Lord Denning, who was concerned with the overall effect of the negotiations, their Lordships thought the issue was simply one of deciding who had offered and who had accepted. The sellers had offered, but by returning the form had seemed to accept the buyers' counter-offer. Their accompanying letter was held only to identify the goods and refer to the price first quoted, and so in the event it made no difference to their position.

2.21 But if the sellers' letter had in fact revived their original terms the contradictions between the two sides' forms would almost certainly have meant that no contract had come into existence, and so either side could have withdrawn at that point without fear of liability. The situation would have been different, however, if the sellers had gone on to deliver the goods, perhaps believing that their own terms were still effective. It would be more difficult at that stage for a judge to deny the existence of a contract, which would presumably consist of such terms as had been agreed, i.e. without the price variation clause. Alternatively the buyers might have been ordered to pay for the goods on quasi-contractual grounds, as in *British Steel Corporation* v. *Cleveland Bridge Co.*, 1984: para. 1.25.

2.22 We have seen from the *B.R.S.* case that when the seller delivers goods after receiving the buyer's standard form he is taken thereby to agree to the buyer's terms. We have also seen in *Butler* that when one side goes so far as to return the other's acknowledgment form he loses the advantage of having said in the first place that his terms alone shall govern the contract. Can that particular advantage likewise be lost just by delivering the goods after receiving the other side's standard form? What if the 'first shot' form uses some such comprehensive wording as this: 'Each order is subject to these conditions of sale to which the buyer shall be deemed to assent. No order shall be subject to other conditions unless the seller agrees thereto in writing and the seller shall not be deemed to accept such other conditions nor to waive any of these conditions *by failing to object* to provisions contained in any purchase order or other communication from the buyer'? There is as yet no definite answer to this important question. Cases such as *Butler* suggest that the seller's subsequent actions might still nullify such wording, yet it is hard to see why he should not be allowed simply to ignore

41

the other's terms if that is what he said he was going to do. A usual way round the problem is to require the other party to sign and return an acknowledgment form, as in *Butler* and *Chichester Joinery* v. *Mowlem*, 1987.

2.23 Another weakness of the 'last in time' principle is that it can obviously cause injustice. It would be all too easy for one of the contracting parties – the buyer, say – to take advantage of the other by slipping in another clause at a very late stage in the negotiations and hoping it would not be noticed. Subsequent delivery of the goods might look like agreement with the new term, but could equally well be seen as consistent with the seller's expectation that terms already agreed would not be changed or added to. In the Canadian case of *Tywood* v. *St. Anne Co.*, 1980, the court held that delivery in these circumstances did not establish beyond doubt that this particular seller knew of or agreed to the new term, and therefore that he was not bound by it.

2.24 The 'last in time' rule can in any case only help us to say whether an offer has been accepted. It has no application after agreement is reached. Once the contract has been made, any purported variation by one party could amount to a breach of contract, and certainly the new term would be of no effect. So in *Evans* v. *Merzario*, 1976, it was held that a later standard form did not affect an existing oral agreement on different terms. *See also* para. 7.9.

2.25 The American solution to the battle of the forms is different from the English. Section 2–207 of the Uniform Commercial Code says that a definite expression of acceptance of an offer creates a binding contract even though new terms are thereby introduced, subject to three vital rules. First, the offeror's original terms may make it clear that any subsequent amendment is of no effect (thus reaching the opposite conclusion to that in *Butler*); second, if the new terms 'materially alter' those in the offer, that of itself ensures they are not binding (which admittedly begs the question, but so far as it goes rejects the *B.R.S.* decision); and third, the offeror's express objection within a reasonable time of receiving the new terms likewise nullifies them. In contrast with the English rules, therefore, the American position seems to be that the man who fires the *first* shot should win. The rule in Article 19 of the Vienna Convention on International Sale of Goods, not yet part of English law, is very similar to that in the U.C.C.

2.26 The American answer may have much to commend it. It recognises that a person who opens negotiations on the basis that his terms alone will govern the transaction probably means what he says, and ought to be allowed to rely on his foresight in making that provision, rather than be deemed by his subsequent (understandable) silence to have agreed precisely the opposite.

iii. Communication of acceptance

2.27   Normally the offeree must tell the offeror directly and expressly that he has accepted his offer. Failure to use the 'proper channels' may invalidate acceptance. One should not give one's letters to the postman, for example, because it is his job to deliver letters, not to post them: *Re London Bank*, 1900. Applications for employment should be accepted by the employer, not by some unauthorised employee: *Powell* v. *Lee*, 1908.

2.28   Where communication of acceptance should be direct and instantaneous, spoken face-to-face or by telephone or telex, but is not heard or received by the offeror, no contract comes into existence. A contract made by telex or, presumably, by fax, is made where the message is received: *Brinkibon* v. *Stahag Stahl*, 1982. *Where acceptance is communicated by letter, the general rule is that a contract exists as soon as the letter is posted*. The common law thus reaches a different answer from that of many other legal systems, which require the letter to be received before a contract can be made. Both the Uniform Laws on International Sales Act 1967 and Article 18 of the United Nations Vienna Convention on Contracts for the International Sale of Goods likewise require receipt. But whichever rule is adopted, it is necessarily arbitrary and capable of causing uncertainty and injustice. In practice it would probably be more accurate to describe the English position as a presumption rather than a rule, which the circumstances of the case might clearly make inapplicable. In *Holwell* v. *Hughes*, 1974, Lord Justice Lawson said: 'The factors of inconvenience and absurdity are but illustrations of a wider principle, namely that the rule does not apply if, having regard to all the circumstances, including the nature of the subject matter under consideration, the negotiating parties cannot have intended that there should be a binding agreement until the party accepting an offer or exercising an option had in fact communicated the acceptance or exercise to the other'.

2.29   The basic position under English law is illustrated in *Household Fire Insurance* v. *Grant*, 1879, where a company posted a letter accepting an application for shares. The applicant never received the letter, but was nonetheless held liable to pay for the shares. Where the offer itself says that acceptance is only effective when received, then the postal rule above is displaced – *Holwell*, above – as it may be also where delivery is delayed by the offeree's own carelessness in misdirecting the letter: *Getriede Import* v. *Contimar*, 1953.

2.30   The common law seems uncertain as to who should bear the risk of mistakes in transmissions by telegram or telex. In *Northland Airlines*, above, it was the sender who was bound, in the sense that because of a mistake in transmission – which appeared to introduce a new term – he could not enforce the contract he had intended to make. In *Henkel* v. *Pape*,

1870, however, the sender was held entitled to enforce the contract in the terms he intended, even though they were altered in transmission.

iv. Form of acceptance

2.31   Expressly or by implication, the terms of the offer may require a particular method of acceptance. Buyer or seller may insist upon completion and return of the order form, without which no agreement can be reached: *Compagnie de Commerce* v. *Parkinson*, 1953; para. 1.34. Since business contracts are commonly made by means of standard forms, such forms will generally have contractual effect even though arising out of earlier oral agreement: *British Crane Hire* v. *Ipswich Plant Hire*, 1974 (*but see also* para. 7.8). Standard form conditions of sale typically lay down periods of time within which the buyer may accept the offer. They may also say that no contract comes into existence until the buyer's 'acceptance' has been confirmed in writing by the seller, as in *Cie. de Commerce* – in which case the purported acceptance is still only an offer. And as mentioned above, a party who invites a contractor to tender might say that his invitation constitutes an offer which is thereupon accepted by anyone whose tender is successful – *Northern Construction* v. *Gloge*, 1986 (Canada) – or, again, he might make it a condition that the tender is irrevocable pending acceptance: *Calgary* v. *Northern Construction*, 1987 (Canada).

2.32   Often enough the surrounding circumstances dictate the form of acceptance. An offer made by telegram indicates that an equally prompt form of acceptance is required: *Quenerduaine*, above. Getting in line at the entrance to an automatically controlled car park is the appropriate way of accepting the advertised terms: *Thornton* v. *Shoe Lane Parking*, 1971. As this latter case suggests, many offers do not require express communication of acceptance. The offeree's conduct may suffice to prove his acceptance, as with B.R.S.'s failure to respond to *Crutchley*'s counter-offer, above. Where a tenant stays on after the rent has been increased, or an employee remains at work without objecting to new conditions, his or her acceptance is presumed: *Harvey* v. *Johnston*, 1846; *Shields* v. *Goff*, 1973. A businessman who refused to sign a printed contract form, but nonetheless took the benefit of work done under it, was held to have accepted the contract by silence: *Empirnall* v. *Machon*, 1989 (Australia).

2.33   These examples lead in turn to the question whether silence alone, as distinct from acquiescent conduct, may constitute acceptance. It is difficult to draw the line between the two, as in the *B.R.S.* case above, but sometimes necessary to do so because the common law is reluctant to accept that the offeree's silence – which is essentially ambiguous – may commit him. The question is particularly important as regards notification and acceptance of exclusion clauses: para. 7.5. Difficulties have arisen also in several commercial disputes where one side has demanded arbitration and then done nothing for several years, thus encouraging the other to believe the claim had been abandoned. If the plaintiff then revives his claim, what are the defendant's rights? In *The Golden Bear*, 1987, the High Court held that the plaintiff's delay amounted to an offer to withdraw his claim which the defendant accepted by his own inactivity, so that both sides' silent conduct combined to make a contract preventing the plaintiff from reviving his claim. The House of Lords has disapproved of this line of argument in arbitration cases: *The Leonidas D*, 1985; Chapter 5. It might seem preferable to interpret such situations in terms of reasonable inferences and/or estoppel (Chapter 3), rather than implied contracts.

2.34   The fact that an offer can sometimes be accepted by silent acquiescence does not of itself enable an offeror to say that unless he has a reply from the offeree he will regard his offer as accepted. Such an offer seeks to compel a reply. The common law regards such offers as against public policy and void: *Felthouse* v. *Bindley*, 1862. 'Hard-sell' techniques of this kind – 'inertia sales' – are in effect forbidden by the Unsolicited Goods and Services Act 1971. The Act makes it illegal to demand payment for goods delivered without prior request by the recipient. The goods belong to the recipient after six months, or within one month of his giving the sender notice to collect them, whichever is the sooner. He has no special duty of care of the goods in the meantime.

v. Unilateral contracts

2.35   The offer and acceptance needed to make a contract usually result in an exchange of promises, along the lines of the formula mentioned earlier: 'I promise to do this for you if you promise to do that for me'. These reciprocal obligations are called bilateral or synallagmatic – two-sided – contracts. There is another kind of contract, however, where the offeror alone is bound by his promise, and where he becomes so not by another promise given in return but by the actual fulfilment of the terms of his offer. Such one-sided commitments are called unilateral or option contracts. A simple example is that of an advertisement for a lost dog. The advertiser promises to pay a £5 reward to anyone who brings the animal back. Clearly he does not expect or want interested members of the public to write to him or tell him of their acceptance of his offer by promising to go out and look for his dog. All he is concerned with is its return, and not until that happens is anyone entitled to the £5. One must be careful, however, to distinguish between a unilateral contract and a conditional gift e.g.: 'I will give you £100 if you call at my house tomorrow' – which on the face of it would be unenforceable. The action called for in return for the offer must be something of economic significance, as explained in Chapter 3. We observe again that if the act is done without knowledge of the offer, as where a person returns a lost dog without knowing of the reward, there is no acceptance.

2.36   An important example of a unilateral contract is the famous case of *Carlill* v. *Carbolic Smoke Ball Co.* 1894, where, as we described in Chapter 1, the company promised £100 to anyone who took their medicine but nonetheless caught influenza. Mrs. Carlill did not need to write to tell the company she had bought or was using the preparation; she was required only to prove that she had used it in accordance with the advertisement, and caught flu. She did so, and her claim was upheld.

2.37   Since in a unilateral contract acceptance does not need to be communicated, and is complete and effective only when the terms of the offer are fulfilled, it should follow at least in theory that the offer can be withdrawn at any time before then – as in *Routledge* v. *Grant*, above. But that theoretical answer would be most unjust. A newspaper might, for example, offer £10,000 to the first person to swim the Channel this year. A competitor might swim to within a few metres of the French coast, and then be told by a newspaper representative following him in a boat that the offer has been withdrawn. The competitor would then – again in theory – not be entitled to anything because the terms of the offer have not yet been fulfilled or, therefore, accepted. It is not an offer of £9,999 to anyone who swims 99.99 per cent of the way.

2.38   The problem was confronted in *Errington* v. *Errington*, 1952, where the elderly parents told their children they could have the house if they paid off the mortgage. They did not promise to pay it off, but nonetheless began making payments. The parents died before payments were completed. It was held that the children were entitled to stay in the house for as long as they continued the payments, on the basis that once an offeree has begun to fulfil the terms of an offer the offer cannot then be revoked. This rule might perhaps be justified as an implied term of the contract – *Daulia* v. *Four Millbank Nominees*, 1978 – which takes effect when the offeree begins to fulfil the contract. The American Uniform Commercial Code sees beginning upon the contract as a form of acceptance which at least prevents revocation: Section 2–206. This Section also says that the offeree should notify the offeror that he has begun.

vi. Revocation of acceptance

2.39   We have said that an acceptance by post is usually complete when the letter is posted. But could the offeree then change his mind and revoke his acceptance before it reaches the offeror, e.g. by telephoning or sending a telegram? If so, he could both accept and then revoke, whereas the offeror could not revoke once the letter of acceptance had been posted. But probably the offeror would be justified in relying on the telephone call or telegram and contract with someone else if he wished. The offeree would be estopped – prevented – from 'blowing hot and cold' and suing to enforce his letter, as described in Chapter 3. Revocation of acceptance at any later stage is inevitably a breach of contract – the consequences of which are discussed in Chapter 13 – except where the offeree exercises the cancellation rights given by the Consumer Credit Act 1974 or Consumer Protection (Cancellation of Contracts Concluded Away from Business Premises) Regulations 1987 to protect him against high-pressure 'doorstep' sales. A draft European Union Directive currently (1995) gives consumers who order goods as a result of distance selling pressures seven days to withdraw from their contracts.

Danish law

2.40   Danish law recognises the distinction between an offer and an invitation to treat, but nonetheless holds that a statement of price attached to goods generally constitutes a binding offer – unless, e.g., clearly mistaken – as in a Supreme Court judgment in 1985 (UfR 877). The same may be true of price statements in advertisements if sufficiently precise. An offer to the general public is binding when made public. If a reward is offered it can be claimed by anyone fulfilling its terms, whether or not he knew of them at the time in question – as laid down in a High Court case on advertisements in 1954 (UfR 818).

2.41   A supplier of services can usually claim payment only for doing work expressly required of him, but exceptionally may demand payment in accordance with the principle of *negotiorum gestio*, which is recognised by Danish law.

2.42   Under Danish law the obligation of a party is based on his promise, whether or not it requires anything in return. The offeror is therefore bound by his offer when it comes to the offeree's attention. An offer can be revoked, but only if the revocation reaches the offeree before or at the same time as he becomes aware of the offer.

2.43   The 'battle of the forms' has not yet led to any important cases in Denmark. Contradictory forms may prevent the formation of a contract. But if the contract has been fulfilled, the offeror's failure to object to contradictory terms put forward by the offeree will usually mean that the offeree's terms prevail – but not if the result is unfair. If the parties know or should know that their terms are different, but carry on nonetheless with the problem unresolved, neither side's terms will necessarily apply. The general rules of law and implied terms may resolve the problem.

2.44   An offer must be accepted within the time specified, or if no time is specified then within a reasonable time, which in the case of an oral offer is immediately. Although the offer is binding, no contract exists until acceptance is received, but thereafter it is binding for both parties.

2.45   Under the Consumer Contracts Act 1978 consumers are entitled to keep unsolicited goods without payment, provided they were not sent to them by mistake.

Dutch law

2.46   The new Dutch Civil Code is explicitly based on the model of formation of contract where offer and acceptance are of major importance. In contrast with the English system, Dutch law holds that an offer or promise stated to be valid for a specified period of time is binding for that period: Article 6.219. The Code also recognises the principle of *negotiorum gestio*: Article 6.198–201.

2.47   As for the battle of forms – para. 2.15 – Dutch case law has precedents for both 'first shot' and 'last shot' theories. Article 6.225 of the new Code says shortly: 'An acceptance which deviates from the offer is considered to be a new offer and a rejection of the original offer. Unless the offeror objects to the differences without delay, where a reply intended to accept an offer only deviates from the offer on points of minor importance, the reply is considered to be an acceptance and the contract is formed according to the latter. Where offer and acceptance refer to different general conditions, the second reference is of no effect unless it expressly rejects the general conditions in the first reference'. An arbitration award reported in *Bouwrecht* 1995, 153, held that a printed reference to the buyer's general conditions on the back of his order form was not effective to reject the seller's printed terms, expressly referred to in his letter of confirmation.

2.48   Unlike English law, the Code considers an acceptance by post complete only when it reaches the addressee: Article 3.37. The Door to Door Sales Act or *Colportagewet* 1973 gives a right of cancellation. The government is considering the introduction of such a right for all real property contracts. There is no general right of cancellation under consumer credit law. Unsolicited goods may be treated as gifts: Article 7.7.

French law

2.49   An offer to contract is one which shows clearly the intention of the offeror to enter into a binding contract on the terms set out, and which contains the essential elements of the contract, whose acceptance without reserve by the other party creates the contract: Com. 6 March 1990. It is distinguishable from a letter of intent or offer to start negotiating, which may create only an obligation to negotiate in good faith and therefore possibly give rise to a quasi-delictual liability if the negotiations are not made in good faith or are arbitrarily ended: Com. 20 March 1972.

2.50   An offer may be inferred from conduct. Displaying goods with their prices usually constitutes an offer for sale: T.C. Seine, 28 May 1981. A taxi waiting at a taxi rank thereby offers a contract of carriage: Civ. 2 December 1969. An offer may be to the general public or a particular individual; for a certain time or not. An offer open for a certain time cannot be revoked before the end of that time: Civ. 10 May 1968. Early revocation usually gives rise to quasi-delictual liability in damages, although certain commentators say the appropriate remedy should be specific performance where the offeree can show he intended to accept the offer within the prescribed time. An offer of indefinite duration can be revoked at any time if made to the general public, or within a reasonable time (*'delai raisonnable'*) if made to a given individual.

2.51   Acceptance must be of the offer as a whole. Reservations or modifications of the terms of the offer constitute counter-offers: Civ. 2 March 1962. Generally, mere silence does not constitute acceptance – Cass. 2 May 1870 – but there are many possible exceptions. Acceptance may be implicit, as where the terms of the offer are fulfilled (Civ. 21 June 1983), or there is a continuing business relationship between the parties and the proposed contract is of the kind regularly implemented between them. Trade usages may also indicate acceptance despite the absence of any response to an offer: Com. 21 May 1951. On the vexed question of consumers' acceptance of standard business forms, *see* paras. 7.63–9.

2.52   There is no overall solution to the 'battle of the forms'. The judges infer the common intention of the parties on a case by case basis. If the forms cannot be reconciled, the relevant clause is deemed not agreed and/or the contract not formed: Com. 17 July 1967. Where the parties' express agreement is required by law, e.g., on reservation of title clauses, the contradiction between the vendor's terms providing for reservation and the purchaser's terms nullifying any such term in advance negatives agreement. The vendor's reservation of title is therefore unenforceable: Paris, 20 June 1990.

2.53   As regards the time of acceptance, the question whether a contract is made when acceptance is posted or when the offeror receives it (which is important in determining whether the offer can still be revoked) has occupied the French courts more than the battle of the forms. The issue is still treated case by case, although the courts tend generally to hold that acceptance is given, and thus the contract made, when it is posted: Com. 7 January 1981.

German law

2.54   German law recognises the distinction between an offer and an invitation to treat, or *invitatio ad offerendum*. Goods displayed and priced in shop windows represent only an invitation. But the courts have not yet decided whether the display of goods in a self-service store should be regarded as an offer.

2.55   Where one person spends his own money to help another without being asked to do so, e.g. where he makes his absent neighbour's house safe after a fire, German law entitles him to reclaim his expenditure. This is a legal obligation arising independently of contract. Article 677 BGB recognises this right in *negotiorum gestio* or *Geschäftsfürung ohne Auftrag* – in contrast with English law (paras. 2.6–7).

2.56   Again in contrast with English law, in principle once an offer has been received by the offeree, it must unless otherwise stated remain open for a reasonable time and cannot be withdrawn before acceptance: Articles 130 and 145. If the offeror does not wish to be bound by his offer he must say so expressly, e.g., by the formula *'Angebot freileibend'* ('offer not binding') or *'Zwischenverkauf vorbehalten'* ('subject to prior sale'). The legal effect of a counter-offer is the same as in English law. By Article 150, conditional acceptance of an offer is a new offer which the other party may then accept or refuse.

2.57   The 'battle of the forms' (para. 2.15) is a problem in Germany also, but the solutions may differ. While generally German courts have followed the 'last shot' rule, they may nonetheless be willing to recognise the existence of a contract 'core' without applying this rule, if and insofar as both parties act as if agreed: Articles 154–5. The effect may be to enforce the terms first put forward, except so far as contradicted by the other party. Terms in conflict are invalid. Gaps in the contract are bridged by applying the BGB. In an important case in 1985 (NJW 1838) the buyer ordered goods on his standard form which said, as in *Butler* (para. 2.18), that his terms alone were the basis of the contract. The seller replied in his own standard form, which likewise purported to govern the whole transaction. His terms were fundamentally different from the buyer's in that they included a retention of title clause (*see* paras. 8.22–36), but the buyer raised no objection to them. After the goods were delivered the buyer became insolvent. The seller then sought to repossess his goods in accordance with his standard form. The court held that the contract was made exclusively on the buyer's terms. The retention of title clause was invalid because it was inconsistent with the buyer's terms and had not been expressly or impliedly agreed. Retention clauses in particular will not be enforced without proof of agreement.

2.58   When an offer is to be accepted by letter, acceptance is complete only when the letter reaches the offeror's premises, even if he does not read it: Article 130. Acceptance may be made by conduct or silence: Article 151. So if a person books a holiday and some days later receives a confirmation different from his booking he is not bound because the 'confirmation' is a new offer. But if he starts his journey without objecting to it he will probably be taken to have accepted the new offer. The courts' willingness to interpret silence as acceptance may sometimes oblige a business party expressly to reject an offer if he is to avoid liability for having accepted it.

2.59   German law recognises a type of unilateral contract known as the *Auslobung*: Article 657. This means a reward offered by public notice for the performance of an act or the bringing about of a particular result, such as the return of a lost dog. Article 657 provides – contrary to English law, para. 2.35 – that whoever does the act or achieves the result is entitled to the reward even though unaware of its existence at the time in question. Unlike a normal offer, an *Auslobung* may be withdrawn at any time. The facts of *Carlill's* case, para. 2.36, would be interpreted as an ordinary bilateral contract, as with manufacturers' guarantees in general. *Auslobung* does not play an important role.

Italian law

2.60   The basic position as to the formation of a contract under Italian law is stated in Article 1326 of the Civil Code: 'A contract is formed at the moment when he who made the offer has knowledge of the acceptance of the other party'. Both offer and acceptance take effect from the time when they come to the notice of the other party: Article 1334. The other party is deemed to know of the offer, acceptance or revocation, as the case may be, at the moment it reaches his address, unless he can prove that without fault on his part he could not have known of it: Article 1335. The contract is made at the place where the offeror learns of the offeree's acceptance. Acceptance may be made by conduct, or as requested by the offeror, or according to the nature of the transaction or by usage. The court will enforce an agreement if the parties act as if bound by it, although all the details may not yet be decided: Corte di Cassazione, 7 October 1992. Even without offer or acceptance, one person may be liable to reimburse another who has voluntarily managed his affairs in his absence and for his benefit: Articles 2028–32.

2.61   Subject to Article 1329, below, an offer can be revoked at any time before acceptance. But if an offeree begins in good faith to perform the contract before learning of the revocation, the offeror must reimburse his expenses: Article 1328. Acceptance must reach the offeror within the time he has specified, or otherwise within a reasonable time. An acceptance can be revoked only by a second communication, e.g. a telegram, which reaches the offeror before the original letter of acceptance. Exceptionally, and in contrast with English law, if the offeror promises to keep his offer open for a certain time, his offer is irrevocable once it comes to the other's notice: Articles 1329–30. It may, however, lapse through passage of time. An offer in the form of an option – a promise binding on the offeror but which the offeree may accept or refuse at his discretion – is likewise irrevocable for the period stated or determined as reasonable by the court: Article 1333. Italian case law on the battle of the forms takes the strict view that if the parties are not expressly agreed on exactly the same terms, there is no contract. So a purported acceptance which does not conform exactly with the offer is seen as a counter-offer, although it may involve only minor modifications of the offer: Article 1326; Corte di Cassazione, 7 January 1993. The court cannot make a contract for the parties out of whatever common ground may appear between them.

2.62   Italian contract law requires parties negotiating a contract to act in good faith – an obligation which may sometimes require the supplier to disclose facts affecting the value of the subject matter of which he knows or ought to know: Article 1337.

Spanish law

2.63   Article 1262 of the Spanish Civil Code says that consent is shown by the concurrence of offer and acceptance of the thing in issue and the *causa* which together constitute the contract. An offer should be precise and complete and intended to be binding. A Supreme Court decision of 10 October 1980 states: 'Once the offer of contract or proposal, with all necessary elements for the future contract, has been made, the contract comes into being with the assent of the other party'.

2.64   Acceptance must be clear and unequivocal, and directed to the offeror. It may be express or implied, but must show the intention to complete the proposed contract. Acceptance may be inferred from silence in appropriate circumstances, as discussed in a Supreme Court case of 13 February 1978. A purported acceptance which in fact modifies the offer or makes it subject to a new condition is only a counter-offer: Supreme Court, 14 March 1973. A seller's delivery of goods is normally conclusive evidence of his acceptance of the buyer's counter-offer: Article 1445 of the Civil Code; Article 339, Commercial Code.

2.65   A commercial contract by exchange of letters is complete when the acceptance is posted: Article 54 of the Commercial Code. In ordinary 'civil' contracts the rule is different; completion does not occur until acceptance comes to the notice of the offeror: Article 1262 of the Civil Code.

Swedish law

2.66   With regard to questions of offer and acceptance generally, the problem of the battle of the forms remains unresolved in Swedish law. As well as the theories concerning the first and last shot, it is argued that no effect at all should be given to contradictory standard form contracts. The contract should instead be interpreted according to non-mandatory rules, i.e., the general clauses of the Sale of Goods Act, trade usages, etc. There are also theories that one should try to combine the two forms and in areas where this is not possible, apply non-mandatory rules. Since Swedish courts often fill in gaps in parties' agreements, it is possible to take a more objective view as to the intentions of the parties.

2.67   The risk of mistakes in transmissions are on the sender, except when the message is delivered by someone who simply passes it on or it is delivered as a telegram. But when the sender learns of the mistake he has to give notice to the recipient in good faith: Article 32, Contract Act.

Chapter 3

Consideration and estoppel

3.1   We come now to the vital question of contract law which all legal systems have to resolve – how to decide which promises shall be enforced and which shall not. One might think that if a judge were satisfied in any particular case that the parties intended to be legally bound and had expressed themselves clearly enough, with an offer on one side and acceptance on the other, as discussed in Chapters 1 and 2, he should then be able to enforce their agreement. He might well do so under other systems of law, but not, unfortunately, under the English system. For historical reasons, notably the late development of contractual remedies out of the law of tort, or delict, requiring evidence of loss or damage, English law demands proof of a further vital element in the parties' relationship, known as *consideration*. This requirement is possibly the most fundamental respect in which English contract law differs from Continental systems – and even from the Scottish.

A. Valuable consideration

3.2   The basic rule is that *a person cannot enforce a promise unless he has given consideration for it*. Consideration – or, strictly, valuable consideration – is a requirement peculiar to Anglo-American law, and correspondingly difficult to translate into the language of other legal systems. The basic idea is that of mutuality or reciprocity; a *quid pro quo*; something of economic value which must be given or done or undertaken by the promisee, or some form of loss he suffers, *in return for* the other's promise. In effect *it is the price he agrees to pay or benefit he confers for the other's promise*. Without that agreement the promise is unenforceable. One can only validly accept an offer, therefore, by undertaking to do – or actually doing – something in return for it. The law is concerned, in other words, with the enforcement of bargains – 'I will do this for you if you will do that for me' – rather than enforcement of agreements with promises on one side only. In commercial contracts in particular, therefore, it is most desirable to state clearly what consideration is given on each side; e.g., 'In consideration of

payment of the sum of £10,000 the seller hereby agrees to sell to the buyer
. . .', or 'In consideration of the buyer's promise to pay £1,000 . . .'

3.3 Conversely, what English law calls a bare promise – a *nudum pactum* – is a promise unsupported by consideration, i.e., to do something for nothing. So a promise to make a gift is generally of no legal significance. Curiously enough, then, when Englishmen have gone round the world saying: 'An Englishman's word is his bond', English law has always denied that that is so. But exceptions to the bare promise rule arise where the promise is made in the form of a deed, and, more importantly, where it is affected by estoppel. Both issues are discussed below.

3.4 It will be appreciated that the consideration requirement is not the same as the *causa* – a Continental rule, apparently of uncertain application, as to the 'justification' for the contract. Justification is an inquiry which is not as such pursued by English law. Instead English law looks for what might be seen in other legal systems merely as evidence as to whether a contract has been made – *viz.* the presence of reciprocal obligations – and converts that important item of evidence into a requirement of substantive law. Normally, of course, contracting parties do enter into such obligations – to work in return for wages, or to deliver goods in return for money – and so the rule is usually a sensible test of contractual intention. But it may also mean that the answers given by English contract law are given for reasons different from those which a Continental judge might give, and occasionally that the answers are very clearly unsatisfactory and almost certainly unacceptable to Continental lawyers.

3.5 We shall note first some leading cases illustrating the basic rule, and then discuss details of the rule. An early example which helped to shape the law was *Price* v. *Easton*, 1833. Here A promised B that if B did certain work for him, he, A, would pay money to C. B did the work, but A failed to pay C. It was held that C had no claim against A because he had done nothing in return for A's promise. The agreement could of course be enforced by B if he wished, but he might have no reason to do so. *Dunlop* v. *Selfridge*, 1915, concerned an attempt to enforce a resale price maintenance agreement. The manufacturers supplied goods to wholesalers – middlemen – on condition that they would only resell at certain prices and would extract promises from their purchasers – the retailers – to do the same. The retailers gave that promise, but broke it. Since the wholesalers had no interest in enforcing the promise the manufacturers tried to do so. The House of Lords held that the manufacturers had no claim because they were seeking to enforce a promise which was not made directly to them and for which they had given no consideration. The retailers were therefore free to break a promise given in a commercial context, which they knew they had given at the manufacturers' request and for their benefit. We observe in passing that nowadays the Resale Prices Act 1976, below, reaches much the same conclusion as to the unenforceability of such agreements – but on broader grounds of public intent.

3.6   The principle is illustrated again in two very important modern cases – *Beswick* v. *Beswick*, 1967, and the Australian case of *Coulls* v. *Bagot's Trustee*, 1967. In *Beswick* the elderly owner of a small business offered to hand over the business to his nephew if in return, *inter alia*, he would promise to pay a pension of £5 a week to his aunt if his uncle died before she did. The contract was made and the business changed hands. After the uncle's death the nephew made one payment of £5 to his aunt, and no more. She sued. It is hard to believe that any system of law other than that of England would have any difficulty in upholding the aunt's claim, but under English law the fact remained that she had given no consideration to her nephew for the promise she sought to enforce, and therefore had no claim as a contracting party. By chance, however, she was her husband's executrix, responsible in this capacity for paying the debts and enforcing the claims of his estate. Her husband had given consideration for the nephew's promise by promising to transfer the business to him, and so 'standing in her husband's shoes' she eventually won her claim, which she had to take as far as the House of Lords.

3.7   In *Coulls* a man owned some land which he wished to lease to a mining company. He and his wife signed an agreement with the company, the vital term of which was that after his death the company would continue making payments to his widow. The company's right to make these payments was challenged by the husband's executors, which resulted in the widow losing her money. The mere fact that she had signed the contract did not make her a party to it – contrary to most people's expectations. She could only become a party if the company's promise had been made to both husband and wife and both had given consideration, or to her alone and she had given consideration for it. But on the facts the promise was made to her husband, though for her benefit, and he alone, as the land owner, gave consideration for it. That is not to say that two or more people on each side cannot make a contract or that one person cannot give consideration on behalf of another (*McEvoy* v. *Belfast Banking*, 1935); only that that is not what happened here. Thus far the case is like *Beswick*, but it did not have the same happy ending, because – again by chance – the widow here was not the husband's executrix and so could make no claim in any representative capacity. In *White* v. *Jones*, 1995, a solicitor failed to prepare a will in accordance with his client's instructions before the client died. The beneficiaries therefore lost their inheritance. The House of Lords held that they had no claim against the solicitor in contract, but allowed a claim for negligence (*see* para. 6.68). Lord Goff's judgment in this case is of particular interest in drawing extensively on Commonwealth and Continental law. These cases show all too clearly the rigour of contract law, and the profoundly unsatisfactory answers it can give. Exceptions to the rule are noted under 'Privity', below.

3.8   Since commercial parties do not always appreciate the refinements of English contract law, the courts sometimes find difficulty in making the facts of deserving cases conform with legal requirements – but only by doing so can they give the kind of answer which the commercial world would find acceptable. An example is the leading case of *New Zealand Shipping* v. *Satterthwaite*, 1975. A shipping firm agreed with cargo owners that the independent parties – the stevedores – who would eventually unload the cargo would have the benefit of the same limited liability for loss or damage that the shippers had negotiated for themselves (under a so-called 'Himalaya' clause). The stevedores damaged the goods and claimed the benefit of the clause. The legal problem was that they appeared to be trying to enforce a promise which was not made to them and for which they had not given consideration. The Privy Council held that the cargo owners' agreement with the shippers was at the same time an offer to anyone who might unload the ship, which the stevedores accepted by unloading it (and so entitled themselves to the benefit of a unilateral contract, Chapter 2). In welcome contrast with this tortuous reasoning is the decision of the Court of Appeal in *Norwich City Council* v. *Harvey*, 1989. The Court upheld a sub-contractor's right to take the benefit of terms negotiated between the main contractor and the employer – the city council – on the purely practical basis that all the parties knew their relationships were intended to be governed by those terms. *London Drugs* v. *Kuehne International*, 1993, is an important Canadian case relieving a contractor's employees of liability on the ground that the exclusion clause expressly or impliedly benefited employees and that the loss or damage was caused by employees doing the work stipulated in the contract.

3.9   *N.Z. Shipping* is notable for the apologia of Lord Wilberforce, seeking to justify the complex reasoning needed to enable the stevedores to take advantage of a contract which was obviously intended to benefit them: 'If the choice, and the antithesis, is between a gratuitous promise and a promise for consideration, as it must be in the absence of a *tertium quid* [third party right], there can be little doubt which, in commercial reality, this is. The whole contract is of a commercial character, involving service on one side, rates of payment on the other, and qualifying stipulation as to both. The relations of all parties to each other are commercial relations entered into for business reasons of ultimate profit. To describe one set of promises, in this context, as gratuitous, or *nudum pactum*, seems paradoxical and is *prima facie* implausible. It is only the precise analysis of this complex of relations into the classical offer and acceptance, with identifiable consideration, that seems to present difficulty, but this same difficulty exists in many situations of daily life, e.g. sales at auction; supermarket purchases; boarding an omnibus; purchasing a train ticket; tenders for the supply of goods; offers of reward; acceptance by post; warranties of authority by agents; manufacturers' guarantees; gratuitous bailments; bankers' commercial credits. These are all examples which show that English law, having committed itself to a rather technical and schematic doctrine of contract, in application takes a practical approach, often at the cost of forcing the facts to fit uneasily into the marked slots of offer, acceptance and consideration.'

3.10   It will be seen that this 'technical and schematic doctrine' leaves many substantial areas of doubt, despite the judges' supposedly 'practical' approach. An interesting hint of dissatisfaction with the rule was given by Lord Goff in *White* v. *Jones*, above: 'Our law of contract is widely seen as deficient in the sense that it is perceived to be hampered by the presence of an unnecessary doctrine of consideration and (through a strict doctrine of privity of contract) stunted through a failure to recognise a *jus quaesitum tertio* [third party right].'

i. Consideration must not be past

3.11   Consideration can be classified as executory, executed or past. Executory consideration is a promise of future action, e.g. to pay for or to deliver goods. Executed consideration is that which is performed or fulfilled – e.g. delivery of the goods in return for the promise. These are both valid forms of consideration. Past consideration, on the other hand, refers to an act done or promise given without any contractual intention, but which in fact leads to a promise by the other side. The rule is that that later promise cannot be enforced by the promisee, because his original act or promise was not done or given in return for the other's promise. Thus if I rescue from drowning someone who then promises me a reward, but – such is human nature – does not pay me, I cannot enforce his promise because my act of rescue is past consideration, i.e. it was not undertaken with contractual intent or in return for the promise of reward.

3.12   *Roscorla* v. *Thomas*, 1842, remains a useful illustration of the rule against past consideration. B contracted to buy a horse from S. After the contract was made S promised B that the horse was not vicious. The promise was broken, but B could not claim compensation because he gave nothing in return for that promise. He had given consideration originally in promising to pay for the horse, but this was past consideration because it was for a bargain made without reference to S's later promise. We note below how this conclusion may affect the enforceability of manufacturers' guarantees. We observe also that American law rejects the rule by Sections 2–209 and 303 of the Uniform Commercial Code, which make subsequent promises or 'warranties' enforceable even without consideration, if in reality they are 'part of' a business transaction.

3.13   Consideration is not to be regarded as past simply because the act or promise in question is not immediately followed by a new promise given in return by the other side. It is not just a matter of showing the chronological sequence of events, but of examining the overall course of dealings between the parties and of deciding what was involved in each offer and acceptance. In *Re Casey's Patents*, 1892, for example, an employer promised an employee a certain payment 'in consideration of [his] past services', but then broke his promise. On the face of it the employee's services were given before the promise and so appeared to be past consideration. In fact, however, both parties understood from the time the employee began work that he would receive some such payment as was now promised. All the employer did by making his new promise was to specify exactly the sum he already owed. He was liable accordingly.

3.14   Similarly, when a person guarantees payment of an existing debt, his promise is void if it is based on past consideration, i.e., the credit previously given by the creditor to the debtor: *Astley* v. *Grimston*, 1965. But again the whole sequence of events must be examined. In *Pao On* v. *Lau*, 1979, B bought shares in a company from S. Later the same day S promised B to make good, within various limits, any losses B might suffer if the shares lost value. When the losses duly occurred S refused to pay, arguing that the sale had been completed by the time he made this promise, and that B had given no new consideration for it. But on the evidence before it the court found that what appeared to be two separate transactions were in fact one. B proved that he had only bought the shares on the basis that S would protect him against loss. By buying the shares he had given the consideration necessary to make S's subsequent detailed commitment binding. Scots law, untroubled by the consideration rule, would evidently have correspondingly less difficulty in enforcing a guarantee of an existing debt.

ii. Consideration must move from the promisee

3.15   With exceptions noted below under the heading of 'Privity', a person who seeks to enforce another's promise – the promisee – must show the promise was made to him and that he gave consideration for it. That means that he must show he has suffered some loss or detriment in return for the promise. Usually the promisor benefits accordingly, but the mere fact of loss or benefit does not prove that consideration was given. The basic rule is that *consideration must move from the promisee, but not necessarily to the promisor.* Thus part of the consideration given by the nephew in return for his uncle's promise in *Beswick*, above, was that he would pay a pension to his aunt. More recently it has been held sufficient if the promisor gains a benefit *without* the promisee necessarily suffering any detriment: *Williams* v. *Roffey*, below.

iii. Manufacturers' guarantees

3.16   Manufacturers' guarantees are such a normal part of commercial contracts that it may seem strange there could be any doubt in English law about their legal status – but there is a doubt, and it is caused by the consideration rule. A guarantee is usually a promise to perform certain services. A consumer trying to enforce that promise must show, as must anyone seeking to enforce a promise under English law, that he or she has given consideration for it. But what did the consumer give or do or suffer in return for the manufacturer's promise?

3.17   One possible answer is for the consumer to show that in response to the manufacturer's promise he bought the goods from a retailer, or, as in *Carlill* v. *Carbolic Smoke Ball Co.*, Chapter 1, used them as instructed by the guarantee. In effect then the terms laid down by the manufacturer are: 'If you buy goods from a retailer, or use them as directed, I promise to provide these services' – thereby benefiting the retailer directly and himself only indirectly. Insofar as the guarantee requires a purchase from a retailer, the consumer's argument makes use of the 'collateral contract' theory. A collateral contract was defined by Lord Moulton in *Heilbut Symons* v. *Buckleton*, 1913, as one for which the consideration is the making of some other contract; e.g.: 'If you will make such and such a contract I will give you £100'. His Lordship warned against using this concept as a means of altering or weakening a primary contract, and said that collateral contracts had to be strictly proved.

3.18   Guarantees need not be in writing, nor need the manufacturer's assurance or promise be given expressly as a guarantee: *Shanklin Pier Co.* v. *Detel Products*, 1951. In *Wells* v. *Buckland Sand*, 1964, for example, a professional flower grower sought advice from a quarrying company as to the best sand for his flowers. Not surprisingly he was told the company's sand was the best. In due course he bought some of it from a retailer. It proved unsuitable and harmful. He had no claim against the retailer, since he had got from him exactly what he asked for, and so his only possible claim was against the quarry company. The court agreed that despite appearances there was a contract between the plaintiff and the company, collateral to or alongside that between the plaintiff and the retailer. When the company's representative gave the information the plaintiff had wanted, what was actually intended and understood, said the court, was a contractual commitment: 'If you buy our sand from a retailer we promise it is the best for your needs.' The plaintiff's purchase was therefore consideration given in return for the promise and not merely an act in reliance on it.

3.19   Similarly in *Andrews* v. *Hopkinson*, 1956, when an over-optimistic car dealer told a prospective customer: 'It's a good little bus: I would stake my life on it', what he actually meant, according to the judge, was: 'If you will enter into a hire purchase agreement with a finance company I will promise this car is in good condition.' The customer entered into that agreement, and in so doing gave consideration for the dealer's promise, which in due course led to the dealer becoming liable for breach of his promise. In *Bowerman* v. *Association of British Travel Agents*, 1995, the terms of an ABTA notice displayed in a tour operator's office were held to constitute an offer to customers which they could accept by doing business with the operator.

3.20   But not every advertisement or recommendation can be given contractual significance. In *Lambert* v. *Lewis*, 1981, for instance, the Court of Appeal held that a manufacturer's advertisement that his goods were safe – a claim which was not made in answer to any specific inquiry – did not amount to a promise to reimburse any retailer who might sell the goods and then be held liable to a buyer for resulting injury. This particular decision, reversed by the House of Lords but on different grounds, is therefore very unsatisfactory in seeming to allow manufacturers to make unfounded claims as to the safety of their products. Although it was a feature of the relevant precedents, it is not clear why as a matter of principle a specific inquiry should always be necessary in order to create a contractual obligation, as the Court of Appeal had held. Again on principle, it must be 'in general undesirable to allow a commercial promoter to claim that what he has done is a mere puff, not intended to create legal relations' – as Lord Simon said in *Esso* v. *Commissioners of Customs and Excise*, 1976. American practice accords with Lord Simon's view: *Baxter* v. *Ford*, 1934 – manufacturer liable to injured buyer for falsely advertising windscreens as 'shatterproof'.

3.21   Despite the judges' apparent readiness to find and enforce guarantees in *Carlill*, *Shanklin Pier*, *Wells* and *Andrews*, however, the position is still doubtful. In all these cases the plaintiff knew of the manufacturer's promise before he or she bought or used the goods, and so could be said to have bought or used them in return for that promise. But normally the buyer is unaware of the existence of any guarantee, and comes upon it only when he has taken his purchase home and opened the box. In legal theory the buyer must then find it difficult to enforce the guarantee, because on those facts he did not buy the goods in return for it. His only contract is with the retailer, who is not usually seen in English law as the manufacturer's agent and so is not responsible for fulfilling the guarantee. It seems therefore that the enforceability or otherwise of a manufacturer's guarantee could depend on the precise moment in time at which the buyer became aware of it – i.e., before or after purchase – an answer so arbitrary that one must hope it is incorrect.

3.22   Though there are no decided cases on the point, these difficulties might be avoided if the buyer could argue that he made his purchase on the assumption that the goods were guaranteed, or alternatively that he afterwards returned the guarantee form – an action which might perhaps amount to consideration. In theory the buyer's remedies against the seller should be sufficient, as described in Chapter 5, and he should have no need to rely on the manufacturer's guarantee. In practice, both consumers and retailers often rely on manufacturers for repair services. But while most manufacturers keep their promises, the overall position remains unsatisfactory and open to abuse. In 1990 the National Consumer Council sponsored a Consumer Guarantee Bill to end the uncertainty and to make enforceable certain minimum terms of any guarantee given by a manufacturer. Consumers were to be entitled under such guarantee to the free repair of defective goods within one year of purchase, and to replacements if repairs were unsuccessful or delayed. The Bill was defeated by government opposition. In Ireland reform has already taken place through the Sale of Goods and Supply of Services Act 1980, which makes sellers liable on manufacturers' guarantees and also enables buyers to sue manufacturers directly on them. A European Commission Green Paper of 1993 proposed harmonisation and strengthening of the law on guarantees. Australia's Trade Practices Act 1974 and New Zealand's Consumer Guarantees Act 1993 impose the same statutory liabilities on manufacturers as on retailers, and also enable consumers to enforce express guarantees.

iv. Consideration must be sufficient, but need not be adequate

3.23   This apparently self-contradictory – or even seemingly quite meaningless – statement in fact tells us that while *consideration must be of some economic value* ('sufficient'), *it need not be equivalent* ('adequate') *to the promise it secures.* These twin propositions are of the utmost importance. If consideration need not be adequate then it may only be a token – a penny or even the proverbial peppercorn – if that is agreeable to the promisor. It will still suffice to make a binding contract for something far more valuable given in return – presupposing, of course, there is no question of fraud or duress, as to which *see* Chapter 11. An example is in the practice of inviting tenders and offering the tenderer £1 to keep the tender open without alteration (which could equally well be achieved by making it a condition of tendering that the terms will not be altered). The presence or absence of consideration or its adequacy may be largely a matter of chance, and yet the enforceability of the whole agreement turns upon it.

3.24   Cases on the adequacy of consideration include *Chappel* v. *Nestle*, 1959, where it was held that chocolate wrappers which were thrown away on receipt were nonetheless part of the consideration in a sales promotion scheme. Taking part in a newspaper promotion scheme by asking for advice from the paper gave the reader a claim for damages for breach of contract when the adviser proved unqualified: *De La Bere* v. *Pearson*, 1908. Merely taking medicine was consideration in *Carlill*, as was an agreement to vote for another's nominee in *Bolton* v. *Madden*, 1873, and an agreement not to pursue a legal claim in *Alliance Bank* v. *Broome*, 1864. In *Paulger* v. *Butland Industries*, 1989 (N.Z.), a company director who gave a creditor a personal guarantee of payment within 90 days was held to have made an offer which the creditor impliedly accepted by forbearing to sue the company until the end of that time. In *Pitt* v. *P.H.H. Asset Management*, 1993, a house buyer gave consideration for the seller's promise not to offer the house to anyone else by promising to complete the purchase within two days. Such cases are sometimes seen as examples of judges' willingness to 'invent' consideration when it seems necessary to do so, but of course no one can predict when that might be. And conversely, if Mrs. Beswick, above, had given her nephew as little as a penny to secure to herself his promise to pay her a pension, he would have had no defence at all to her claim.

3.25   The other major consequence of the same rule is that insofar as the common law finds nothing objectionable in a person contracting to give very little in order to obtain a great deal, on principle it is not concerned with the *fairness* or otherwise of bargains. Its basic attitude is still that of nineteenth century *laisser-faire* philosophy. It is a law for merchants and businessmen, supposedly bargaining on equal terms, each free to get the better of the other if he can. Once made, the bargain is binding, for better or worse. The law will not rewrite people's contracts for them in the interests of abstract ideals of fairness or justice. English law is thus unique among legal systems in having no general rule against unconscionable contracts, or in refusing to imply obligations of good faith between contracting parties. There are many exceptions and reservations to this position, particularly as regards the Unfair Contract Terms Act 1977 and the Unfair Terms in Consumer Contracts Regulations 1994, Chapter 7, but they have not yet changed the basic philosophy.

v. Insufficient consideration

3.26   Certain types of promises are now clearly established as being legally worthless. They are therefore unenforceable in themselves, or, as the case may be, cannot be relied upon to enforce someone else's promise. Thus the mere fact that a promise expresses an existing moral obligation, or is undeniable because and insofar as it is in writing, does not of itself make that promise enforceable. It would only become so if required and given in return for another's promise or act. A promise to fulfil, or actually fulfilling, a duty which the promisor is already obliged by law to fulfil is evidently of no economic value and so is not good consideration. So, for example, the police cannot enforce a promise to pay them for services they are legally required to provide. But if by request they were to provide additional services they could charge accordingly: *Glasbrook* v. *Glamorgan C. C.*, 1925. In *Harris* v. *Sheffield United F.C.*, 1988, the police recovered the excessive costs incurred in trying to control football hooliganism.

3.27   On the same principle, a promise to fulfil – or actual fulfilment of – an existing *contractual* duty to the promisee should be economically worthless, and so should not bind the promisee to any new promise he might give in return. But this argument was doubted in *Williams* v. *Roffey*, 1989. A contractor here promised his sub-contractor an extra payment to help him over his financial problems, and so make sure he finished his work on time. The sub-contractor completed the work, but the contractor refused to pay the additional sum. The Court of Appeal said that in return for his promise the contractor had secured a new benefit for himself, in avoiding liability to his own employer for breach of contract. On this ground, and emphasising that there was no duress on the part of the sub-contractor, the Court held the contractor's promise binding, even though strictly speaking the sub-contractor had given nothing in return. The decision may be commercially convenient, but seems contrary to established principle. On the other hand again, the principle itself may sometimes seem unattractive, as in *Stilk* v. *Myrick*, 1809. This case arose out of desertions from a ship on a voyage to the Baltic. The captain promised the rest of the crew that he would divide between them the pay due to the deserters if they would work the ship back to London. His promise was held void for lack of consideration, since the men were already bound to work the ship back. In his judgment in *Williams*, Lord Justice Glidewell did not explain exactly why the rule in *Stilk* did not apply, but said it was 'not surprising that a principle enunciated in relation to the rigours of seafaring life during the Napoleonic Wars should be subjected during the succeeding 180 years to a process of refinement and limitation' – an interesting line of reasoning which would enable one to dispense with a great deal of the common law if need be. In *Musemeci* v. *Winadell*, 1994 (Australia), the court followed *Williams* in enforcing a landlord's promise to reduce a tenant's rent in order to keep the property occupied. In theory the tenant's promise to pay less than he had originally agreed was not good consideration, but the landlord was held to have benefited by maintaining the value of the property and avoiding possible legal proceedings by the tenant. *Stilk* was said to be explicable on grounds of duress by the crew (Chapter 11).

3.28   The basic rule as to the invalidity of promises to fulfil existing duties has important practical consequences. A contracting party may find it has become more difficult or expensive for him to supply goods at the agreed price, or shortages may enable him to demand a higher price. He might then refuse to fulfil his contract unless he is paid more. The effect of the consideration rule is that the buyer's unwilling promise to pay more for the goods (as distinct from the 'voluntary' promise in *Williams*, above) is not binding upon him, because the seller gives no consideration for it by his (second) promise to deliver them. On the same grounds, any extra payment actually handed over is recoverable, as long as the claim is made without delay. Consideration thus answers problems which might otherwise involve more difficult issues of economic duress, though this concept still has a part to play: *North Ocean Shipping* v. *Hyundai*, 1978 (Chapter 11). Similar issues often arise in employment. As *Stilk*, above, shows, an employee is not entitled to more pay for doing what his contract already obliges him to do. So in *Cresswell* v. *I.R.C. 1984*, a tax assessor's claim for more pay for using new technology was rejected, since his work with the new equipment was still that of a tax assessor (though he might, of course, properly demand more pay for substantially different duties). In *Swain* v. *West*, 1936, an employer promised not to dismiss an employee if he would give him the names of other employees who were defrauding the firm. The employee did so, but was still dismissed. He lost his claim against the employer, because he was already bound by his contract to give such information.

3.29   Contracting parties are, of course, free to vary or re-negotiate their agreements *voluntarily*. In theory, new terms require new consideration, but in everyday commercial practice this requirement is ignored – or would at least be very difficult to prove. Where an employer agrees to increase pay, for example, he does not always demand longer hours or higher production in return, but his promise is still binding. In *Woolworths* v. *Kelly*, 1990, an Australian court enforced a company's promise to pay an additional pension to a director on his retirement, without finding it necessary to decide on what, if any, consideration he had given for this new benefit. Perhaps the consideration given by employees in such cases is that they continue in employment: *Lee* v. *G.E.C.*, 1993. Contracting parties may abandon their agreement altogether if each gives up his rights against the other: *Morris* v. *Baron*, 1918. A new agreement is called a 'novation', a term more specifically used where it is agreed to replace an existing party with a new one. New agreements involve 'accord and satisfaction'. The accord is the new agreement, and the satisfaction is the new consideration needed for it.

vi. Part payment in full settlement

3.30   A particular point of controversy arising from our previous discussion, but needing separate treatment, is that of a creditor's promise to accept – or his actual acceptance of – part payment in full settlement of what he is owed. A creditor who makes such a promise usually gets nothing new – i.e. no consideration – in return for it from the debtor, and so under English law can at any time break his promise and sue the debtor for the amount still owing. A leading case on the point is *Foakes* v. *Beer*, 1884. The plaintiff here obtained a court order against the defendant for repayment of a debt. She subsequently agreed to accept the repayment in instalments.

The debtor duly repaid the debt, but the plaintiff then sued for interest on the debt. The House of Lords held that the plaintiff had received nothing in return for her apparent agreement to forgo interest, and so upheld her claim. *Foakes* was followed in *Re Selectmove*, 1995, where a debtor was held unable to enforce a creditor's promise to accept repayment of an existing debt by instalments, because, again, the debtor had given no consideration for the promise. Since the ruling in *Foakes* was that of the House of Lords, it could not be overridden by the reasoning in *Williams*, and only a new decision of the House could change it. In the meantime, and for no very obvious reason, the position seems to be that a promise to accept less than is already owed is of no effect, while a promise to pay more is binding.

3.31   It seems perfectly agreeable that a creditor should not be bound by his promise to accept less than he is owed, when the debtor knows the creditor is in financial difficulties and refuses to pay him anything at all unless he agrees to accept part payment in full settlement – as in *D and C Builders* v. *Rees*, 1965. On the other hand it might be better for the creditor to get some of his money back rather than none at all if it is the debtor who is in difficulties. In that case perhaps the creditor should be bound by his word. But whatever the merits of the argument, the fact that in neither case has the debtor given consideration enables the creditor to go back on his promise and claim everything he is owed. He is still not debarred from doing so if under protest he pays the part payment into his bank account: *Aurjema* v. *Haigh*, 1988; *Stour Valley Builders* v. *Stuart*, 1993.

3.32   As exceptions to this general rule, a creditor's promise to accept part payment in full settlement *is* binding upon him if in return the debtor agrees to give new consideration by paying the smaller sum before the date originally agreed, or if, again at the creditor's request, the debtor repays the debt in the form of goods or services, possibly of a lesser value, or in some other way suffers a detriment not previously agreed: *Couldery* v. *Bartrum*, 1881. The creditor is also bound if he agrees to take the smaller sum in full settlement from a third party, since otherwise he would defraud that person: *Hirachand Punamchand* v. *Temple*, 1911. Another exception arises – although it is difficult to find the requisite consideration – where a creditor makes such an agreement jointly with other creditors and the debtor, e.g. to accept a settlement of 50p in the pound. This is called a 'composition agreement'.

B. Estoppel

3.33   The word 'estoppel' is not one in common English usage. Its effect is much the same as 'stop', but the root of the word is entirely different. It comes from the Latin *stupa*, meaning hemp or tow, and thence something used to fill or block a hole or gap. The legal principle involved is a most important one, that of preventing or estopping a person from going back on his word or repudiating his previous conduct when someone else has relied upon it. All legal systems, including the English system, recognise that one cannot change one's mind in commercial dealings whenever one pleases – but in English contract law the application of this elementary rule is complicated by the requirement of consideration.

3.34   We have seen that a promise is of no legal significance unless 'bought' by consideration given by the promisee. In theory, therefore, if the promisee *believes* the promise and acts in reliance upon it, but does not actually give or do anything *in return for* it, he should be unable to stop the promisor from breaking his promise, whatever the loss which he, the promisee, may suffer thereby. That is indeed the position under English contract law, but how can that answer be reconciled with the principle of estoppel? Are there two separate rules as to when promises are binding, or is there only one?

3.35   Both problem and answer are best explained by reference to the leading cases. Simplifying the facts of *Central London Property Trust* v. *High Trees House*, 1947, the position was that a landlord leased certain property in London to tenants before the last war. During the war some of the tenants left the property. To help to keep it occupied the landlord reduced the rent for the remaining tenants. After the war the landlord wished to restore the rent to its previous level, and also to claim arrears of rent – i.e. the amount lost by the reduction. There was no difficulty about the first claim, since the reduction had been only for the duration of the war, but the claim for arrears raised fundamental questions whose solution has made this case one of the most important in English contract law.

3.36   How could the landlord have thought, having reduced the rent and encouraged the tenants to stay there and adjust their incomes and expenditure accordingly, that he could go back on his word and demand arrears? The answer is that the tenants gave no consideration for the reduction. There was no bargain. The landlord did *not* say: 'I will reduce the rent if in return you will promise to stay here for the duration of the war'. The tenants did not give or do, and were not required to give or do, anything in return. They were free to stay or go as they pleased, though naturally those who stayed relied on the landlord's assurance. Since they gave no consideration it should have followed that the landlord's promise to reduce the rent was unenforceable, and therefore could be revoked at any time and its effect repudiated. But this conclusion would, of course, have been most unjust in view of the tenants' reliance upon the promise.

3.37   The case came before Mr. Justice Denning, as he then was, who set himself accordingly to find a more acceptable answer. With all due reference and deference to precedent he invented the doctrine of 'equitable' or 'promissory' estoppel. We noted in the introduction the difference between common law and equity, and need only observe here that the existing common law rule of estoppel turned on representations of *fact*. His Lordship extended the rule to make it cover promises as to future conduct – here, the landlord's promise to reduce the rent.

3.38   The rule of equitable estoppel developed in the *High Trees* case may now be broadly stated as follows: *If a person by words or conduct makes a promise or representation which he intends another person to act upon, and that other person does act upon it as intended, then the promisor or representor cannot deny his promise or representation if it would be unfair to do so.* The landlord in *High Trees* intended the tenants to believe him and to stay in the property; they did believe him and stayed; he could not then renounce his promise. It will be seen that this rule is a vital one to protect the interests of those who rely on others' promises *even though they have given no consideration for them*. But if we say that *reciprocity* is the only basis on which promises will be enforced, how can we now say that mere *reliance* will do equally well?

3.39   This crucial question was resolved, at least in part, in *Combe* v. *Combe*, 1951. A husband promised to pay his wife maintenance when they separated – but broke his promise. Some years later she sued for the arrears. Again the case came before Lord Denning. He rejected her claim for breach of contract because she had given no consideration for her husband's promise. It had not been given in return for any action or forbearance on her part. She argued in the alternative that since she had *relied* upon the promise by not seeking a court order against her husband, as he must have intended, he was thereby estopped under the *High Trees* principle from denying his promise. Lord Denning rejected that argument also. He reaffirmed the basic rule that a plaintiff could only enforce a promise if he or she had given consideration for it. Estoppel by itself did not give rise to a cause of action – a right to sue – but was only a defence. A promisee could not sue on an estoppel, in other words, but could stop himself being sued. *Estoppel*, in short, as Lord Denning put it, *is a 'shield but not a sword'*.

3.40   Several more recent cases show how the rule works. We refer again to *D and C Builders*, above. It might be thought that since the builders agreed to accept part payment in full settlement they should have been estopped from claiming the remainder, but we have seen that they were not. The reason was that the debtor had taken advantage of their financial difficulties, and so their promise was not a voluntary one. Estoppel clearly cannot apply to statements made under duress or deception by the other side; only to those made voluntarily – even if mistakenly. In *Avon County Council* v. *Howlett*, 1983, a bank mistakenly overstated the sum in a customer's account. The bank could not recover the amount overstated once the customer has reasonably supposed the statement was correct and had spent the money. Where a finance company assured a customer both in writing and by word of mouth that he owed the company only £1,000 on his car, in reliance on which he sold it, the company could not reclaim the £6,000 he actually owed: *Lombard* v. *Stobart*, 1990.

3.41   Basically the question involved in estoppel is whether it would be unjust to allow a person to go back on his word. No injustice will be done if no clear and definite representation has been made. So in *Banning* v. *Wright*, 1972, it was held that a creditor who did not immediately insist upon prompt repayment was not thereby estopped from demanding repayment without notice when his debtor continued in default. A delay in pursuing a legal claim does not usually amount to a representation that the claim has been abandoned: *James* v. *Heim*, 1980. In *Ajayi* v. *Briscoe*, 1964, a finance company supplied a trading company with lorries on hire purchase. The trading company complained that the lorries were defective. The finance company at first agreed that hire purchase payments should be suspended while the lorries were being repaired, but then demanded payment as it fell due. The Privy Council held that the finance company was free to change its mind, since the trading company had not in any way altered its position in reliance upon the finance company's initial indulgence. We should note that the possible effects of waiver or suspension of rights are sometimes dealt with in the contract itself, as, e.g.: 'Any indulgence, extension of time for repayments, or delay in enforcing the terms of this agreement on the part of the company shall in no way prejudice the company's right to enforce the strict terms of the agreement.' Or again: 'Any waiver by the company of any breach of this contract by the buyer is limited to the particular breach. No delay by the company to act upon a breach shall be deemed a waiver.' Buyers' standard forms may expressly provide that payment for the goods does not preclude a claim for breach of contract.

3.42   In contrast with *Ajayi* is *Brikom* v. *Carr*, 1979. Here a landlord promised to pay for certain repairs to property himself in order to encourage his tenants to renew their lease. The tenants renewed the lease, whereupon the landlord sued to recover the cost of repairs. It was found that the tenants had not suffered any loss or detriment by renewing the lease, because the evidence showed they had in any case intended to renew it. The landlord's claim was nonetheless estopped, because his promise was clear and as a matter of principle he could not be allowed to 'blow hot and cold'. Thus while proof of detriment is normally required, it seems it is not always essential.

3.43   Whether or not there has been a detrimental reliance, it is clear that a public authority cannot be estopped by its statements or actions from fulfilling its legal duties: *Western Fish* v. *Penrith D. C.*, 1981. Likewise, a government minister is not bound to follow his own previous indications of government policy: *R* v. *Secretary of State, ex p. Barratt*, 1989. But a specific assurance given to a member of the public by a responsible officer in return for full disclosure and with knowledge of intended reliance upon that assurance is thereby binding: *R* v. *Commissioners of Inland Revenue*, 1989.

i. Proprietary estoppel

3.44   The rule that estoppel is only 'a shield and not a sword' has been widely criticised. Several judges have suggested that a person who relies on a promise as the promisor intended him to should for that reason alone be able to enforce that promise: *Amalgamated Investment* v. *Texas Bank*, 1981. So far, however, only one major exception to the general rule has been recognised, which is in cases of proprietary estoppel. *Where A leads B to believe that he has or will have rights in or over A's land, and B incurs expenditure in reliance on that assurance, B can sue to protect his interest even though he gave no consideration for it.* So if A lets B build on his land, or if he gives or promises B a right of way over the land, B can sue A if he threatens those rights: *Crabb* v. *Arun District Council*, 1975. In *Durant* v. *Heritage*, 1994, a niece who for many years was tenant of her uncle's run-down property spent large sums of money renovating the property in the belief, encouraged by the uncle, that he would bequeath it to her. He left it instead to someone else. The niece successfully claimed ownership of the property on the basis of proprietary estoppel.

3.45   If justifiable reliance can give rise to a right to sue in connection with land there seems no logical reason why it should not do so in other cases. We saw in Chapter 1 acceptance of a similar principle in quasi-contract cases. Section 90 of the American Restatement of the Law of Contract suggests the need for overall reform in this area of English law. It states a general rule of enforcement of promises on grounds of reliance, supplementing the requirement of consideration: 'A promise which the promisor should reasonably expect to induce action or forbearance on the part of the promisee, and which does induce such action or forbearance, is binding if injustice can be avoided only by the enforcement of the promise'. So where a main contractor relies on terms offered by a sub-contractor in tendering for the overall contract, he can stop the sub-contractor from withdrawing his offer even though he has not formally accepted it: *Drennan* v. *Star Paving*, 1958. American legal doctrine is thus well in advance of English law and broadly in line with Continental practice. In England, Professor Atiyah, one of the most distinguished modern writers on contract, has argued vigorously that both reciprocity – consideration – and justifiable reliance should generally be accepted by the law as sufficient 'good reason' to make promises enforceable.

ii. Other promises binding without consideration

3.46   In a few other exceptional cases promises may be binding despite the absence of consideration or any question of estoppel. Promises made in

71

deeds, i.e. documents signed, witnessed and delivered – not just 'in writing' – are enforceable because of their formality. The remedy of specific performance, Chapter 13, however, is not available for breach of such promises. Bankers' confirmed credits, covenants running with land, and trusts are among other exceptions discussed immediately below.

C. Privity of contract: Exceptions

3.47   The fundamental rule, despite the doctrine of estoppel, is that a person can only enforce or be bound by a contract to which he or she is a party – or, in old English, if he or she is privy to it. (We observe in passing that in old English usage a privy also means a lavatory, but with a little care it should be possible to avoid confusion. Both meanings derive from the original sense of 'privacy'.) In principle, *a person is a party to a contract if a promise is made to him, for which he gives consideration, or it is given on his behalf.* Cases such as *Beswick* and *Coulls*, above, show that the common law's reluctance to recognise the rights of a person who does not come within this definition can frustrate various reasonable contractual expectations and cause injustice. Over the years, therefore, a number of exceptions have been developed, some by the judges, others by Parliament, conferring rights or occasionally duties on non-contracting parties. But piecemeal exceptions, meeting problems as they arise, do not encourage the development of a rational or coherent legal system, and there are signs of continuing dissatisfaction with the privity rule in both judicial and other legal circles. We have noted already, for example, the Court of Appeal's purely pragmatic solution to the problem in *Norwich City Council* v. *Harvey*, para. 3.8. Another important decision is that of the Australian High Court in *Trident Insurance* v. *McNeice*, 1988. The Court held that a third party beneficiary's claim under a public indemnity policy which was stated to be for his benefit could not be barred by the privity rule. The rule itself was criticised by the Court as unjust and not in line with current statutory developments. In 1994 the UK Law Reform Commission recommended enforcement of third party rights, but so far to no effect. In the meantime we list the recognised exceptions to the rule, starting with those of the common law.

i. Agency

3.48   This exception is perhaps more apparent than real, in that when the agent makes a contract under which his principal becomes liable, the basis of the principal's liability is that he and the agent are seen as one person. But whether real or apparent, the courts are reluctant to imply an agency simply to circumvent the privity rule. A retailer, for example, does not usually sell as manufacturer's agent, so as to make the manufacturer liable if the goods are faulty, even though the retailer may advertise as authorised or franchised dealer. He is probably still a separate and independent commercial entity (but *see* Consumer Credit, below). Likewise, a representative of a group does not necessarily contract on behalf of or as agent of that group, but – anomalously – a man booking what proved to be a very disappointing holiday for himself and his family was held entitled to claim compensation for the family's disappointment as well as his own: *Jackson* v. *Horizon Holidays*, 1975. Lord Denning's decision here, indirectly recognising third party rights, was severely criticised by the House of Lords in *Woodar* v. *Wimpey*, 1980, but no satisfactory alternative rule was offered. The particular problem in *Jackson* is now resolved by the Package Travel Regulations 1993, following a European Union Directive. The Regulations entitle any member of a holiday group to sue the tour operator for damage or loss suffered in the circumstances defined therein.

3.49 One aspect of agency mentioned earlier merits further attention here. It will be recalled that the problem in *New Zealand Shipping* v. *Satterthwaite* was whether stevedores could take advantage of a limitation of liability in a contract negotiated between the owners and shippers of goods, and said to be for the benefit of the shippers and their employees, agents and contractors. The difficulty was that the contract expressly provided that the shippers were acting as agents of their own agents – the stevedores – in negotiating limited liability for them. The stevedores therefore had to prove that they were in fact principals, and the shippers their agents. The Privy Council agreed that an agency would be established if, as here, the contract made it clear that a specific third party was to be benefited; that the contract was made by that party's agent; the agent had that party's authority to make the contract, and that third party gave consideration for the promise in question (here, by unloading the goods). *See also London Drugs*, para. 3.9.

ii. Assignment

3.50 Contracting parties may in certain circumstances assign or pass their rights or, exceptionally, duties, to others. A creditor, for example, may assign his contractual rights against the debtor to a third party, as is commonly done when a person who has a credit account at a bank owes money to someone else and writes a cheque in favour of that person. Here again the third party's rights derive from his standing in the shoes of the assignor. Rights which can only be enforced by legal action and not by taking physical possession, notably rights to money, are still called in medieval English 'choses in action'. They can be assigned in the written form laid down by Section 136 of the Law of Property Act 1925, requiring written notice to the debtor, or informally under equitable rules. In *The Albazero*, 1976, the House of Lords accepted as a rule of commercial convenience that where goods are bought for resale, the original buyer could be deemed to have contracted on behalf of subsequent purchasers and so could bring on their behalf any claim for damages for breach of contract which they might have against the original seller. Rights and duties relating to the performance of contracts of personal service cannot be assigned, although rights to benefits under such contracts (e.g., claims for damages for breach) may be: *Linden* v. *Lenesta*, 1992; *Darlington B.C.* v. *Wiltshier*, 1994. As a general rule, duties under a contract can only be assigned or delegated to others to fulfil if the contract itself so provides, or if permission may be inferred from the non-personal nature of the contract: *Davies* v. *Collins*, 1945. Leases, hire purchase and hire contracts usually contain clauses prohibiting assignment, as e.g.: 'The hirer shall not assign this contract or part with, share possession or control of or encumber or otherwise deal with the equipment, or allow it to be seized for the satisfaction of debt.'

iii. Bankers' confirmed credits

3.51   Under this system a buyer in one country can assure a seller in another that the buyer's bank will pay him on receiving documents of title to the goods. Despite the absence of any express contract between the seller and the buyer's bank, the common law upholds the validity of this long-standing commercial practice: *Malas* v. *British Imex*, 1958.

iv. Trusts

3.52   The concept of the trust as developed by the Court of Chancery is that of a person – the trustee – having rights over land or money which he is bound by agreement with the maker or settlor of the agreement – the trust – to exercise on behalf of another – the beneficiary. Contrary to the basic requirements of consideration and privity, the beneficiary can enforce his entitlement under the trust against the trustee. The common law courts are reluctant to use this concept and to regard a person as a trustee liable to a third party merely because he has agreed with another to do something for that third party. They will recognise a trust only if the commitment between settlor and trustee passes legal ownership or control of the property in question to the trustee, and is irrevocable: *Re Webb*, 1941. For these reasons they refused to find that the agreement in *Beswick* was essentially a trust for the aunt, rather than a commercial deal between the uncle and the nephew.

v. Quasi-contract

3.53   Rules under this somewhat nebulous heading, noted in Chapter 1 with regard to liability for work done in response to letters of intent, may in exceptional circumstances allow a third party to enforce a claim without proof of either a contract or trust, but essentially on moral grounds. So where A gives money to B to pay to C, C can sue B for non-payment because otherwise B would be 'unjustly enriched': *Shamia* v. *Joory*, 1958.

vi. Restrictive covenants

3.54   Certain contractual restrictions on the use of land are said to 'run with the land' – in effect to be part of the land – and are enforceable between assignees of the original vendor or purchaser or of the original landlord or tenant, whether or not they know of the restriction. Thus a landowner might sell part of his land to a purchaser on condition that the purchaser will not use it for industrial purposes. The landowner or his successor could then enforce that restriction against that purchaser or any subsequent purchaser from him: *Tulk* v. *Moxhay*, 1848.

3.55   The position as regards property other than land is not equally clear. If A agrees to let B use his, A's, goods in a certain way, and then sells them to C, is C bound to let B carry on using the goods as agreed with A? Restrictions on the use of goods do not 'run with the goods' as they do with land. The answer may depend on C's knowledge of the restrictions when he buys the goods. *De Mattos* v. *Gibson*, 1858, one of several cases on the rights of buyers of ships under charter, is generally accepted as establishing that a person who acquires property knowing of an existing contract affecting the use of the property cannot then use that property in a way inconsistent with the contract. In some cases, however, the new owner may be bound by existing proprietary rights over the goods, whether he knows of those rights or not. If, for example, A was a finance company from which B obtained goods on hire purchase, B has proprietary rights over the goods which he can assert against C, who buys out A and becomes the new owner of the finance company. C's liability, if any, is negative – i.e., he can be stopped by injunction from breaking the existing contract, but he cannot be compelled positively to fulfil it: *Law Debenture Trust* v. *Ural Oil*, 1992. Even if not liable under contract law, anyone who knowingly and without lawful excuse interferes with another's contracts may commit a tort, or be subject to some 'equitable equivalent' remedy such as the duty to return a security for a loan when he knows the security has been pledged to a third party: *Swiss Bank* v. *Lloyd's Bank*, 1981. Protection of both contractual and equitable interests requires some specific asset capable of protection. So a subsequent creditor's claim is not affected by his knowledge of his debtor's existing *unsecured* liabilities: *MacJordan* v. *Brookmount*, 1991.

3.56   Many exceptions to the privity rule have also been made by Act of Parliament, generally to meet commercial needs. The main ones affect:

vii. Insurance

3.57   Miscellaneous Acts grant third party rights, particularly as regards life, land and motor vehicle insurance – Married Women's Property Act, 1882; Law of Property Act 1925 and Road Traffic Act 1972 – and more generally where claims against an assured person, e.g. a car driver, cannot be met because of his insolvency: Third Parties (Rights Against Insurers) Act 1930.

viii. Land

3.58   Section 56 of the Law of Property Act 1925 enables a person to claim 'an interest in land or other property, although he may not be named as a party' to the contract transferring that interest. The effect of this curiously worded provision is not completely clear, but at all events the House of Lords decided in *Beswick*, para. 3.7, that whatever else the expression 'or other property' might mean, Section 56 did not nullify the privity rule in contracts not affecting land.

ix. Carriage of goods by sea

3.59   When goods are sent by sea, the carrier – the ship owner or charterer – issues a bill of lading to the consignor of the goods. The bill acknowledges receipt of the goods on board, states the terms of the contract of carriage, and serves also as a document of title to the goods. The consignor must therefore transfer the bill and accompanying insurance policy to the consignee when he sells the goods to him. The consignee in turn must transfer the bill as and when he sub-sells. Sub-purchasers' rights and duties under the contract of carriage and the insurance policy, which would otherwise be affected by the doctrine of privity, are now safeguarded by the Carriage of Goods by Sea Act 1992. The Act entitles any subsequent lawful holder of a bill to enforce the contract against the carrier, and conversely makes the holder liable to the carrier for freight.

x. Patents

3.60   The Patents Act 1977 enables a patentee to impose limited restrictions on anyone selling or using the patented goods. The Act also gives employees rights to benefit from their own inventions even though patent rights belong to their employers, but only where the invention has been of exceptional value to the employer. This requirement has been interpreted very restrictively by the courts.

xi. Resale prices

3.61   At common law a manufacturer could not compel a retailer to sell at a certain price unless there was a contract between them to that effect. The position is now governed by the Resale Prices Act 1976. The Act permits resale price maintenance only in accordance with strict public interest criteria. Where such criteria are fulfilled, as has happened with books and pharmaceutical goods, the producer can insist upon sale at list price even though he has no contract with the retailer.

xii. Consumer credit

3.62   When a consumer obtains goods on credit he usually does so by means of credit supplied by a finance house, not by the dealer who provides the goods. The consumer may think he is contracting with the dealer, but in fact he contracts with the creditor – the finance house. But the creditor cannot therefore deny all responsibility for what the dealer says and does on his behalf. Section 56 of the Consumer Credit Act 1974 makes the creditor liable to the consumer for anything said or done by the dealer in the course of negotiations leading up to the making of the credit agreement. And if a creditor provides a consumer with credit to enable him to buy goods from a dealer under pre-existing arrangements between creditor and dealer, Section 75 gives the consumer the same rights against the creditor as he has against the dealer if the dealer breaks his contract: *U.D.T.* v. *Taylor*, 1980. This rule affects purchases of between £100 and £30,000 in value, and covers credit card purchases other than those made by American Express or other cards – charge cards – requiring prompt repayment in full. Where charge cards are used their effect is to end any continuing interest in or responsibility for the goods which the finance company would otherwise have.

xiii. Housing

3.63   Under the Defective Premises Act 1972 a house builder has a duty to ensure the fitness of the house which he owes not only to the first purchaser but to anyone else taking a legal or equitable interest in the property. The duty lasts for only six years from completion of the building.

xiv. Conclusion

3.64   So many exceptions for so many different purposes must make one doubt both the value and the validity of the privity rule. Comprehensive reform to recognise third party rights was recommended by a Law Review Committee as long ago as 1937, and in 1994 by the Law Commission, but still nothing has been done. The problem of privity lives on to a larger or smaller extent in all common law jurisdictions, but has been substantially overcome in America by Section 302 of the second Re-statement of the Law of Contract and Section 2–318 of the Uniform Commercial Code, para. 6.79, and all but eliminated in several Australian states, Quebec, and New Zealand. New Zealand's Contracts (Privity) Act 1982 shortly entitles third party promisees to enforce contractual promises in their favour.

Danish law

3.65 Consideration is not required by Danish law. Without such a rule, Danish law is willing to recognise contracts for the benefit of third parties. If the purpose of an agreement between A and B is to support C, C can enforce the agreement. So in cases like *Beswick* and *Coulls*, paras. 3.7–8, the widow would be entitled to fulfilment of the contract. But A and B may revoke their agreement without C's consent, unless a promise has been made directly to C. Since consideration is not necessary it does not matter whether the promise relates to a past event. In a case like *Roscorla*, para. 3.12, the seller would be bound by his later promise.

3.66 Another consequence is that there is no need for an estoppel principle. Since promises are generally binding, the promisor can go back on his promise only where it would be unjust to hold him to it. The question is decided by reference to Article 36 of the Contracts Act 1975, as amended – a most important general clause noted again in our commentaries on later chapters. The Article says that 'an agreement may be set aside or changed, in whole or in part, if its enforcement would be unreasonable or contrary to principles of fair conduct'.

3.67 Manufacturers' guarantees run with the goods. They are valid only if they improve consumers' existing legal rights. They are seen as bilateral agreements, since the cost of them is included in the price of the goods, and enforceable as such. A guarantee of safety may be the basis of a claim for damages for personal injury.

3.68 Creditors' promises to accept part payment in full settlement are also binding, unless obtained by economic duress: Article 31 of the Contracts Act.

3.69 Agreements on resale price maintenance are unenforceable unless approved by the Competition Control Authority.

3.70 There is no special legislation on defective premises or the responsibility of house builders towards subsequent buyers. But it follows from the general principles of contract and tort law that if a contractor's work is defective a subsequent buyer can claim compensation from the contractor. Claims may be made up to 20 years after the work was done or up to 5 years after the defect became apparent, whichever occurs sooner.

Dutch law

3.71   The concept of consideration is unknown in Dutch law. Under the new Code even the slightly similar requirement of *causa*, as provided for in the previous Code of 1838, is no longer necessary. Estoppel has no exact Dutch equivalent, although the concept of *rechtswerking* which is based on the general duty to act in accordance with equity and good faith (*redelijkheid en billijkheid*: Article 6.2) sometimes leads to similar results.

3.72   Dutch law, as to privity of contract, is generally in line with English law, though the law expressly recognises the right to make a contract for the benefit of a third party, enforceable by the third party once he has accepted the terms of the contract: Articles 6.253–4. The concept of the trust is foreign to Dutch law. Case law allows some much discussed exceptions to the rule that a third party cannot be obligated or disadvantaged by a contract. In *Securicor* v. *Nationale Nederlanden N.V.*, NJ 1979, 362, the *Hoge Raad* (High Court) held a limitation of liability clause binding on a third party – a possibility confirmed in later cases. Conversely, the Code expressly allows an employee or agent to take the benefit of a 'Himalaya clause' (para. 3.9), limiting his employer's liability for him: Article 6.257.

French law

3.73   Article 1108 says that the obligation of a party must have a 'lawful cause', and Article 1131 provides that 'an obligation without cause, or arising from a false cause or an illegal cause, has no effect'. The concept of 'cause' under French law is twofold, depending on the purpose of the inquiry. The question may be whether it exists, or whether it is illegal. In the first case, the cause of the obligation is merely the existence of a reciprocal obligation on the part of the other party in bilateral contracts, and will always be the same for a given category of contract. So the cause of the purchaser's obligation in a contract of sale to pay the price is the corresponding obligation of the vendor to deliver the thing which is the subject-matter of the contract, and *vice versa*: Civ. 30 December 1941. In unilateral contracts, however, where there is an obligation on one party only, the cause of his obligation is the *intention libérale* (*animus donandi*): Civ. 6 October 1956. In groups of contracts, or with respect to *actes abstraits* (abstract acts) such as guarantees, where the guarantor undertakes to make payment as the primary obligor, despite the lack of corresponding obligation on the part of the beneficiary, the cause of the obligation is in the overall benefit the promisor receives from the entire transaction (*see* Ghestin; *Traité de Droit Civil: Le Contrat*, paras. 714 *et seq.*; Cabrillac, *Droit des Obligations*, paras. 83 *et seq.*).

3.74   But when considering whether the cause of an obligation is lawful, the judges look at the reasons and purposes of the parties. A contract to buy a house for the purposes of prostitution is void despite the existence of reciprocal obligations of the parties because the purposes of the parties are illegal: Com. 27 April 1981. Similarly, a transaction purporting to effect a preferential payment by an insolvent company, or otherwise to breach the rule of equality between the creditors of a bankrupt business, has illegal purposes and therefore an illegal cause.

3.75   A major difference between the French system and the English concept of consideration lies in the possibility of creating under French law rights in favour of a third party. By way of exception to the rule in Article 1165, whereby 'contracts have effect only between the contracting parties', Article 1121 provides that one can contract for the benefit of a third party, and thereby create for the beneficiary a direct right against the undertaking party (*stipulation pour autrui*). The main application, now codified in the Code of Insurance, relates to insurance contracts. The beneficiary here has, by virtue of the contract between the insurer and the insured, a direct right of action against the insurer and over sums payable by it upon the occurrence of the insured loss. It is not required, as would theoretically be the case under English law, that the beneficiary supplies any sort of consideration. The obligation of the insurer to make payment to the beneficiary rather than to the insured has a cause which is the payment of the premiums by the insured.

3.76   The cause is not the monetary equivalent of the obligation of the other party. It is only if that latter obligation is so small as to be almost non-existent that the courts may nullify the contract for 'lack of cause'. The Civil Code recognises that in certain exceptional cases a gross disparity between the obligations of creditor and debtor might make a contract voidable on grounds of *lésion* ('injury'). The only important case is that of sale of land at a gross undervalue: Article 1674.

3.77   The principle of estoppel is unknown under French law, under which the situations described in paras. 3.33 *et seq.* would probably be analysed as creating implicit contracts or quasi-contracts, or as involving the liability in tort of the party against whom estoppel is raised.

German law

3.78   German law has no rules equivalent to those of consideration or estoppel. Promises without consideration are on principle enforceable as contracts. A contract is valid as soon as the parties agree on all the provisions they want included in it. An attempt to deny or vary the effects of words or conduct which have reasonably been relied on might be a *Rechts-misbrauch* – an abuse of rights – which would make the rights unenforceable.

3.79 In the absence of any requirement as to consideration, there is no great difficulty over contracts for the benefit of third parties. Article 328 provides that a contract may stipulate performance for the benefit of a third party, so that the third party acquires directly the right to demand performance. Such rights may sometimes be implied. Members of a tenant's family, for example, might have contractual rights against the landlord: BGHZ 66, 51; paras. 5.71–2. A traveller who contracts with a tour operator might enforce the contract between the operator and the airline. An implied contractual right of this kind is said to arise under a *Vertrag mit Schutzwirking für Dritte* – a contract with protection for a third party. *See also* the overlapping principle of *Drittschadensliquidation*; para. 8.55. Contracts to the detriment of third parties are not binding on them.

3.80 A party who no longer wishes to supply goods or services at the agreed price can nonetheless be compelled to do so, unless, of course, the other party accepts an increase because of economic pressure or a price escalation clause in the contract. *See also* para. 9.36. A creditor's written agreement to accept part payment in full settlement is binding upon him.

3.81 Manufacturers' guarantees are seen in German law as contracts completely separate from the contract of sale, and are directly enforceable – another rule completely different from English law. Manufacturers' guarantees must meet the standards of the *Gewährleistung* (legal responsibility) of the seller: paras. 5.66 and 6.103.

3.82 Assignment is regulated by Article 398 *et seq*. BGB. Only a creditor may assign. The debtor has no right of objection if assignment was permitted by the original contract.

Italian law

3.83 A contract's validity under Italian law depends not on reciprocity of obligation, as under English law, but on the fact of agreement, lawful subject-matter, appropriate form (*see* Chapter 4), and in particular on the concept of *causa*: Article 1325. This expression has no precise English equivalent, but can be defined as the social and economic function of a contract. To be enforceable, an agreement must perform a social and economic function deemed useful and worthy of protection by the law: Articles 1322–5 of the Italian Civil Code. So, for example, the *causa* of a contract of sale is the transfer of ownership. By Article 1418, an agreement which lacks *causa* or in which the *causa* is illegal is void. An example is a recent decision of the Supreme Court, declaring void a contract which purported to transfer an exclusive property right without giving any indication of the price for any underlying interest or reason for the deal: decision n. 12401, 20 November 1992.

3.84   An agreement may lack *causa* because it is ineffective, as where by mistake a person contracts to buy that which is already his. *Causa* should not be confused with the parties' reasons for making their contract, which are normally of no interest to the law. But if both parties intend to make an illegal agreement, the absence of *causa* itself makes the contract void: Articles 1345, 1418. An agreement is illegal if it is contrary to an express prohibition, public policy or accepted standards of morality: Article 1343 (and *see* Chapter 11).

3.85   If for want of *causa* or any other reason a contract or some part of it is declared void, invalidity runs from the time the contract was made. The court may, however, order that the parties be bound by what they would have agreed to but for the nullity: Article 1424. In practice, very few contract cases ever involve any discussion of the meaning or effect of *causa*.

3.86   It will be seen that the *causa* requirement is not the same as the English consideration rule, which does not exist in Italian law. It is therefore easier to make contracts in favour of third parties, as expressly authorised by Article 1411. It follows also that there is no such rule as estoppel under Italian law.

Spanish law

3.87   Spanish contract law has no requirement of consideration. The nearest rule is that relating to *causa*, specified in Article 1261; Chapter 1. *Causa* is like consideration in that it may be the 'lending, granting or promise of a thing or service by the other party', but is quite distinct in that it may exist also in gratuitous promises. In such cases it is 'the mere liberality of the benefactor': Article 1274. *Causa* is presumed to exist and to be legal in contracts even when not expressed, so long as the debtor cannot prove the contrary: Article 1277. Contracts without *causa* or with unlawful *causa* are of no effect: Article 1275. Consistently with the broad effect of *causa*, Spanish law permits enforcement of promises for the benefit of third parties. Article 1257 states: 'If the contract contains any stipulation in favour of a third party, the latter may demand its performance, whenever he has made his acceptance known to the obligee before the stipulation has been revoked'.

3.88   There is no specific rule of estoppel in Spanish law. But the general requirement of good faith in contracts – Article 7 – prevents a person from denying his own words or conduct in circumstances where what he has said or done was clearly intended to affect his legal rights. It is a basic principle that no-one may avoid the consequences of his own acts. On 21 December 1984, the Supreme Court held that a party who had made a payment on account in pesetas could not deny all liability under a contract requiring payment in German marks (which had become illegal because of foreign exchange controls).

Swedish law

3.89   As with Danish law, there is no rule of consideration in Swedish law. The Contract Act requires only an acceptance in accordance with an offer for a contract to be binding. A person may, however, be liable as if there were a contract when he knowingly allows another to act in the mistaken belief that a contract exists between them: NJA 1977 s. 92.

3.90   Obligations may arise towards persons who are not parties to the contract; e.g., in contracts for the benefit of third parties. But a manufacturer's guarantee given to a dealer is not binding towards consumers. The manufacturer's obligation towards the consumer is regulated by the Product Liability Act and it is irrelevant whether he has given a guarantee or not. Contrary to the rule in the UK Defective Premises Act (para. 3.63), a house buyer under Swedish law cannot make a claim directly against the builder, if the buyer is not party to the building contract. The claim has to be made against the seller, who in turn may claim against his seller, and so on back to the builder. Normally the claim may be made up to 10 years after the sale or after the construction. The claim must be made as soon as the defect is discovered.

Chapter 4

Writing and capacity

A. Writing

4.1   A judge's decision whether to enforce an agreement depends in English law essentially on the parties' apparent intentions, certainty as to the terms of their agreement, offer and acceptance and consideration, as discussed in the previous Chapters. None of these elements in itself requires writing or signature to prove agreement, desirable though that may be in practice. Only relatively rarely are there any more specific requirements as to the form of the contract or the contractual capacity of the parties. In this chapter we summarise these exceptional cases, and consider also certain problems as to the evidence which may be given when a contract is in writing.

4.2   We distinguish first between so-called 'simple' contracts and 'specialty' contracts. A simple or informal contract is one which is not made in the form of a deed, below. Simple contracts may be made in writing or by word of mouth – oral or 'parol' – or even by conduct – e.g. by getting on a bus – and may be correspondingly complicated or quite straightforward. A specialty contract is one made in the form of a deed or bond. Before the Law of Property (Miscellaneous Provisions) Act 1989 a deed had to have a seal or, in more recent practice, an indication of a seal such as a printed circle with the letters 'L.S.' – *locus sigilli*, the place of the seal. The new Act abolishes this requirement. It defines a deed as an instrument – a document – which makes clear, by using the word 'deed' or otherwise, that it is intended as such by the person making it. The document must either be signed by the person making it, and his signature attested – supported – by a witness, or it may be signed on the grantor's direction by someone else whose signature is attested by two witnesses. It must then be 'delivered' by or for the grantor. Delivery involves an act or statement proving the intention to be bound by the deed. A deed delivered as an 'escrow' is one intended to take effect only in certain specific circumstances. Deeds are binding because of their formality or solemnity, and so consideration is not required in return. They are necessary, therefore, for the enforcement of any promise not supported by consideration, notably for promises of gifts to charity.

4.3   Transfers of interests in land may involve both simple and specialty contracts. Section 2 of the 1989 Act, above, says that contracts for the sale of land or affecting other interests in or over land, including the proceeds of sale of land, must be in writing. All expressly agreed terms have to be incorporated in the written agreement, in full or by reference to another document. Letters of offer and acceptance are not sufficient: *Commission of the New Towns* v. *Cooper*, 1995. There are certain exceptions to the rule, including leases for less than three years, and it is still possible for interests in land to be created by estoppel or implied trust: Chapter 3. The actual conveyance or completion of the contract must be by means of a deed. Deeds are sometimes used also in building contracts because they can be sued on for twelve years from breach, whereas liability for breach of a simple contract ends after six years. Obligations in a deed may be changed or abandoned by written or spoken agreement. Equivalent rules for Scotland are to be found in the Requirements of Writing (Scotland) Act 1995.

4.4   Various Acts of Parliament require that particular kinds of simple contract must be in writing, or, as the case may be, evidenced in writing. The consequences of failure to comply depend on the Act in question. Some unwritten agreements are declared void; others unenforceable; others enforceable only with the approval of the court; others again – as in employment, below – are not affected at all, except that the terms may be that much more difficult to prove.

4.5   The most common commercial transactions required to be in writing are hire purchase and other consumer credit contracts regulated by the Consumer Credit Act 1974. The Act provides that where an individual (whether or not in business) is given credit up to £15,000 he and the creditor must sign the agreement, which must set out details of payments and state the debtor's various rights – including that of cancellation in certain 'doorstep' transactions. A credit contract which is not in proper form and duly signed is enforceable only by a court order. Written notice of cancellation rights is required also in 'doorstep' contracts regulated by the Consumer Protection Regulations of 1987 and by the Timeshare Act 1992. Under Section 1 of the Employment Protection (Consolidation) Act 1978 employees are entitled within eight weeks of starting work to written particulars of their pay, hours, holidays, sick pay, disciplinary procedures, notice and pension rights. The Commercial Agents Regulations 1993 entitle such agents to written particulars regarding commission, termination, etc. Bills of exchange and promissory notes such as cheques must conform with requirements as to writing in the Bills of Exchange Act 1882. Mortgages of goods (or in Scottish law 'hypothecs') are valid only if included in the written form laid down by the Bills of Sale Acts 1878–82. Miscellaneous other requirements as to writing include those of the Marine Insurance Act 1906.

4.6   Several very wide requirements as to writing were laid down originally in the Statute of Frauds 1677. These included contracts for the sale of goods for more than £10 and contracts which would take more than one year to complete. The need for written evidence in these and other cases was soon found to cause fraud rather than prevent it, so that the Act became widely known as the Statute *for* Frauds. Once the evils were perceived, English law moved with customary speed to remedy them. By the Law Reform (Enforcement of Contracts) Act 1954 most of the 1677 Act was repealed, including the £10 and one year rules. We mention these particular rules in passing, however, because the Statute was adopted in many common law countries, including America, where with local adaptations these rules live on.

4.7   The only part of the Statute still remaining in English law is Section 4, which concerns certain contracts of guarantee or insurance. A promise to answer for the 'debt, default or miscarriage' of another is unenforceable unless evidenced in writing. The section applies where another person is the principal or primary debtor and the guarantor's liability arises upon that other's failure to pay. The intention of the party signing the guarantee is irrelevant. So in *Elpis* v. *Marti*, 1991, the House of Lords held that an agent who signed a guarantee on behalf of his principal thereby made himself personally liable. Section 4 does not apply, however, where the guarantee is given as part of a larger contractual commitment entered into for a different purpose, e.g., in order to obtain employment as an agent in the first place.

4.8   Apart from these special cases, English law does not require contracts to be in writing. In commercial practice, of course, writing is the norm, and sometimes its absence may suggest lack of contractual intention: para. 1.14. In commerce, each side commonly deals with the other by using standard forms of sale or purchase, drafted by their own or their trade association's lawyers, within which they seek to define and limit their contractual obligations. Typically, the forms define the parties to the contract, specify the goods or services required, deal with the price and possible increases, provide for tests of, defects in and repairs to the goods, delivery dates, risk of accidental loss or damage, liability for breach, bankruptcy of the other party, arbitration, choice of legal system – and so on. Many of these issues are discussed in detail in the following chapters.

i. Parol evidence

4.9   The question which may then face the court is whether to regard such apparently detailed provision as complete and exhaustive, or whether it should admit evidence of other alleged written or spoken terms. The basic answer is that given by the so-called parol ('spoken') evidence rule, though the rule covers both written and oral evidence. If a written contract appears as a complete record, then evidence will not be admitted which may add to it, or vary or contradict it: *Jacobs* v. *Batavia Trust*, 1924. That general principle is subject to many exceptions, and in itself begs the question: was the contract a complete record? If as often happens the contract is made partly in writing and partly by word of mouth, evidence of the oral part will be accepted. Much depends on the court's view of the importance of the alleged oral term. In *Birch* v. *Paramount Estates*, 1956, for instance, a builder promised orally that the house he was building and selling would be as good as the show house. This promise did not appear in the written contract of sale, but was nonetheless seen as vital and enforced as a term of the contract. The court must in any case accept evidence of mistake or misrepresentation or fraud: *Curtis* v. *Chemical Cleaning Co.*, 1951; *Lowe* v. *Lombank*, 1960. An express oral agreement will override a written provision to the contrary: *Evans* v. *Merzario*, 1976. This should still be so despite any contractual provision such as an 'entire contract' clause excluding previous or subsequent negotiations or representations: para. 7.44.

4.10 Evidence may also be given to explain ambiguities or to show when the contract takes effect, or that it was later varied or rescinded. The court may accept an oral agreement as a collateral or subsidiary contract, which may in fact substantially alter or add to the effect of the written contract in question, as in *Evans*, above. But evidence of preliminary negotiations, or of the parties' general intentions, or their conduct after making the contract, will not be admitted if and insofar as it seeks to give a different meaning to words which are otherwise clear: *Miller* v. *Whitworth Estates*, 1970. The exceptions seem almost to invalidate the rule, but in its report in 1986 the Law Reform Commission thought that no change was necessary.

B. Capacity

i. Corporations

4.11 There are very few restrictions in English law on a person's capacity or legal ability to make a binding contract. In commerce the only one of any recent significance was the doctrine of *ultra vires*. This doctrine was devised in the nineteenth century to protect shareholders against companies using their money for unauthorised purposes. The basic rule was that a contract made by a company acting in breach of the objects and powers laid down in its memorandum and articles of association was void. Such a contract could not be ratified and enforced even with the consent of all the shareholders: *Ashbury Railway Carriage Co.* v. *Riche*, 1875. As applied in this case and others like it, the rule was no doubt beneficial for shareholders, but clearly unjust for other contracting parties dealing with the company in good faith.

4.12   The strictness of the rule was gradually reduced, first by judicial acceptance of very widely drawn objects clauses which gave companies the power to undertake whatever principal activities their directors thought fit – *Bell Houses* v. *City Wall*, 1966 – and then by statute. So far as it affects company law, the doctrine is for practical purposes abolished by Section 35 of the Companies Act 1985, as amended by Section 108 of the Companies Act 1989. Section 35A says that a person dealing with a company in good faith, i.e. unaware of any restriction, is entitled to assume that the power of the board of directors to bind the company, or to authorise others to do so, is free of any limitation under the company's constitution. Any payment he may make is recoverable. The directors themselves remain liable to the company for their breach of duty in such cases. Apart from company law, the doctrine of *ultra vires* may still affect contracts made by other statutory bodies such as local authorities: *Kleinwort Benson* v. *Glasgow D.C.*, 1994.

4.13   Another aspect of company law which should be borne in mind here, though not directly concerned with the company's own capacity to make a contract, is that of the relationship between companies and those who make contracts on their behalf. English law regards incorporated companies as having independent legal existences, quite separate from their directors and owners and separate also from other companies in any group of which they may form part: *Salomon* v. *Salomon & Co.*, 1897. The result of this rule is that if a company fails to pay its debts it is not usually possible to sue the board of directors or any individual director, even where it is a one-man company wholly owned and directed by a particular individual whose private resources could easily pay the debts. Holding companies are likewise generally immune from liability for the debts of their subsidiaries, in the absence of agreement to the contrary (as illustrated in *Kleinwort Benson*, para. 1.26). It is thus a common occurrence for directors to put insolvent companies into liquidation and then to start their businesses again with new companies which have no liability for the debts of the old ones – and cheat their creditors accordingly.

4.14   Only in the most obvious cases of fraud and to compel payment of income tax will the courts 'pierce the corporate veil' and make individual directors or holding companies liable accordingly, but English judges have failed to develop any coherent principles of law in this area. American judges intervene more readily and expressly on the merits of the case, much as in civil law systems. The UK Companies Act and Insolvency Act 1986 make it a crime to run a company knowing it cannot pay its debts, but it is doubtful how far these provisions are effective to prevent the abuse.

ii. Partnerships and sole traders

4.15   Contracts made by or with the actual or apparent authority of unincorporated associations such as partnerships are enforceable against the individuals concerned to the full extent of their personal assets: Section 9, Partnership Act 1890. The same is true of contracts made by or on behalf of individual traders who have not protected themselves by the formalities of incorporation under the Companies Act.

iii. Minors

4.16   Since the Family Law Reform Act 1969 a young person has become an adult for the purposes of English law on his or her eighteenth birthday. If he or she wishes to take legal action before coming of age, it must be undertaken by an adult, his or her 'next friend'. The next friend is liable in costs if the action fails, but is entitled to be indemnified. When a young person is sued the case is defended on his or her behalf by a 'guardian *ad litem*'. A parent is not liable for a child's debts unless the child acts as agent for the parent, or the parent agrees in writing to act as guarantor.

4.17   The policy of the law towards minors – or infants, as the law used to call them – has always been to try to stop adults from taking advantage of their inexperience. This has been done by declaring many minors' contracts void and unenforceable. Unfortunately it was never quite clear which contracts would be treated in this way nor what exactly were the consequences. On occasion it was the adult party who needed protection – but could not get it.

4.18   The position is now regulated by a combination of mainly nineteenth century – or earlier – cases, with little or no relevance to current trading conditions, and a partial reform of the law in the shape of the Minors' Contracts Act 1987. The effect of these rules can be very shortly summarised as follows.

4.19   First, executed contracts for 'necessaries' are *binding* upon minors. An executed contract is one which has been fulfilled, as e.g. by the delivery of the goods or services required. Necessaries – a legal expression not in common use – are defined more broadly than necessities. They are goods or services suitable to the young person's social position and actual needs. Even so, he or she is obliged only to pay a reasonable price for necessaries received, which may not be as much as the agreed price. Contracts of employment and apprenticeship and for education are within the definition of necessaries, if on the whole for the minor's benefit: *Chaplin* v. *Frewin*, 1965. Strangely enough, however, contracts made by minors in the course of their trade or businesses are not binding on them, a rule which is perhaps intended to ensure that their entire assets should not be at risk. So in

Cowern v. *Nield*, 1912, a young trader was not liable for damages for selling defective goods; nor at that time could the buyer recover his advance payment for other goods which he had ordered, but which the minor had failed to deliver to him.

4.20   Second, certain other contracts with minors which give them continuing benefits and impose continuing obligations, particularly leases of land and purchases of shares, are *voidable*. That is to say, they are binding upon minors unless and until they repudiate them. Such contracts can be avoided at any time during minority or within a reasonable time of becoming eighteen. But a minor cannot recover money he has paid under a voidable contract unless he has received nothing at all in return: *Steinberg* v. *Scala*, 1923 – partly paid shares repudiated – the part payment was held irrecoverable.

4.21   Third, contracts which are neither for necessaries nor of continuing obligation, above, are on principle *unenforceable* by the adult party. The adult may be sued for breach of contract, but cannot sue the minor unless he or she ratifies the contract on becoming eighteen. On the other hand the minor cannot recover goods delivered or money paid under such a contract unless he has received nothing in return, and he can pass a good title to any property he may own. Traders concerned to avoid losing money under unenforceable contracts normally require an adult to give a written guarantee of payment. A guarantee is binding if given in return for future credit facilities but not if based on past consideration: paras. 3.14 and 4.7.

4.22   One of the purposes of the Minors' Contracts Act was to improve the rights of an adult who makes a voidable or unenforceable contract with a minor. Section 3 seeks to ensure that minors are not unjustly enriched by keeping goods obtained under such contracts without paying for them. It says that if it is just and equitable to do so the court can order a minor to return property 'or property representing that property' to the supplier. This wording presumably covers the proceeds of sale of the property, if they can be traced, or, e.g. goods bought with money borrowed under unenforceable loans. But if the minor has spent the money or consumed the goods, there is nothing to restore and he is still not liable to repay. It will be seen there are still traps for the unwary in this area of law. In contrast, following reform in 1991, Scots law says much more simply that children over 16 have full contractual capacity, but that contracts made between the ages of 16 and 18 can be set aside by the court if proved substantially prejudicial.

iv. Mentally disturbed and drunken persons

4.23   The basic rule as to the contractual capacity of a mentally disordered or drunken person is that it is for him to show he was not responsible for his actions at the time of making the contract and that the other contracting party knew or should have known that was so: *Hart* v. *O'Connor*, 1985. The contract is then voidable, except with regard to necessaries, for which a reasonable price must be paid.

4.24   Contracts made by the aged or infirm may also be set aside on the grounds of *'non est factum'* – 'this is not my deed'. This defence is open to a person who despite taking reasonable care has nonetheless been tricked into signing a document whose effect is fundamentally different from what he believed it to be: *Saunders* v. *Anglia Building Society*, 1971; para. 10.16.

Danish law

WRITING

4.25   There are no general requirements as to form in Danish law, but a few agreements must be in writing, e.g. memoranda of association and marriage settlements – and written information as to credit terms must be given for hire purchase and other consumer credit contracts. The parol evidence is unknown in Danish law. Whether a contract is written or spoken, evidence can be given of preceding negotiations, marketing material, previous agreements between the parties and other preceding and subsequent circumstances to establish the meaning of the contract.

CAPACITY

4.26   Legal capacity is reached at the age of eighteen. Minors' contracts are invalid and each party must return what he has received or refund its value, though the minor need only pay for what has been useful to him unless he obtained the benefit by fraud. A similar rule applies to contracts with mentally disordered persons.

4.27   An *ultra vires* contract is binding on a company if the other party acted in good faith.

Dutch law

WRITING

4.28   Dutch law, like English law, does not require contracts to be in writing. The exceptions to the rule are very similar. Unlike English law, Dutch law does not require a contract for the sale or lease of land or housing to be in writing. However, a Bill introducing a requirement of writing for consumer sales of housing is currently before Parliament, and a notarial deed is necessary for the transfer of property in land or housing.

4.29   Once there is a contract in writing, Dutch and English law differ as to its consequences. The parol evidence rule is unknown to Dutch law. The prevailing rule is that of *Ermes* v. *Haviltex*, NJ 1981, 635. This case says that the meaning and effect of written terms and the question whether there are gaps to be filled is not resolved by mere grammatical construction of the terms of the contract. Instead the court seeks the construction which both parties might reasonably give to such terms and what they might reasonably expect therefrom.

CAPACITY

4.30   As in English company law, Dutch law had the doctrine of *ultra vires*. But as a consequence of the EC Directive on company law, this no longer holds true.

4.31   Contracts made by minors and mentally disturbed persons under guardianship are voidable under Dutch law. This is not the case, however, when the minor has acted with the consent of his parents or with funds they have put at his disposal: Article 1.234 of the new Civil Code.

French law

WRITING

4.32   Under the fundamental *principe du consensualisme*, a contract is essentially a matter of mutual consent. It is made as soon as the parties have agreed the subject-matter and terms of the contract, irrespective of whether the agreement is implicit, e.g., by opening the door of a taxi in a taxi rank (Civ. 2 December 1945), or explicit, or whether expressed in writing or orally. But there are two sets of exceptions. A limited number of contracts must be made according to certain written forms (*acte authentique*: notarised deed, or simply a written deed), and rules of evidence may require the production of written documents.

4.33   Contracts whose validity requires the execution of a notarised deed or a deed in writing are called '*contrats solennels*'. They cover a variety of situations: substantial gifts, marriage contracts and mortgages on real property. Other contracts requiring writing include guarantees – *cautionnements* – or the indication of the 'global effective rate' in a loan agreement, or of the turnover and profits for the last 3 years in a contract for the sale of a business. Non-compliance with the rule usually results in the nullity of the contract. In certain circumstances, the sanction can be different (nullity of the relevant clause; for instance, of an interest clause if the 'global interest rate' has not been stated). Standard form contracts aimed at the public at large are increasingly subject to such requirements: life insurance contracts, contracts of loan for the purchase of real property, consumer credit, door to door sales, etc. The law specifies on each case the writing that is required and the penalty for non-compliance.

4.34   The requirements above must be distinguished from those relating only to the bringing of evidence. Under Article 1341, any contract whose subject-matter is in excess of FRF. 5,000 must be evidenced in writing. It is not generally possible to prove such contracts by way of oral testimony. There are three major exceptions. Contracts between *commerçants* (traders, including commercial companies) may be proved orally: Code of Commerce, Article 109. Contracts even between non-traders can be proved orally if at least partly evidenced in written documents, e.g., correspondence from the defendant: Civ. 29 February 1972. The third exception is in Article 1348, which says that writing is not necessary where it is essentially impracticable to insist upon it. This exception takes account of commercial practice, family relationships, and other, more extreme, circumstances. Each party with a distinct interest should have an original copy of the contract: Article 1325. The practice of initialling each page of a contract has no legal basis; it is only a widely accepted custom adopted to avoid problems of evidence.

CAPACITY

4.35   As under English law, companies and other legal persons have their own legal personality separate from that of the shareholders or directors or of other companies in the same group. Companies, etc., usually contract in their own name, and the obligations undertaken by them are not binding personally on their shareholders or directors or on associate companies. One can contract on behalf of a third party, but if the latter does not ratify the undertaking and agree to be bound by it, the promisor is liable to damages: Article 1120; *porte-fort*. The courts have recently held that a contract made with one company in a group of companies can create obligations not only for the particular company but for others in the group, or at least the parent company. This could occur where the contracting party could legitimately believe that the contract was made also with the parent company or with the group because of confusion created by the group or the parent company – for instance, where the confusion was created by the use of common trademark, common letterhead, common directors, etc. (Lyon, 8 June 1990; use of a common logo and letterhead). The *ultra vires* doctrine is not known in French law. The company is bound by the *mandat apparent* of its directors and officers.

4.36 People under 18 years of age and those whose capacity is restricted because of their mental health or age cannot validly contract: Article 1124. Their contracts must be made by their legal representatives or, as the case may be, they must be assisted by such representatives.

German law

WRITING

4.37 As in English law, writing is not usually necessary to make a contract valid under German law. But there are exceptions. Writing is required in contracts between landlords and tenants (Article 566 BGB), contracts of financial guarantee (Article 766), and consumer credit contracts, including hire purchase contracts (Article 4 Consumer Credit Act 1991). Contracts for transfers of interests in land, including mortgages, must be authenticated by a notary. Although Article 125 BGB makes contracts void which are not in writing as required, the effect of the rule is limited by principles of good faith. Tenants are not immediately evicted, and buyers under credit contracts may keep the goods delivered but need pay only the cash price.

CAPACITY

4.38 German law like English law regards corporations (*Aktiengesellschaft*, AG; *Gesellschaft mit beschränkter Haftung*, GmbH) as legal persons, and so they and not the directors or shareholders must be sued. Exceptionally the court may pierce the corporate veil – *Durchgriffshaftung* – and allow action against shareholders. A registered association – *eingetragener Verein*, e.V. – such as a consumer association is also a legal person. But there is nothing similar in German law to the doctrine of *ultra vires*. A corporation can only be bound by a contract signed by a person who has the power to represent it. The power to act as agent is called *Vollmacht*: Article 164 *et seq.* BGB. There are two special types of power. *Prokura* is the power to act in all transactions in the scope of mercantile trade. The person so empowered must be named in the Commercial Register. The holder of a commercial power of attorney – *Handlungsvollmacht* – is authorised only to enter into transactions within the corporation's particular trade.

4.39 The rules on *Prokura* and *Handlungsvollmacht* apply also to partnerships, whether general – *Offene Handelsgesellschaft*, OHG – or limited – *Kommanditgesellschaft*, KG. But both the partnership and the individual partners can be sued, unless the latter's liability is limited.

4.40   The age of majority in Germany is 18. A contract with a child under seven is void. Contracts with minors aged between seven and eighteen are valid only if their legal representatives – normally, their parents – confirm the contracts: Articles 105–7, BGB. The BGB seems generally to give minors better protection than English law.

Italian law

WRITING

4.41   Under Italian law most contracts can be made 'in free form' – by conduct or spoken or written word, as preferred by the parties. There are, however, certain 'formal' contracts, which are void if not in writing. Formal contracts divide between those made by public act and those made by private writing.

4.42   A 'public act' is a document drawn up by a notary or other authorised official: Article 2699 of the Italian Civil Code. The notary certifies the parties' identity and signatures made in his presence, but not the truth of the document. A private writing requires the signature of the contracting party or parties, but may be upheld in favour of a party who has not signed if he can produce the agreement in court.

4.43   Contracts requiring public acts include substantial gifts (Article 782), articles of association (Article 2328) and marriage agreements (Article 162). Private writing is required for all contracts affecting ownership of land and interests in land and leases for more than nine years: Article 1350. If parties agree to make a contract in the future in a certain written form, the contract will be void if not in that form: Article 1352.

4.44   In certain other cases writing is required only by way of evidence of agreement, and its absence does not affect the validity of the contract. Examples include transfers of businesses: Article 2556.

CAPACITY

4.45   In Italy full contractual capacity is acquired at the end of one's eighteenth year: Article 2. Contracts made by minors or persons suffering habitual mental infirmity are voidable: Articles 414, 1415, 1426. Drunkenness, drug addiction or other such infirmity may also be grounds for annulling a contract: Article 428.

4.46   Italian company law has no rule of *ultra vires* like that until recently characteristic of English law. It is now accepted that unincorporated associations may own land and buildings: Corte di Cassazione, 23 June 1994, n. 6032.

Spanish law

WRITING

4.47   Article 1278 of the Spanish Civil Code allows parties to contract in whatever form they prefer. The same general rule applies also to commercial contracts: Article 51, Commercial Code. Writing is, however, needed for contracts of carriage of goods, guarantee, charter-party, and marine insurance, among others. Contracts under seal do not exist in Spanish law, but certain agreements must be sworn before a notary public to be fully effective. These include agreements affecting land, mortgages, and setting-up companies. Absence of writing does not necessarily invalidate the contract. If the agreement can be proved, one party can oblige the other to fulfil the legal requirements: Article 1279.

CAPACITY

4.48   Minors and persons physically or mentally ill and under legal guardianship cannot make valid contracts: Article 1263. There are restrictions on the contractual powers of certain persons such as guardians, executors, and civil servants. Any adult entitled to dispose of his own goods has the legal capacity to carry on business: Article 4, Commercial Code.

4.49   The Spanish rule as to a company's contractual capacity is similar to that in the UK Companies Act 1985. The basic rule is that a business agent makes his principal liable on all matters within the customary extent of the business: Article 286 of the Commercial Code. In company law, the general powers of representation laid down in the Mercantile Register assure contracting parties that the company is likewise bound by all transactions within its normal business. Against third parties relying in good faith on a company's acts, the company is bound even if the act is beyond its powers: Article 129, Companies Act.

Swedish law

WRITING

4.50   Swedish law does not, apart from some special cases, require contracts to be in writing. A promise to make a gift will be binding only if in writing or otherwise made publicly known. Sale of land must be made in a written contract, signed by both seller and buyer. Apart from the price, the specific terms in a contract for sale of land do not have to be in writing. Memoranda of association and wills are other examples of obligations that require written form. Swedish law does not have the parol evidence rule (paras. 4.9–10). Evidence may be given of any oral or written statements which may assist the court in interpreting a contract.

CAPACITY

4.51   As for capacity, the rules of English law in paras. 4.13–4 are parallel to those of Swedish law. In Swedish law a person under 18 years is a minor and not able to be party to a contract without the consent of a guardian. This consent may be given at or after the making of the contract. If the other party acted in good faith and was unaware that the person was under 18 years of age, there might be a responsibility to compensate that other party for benefits he gave to the minor which cannot be returned, such as food.

Chapter 5

Conditions, warranties and innominate terms: Express and implied terms

A. Conditions and warranties

5.1   In the previous chapters we have considered what is required under English law to make an agreement enforceable. In this chapter we begin an examination of the terms of contracts; their meaning and effects. This chapter discusses contract terms in general. It seeks to explain the language used by English law in classifying contractual obligations, and the practical consequences of those classifications. We consider the issues first by reference to the importance of the obligations in question, and second according to whether they are obligations expressly agreed between the parties or implied by law.

5.2   Before we go into detail we should recall briefly two points of vocabulary already mentioned. Statements of opinion about the worth or value of goods or services, such as are found in most advertisements, are known as *puffs* and have no legal effect. Statements of fact which help to bring about a contract but do not necessarily form part of the contract are called *representations*. Remedies for misrepresentation overlap with but are not the same as those for breach of contract, as will appear from the present chapter and Chapters 11 and 13. In this chapter we are concerned only with the terms of the contract as such.

5.3   The rights or duties granted or imposed by the contract have traditionally been divided by English (but not Scottish) law into *conditions* and *warranties*. Conditions are regarded as basic or essential terms, while warranties are usually minor or ancillary provisions. The point of this division is that it determines the remedies of the innocent party. If he is the victim of a breach of condition then in the law's eyes he has been deprived of the essential point and purpose of the contract, and so is entitled to repudiate it. That means he can refuse to fulfil his own part of the contract, can give back what he has received (unless he has 'accepted' it: para. 6.4), and demand the return of his own goods or money. Alternatively or additionally he may claim damages for loss. But if a warranty only is broken, then in effect the injured party has received nearly what he asked for, and so cannot repudiate the contract. Instead his remedy is a claim for damages, basically for the difference in value between what he asked for and what he got. The distinction between conditions and warranties has not been adopted throughout the Anglo-American system. Section 2–313 of the American Uniform Commercial Code classifies all statements and promises which are part of a contract as warranties.

5.4   In the English system these classifications and their consequences are the basis of countless common law cases, and they have been adopted also by certain statutes. The most important of these statutory provisions for our purposes are the conditions as to quality and fitness of goods in the Sale of Goods Act 1979, as amended, and in certain other Acts affecting transfer of goods, as described at length in Chapter 6. The possibilities of avoiding liability for breach of condition or warranty are mentioned below and discussed in more detail in Chapter 7.

5.5   The classifications are easy to explain, but abound with practical difficulties. Some are problems of law, others arise simply out of the use of words. We consider this latter question first. The difficulty here is that the legal meanings of the words 'condition' and 'warranty' are altogether different from their meaning in ordinary English usage, and even in law are often used interchangeably. Among its other meanings, for example, a condition may be a 'state of affairs', as in: 'Is this fruit in good condition?' Or it may be any term at all in a contract, major or minor, as in the phrase 'conditions of sale'.

5.6   Another possibility is that a 'condition' may signify an essential preliminary of contractual liability – more accurately a *condition precedent.* This might in turn affect events which must occur either *before* any contract can be made, or, as the case may be, circumstances pre-determining liability *within* the contract. An example of the former would be: 'If I can borrow £5,000 from the bank I will make a contract with you'. There may then be a duty to try to borrow the money, but no question of liability for breach of the proposed contract itself: *Ee* v. *Kakar*, 1979. An example of a pre-condition within the contract would be the following, after a clause by which the seller promises to replace defective goods: 'It is a condition precedent to the seller's liability under this clause that the buyer satisfies the seller that the goods have been properly handled, stored and maintained, and that a note of such defect is received by the seller within 21 days of delivery.' In contrast is the *condition subsequent* – a future event whose occurrence is stated in the contract to affect the application of the contract in a particular way – usually by bringing it to an end.

5.7   Similar difficulties may arise over the word 'warranty'. In older English usage a warranty means a promise of any kind, whether fundamental or incidental, and in current use it usually means a manufacturer's guarantee – which as we saw in Chapter 3 may be of no legal significance at all. When a party promises in effect that everything he has said is true, that promise is often called a warranty. So in insurance contracts, the insured party's replies and disclosures are described as warranties, and yet breach of them may nullify the contract (even though such breach was not the cause of the insured's loss: *Forsikringsaktielskapet Vesta* v. *Butcher*, 1989). Similarly, the answers a seller of land or of a business gives to the buyer's preliminary inquiries as to, for instance, title to the land or the profits of the business (sometimes known as 'due diligence' inquiries) are also commonly called warranties, although inaccurate replies might well justify the buyer in repudiating the contract. Not surprisingly then the judges recognise that they have to be very careful in interpreting 'condition' and 'warranty' whenever they come across these expressions in contracts, with the varying consequences we discuss below.

i. Innominate terms

5.8   From the strictly legal point of view the main difficulty is of course to decide, in cases where the statutory classifications, para. 5.4, do not apply, which terms should be regarded as conditions and which as warranties. What is the effect, for example, of a late or faulty delivery of one instalment in an instalment delivery contract, or of one late payment in an instalment payment contract? Can the other side repudiate, or has he only a claim for damages? This particular issue was discussed in *Maple Flock* v. *Universal Furniture*, 1934, where the common sense answer was given that everything depended on which instalment was in arrears, how long the delay, and how likely its repetition. Clearly a month's delay in the first instalment is more likely to justify repudiation than a day's delay with the last. Even a long delay in making the final payment did not justify rescission in *Cornwall* v. *Henson*, 1900. But the parties are free to make express provision to the contrary, as we see in Chapter 13. *See also Standard Precast* v. *Dywidag*: para. 13.10.

5.9   It follows that usually it is for the judges to decide how to classify any particular term in a contract, and then to give the appropriate remedy. It follows also that their decision may turn on the nature and consequences of the *breach* of contract rather than on a classification beforehand of the importance of any given term. The importance of the distinction between these two possible approaches was very clearly brought out in the leading case of *Hong Kong Shipping* v. *Kawasaki*, 1962. This concerned a contract of hire – a charter-party – of a ship for 24 months. One of the terms of the contract was that the ship should be 'seaworthy'. On the face of it, seaworthiness was a vital term and therefore a condition, so that in theory

101

any breach by the owners would enable the hirers to repudiate. But the Court of Appeal observed that there were many very different reasons why a ship might not be seaworthy, ranging from the trivial and quickly and easily remediable to the most fundamental and difficult to overcome. That being so, said the Court, it would be absurd to give the hirer in every case the right to exercise the drastic remedy of repudiation. If the consequences of the breach were trivial, damages would suffice. If they were serious, or potentially so, then and only then would repudiation be justified. This more flexible approach is essentially that adopted by the 1980 Convention on Contracts for the International Sale of Goods which permits repudiation only where the buyer or seller is in fundamental breach of contract. A fundamental breach is there defined as one by which the innocent party has been substantially deprived of the benefit of the contract in circumstances which were not reasonably foreseeable. Section 2–608 of the American Uniform Commercial Code takes a similar view of the right to repudiate.

5.10   In the *Hong Kong Shipping* case itself, the hirers' grievance arose out of faults in the ship which kept it out of use for four months. The Court decided that the hirers could not repudiate because they still got twenty months' use out of twenty four, which was nearly what they wanted. Damages were therefore a sufficient remedy. One might not necessarily agree with that final assessment of the consequences of the breach, but it was reached by the Court in the light of the hirers' requirements as they appeared in the contract.

5.11   In effect then the obligation as to seaworthiness in the *Hong Kong Shipping* case was originally neither a condition nor a warranty. It was a term whose precise significance could not be determined until after it had been broken. The Court described such terms as *innominate* or *intermediate*. Once a court feels able to interpret a term in this way, it gives itself a very wide discretion as to the appropriate remedy for the injured party. In theory at least the approach has much to commend it, in the sense that the remedies are or ought to be tailored to what actually went wrong and are not decided by some possibly arbitrary pre-determination.

5.12   Illustrations include *Cehave* v. *Bremer*, 1976. The contract here required shipment of cattle food 'in good condition' – an obligation which again one might think so important as necessarily to be classified as a condition. Part of the consignment was not in good condition, but despite the faults the buyers were able to use the goods in almost exactly the same way as if they had been perfect, and in fact suffered no financial loss. The Court of Appeal held that 'in good condition' was only an innominate term, and that in the circumstances the breach of this term did not allow the buyers to repudiate the contract. In *Reardon Smith* v. *Hansen Tangen*, also in 1976, the House of Lords held that in a contract for the hire of a ship a stipulation as to the yard in which it was to be built was again no more than an innominate term, and that if in all other respects the ship was built in accordance with specifications, as it was here, the hirer had got what he said he wanted and could not then reject the ship.

5.13   These decisions seem eminently reasonable on their own facts. But the innominate term approach also has its disadvantages. The most important is that the parties cannot know beforehand the significance of the terms they have agreed on, but must wait until they are broken. If as businessmen they wish to avoid this kind of uncertainty, they are, of course, free to adopt for themselves the methods of the Sale of Goods Act and specify in advance which terms are crucial and which less so – though not necessarily just by calling them conditions or warranties, as we see below – and what the remedies shall be if they are broken. A typical hold-all provision is: 'Each and every condition herein set out is hereby declared to be of the essence of every contract made by the company'. If by such wording the parties' intentions are clear – and legal – the judges may have no choice but to enforce them.

5.14   In general, if the terms of a contract are clear, a judge has no power to substitute his own view as to what might seem more reasonable in the circumstances: *Adams* v. *British Airways*, 1995. But if the terms are ambiguous, he might doubt whether the parties actually meant what they said, and so refuse to give effect to their apparent intentions. This alarming situation was very well illustrated in *Schuler* v. *Wickman*, 1974. A German machine tool manufacturer agreed with an English agent that the agent would call on a certain list of clients once a week. This was stated to be a condition of the contract, which also provided that any 'material breach' of the contract would entitle the manufacturer to end it thereupon. The agent failed to call as agreed, and some two years later the manufacturer purported to end the contract because of his default. The English agent then sued him for damages for wrongful repudiation.

5.15   By a majority the judges in the House of Lords upheld the agent's claim. Their argument was essentially that the word 'condition' was ambiguous – as explained above – and that since it was ambiguous there was a problem of interpretation, which in turn confronted the judges with a choice between reasonable and unreasonable meanings. If 'condition' was interpreted in its strict legal sense, that would mean that the parties intended that any and every failure on the agent's part, however small or unavoidable or unintentional, would entitle the manufacturer immediately to end this valuable contract. Interpreting the word to mean only 'a term', on the other hand, would allow for the possibility of an occasional imperfection – which their Lordships found the more fair, rational and likely explanation of the parties' intentions. Influenced also by the manufacturer's delay in exercising his supposed rights, their Lordships gave judgment accordingly in the agent's favour. In passing we might note the view of Lord Wilberforce, the dissenting judge in *Schuler*, who said that if the German manufacturer cared to say that all his customers must be called on every week that was presumably what he meant – but as we have seen the majority preferred on this occasion a more relaxed – English? – approach.

5.16   We have seen in *Schuler* that not every breach of 'condition' will necessarily be treated as 'material', i.e., such as to justify repudiation of the contract – contrary to the general rule. The same practical answer may sometimes be given by the judge refusing, in the exercise of his discretion, to give redress for a very trivial grievance or wrong – the *de minimis* rule. So in *Golby* v. *Nelson's Travel Agency*, 1967, a booking on a particular flight was said to be a condition of a package holiday contract. In the event, that flight was overbooked and a relief flight provided. When the plaintiff was told of the new arrangement he repudiated the contract and claimed repayment of his deposit. The Court of Appeal held that even if there had been a breach of condition, which it denied, the breach did not go to the root of the contract and so repudiation was unjustified. The question is clearly a difficult one. Many commercial contracts expressly require exact compliance with the agreed terms and all warranties or representations. In trying to give effect to the parties' wishes, the judges will be guided by observations such as these: 'Parties may think some matter, apparently of very little importance, essential; and if they sufficiently express an intention to make the literal fulfilment of such a thing a condition precedent, it will be one': *Bettini* v. *Gye*, 1876. And again: 'The more unreasonable the result the more unlikely it is that the parties can have intended it, and if they do intend it, the more necessary it is that they shall make that intention abundantly clear': *Schuler* v. *Wickman*, 1973.

5.17   Another example of the uncertainty of both law and language in this area was in *Skips* v. *Syrian*, 1983. The question was whether a bill of lading which was said to incorporate 'all conditions of the charter-party' thereby incorporated the arbitration clauses in the charter-party. Did 'conditions' mean 'terms', which would include arbitration, or only 'conditions properly so called', which would exclude all provisions other than the consignee's obligations on the ship's arrival? A precedent on this problem of interpretation was *The Astro Valiente*, 1982, where the judge deplored the courts' sometimes over-technical approach, which he said was not appropriate to a commercial relationship and should if possible be avoided. 'So too', he said, 'should the interpretation of an ordinary English word, "conditions", in a sense different from that which it naturally bears, particularly in a document which may well not be prepared by a lawyer, or at any rate by an English lawyer'. But this plea fell on deaf ears in *Skips*. The Court of Appeal held that 'the conditions' were those under which the goods were loaded, stored and discharged, and so excluded the arbitration clauses. This narrow interpretation was said to be justified by the great importance commercial men attached to certainty in their dealings. The Court said it was not the law's policy to change established meanings and effects even when there might be a case for doing so. But why then should the parties have troubled to agree on arbitration in the first place?

ii. Entire and severable contracts

5.18   We should mention here another possible complication, the concept of the 'entire' contract (not to be confused with an 'entire agreement' clause: para. 7.44). An entire contract is one under which no payment at all is due to the seller or supplier of services unless and until he has fulfilled all his commitments exactly in accordance with the contract – as distinct from the (more common) 'severable' contract, under which part payment is due for each stage of completion of the contract. In theory a strict interpretation of the requirements of an entire contract would mean that even the smallest deficiency or defect in the seller's performance of the contract would in effect be a breach of condition which justified the buyer in repudiating the contract. But that would seem an unreasonable solution, particularly because the buyer might not always be able to return what he had received under the contract, as illustrated below, and so might make a considerable and unjustifiable profit. The potential injustice of this situation is reduced by the judges' rule of 'substantial performance', which in appropriate cases restores the situation to that of breach of warranty, and by their overall reluctance to interpret contracts strictly as entire contracts. In *Baltic Shipping* v. *Dillon*, 1993 (Australia), for example, the court rejected a cruise ship passenger's claim for all her money back after the ship sank during the cruise.

5.19   Examples of the difficulty of drawing the line in these cases include *Hoenig* v. *Isaacs*, 1952, and *Kiely* v. *Medcraft*, 1965. In *Hoenig* a contractor agreed to decorate a flat for £750. There were faults which would have cost £55 to remedy. The contractor was held entitled to £695. In *Keily* it would have cost £200 to remedy the faults in a contract for work worth £520, but the customer still had to pay £320.

5.20   To the contrary was *Bolton* v. *Mahadeva*, 1972, which concerned a contract to instal a central heating system for £560. The work was badly done, with complaints of fumes and some rooms left unheated. Repair work would have cost a further £174. In the circumstances this was more a failure to do the job at all than a substantial but imperfect performance, and so the contractor was not entitled to any payment whatever for his work. The same decision was reached in the Australian case of *Simpson* v. *Spencer*, 1964. The contractor here promised to build a shed of a certain size and using certain materials for £2,159. The completed shed was the wrong size and did not use the right materials. It would have cost £720 to put it right. The buyer's refusal to pay anything was upheld by the court, though the judge

105

said he regretted the decision because the buyer had undoubtedly received something of value for which he paid nothing.

5.21 Curiously enough, however, if the buyer in such a case as *Bolton* or *Simpson* had paid in advance he would not be able to recover all his money. At common law a whole sum of money can be recovered only if there has been a total failure of consideration, i.e. if the buyer received nothing at all in return – which would not be so in these cases.

iii. Terms as to time

5.22 In the midst of all these varying approaches it may come as a relief to know that there is one particular type of contract whose significance and effect is virtually beyond doubt – for better or worse. English judges say that *terms as to times and dates in shipping contracts are self-evidently vital*, so that any breach will necessarily be treated as a breach of condition. It is not necessary for the innocent party expressly to make time of the essence in these cases, nor to show any loss or damage actually arising or even likely to arise from the breach.

5.23 The position is very clearly illustrated in *Bunge* v. *Tradax*, 1981. The contract here required a buyer of goods to give fifteen days' notice of readiness to load, but he gave only thirteen – whereupon the seller repudiated the contract. In the High Court the judge held that the notice requirement was an innominate term, and that in the event the delay did not go to the root of the contract. This view was rejected by both the Court of Appeal and House of Lords, each stressing the need for commercial certainty. 'It can fairly be said that in mercantile contracts stipulations as to time not only may be but usually are to be treated as being "of the essence of the contract", even though this is not expressly stated in the words of the contract', said Lord Justice Megaw.

5.24 In *Gill* v. *Société pour L'Exportation des Sucres*, 1986, the defendant had to nominate a port by 14 November 'at latest', but in fact nominated one on 15 November. The plaintiff repudiated the contract and the defendant alleged wrongful repudiation. Sugar trade arbitrators found in the defendant's favour, noting that no loss had been caused by the day's delay. They said: 'In the refined sugar trade it would be customary for a trader in such circumstances to give . . . notice before . . . being able to treat the contract as repudiated. Indeed though certainty in certain terms in many mercantile contracts is essential we believe that was a clause such as this to be considered a condition making time of the essence of the contract, the trade in refined sugar would become extremely difficult. Such slippages as in the present case frequently occur. It is not the custom of the trade to treat such slippages, without the service of notice on the party in default, as grounds to cancel the contract'. The Court of Appeal nonetheless held that the practical difficulties and contrary trade practices were not enough to displace the law's strict requirements as to time in commercial contracts. In *Société Italo-Belge* v. *Palm Oils*, 1982, a term requiring a declaration of ship 'as soon as possible' was held not to be an innominate term, regardless of its inherent uncertainty, and so a declaration made one month after the ship sailed again justified repudiation. A seller's three day delay in readiness to load a ship entitled the buyer to end the contract in *Compagnie Commerciale des Sucres* v. *Czarnikow*, 1990 (House of Lords).

5.25 Section 10 of the Sale of Goods Act says that terms as to time of *payment* (Chapter 8) are not normally 'of the essence'; i.e., they will not normally be treated as conditions. In shipping cases, however, the courts may well reach the opposite conclusion. So in *Scandinavian Tanker* v. *Flota*, 1982, the House of Lords held that one day's delay in payment under a charter-party justified the owner in forfeiting – withdrawing – the ship. Their Lordships emphasised that the agreement in question was a time charter which gave the charterer no rights over the vessel but was a contract for services to be provided by the ship's owner. The Court therefore thought that if forfeiture was not allowed the owner would in effect be compelled to fulfil these services, possibly without payment.

5.26 We see then that the courts attach the greatest importance to what they believe to be the commercial need for certainty, albeit more in the shipping context than elsewhere, and even there with consequences which one might think are not always those envisaged by the parties. In this context the judges seem intent on upholding every word of a contract to the letter. Their underlying philosophy was roundly proclaimed by Lord Bridge in *The Chikuma*, 1981: 'This ideal [of certainty] may never be fully attainable, but we shall certainly never even approximate to it unless we strive to follow clear and consistent principles and steadfastly refuse to be blown off course by the supposed merits of individual cases.'

5.27 We observe in passing that this seems very much an English attitude. Professor Goode, a foremost authority on commercial law, has written in *Legal Studies*, 1983, that 'the strictness of English contract law, its insistence that undertakings in commercial agreements must be fully and timeously [punctually] performed, may be repellent to lawyers trained in the civil law tradition with its emphasis on good faith and fair dealing. Yet it is the very rigour of the common law of contract and its preference for certainty over equity that have made English law . . . one of the most commonly selected systems in choice of law clauses in international contracts.'

5.28 Whether the basic reason for the general use of English law and English legal forms is indeed the courts' insistence on exact compliance with times and dates is open to question. One might wonder whether commercial men – and particularly those in continental Europe whose legal systems at least appear to attach more importance to the claims of morality than the English – regard strict adherence to every word as the basis of their contracts. May they not take more account of convenience, mutual reliance and the like, which might perhaps call for a more flexible approach to their dealings by the law? Is it true that merchants, out of all members of society, prefer that the law should be certain rather than that it should examine the 'supposed merits' of their cases? Be that as it may, however, there is no doubt that here again we see English law as philosophically a system designed to uphold what it sees as businessmen's self-interest.

5.29   The courts' attitude in shipping cases contrasts sometimes quite remarkably with that taken in other commercial situations, where terms as to time are not usually regarded as vital. In *Amherst* v. *Walker*, 1983, for example, the Court of Appeal held on the facts that a landlord's right to exercise a rent review clause in December 1974, as required by the lease, was not affected by delay until May 1979. And conversely a landlord could not deny his tenant's right to renew the lease merely because the tenant did not pay on time, as long as all payments were made by the end of the term: *Bassett* v. *Whiteley*, 1983.

5.30   To put the matter beyond doubt, the parties can as we have said expressly make time of delivery or payment 'of the essence' in their original contract, with consequences discussed further in Chapter 13. Otherwise, the contract must usually be carried out within a reasonable time, as is provided for contracts for services by Section 14 of the Supply of Goods and Services Act 1982. What is a reasonable time is a question of fact in each case. If the goods are known to be perishables, or the business subject to rapid fluctuations in activity or value, it must of necessity be a very short time. In *McDougall* v. *Aeromarine*, 1958, boat builders contracted to 'use their best endeavours' to build a boat by 1 May 1957, but said in the contract that because of delays and shortages they could not guarantee a delivery date. The boat was defective and still not deliverable in September of that year. The buyer was held entitled then to repudiate the contract because the boat should have been ready within a reasonable time of 1 May.

5.31   Another possibility is that at some stage after the contract has been made one side may give the other due notice that he intends to make time of the essence, and so bring to an end the other's delays. This is not a unilateral variation of the contract, which would be of no effect, but an enforcement of the implied obligation to complete within a reasonable time. An example is *Rickards* v. *Oppenheim*, 1950, where, after accepting repeated delays by the seller in delivering a new car, the buyer was held entitled to say that he would not take it if it were not delivered by a certain date. He must give reasonable notice of this date: *Behzadi* v. *Shaftesbury Hotels*, 1990. The reasonableness or otherwise of the time thus settled is not affected by the supplier's financial or administrative difficulties: *British Group* v. *Quadrex*, 1988. Conversely, of course, as illustrated in *McDougall*, above, strong sellers often seek to avoid the constrictions of times and dates by using *force majeure* or other such provisions. The validity of their attempts to do so is judged by Section 3 of the Unfair Contract Terms Act, discussed in Chapter 7.

5.32 Related issues dealt with in other chapters include the possibility of conflict between buyers' and sellers' standard forms, as to which *see* our discussion in Chapter 2. Whether one side's apparent repudiation of the agreement can be treated as a breach of condition justifying the other in repudiating is discussed in Chapter 13.

B. Express terms

5.33 Our main concern thus far in this chapter has been to divide contractual terms into the major and the minor, and to examine the consequences of that division. We now re-divide and re-examine the terms according to whether they are expressly agreed between the parties or implied by law.

5.34 As regards express terms there are, of course, many possible ancillary provisions apart from the basic duties of delivery and payment which each party undertakes and whose main effects are discussed in the following chapters. It is not the English way simply to state these basic objectives and leave the rest to chance or good will. English commercial contracts usually contain many detailed subsidiary provisions, sometimes in the form of Schedules at the end of the contract containing technical data, specifications, etc. The terms may include, for example, an 'entire agreement' clause, making it clear that the contract document excludes any other written or oral agreements between the parties (Chapter 7); clauses allocating risk (discussed in Chapter 8); clauses excluding or limiting liability for breach of contract, (examined at length in Chapter 7); clauses governing arbitration and choice of law, and provisions as to notice or on ending the contract on the buyer's bankruptcy or liquidation. It is convenient to deal here with these latter three standard form provisions.

i. Arbitration terms

5.35 English businessmen may indeed be as impressed by the principles of English law as Professor Goode asserted, above, but if so they seem to have little or no faith in English courts or lawyers. Their fears, no doubt, are of astronomical costs, appalling delays and confrontational litigation arising out of excessively technical or legalistic approaches to business affairs. These fears are well founded. The English system, accepted by most English lawyers as the best in the world, is one of the slowest in Europe, after Italy and Ireland, according to *'Civil Procedures in EC Countries'*, a survey by McIntosh and Holmes, published in 1992. Lord Woolf, advocating the reforms noted in para. 0.14, has said that Continental systems of justice had the advantage of speed and cheapness and were more attractive to commercial firms than the English system (*Law Society Gazette*, 11.5.95). But whatever the reasons or their validity, businessmen usually include terms such as these in their contracts: 'If at any time any question, dispute or difference whatsoever shall arise between us and the customer in connection with this contract, either party may give to the other notice in writing of the existence of any such question, dispute or difference and the same shall be referred to the arbitration of a person to be mutually agreed upon, or failing agreement within 14 days of receipt of such notice, of some person appointed by the President for the time being of the [relevant] Institute'. Or, more simply: 'Any dispute arising under the contract shall be referred to arbitration under the Arbitration Act of 1950 or any statutory modification or re-enactment thereof.' The contract may nominate an arbitrator, e.g. one of the Official Referees of the High Court. Ideally also the contract should specify the place of arbitration, the procedure and time limits, and in international contracts the choice of law and language of the proceedings. If a party refuses to co-operate in choosing an arbitrator, the court may decide the matter for him: *Sudbrooke* v. *Eggleton*, 1982. An arbitration clause is seen as a self-contained contract, which may therefore enable an arbitrator to decide on the validity of the contract itself: *Bremmer Vulcan* v. *S. India Shipping Corp.*, 1981; *Ferris* v. *Plaister*, 1994 (Australia).

5.36   There is obviously much to be said for arbitration provisions, perhaps more in deciding matters of fact such as the quality of goods rather than questions of law. But such provisions do not necessarily solve all the parties' problems. Although arbitrations are private and informal, they are not necessarily cheaper or quicker than court proceedings, nor can they always give effect to the parties' wishes. Pending proposed reform, the arbitrator does not have under English law the role of *'amiable compositeur'* or 'compromisor' allowed to him by both Continental and American systems. He cannot give whatever decision appears most fair and reasonable and agreeable to the parties, even if expressly authorised to do so by the arbitration clause: *Overseas Union* v. *A.A. Insurance*, 1987. He may, however, be given more latitude in interpretation of documents than a court would give: *Home Insurance* v. *Mentor*, 1988. His decisions must be in accordance with English law, otherwise they will not be enforced by English courts (though our courts will enforce foreign awards made on an *amiable compositeur* basis). We observe also that the parties may use the threat of arbitration proceedings as they use the threat of court proceedings, as a bargaining counter. The result may be long delays and uncertainties, defeating the whole object and benefit of arbitration. One particular problem has been that English arbitrators had until recently no legal authority either to compel the parties to expedite proceedings or to declare them formally abandoned.

5.37   This latter deficiency led to a number of unsatisfactory court cases where one side or the other belatedly tried to revive an apparently dead dispute or, as the case may be, to have the dispute officially buried. As we saw in Chapter 2 it has been argued that a very long delay in pursuing a claim, leading the other party to believe it had been abandoned, could be interpreted as a tacit but binding contract to that effect. But in the leading case of *Paal Wilson* v. *Partenreederei; The Hannah Blumenthal*, 1983, the House of Lords said it was not possible to make an agreement this way, and held that both parties to an arbitration were legally obliged to try to pursue the dispute to completion. The decision was criticised as bearing no relation to commercial reality, but was confirmed by their Lordships in *The Leonidas D*, 1985. The impasse was resolved by s. 86 of the Courts and Legal Services Act 1990, which enables arbitrators to dismiss excessively delayed claims.

5.38   At common law and by statute, arbitration clauses cannot stop a party from going to law. The Consumer Arbitration Agreements Act 1990 expressly annuls agreements taking away consumers' rights to use the small claims procedure (para. 0.18). An arbitration agreement may contain a '*Scott* v. *Avery*' clause, purporting to stop either party from taking legal action before the award is made. But whether or not such a clause is included, the courts will usually delay action until after the arbitrator has given his award. The courts' powers to 'stay' or stop proceedings at any earlier stage are given by Section 4 of the Arbitration Act 1950 as regards domestic arbitrations (with one or both parties being British and the claim subject to English law), and by Section 1 of the Arbitration Act 1979 in other cases. But applications to the court may be made by one party and the arbitrator or by both parties for a ruling on a preliminary point of law, and appeals to the High Court and above are allowed on substantial points of law unless expressly excluded by the terms of the agreement. Appeals can, of course, nullify the advantages of arbitration. They are allowed only where there is some real ground for saying the arbitrator was wrong in law: *Ipswich B.C.* v. *Fisons*, 1989. Applications for leave to appeal must be made promptly: *Secretary of State* v. *Euston Centre*, 1994. The court will enforce an arbitration award under a written agreement as if it were an order of the High Court.

ii. Choice of law terms

5.39   Standard forms for contracts which may have effects outside the United Kingdom, or one of whose parties is foreign, almost invariably contain a 'forum' or *lex loci* clause: 'This contract shall in all respects be construed and operate as an English contract and shall be governed by English law' – or words to that effect. The clause may expressly require a foreign party to submit to the jurisdiction of English courts and perhaps also state that in case there is a conflict between translations of the contract the English language version shall prevail. Usually the clause expresses the will of the stronger contracting party, invoking whichever legal system seems more likely to protect his interests. Sometimes the law of a 'neutral' country which is not otherwise concerned with the contract may be chosen. In general such choices will be upheld by English courts, unless perhaps there is some evidence of bad faith in a wholly unreasonable choice – requiring, say, English and French parties to go to arbitration in Japan – or a wish to avoid the legal obligations normally attached to a contract: *Vita Food Products* v. *Unus Shipping*, 1939; *The Hollandia*, 1982 (House of Lords decisions).

5.40   The Contracts (Applicable Law) Act 1990 is intended to resolve 'forum' problems for European Union countries. The Act incorporates the 1980 Rome Convention on contractual obligations which are subject to conflicts of law. Questions of status, wills, matrimonial and family relationships, negotiable instruments, arbitration agreements, company law, agency duties, trusts and certain insurance contracts are outside the scope of the Convention. With these exceptions, the Convention says that contracts are governed by the system of law expressly or by clear implication chosen by the parties. If their choice is not clear, the law applicable is that of the country most closely connected with the contract. This is determined first by reference to the liable party's habitual place of residence or business. If land is involved, the country most closely connected is that where the land is situated. Article 5 of the Convention makes special provision for consumer contracts. It says that choice of law clauses cannot take away the protection of the consumer's own legal system if he made the contract in his own country after a specific invitation or advertising by the other party, or, *inter alia*, if the contract is for a package holiday. But contracts of carriage and contracts for services to be supplied in another country (such as car hire or time-share agreements) are not protected in this way. We note here also that the Brussels Convention on Jurisdiction and Enforcement of Judgments, 1968, given effect in the UK in 1982, makes judgments in EU States reciprocally enforceable.

5.41   In practice it is most important to decide expressly upon the appropriate system of law and procedure where there is any foreign element in the contract. A classic example of the kind of problem which can otherwise arise is in *The Assunzione*, 1954. After negotiations in France and Italy, French carriers chartered an Italian ship to carry goods from Belgium to Italy. The contract was made in France, but on an English standard form which said nothing as to the governing law. The Court of Appeal held that since the contract was to be performed in Italy it should be governed by Italian law. Another example is *Amin Rasheed Shipping* v. *Kuwait Insurance*, 1983. Insurers under an English language Lloyd's Standard Marine form policy issued and signed in Kuwait, but payable in London, denied liability when the ship was lost. The owners tried to sue them in England, but were refused leave. In the House of Lords it was held that the contract had to be interpreted according to English law, but by a Kuwaiti court. Lord Diplock said it would be 'wholly wrong for an English court with quite inadequate experience of how it works in practice in a particular country to condemn [the civil law system procedure] as inferior to our own'. The 'natural prejudice in favour of a familiar system' was not a relevant consideration in deciding on jurisdiction. English may be the language of commerce, but for better or worse the use of it does not guarantee access to English courts. Even an express provision for arbitration in England does not necessarily prove that the English courts have jurisdiction over the dispute: *Compagnie d'Armement Maritime* v. *Compagnie Tunisienne de Navigation*, 1971. 'Judicial comity' between nations must be respected: *Spiliada Maritime* v. *Cansulex*, 1986.

5.42   The problem arose in a different form in *Seashell Shipping* v. *Mutualidad de Seguros*, 1988. The plaintiff was a Panamanian corporation and the defendant a Spanish insurance company. Their contract was written in English but contained no *lex loci* clause. If the case were to be tried under English law the contract would probably be held enforceable; under Spanish law, unenforceable. Since there were no other matters in dispute, the issue was simply whether the parties had chosen English law or Spanish. The Court of Appeal held that where the question was essentially as to the true meaning and effect of documents written in English, an English court was better qualified than a Spanish one to interpret those documents. It was relevant also that Spanish law might enable the defendant to avoid his liability under the contract and so defeat its apparent purpose. An English court's decision as to the proper law of a contract may thus depend to some extent on whether the other legal system involved recognises and protects interests recognised and protected by English law. Considerations of speed and cost may be particularly important: *The Al Battani*, 1993. In *Roneleigh* v. *M.I.I.*, 1989, for instance, the fact that a successful plaintiff could not recover his costs in an American court led the Court of Appeal to hold that the case should be tried in England. 'There must be cases where a judge could reasonably and properly come to the conclusion that substantial justice would not be done via proceedings in a foreign forum, if the success of a plaintiff in monetary terms would necessarily and substantially be diminished by costs which he would have to pay there but would not have to pay here.' But the Court has also held that the availability or otherwise of legal aid could not of itself determine the appropriate court, even though the practical result might be that the plaintiff could not afford to bring his claim in another country: *Connelly* v. *RTZ Corp.*, 1995.

5.43   On a more specific point, it was decided in *Attock* v. *Romanian Bank*, 1989, that a performance bond or letter of credit was usually governed by the law of the place where payment was due. The bond or letter was a separate transaction, not necessarily affected by the proper law of the rest of the contract. The decision was said to be in accordance with the banking rule that a current or deposit account was governed by the law of the place where the account was kept: *Libyan Bank* v. *Manufacturers' Trust*, 1988.

iii. Termination

5.44   Contracts involving any kind of continuing relationship between the parties should state expressly the circumstances in which they can be ended or the obligations in them cancelled. Commercial contracts usually provide for termination by either side with due notice, or on the occurrence or non-occurrence of a certain event (e.g., failure to obtain a licence). If no period of notice is specified, the law would usually allow for termination on reasonable notice – although it is by no means certain that it will do so: para. 5.53. Typically, the contract will also grant one side the right to repudiate on the ground of the other's breach of contract or bankruptcy. The question whether a breach of contract is serious enough to justify termination may depend either on the precise terms of the contract or on the general principles of law regarding conditions and warranties, as discussed above and in Chapter 13. An example of a term providing for termination on grounds of bankruptcy is given in para. 9.20.

C. Implied terms

5.45   Despite the customary attention to detail in their contracts, commercial parties seem surprisingly often to be confronted by problems for which they have made no express provision. They then commonly seek support for their arguments in the terms which they say are or ought to be implied by law. Such terms may in appropriate cases be added by statute or by common law. The role of statute law is generally to provide obligatory minimum standards for all transactions or relationships of a particular kind. For present purposes the main provisions are those in the Sale of Goods Act 1979 or equivalent legislation on other forms of transfer of goods. These Acts set out various conditions and warranties, as defined above, intended to ensure a buyer's or other transferee's title to the goods, the goods' compliance with description and their quality and fitness for purpose. Other statutorily implied rights and duties concern allocation of risk and rules as to delivery and price. Since we discuss all these rules in detail in ensuing chapters we need make no further reference to them here.

5.46   The judges' approach to the implication of terms in contracts is somewhat different from that of Parliament. In the first place the judges are very reluctant to do what they see as Parliament's job and in effect to legislate for minimum standards in a given area. In the second, the doctrine of precedent and the *laisser-faire* attitudes it has embedded in the common law incline them strongly against any interference – for better or worse – with contractual commitments. They are still much influenced, consciously or otherwise, by the sentiments expressed by a nineteenth century judge, Sir George Jessel: 'If there is one thing more than another which public policy requires, it is that men of full age and competent understanding shall have the utmost liberty of contracting and that their contracts, when entered into freely and voluntarily, shall be held sacred and shall be enforced by courts of justice': *Printing and Numerical Registering Co.* v. *Sampson*, 1875. But even this degree of rugged individualism begs many questions and permits many exceptions, as twentieth century judges have had increasingly to recognise. A third difficulty which should be mentioned in passing is the 'parol evidence' rule noted in Chapter 4. Nevertheless, the fact remains that many contract cases have to be decided according to terms added in by the judges.

5.47   Certain basic contractual relationships such as those of principal and agent, landlord and tenant, and employer and employee are underpinned by terms added in by the judges. These general rules are said to be implied 'in law', as distinct from those which may be implied in and limited to individual contracts, which are implied 'in fact' (below). By way of illustration of terms implied in law, we mention briefly the standards prescribed by the judges in employment contracts. Employees are bound by common law duties of obedience, care, competence and good faith. In *Superlux* v. *Plaisted*, 1958, for example, a salesman was held liable for breach of contract when he left his employer's goods in a locked but unguarded vehicle overnight, when he could have taken them into his house. The judge said the standard of care required of him was as high as if the goods had been his own. The duty of good faith has been invoked to stop employees from doing spare time work competing with their employers. It has also required disclosure of inventions made in the course of employment, as now provided by the Patents Act 1977. It has proved a little more difficult for the judges to lay down employers' duties, but there are now quite stringent common law safety liabilities and an increasing acknowledgement of the need for fair treatment of employees. So, for example, it is a breach of contract by the employer if he wilfully changes terms of employment so as to undermine mutual trust and confidence.

5.48   More to the point, however, is the question of the judges' willingness to vary or add to the express terms of ordinary commercial contracts. Occasionally they can be prevailed upon in this way. Various different arguments have been advanced to justify intervention in particular cases. The best known – and among students perhaps the most misunderstood – is the principle put forward in the case of *The Moorcock*, 1889. An agreement was made to unload a boat at a jetty. When the tide went out the boat grounded and was damaged. The contract said nothing as to the safety of the boat or the requisite depth of water, but the jetty owners were held liable for

115

breach of an implied term that the boat could be left there safely. Such a term was necessary, said the Court of Appeal, to give the contract 'business efficacy'. It was an underlying assumption of the contract. Without it the whole point and purpose of the contract would be defeated; it would be meaningless. But that does not mean that any and every contract could or should be made more effective by adding in a term suggested by one side or the other to resolve a dispute. There was no question of 'improving' the contract in *The Moorcock*; only of filling a gap which would otherwise have left it devoid of all commercial sense. The basis of the implication, in short, was *necessity*, not advantage or improvement.

5.49   It is not always so easy to define what is necessary, nor to distinguish necessity from desirability. A possible test is that of the presumed intention of the parties. '*Prima facie* that which in any contract is left to be implied and need not be expressed is something so obvious that it goes without saying; so that, if while the parties were making their bargain an officious bystander was to suggest some express provision for it in their agreement, they would testily suppress him with a common "Oh, of course"': *Shirlaw* v. *Southern Foundries*, 1939. The 'officious bystander' test, as it then immediately became known, has the obvious weakness that since both parties are now in dispute over the proposed term they would evidently never have agreed to it on a 'common "Oh, of course"' basis.

5.50   The whole question of the grounds on which terms might be implied at common law was examined by the House of Lords in *Liverpool City Council* v. *Irwin*, 1977. The problem here was whether the corporation had any – and, if so, what – duty to maintain its property for the benefit of its tenants. This problem arose because the tenancy agreements stated only the obligations of the tenants and said nothing at all as to any landlord's duties. In the Court of Appeal Lord Denning decided that it would be 'reasonable' to imply certain maintenance duties. But the House of Lords indignantly rejected mere reasonableness as the basis of judicial intervention. Lord Denning's argument, it was said, went a 'long and undesirable way beyond sound authority'.

5.51   Lord Wilberforce explained that there were several different circumstances in which, or bases on which, terms might properly be implied, none of which depended merely on a test of reasonableness – though any term which was implied had to be a reasonable one. A term might be added to an otherwise apparently complete agreement 'on the ground that without it the contract will not work', much as in *The Moorcock*, or to explain a contract by reference, for example, to a trade custom which must have been in the parties' minds and which would give a special or hidden meaning to the words used. Or again the court might be concerned simply to establish what the contract is, the parties themselves not having stated all its terms. The court is then searching for what must be implied to avoid the contract being 'futile, inefficacious and absurd'. It is not perhaps immediately clear why the test of business efficacy would not suffice for all these instances, but at all events their Lordships stressed that in such a case as the present the test was that of *necessity*. On this basis they decided that the tenancy agreement would be unworkable unless the corporation was under a duty to take reasonable care to maintain the property.

5.52   A few brief illustrations of the working of the necessity test may be helpful. In the past few years the judges have found implied terms necessary, for example, to compel a landlord to repair the outside of his property when his tenant was expressly obliged to repair only the inside: *Barrett* v. *Lounova*, 1988; to oblige an employee to pay interest on a loan from his employer when he knew his employer had borrowed from the bank to finance the loan: *Baylis* v. *Barnett*, 1988; to oblige a ship repairer to tell the ship owner of a dangerous fault in the repair: *Stag Line* v. *Tyne Repair*, 1984; and to prevent a contracting party from seeking to influence the decision of an arbitrator: *Essoldo* v. *Ladbroke*, 1976. In *Davey* v. *Cosmos*, 1989, a tour operator was held liable for failing to warn of a pollution problem at a holiday resort. And in *Scally* v. *Southern Health Board*, 1991, the employer was held under a duty to ensure that his employees knew of pension rights available under a collective agreement.

5.53   On the other hand, the judges have said there was no implied obligation on a contracting party to repay a bond paid on his behalf – *Travel Insurance* v. *Barron*, 1988 – nor on a sales agent who had contracted to use his best endeavours to promote the plaintiff's products to refuse to act for the plaintiff's competitors: *Ault* v. *Sure Service*, 1983. In *Ashmore* v. *Corporation of Lloyd's*, 1992, it was held that Lloyd's insurance corporation had no implied duty to its members, who joined expressly on the basis of total liability for losses in a speculative market, to alert them to possible risks to their interests or to monitor and report on the activities of members' agents. A person using travellers' cheques had no implied obligation to his bank to take reasonable care of them: *El Awadi* v. *Bank of Credit*, 1989. There was no implied duty on a seller to keep a buyer's offer secret so as to prevent a rival buyer from making a better offer – *Trees* v. *Cripps*, 1983 – nor on a business tenant to use the land 'in good faith as a commercial venture with a view to income maximisation' (for the benefit of the landlord): *Thomson* v. *Muir*, 1995 (Scot.). A contract with no fixed date of termination and no provision for notice was not necessarily subject to an implied right to give reasonable notice: *Tower Hamlets B.C.* v. *British Gas*, 1983 – but contrast *Staffordshire A.H.A.* v. *S. Staffordshire Waterworks*, 1978. In *Chelsea Football Co.* v. *SB Property*, 1992, the Court of Appeal refused to imply a term in a contract for the sale of land which would ensure compensation for all delay, however caused. There is no implied term in a package holiday contract that the hotel will be reasonably safe: *Wilson* v. *Best*, 1993. In a contract to build a house according to certain specifications there was no implied term that the house should also be habitable: *Lynch* v. *Thorne*, 1956 (a much criticised decision, which should perhaps be read in the light of the cases above suggesting a contractual duty to warn of defects, and negligence cases to the same effect noted in para. 11.9). And as we shall see in our chapters on mistake and misrepresentation, there is not yet any implied obligation on a seller to disclose facts about his property which he knows would be of fundamental importance to a buyer: *Bell* v. *Lever Bros.*, 1932.

5.54   While it seems then that necessity may sometimes be interpreted fairly freely, it is nonetheless a very much narrower basis for the implication of terms than that of fairness, reasonableness or good faith, as expressly required by civil law systems (however difficult it may be to say exactly what good faith means in any given circumstances). It is in fact one of English law's most remarkable characteristics, and one most clearly distinguishing it from its American and Continental counterparts, that it has neither an express requirement of good faith in contracts generally, nor, as we have just seen, any principle of common law by which such a general duty be implied – nor, conversely, any general rule against abuse of rights. In his *Commercial Law* Professor Goode observes: 'The irrelevance of good faith to the entitlement to legal remedies is at once the most remarkable and the most reprehensible feature of English contract law'. This situation may be changing, however. Recent Commonwealth cases suggesting growing acceptance of a good faith principle include *Livingstone* v. *Roskilly*, 1992 (N.Z.), and *GSA Group* v. *Siebe*, 1993 (Australia). In *GSA*, Chief Justice Rogers said: 'In the context of consumer contracts there is certainly an increasing expectation that the stronger party in the transaction will behave fairly . . . The situation of two commercial parties in positions of equal bargaining power is very different . . . [But] it is likely that ultimately Australian courts will embrace the American and civil law concept of the obligation that each contracting party should show good faith in the performance of contractual obligations'. A limited good faith obligation has been imported into English law under European Union influence, in the form of the Unfair Terms in Consumer Contracts Regulations 1994: paras. 7.49–53. If and when the Vienna Convention on Contracts for the International Sale of Goods is adopted in Britain, good faith will become a legal obligation in contracts covered by the Convention unless expressly excluded by the parties.

Danish law

CONDITIONS AND WARRANTIES

5.55   Danish law does not divide contractual rights and duties into conditions and warranties. The remedies of the innocent party depend on the nature and consequences of the breach, not on a preliminary classification of the importance of the various terms. Generally repudiation is allowed only where the breach is material or major. The parties are free to emphasise in their contract the importance of particular terms. In 'entire' contracts (paras. 5.18–21) the remedy does not depend on whether the seller claims payment or the buyer seeks to recover his payment. If the buyer has received anything of value he cannot repudiate the contract, but may claim reduction of the price or damages.

5.56 Article 21 of the Sale of Goods Act 1906 says that delay in delivery in a commercial sale is material, unless affecting only a small part of the whole. Article 28 lays down a similar rule as to payment. Both parties must act with due regard to the other's interests. The innocent party may therefore be prevented from cancelling the contract if that would be especially harsh and if some other remedy would suffice.

EXPRESS AND IMPLIED TERMS

5.57 Parties who have expressly agreed on arbitration cannot take their disputes to court. But an arbitrator's decision is void if clearly wrong in law or procedurally unfair. The contract may enable the arbitrator to base his decision not only on law but on what he considers fair and reasonable.

5.58 When interpreting a contract the court will consider the intention of the parties and the reasonable expectations created by the contract, together with more pragmatic factors such as what is needed to fulfil the parties' interests in a fair and reasonable way. If the parties' wishes are not clear the court will 'fill out' the contract by implying into it that solution which in accordance with trade usages and general principles of contract law, including that of good faith, seems most fair, reasonable and expedient. This 'filling out' process applies in all cases; not merely those of necessity as under English law. In effect the Danish position is that the law has an answer to all problems and that this answer is implied in the contract unless the parties have expressly agreed otherwise. *See also* para. 9.22.

Dutch law

CONDITIONS AND WARRANTIES

5.59 Unlike English law, Dutch law draws no distinction as between terms, conditions and warranties. But the effect is the same since a contract can be repudiated only when the breach is of some real significance: Article 6.265. English law seems to stand quite apart in its general insistence on certainty of contract. Both the old and new Dutch Codes on the other hand have emphasised the importance of good faith between contracting parties, as noted below. According to some Dutch writers, therefore, the interpretation of the significance of contract terms is not only a question of finding the parties' actual intentions but also of establishing what they might reasonably be expected to have intended.

EXPRESS AND IMPLIED TERMS

5.60   Dutch arbitration law, like UK law, has recently been modernised in order to attract more arbitration cases to the Netherlands. But unlike the UK Arbitration Act, Dutch law has more closely followed the Model Law proposed by the United Nations Commission on International Trade Law. As far as choice of law is concerned, Dutch courts apply the 1980 Rome Convention, i.e. the rule that in the absence of express agreement between the parties, their contract will be governed by the legal system with which it is most closely connected – usually the seller's place of residence or principal place of business.

5.61   As regards implied terms, Dutch courts are clearly instructed by the new Code to introduce into contracts whatever rights and duties are necessary to give effect to the requirements of good faith. Article 6.2 is one of the most important of the many references to this overriding standard. It says (in terms no doubt surprising or perhaps even alarming for the English lawyer): 'Creditor and debtor must as between themselves act in accordance with the requirements of reasonableness and equity (*redelijkheid en billijkheid*). A rule otherwise binding upon them by virtue of law, usage or juridical act does not apply to such extent as would in the circumstances be unacceptable according to criteria of reasonableness and equity.' Similarly, Article 6.248 declares: 'A contract has not only the juridical effects agreed to by the parties, but also those which, according to the nature of the contract, result from law, usage or the requirements of reasonableness and equity. A rule binding upon the parties as a result of the contract does not apply to such extent as would in the circumstances be unacceptable according to criteria of reasonableness and equity'. These very extensive powers to add to or vary or subtract from the terms agreed between the parties remain to some extent controversial within the business community.

French law

CONDITIONS AND WARRANTIES

5.62   The traditional distinction in English law between conditions and warranties, with different remedies in case of breach, has no equivalent in French law. An English 'warranty' is treated simply as a term of the contract, breach of which gives rise to damages or specific performance in accordance with the principles in Article 1147 *et seq.* Conditional obligations are those defined in Article 1168 which depend on a future and uncertain event, and are either suspended for so long as such event has not occurred (*condition suspensive*; condition precedent), or terminated upon the occurrence of such event (*condition résolutoire*; condition subsequent). For so long as the condition precedent has not occurred, the obligation is not enforceable. Upon the occurrence of the condition subsequent, the obligation is retroactively ended and the parties must be restored to their original position.

5.63   Breach of a material term of a contract may entitle the innocent party to end the contract. Article 1184 provides that 'a condition subsequent is always implied in bilateral contracts if one of the two parties does not comply with its obligations'. The termination can, however, only be ordered by a court when an express termination clause has not been included in the contract (but also in practice if it was included in the contract, for enforcement purposes and to acknowledge non-compliance by the party in default). The judges have a wide authority to determine whether the alleged breach is one that affects the main terms of the contract and therefore justifies its termination, or whether the breach concerns an ancillary element of the contract which justifies only an award of damages: Civ. 14 April 1891. Despite the use of the words '*condition résolutoire*' in Article 1184, the normal effect of which is the retroactive nullification of the contract, contracts of continuing obligation (*contrats à exécution successive*), such as leases, employment contracts, etc., are not automatically retroactively terminated: termination may be effective for the future only (*résiliation: see* Civ. 28 January 1992).

5.64   The freedom of the judges is limited where the contract has a termination clause providing for automatic termination on the occurrence of certain events. In that case, the judge can only interpret the clause and verify that the events indicated therein have occurred. He cannot, for example, grant additional time for payment: Civ. 4 June 1986. Termination sought by a party on the pretext only of a minor breach of the contractual terms can be 'abusive' and give rise to a claim for damages against that party. We should note that French law prohibits 'perpetual commitments'. It follows that contracts made for an undetermined period of time (including guarantees) can be terminated by either party at any time, subject to any agreed or customary notice requirement and to an obligation of 'reasonableness': Com. 19 January 1983; Civ. 5 February 1985.

EXPRESS AND IMPLIED TERMS

5.65   French contract law makes no provision for implied terms. It does, however, lay down various terms and conditions – *lois supplétives* – which form the basis of a contract unless otherwise agreed by the parties. Article 1135 of the Civil Code provides that agreements oblige the parties not only with respect to what is expressly set out but 'also with respect to the consequences that equity, usages or the law require according to the nature of the obligation'. Article 1134 provides that agreements 'must be carried out in good faith'. Whether these provisions really affect the basic rule in Article 1134, whereby the contract is 'the law of the parties', remains uncertain. While the judges enjoy a certain freedom in interpreting the common intent of the parties, they have no right to supplement a contract even in the case of inadequate or missing provisions, and cannot in any case add to the obligations of the parties: Civ. 8 May 1933. Article 1135 is in fact limited essentially to commercial transactions where contracts defining only the main terms of agreement of the parties are supplemented, in their interpretation, by the customs of the trade: Com. 25 January 1972. The good faith requirement of Article 1134 is regarded generally as no more than a statement of intent. But it may be invoked by the courts, e.g., to punish a party's 'abusive' exercise of a contractual right: Civ. 6 June 1984. The rule has also been used by legal authors to justify the creation by the courts of obligations on one contracting party to inform the other of the progress of the transaction in the negotiation period, or to ensure the adequacy of the product or service offered in relation to the needs of the purchaser and any other disclosure obligations (*see* Ghestin, *op. cit.*; Cabrillac, *op. cit.*, para. 123 *et seq.*; Civ. 27 February 1985; 3 July 1985). This duty to inform is an increasingly important aspect of consumer protection law.

German law

CONDITIONS AND WARRANTIES

5.66　German law does not make the same distinctions as English law between conditions and warranties or between express and implied terms. For the purposes of the Civil Code, the BGB, the important question is whether the goods have been delivered or service supplied, or not. If defective goods have been delivered or a defective service supplied, the BGB gives remedies for breach of promise or warranty – *Gewährleistungsrechte* – according to the type of contract. 'Warranty' does not have the same meaning here as in English law, but signifies a reasonable standard of fitness. The German rules are more complicated than the English ones, because they offer the buyer different remedies with different prerequisites. The buyer can choose between repudiation of the contract or a lower price. In contracts for work and services the law enables him alternatively to demand improved performance; a remedy which otherwise depends on the terms of the contract. If the seller or supplier is at fault, the buyer may also claim damages. His remedies may be limited by standard contract terms, but cannot be excluded altogether.

5.67   Where the seller cannot fulfil the contract, it is cancelled: Article 323, BGB. If his failure is due to negligence, he is liable in damages – Article 325 – as he is also if performance is delayed because of his negligence: Article 286. If performance is delayed even after the buyer has given the seller additional time, the buyer may repudiate the contract and claim damages: Article 326.

5.68   Cases like *Bolton* or *Simpson*, para. 5.20, would not be decided in the same way by a German court. A party who is allowed to repudiate has to return everything he got from the other party. If he cannot do so, e.g. because of installations in his house, he must pay for the value of the things he cannot return.

EXPRESS AND IMPLIED TERMS

5.69   Terms as to time are not usually interpreted as strictly as in the English shipping cases. Such cases do not often come before German courts. Contracts in which time is in fact of the essence are regulated by Article 361, BGB (*Fixgeschäft*). Delay then justifies cancellation of the contract. If the delay is due to fault, a claim for damages may also be made.

5.70   Although, as noted above, German law does not use the concept of implied terms in contracts, the negotiation and execution of contracts is limited by the fundamental requirement of good faith in Article 242. Similar conclusions might be reached by judgments finding a positive violation of a contract duty – *positive Vertragsverletzung*. So, for example, where a customer slips and injures himself in a shop, that might be regarded as a breach of a contractual duty to keep the floor safe. Similarly a seller of electrical equipment might be liable for failing to give instructions as to use, or a travel agent for failing to advise on the need for a visa. Despite what was said in para. 1.48 on the limited role of case law, the rules of *positive Vertragsverletzung* are purely judge-made, and are cited like provisions of the BGB.

5.71   We should note also that case law extends the cover of the contract both to certain pre-contractual situations and on occasion even to non-contracting parties. Thus a shopkeeper could be held liable to a *prospective* customer for injuries suffered in the shop, e.g., because of an employee's negligence: RGZ 78,239. The principle involved here is that of *culpa in contrahendo* – fault in contracting – which has no equivalent application in English contract law. Once a contract is made, its protection may extend to non-contracting third parties for whom the contractor is responsible: *Vertrag mit Schutzwirkung für Dritte*. So a garage proprietor would have to compensate members of a car owner's family injured through his defective repairs to the car. These principles go a long way towards overcoming the complications of German tort law (paras. 6.104, 6.106). On the other hand, liability in contract, unlike tort, is limited to economic loss and does not compensate for pain and suffering unless negligence can be proved. If a claim in tort can be made against the other contracting party, then compensation for pain and suffering can be claimed.

Italian law

CONDITIONS AND WARRANTIES

5.72   Under Italian contract law, much as in English law, *'condizione'* may signify either an uncertain and future fact, whose occurrence or non-occurrence may determine the starting or ending of a contract, or the basic purpose or interest to be fulfilled by the contract. When the contract is brought to an end by non-fulfilment or breach of condition, the parties must so far as possible be returned to their original positions.

5.73   If a term as to time of performance is vital and is not fulfilled, Article 1457 of the Civil Code brings the contract to an end – unless the innocent party declares his willingness to continue despite the delay. If the term is not essential, a claim for damages may be made.

5.74   A warranty may be regarded as a species of condition. It is in effect a promise imposed by law that the contract will be properly performed, as for example the legal obligation to supply goods of the right quality and description. The remedy for breach may be reduction of price or the ending of the contract: Articles 1490–7; 1667–8.

EXPRESS AND IMPLIED TERMS

5.75   Italian law recognises something similar to the implied terms of English contract law in its use of *presupposizione*. Where one party's basic reason for making the contract is known to the other side the contract may be avoided if that basic reason or purpose cannot be fulfilled, even though it has not been made an express term of the contract. It is a question of the judge's interpretation of the parties' intentions.

5.76   Many of the provisions of the Civil Code have the effect of implied terms. Article 1339, for instance, says that terms imposed by law are 'automatically inserted' in the contract, despite any express agreement to the contrary. 'Customary terms' are also included, unless the parties otherwise agree: Article 1340. Contracts are binding not only in their express terms but in all the consequences arising in law, usage or equity: Article 1374. And underlying all contracts is the duty imposed upon the parties by Article 1375 to act in good faith. Similarly Article 1175 says that 'debtor and creditor shall behave according to rules of fairness.' These rules are sometimes used to 'enrich' the main contractual obligations with other (limited) collateral obligations; duties, for example, of co-operation or disclosure of information. In its decision of 13 January 1993, n. 343, the Supreme Court said that good faith might require each party to protect the interests of the other by taking action not expressly required by the contract or by accepting restrictions on his own rights, as long as such action or restriction did not involve a 'valuable economic or personal effort'.

Spanish law

CONDITIONS AND WARRANTIES

5.77   Spanish law draws no such distinction as the English system between 'conditions' and 'warranties', with their respective remedies for breach. The general rule laid down in Article 1124 of the Civil Code is that the right to end a contract is implicit where one party does not fulfil his obligations, and that the injured party can demand either completion or termination of the contract, with the possibility of damages and interest in both cases.

5.78   The Supreme Court has, however, held that an innocent party can repudiate a bilateral contract only if he can show that he has fulfilled his own obligations, that the other side was personally responsible for the breach, and that the breach shows a deliberate intention or wish – *una voluntad deliberadamente rebelde* – to flout or reject the contract, or else creates an insuperable obstacle to its fulfilment. Recent cases suggest that the element of intention may be established by the 'prolonged inactivity or passivity' of the debtor, without the need to prove active hindrance or a degree of deliberation akin to fraud. Repudiation because of delay will not be allowed unless the delay frustrates the practical purpose of the contract.

EXPRESS AND IMPLIED TERMS

5.79   Arbitration agreements are regulated by the new Law of 5 December 1988. Arbitrators may decide cases equitably according to their knowledge and understanding unless expressly required to decide according to law: Article 4. Decisions are final – subject to very limited rights of challenge – and enforceable by the courts.

5.80   Questions of choice of law are resolved by Article 10 of the Civil Code. If the parties do not otherwise agree, their common national law will apply, or alternatively the law of the place where they normally live. In the last resort the law applicable will be that of the place where the contract was made.

5.81   In contrast to English law, there is in the Spanish Civil Code the general provision in Article 1258 that contracts involve the obligation 'not only to carry out what has been expressly agreed but also all those consequences which according to their nature conform to good faith, usage and the law'. This clause is used, particularly in commercial contracts, to fill any gaps caused by failing to state standard terms: Article 1287. The law also adds many standard terms to particular kinds of contract such as company contracts, insurance, freight, and contracts of employment.

Swedish law

CONDITIONS AND WARRANTIES

5.82   Swedish law does not recognise any division of contract terms into conditions and warranties. The consequences of a breach depend upon the interpretation of the contract, and not on any classification of different types of terms. A breach might lead to rescission, damages, price reduction or cure.

5.83   'Entire contract' clauses (*see* paras 5.19–21) are not conclusive under Swedish law, although on principle they will be upheld. However, in exceptional cases oral or other extrinsic evidence may prove that it would be unreasonable to uphold the entire contract clause, and if so, it will be set aside. The Swedish position with regard to cases such as *Hoenig*, *Kiely*, *Bolton* and *Simpson* is that when a builder or other contractor is in breach because he has not performed in accordance with the agreement, the buyer is entitled to demand that the builder corrects his work, or, when this is not suitable, to claim a price reduction. The price reduction could either correspond to the cost of correction or to the difference in value of the work done and the work promised. The buyer is entitled to price reduction whether or not he has already paid.

5.84   According to Swedish law, there are no general assumptions as to when time is of the essence. The type of contract, the situation as a whole, and the terms of the contract are considered when deciding whether the delay is fundamental enough to allow repudiation.

EXPRESS AND IMPLIED TERMS

5.85   Arbitration clauses are common in Swedish contracts. The arbitration clauses often refer to the Stockholm Chamber of Commerce Arbitration Institute, which is an institute concerned with both national and international disputes. Arbitration is probably more widely used in enforcement of Swedish commercial contracts than the courts. Arbitration decisions are binding and subject to very limited rights of appeal to the courts.

Chapter 6

Fitness of goods and services

6.1   Disputes over the quality or fitness of goods or services may be resolved under English law by breach of contract actions, or, if physical injury or damage to property is involved, by actions in tort for negligence or strict liability claims. In these latter cases, no contractual connections between plaintiff and defendant need be established. Contract claims are decided in accordance either with the terms expressly agreed between the parties or with those which may be added by the law to fill the gaps in their agreement.

A. Contract

6.2   In the absence of any more specific contractual requirements set by the parties themselves, the basic standards of fitness are those in the Sale of Goods Act 1979 ('SGA'), as amended by the Sale and Supply of Goods Act 1994, the Supply of Goods (Implied Terms) Act 1973, and the Supply of Goods and Services Act 1982. These deal respectively with sales, hire-purchase transactions and redemption of trading stamps, and hiring and renting of goods and contracts for services.

6.3   The duties imposed on the seller or supplier of goods under all four Acts are in virtually identical terms, though with significantly different effects in hire-purchase contracts, as noted below. Nearly all the obligations in question are classified as either conditions or warranties (though not in Scottish law, where they are described merely as 'terms'). We saw in Chapter 5 that the purpose of this classification is to distinguish between the major and minor terms of the contract and so to give the appropriate remedy for breach. Breach of condition entitles the innocent party to repudiate the contract and/or claim damages; breach of warranty entitles only to damages. Most of the obligations we are about to examine are in fact described as conditions. By definition, then, all breaches of the relevant duties justify repudiation of the contract. It is questionable whether this 'all or nothing' approach is helpful to either party. Where the rule applies, its effect is that there is no such thing as a minor breach of contract which can be suitably recompensed by a small sum of damages. But judges are understandably reluctant to allow contracts to be repudiated for what are in fact minor grievances, and so the result may be that the buyer has no remedy at all. Under the Convention on International Sale of Goods the right to repudiate is given only for substantial and unforeseeable breach. Similar reform in UK sales law has been urged by the Law Reform Commission, and was brought a little closer by the 1994 amendments to the SGA, below.

i. Acceptance

6.4   Even where a seller has clearly broken a condition of his contract, however, the buyer loses his right to repudiate and is limited to a claim for damages once he 'accepts' the goods: Section 11(4) SGA. Sections 35 and 35A explain that acceptance occurs when the buyer tells the seller he will keep the goods, or when after taking delivery and having a reasonable opportunity for inspecting the goods to see that they conform with the contract he acts in a way inconsistent with the seller's continued ownership of the goods, e.g. by keeping the goods for more than a reasonable time without telling the seller he has rejected them. Acceptance of part of the goods does not affect the buyer's right to reject another part if it is faulty.

6.5   It is clearly a matter of common sense that the longer a buyer holds on to goods the more difficult it must be for him to say they are not what he ordered, but the practical application of the reasonable time rule is very unsatisfactory. How long is a reasonable length of time? The amended SGA tells us only that sending goods for repair, or sub-selling them, does not of itself affect the right to reject them. Is the question merely one of the passage of time, or does the concept of acceptance necessarily involve knowledge on the buyer's part of the true condition of the goods? If defects may take months or even years to appear, should the buyer be denied the opportunity to reject at that stage? Lord Denning held in *Guarantee Trust* v. *Gardner*, 1973, that 'a person cannot be said to affirm a contract unless he has full knowledge of the breach and deliberately elects to go on with it'. But it is doubtful whether that is indeed the position of English law, despite recent amendment. Section 34 of the SGA says only that acceptance presupposes a reasonable opportunity to examine the goods, which of itself may reveal nothing.

6.6   Unfortunately current case law seems contradictory and lacking in principle, making it almost impossible to advise on the operation of the 'reasonable time' rule. In *Bernstein* v. *Pamsons Motors*, 1986, for example, the plaintiff bought a new Nissan car. In the next three weeks he drove it some 150 miles. It then stopped suddenly en route because a piece of sealant entered the lubrication system and cut off oil to the camshaft, which then seized up. The plaintiff sought to return the car and recover his money. The judge agreed the car was dangerous and as such in breach of the condition of merchantable quality implied by Section 14 of the SGA, below, but still refused to allow the plaintiff's claim. He was awarded damages only, as if for breach of warranty, on the basis that three weeks' use of the car constituted acceptance. He had had a reasonable time to 'examine and try out the goods in general terms'. The judge said that the nature of the defect and the speed with which it might have been discovered were irrelevant – contrary to what one might have thought were the vital questions. It is not clear whether the 1994 amendments to the SGA, noted above, would necessarily give a different answer, although that may perhaps have been their intention. As is the general Continental approach, the Convention on International Sales of Goods has no acceptance rule as such, but requires buyers to notify sellers as soon as possible if they wish to reject defective goods.

6.7   Other cases sometimes adopt a different standard from that in *Bernstein*. In *Spencer* v. *Rye*, 1972, the buyer's right to reject was upheld despite three months' possession and intermittent use of a car, as it was after four months and several thousand miles driving in *Farnworth Finance* v. *Attryde*, below. In *Laurelgates* v. *Lombard*, 1983, the hire-purchaser sought to reject a new Jaguar car after eight months' continuous and serious complaints against the dealers, after which he had given the manufacturers a final opportunity to try to make it fit to drive. They failed. The judge nonetheless allowed the purchaser to reject, because he had acted reasonably to avoid litigation and had shown commendable patience.

6.8   On the other hand again are cases such as *Lee* v. *York Coach*, 1977, where the court held that after five or six months' limited use knowing of the defects it was too late for the buyer to return the car, and similar decisions in various hire-purchase cases such as *Charterhouse Credit* v. *Tolly*, 1963, and *Jackson* v. *Chrysler*, 1978, where the hirer continued to pay instalments despite his knowledge of major faults and so lost his right to repudiate. It should be noted, however, that there is no statutory 'acceptance' rule in hire-purchase transactions.

6.9   Decisions such as *Laurelgates* seem very much preferable, in the sense that they show a flexible approach and give adequate relief where necessary, while at the same time obliging consumers generally to try to 'make a go' of their contracts – an essential requirement in view of the possible value and complexity of the goods and the market's overall need for stability. The UK Consumers' Association, among others, urges that acceptance should take place only after defects could reasonably have been discovered.

ii. The Sale of Goods Act

6.10   The present Act is still largely a restatement of the first Sale of Goods Act of 1893, which became the model for both Commonwealth and

American legislation. The 1893 Act was repealed by the SGA 1979, as amended in 1994 and 1995. Many of the cases decided under the original Act remain important in interpreting the Act as it stands today.

6.11   Anyone who contracts to sell goods is a 'seller' within the Act, whether he does so as manufacturer, distributor, retailer or private individual. Section 14 of the Act – the vital rule on quality – applies only to business sales, but otherwise all sellers are bound to their buyers by the same terms of the same Act. So far as retailers and distributors are concerned we should note that they are almost always in business on their own account and thus personally or corporately liable on their own contracts. They may well be described in the sales literature as 'manufacturers' agents' or 'franchised dealers', but that does not make them agents in law. Only where one person genuinely contracts for and on behalf of another, or with that other's apparent authority, does he make the other liable as principal for his own breach of contract.

iii. Title

6.12   The first of the relevant rules in the SGA is in Section 12, which requires only brief mention for present purposes. *The section implies into all contracts of sale a condition that the seller has the right to sell the goods.* It adds also warranties of freedom from others' rights over the goods and quiet possession of them, except insofar as any limitations are disclosed before sale. So a seller is liable to his buyer for infringement of a third party's patent rights, whether deliberate or inadvertent: *Microbeads* v. *Vinhurst*, 1975. He would likewise be liable under this section for selling stolen goods, even in good faith: *Rowland* v. *Divall*, 1923. In this case the innocent buyer of a stolen car, which he had to return to the true owners, was held entitled to recover from the innocent seller who had bought the car from the thief the price he had paid for it, without any reduction for use, on the basis that without title to the car he had effectively received nothing of value for his money. The Law Reform Commission has recommended that damages should be reduced proportionately to the buyer's use of the goods.

iv. Description

6.13   Section 13 says that *in sales by description there is an implied condition that the goods will conform with their description*, i.e. that the buyer will get what he was promised. In sales by both sample and description the bulk of the goods must also correspond with the description. In theory, then, any but the most trivial non-conformity will entitle the buyer to give up the whole contract.

6.14   But the word 'description' does not by any means cover everything which a seller might say or write about his goods, nor on the other hand does it presuppose that anything was in fact said or written. Many goods 'describe themselves' by the way they are packed or displayed: *Grant* v. *A.K.M.*, 1936. The judges have held that the 'description' is confined to those express or implied statements which actually identify the goods or are otherwise part of their essential attributes; the sort of thing, one might say, that one would write on a sales or receipt note to define the purchase (but subject to the question of the buyer's reliance on his own skill and judgment, below). Lord Diplock put it this way in *Ashington Piggeries* v. *Hill*, 1972: 'The description by which unascertained [usually generic] goods are sold is . . . confined to those words in the contract which were intended by the parties to identify the kind of goods which were to be supplied . . . Ultimately the test is whether the buyer could fairly and reasonably refuse to accept the physical goods proffered to him on the ground that their failure to correspond with what was said about them makes them goods of a different kind from those he had agreed to buy'.

6.15 Difficulties may then arise in distinguishing between essential and inessential attributes. Statements such as 'immaculate condition', or 'one previous owner' do not identify the goods. But whether goods are new or used, their quantity, measurements, colour, packaging (for example, for resale purposes: *Re Moore*, 1921) are all likely to be essential elements. Their quality also may be a vital part of their description, as illustrated below. But even those requirements may create problems. How, for instance, does one define 'newness'? In *Phillips* v. *Cycle Corporation*, 1977, a motor cycle was sold as new though it was actually five years old. The court held that goods were new if they had not previously been sold by retail, and since that was the position here the seller was not liable. This test seems of doubtful validity in *Phillips* and in other situations may not be relevant at all. In *R* v. *Anderson*, 1987, it was said that a car registered in the dealer's name could not be new, even though the purpose was only to enable him to bring it from the dockside to his own depot. And in *R* v. *Ford*, 1974, the question was whether a car damaged on the way from the factory to the dealer and then repaired by the dealer could properly be sold as new. The answer on this occasion was that everything depended on how substantial the repairs were.

6.16 Conversely if the goods are indeed new or otherwise in accordance with the contract, the fact that they do not work properly does not of itself prove breach of Section 13. In *Grenfell* v. *Meyrowitz*, 1936, for example, the buyer ordered a particular kind of safety glass which broke when he used it and injured himself. He had no claim under Section 13 because he got the type of glass he asked for. Similarly in *Ashington Piggeries*, above, a consignment of 'herring meal' was still within that description even though poisonous for certain of the animals to which it was normally fed. There may, of course, be a point at which an article is so defective that it cannot properly be given the same description as if it were in working order, but such cases must be rare.

6.17   The most obvious application of Section 13 is where a buyer orders item A but receives item B. If he receives A but it is defective, his usual remedy is not under Section 13 but under the quality and fitness rules in Section 14, below. These rules are uncertain in application, however, and so buyers should consider whether they can bring their quality requirements within the scope of Section 13 instead. This can be done by the use of very precise specifications which define or identify the goods – as distinct from, say, a requirement that the goods be 'in good condition' or 'pure': *Cehave* v. *Bremer*, 1977; *Darlington* v. *Gosho*, 1964. A good example is *Tradax* v. *European Grain*, 1983, where the buyer ordered animal feeding stuffs with 'maximum 7.5 per cent fibre content'. On delivery the consignment was found to contain up to 9.25 per cent fibre. The provision as to fibre content was held to be a vital part of the description of the goods, and the buyer thus able to reject them without having to argue as to their suitability or fitness under Section 14.

6.18   But if there is only a very minor variation in quality or quantity the buyer's claim will probably fail. In *Tradax* v. *Goldschmidt*, 1977, a contract for the sale of barley allowed up to 4 per cent impurity. The barley delivered contained 4.1 per cent impurity. The buyer was not allowed to reject the goods on this pretext. Earlier cases allowing rejection for 'microscopic variations', such as *Arcos* v. *Ronnaassen*, 1933, have been criticised as too rigid and an encouragement to buyers to try to get out of unwanted contracts on purely technical grounds: *Reardon Smith* v. *Hansen Tangen*, 1976 – buyer was not allowed to reject a ship built according to specifications but not in the agreed shipyard – shipyard was not an essential part of the ship's specifications.

6.19   We note finally that while goods may still be sold by description even though present and available for examination by the buyer (and even where he has himself selected them, e.g. in a supermarket), nonetheless the more he examines them and satisfies himself of their quality and quantity, the less likely he is to rely on the seller's description of them. There may then be no sale by description at all, or none as regards those aspects of the goods which he examined. So in *Harlingdon* v. *Hull*, 1990, an expert buying on the basis of his own judgment a painting wrongly attributed by the seller to a certain artist had no claim under this section. In *Beale* v. *Taylor*, 1967, two halves of cars were welded together to produce a new car. The buyer tested it, unaware of its divided loyalties, found it satisfactory and bought it. When eventually he discovered what was wrong with it he was still protected by Section 13 because his examination had not been directed towards such structural peculiarities. Goods expressly sold 'as seen' are not within Section 13 so far as their visible characteristics are concerned: *Cavendish Woodhouse* v. *Manley*, 1984. In a consumer sale, it may nonetheless be a criminal offence to exclude this Section: para. 7.32.

v. Business sales

6.20 For product liability purposes the most important duties imposed by the Sale of Goods Act are those in Section 14. We observe first that unlike the duties in Sections 12, 13 and 15, they apply only to sales *in the course of a business*. People buying used goods from private individuals cannot rely on this branch of the law to help them and must ensure for themselves that the goods are what they want. This is the basic *caveat emptor* or 'buyer beware' policy of the law in this connection.

6.21 Difficulties occasionally arise in deciding whether a sale is private or in business. The Act defines business to include a profession and the activities of public authorities, so it is not merely a matter of immediate commercial profit. It is not necessary either to be the manufacturer of the goods in question, nor even to deal frequently in such goods, as where for example a coal merchant might sell his lorry. An overall view is necessary. Illustrations include *Blackmore* v. *Bellamy*, 1983 – a postman who bought, improved and sold cars as a hobby was held here not to have sold them in the course of a business – and *Davies* v. *Sumner*, 1983, where the same decision was reached when a self-employed courier sold his own car, which he had used almost entirely for business purposes.

6.22 The question of the seller's status is important for another reason also. Since businesses have greater liabilities than private individuals their advertisements must declare their business status: Business Advertisements (Disclosure) Order 1977. If a private person sells through a business agent, e.g. an auctioneer, the agent is liable for the quality of the goods unless he tells the buyer that the sale is not the course of business: Section 14(5) SGA.

vi. Satisfactory quality

6.23 Section 14 imposes two main obligations on business sellers of goods. The first, in Section 14(2), is a *condition of satisfactory quality*. The rule does not affect faults pointed out to the buyer before sale, nor those he should have seen in any examination he may have made. He is not obliged to examine the goods beforehand, and indeed very often cannot do so, e.g. because they are sold when in transit.

6.24 The key question is the meaning of 'satisfactory' quality. This is a new requirement, introduced in 1994, replacing the previous test of 'merchantable' quality. While the effect of the new rule is not a great deal clearer than that of the old one, it is evidently intended to meet stringent consumer expectations, as well as possibly less demanding commercial requirements. Section 14(2A) says that goods are of satisfactory quality if they would be so regarded by a reasonable person, taking account of their description, price and other relevant circumstances. Subsection 2B says that the 'quality' of goods includes their state or condition, and takes account of aspects such as their fitness for usual purposes, appearance and finish, freedom from minor defects, safety and durability. We discuss these aspects in more detail below.

6.25   Some of the cases on the previous requirement of merchantability seem still to be relevant. They explore the same basic problem of striking a fair balance between the interests of buyers and sellers. Different questions may arise in resolving these interests in contracts between businessmen, as against those arising in contracts between businesses and consumers. In the business context, for example, what is the appropriate standard of 'sale-ability' when goods are supplied for resale? In *Sumner Permain* v. *Webb*, 1922, goods were bought for export to Argentina. Unknown to the buyer, the Argentine government prohibited the import of such goods. But the fact that he could not sell them there, and the object of his contract thus defeated so far as he was concerned, did not mean they were not saleable. They could be sold elsewhere, though at a lower price. Similarly in *Buchanan-Jardine* v. *Hamilink*, 1983, the buyer's right to resell his goods was delayed by operation of law, but that did not affect their ultimate merchantability.

6.26   Goods which can only be resold at a lower price are not necessarily unsatisfactory or unmerchantable under their original description. The question would be as to the extent of the reduction and the reason for it. The market might have dropped, or the goods might be usable for some other more economical purpose: *Brown* v. *Craiks*, 1970. In either event the goods are still 'satisfactory', despite the loss of profit. Conversely a resale price only just below the original purchase price does not of itself prove that the goods are satisfactory, as illustrated below.

6.27   So far as consumer contracts are concerned, the case of *Bernstein* v. *Pamson's Motors*, 1987, is of interest and importance. The facts are set out in para. 6.6 above. Mr Justice Rougier discussed at length here the standard of quality and fitness which the buyer of a new car might reasonably expect: 'No system of mass production can ever be perfect: mistakes and troubles of one sort or another, generally minor, are bound to occur from time to time, being often referred to as teething troubles. Nowadays the buyer, even the buyer of a new car, must put up with a certain amount of teething troubles and have them rectified, albeit generally under some sort of manufacturer's warranty'. In attempting to define teething troubles, aside from those involving basic safety obligations, his Lordship said: 'The time which is taken and the expense of rectification, evidencing as it does the seriousness of the defect, are relevant considerations. The work of a moment such as would be comprised in attaching a battery lead . . . would hardly, if ever, justify rescission. Many days spent off the road in the repair shop might have a different effect . . . Clearly there could come a stage when an army of minor unconnected defects would be evidence of such bad workmanship as to amount *in toto* to a breach of condition of merchantability'.

6.28 Another interesting issue as to quality and fitness is that of the purely cosmetic or superficial fault, which does not in any way affect the working of the product. A buyer would not pay the full market price for a new but slightly scratched or discoloured product. This very minor fault might therefore make the product unsaleable as new, and so justify rejection on delivery. The Canadian case of *Shcherban* v. *I.B.M.*, 1925, is an instructive example. The buyer ordered a $300 computer scale. It was delivered with a broken dial glass costing 30 cents to repair, but otherwise in complete working order. The buyer rejected the scale as unmerchantable. The court upheld his right to do so – though the defect seems to have been as near as could be imagined to the point when faults are so trivial that no reasonable buyer should take account of them. The question of superficial faults was discussed again by Mr. Justice Rougier in *Bernstein*: 'It may well be that in appropriate cases cosmetic factors will also apply, depending on the description and price applied to any individual car. No buyer of a brand new Rolls-Royce Corniche would tolerate the slightest blemish on its exterior or paintwork; the purchaser of a motor car very much at the humbler end of the range might be less fastidious'.

6.29 The law on these issues of consumer acceptability is now somewhat more helpful than in the past. Following the 1994 amendments, the Act expressly recognises for the first time the importance of 'appearance and finish' and 'freedom from minor defects' as elements of satisfactory quality (– though that still does not mean that every product must be perfect). Section 15A draws a necessary distinction between business and consumer requirements, and emphasises consumers' rights by declaring that buyers who do not deal as consumers cannot reject goods for faults which are so small that it would be unreasonable for them to do so. Even in consumer sales, we have seen that the right to reject must be subject to the *de minimis* rule (para. 5.16), and that it will in any case be lost within a very short time of delivery. In business contracts, the risk of the buyer repudiating may be reduced still further by the seller specifying broad tolerances with which his goods are sold, or by 'anti-technicality' clauses which entitle the seller to repair or replace defective goods before the buyer can exercise any right of rejection he might have.

vii. Reasonable fitness

6.30 Section 14(3) of the SGA says that *where goods are sold in the course of a business there is an implied condition that they will be reasonably fit for any purpose expressly or impliedly made known by the buyer, whether or not that is their normal purpose, unless in the circumstances the buyer does not or should not rely on the seller's skill or judgment.* The

135

requirements of satisfactory quality and fitness for purpose are usually the same, but not necessarily so. As suggested above, goods with cosmetic faults might not be satisfactory, while in all other respects reasonably fit for their purpose. Likewise, goods usable or resaleable in some context other than that intended by the buyer might still be of satisfactory quality, even though not reasonably fit for their original purpose: *Ashington Piggeries*, above. A buyer can reject goods or claim damages if he can prove breach of either requirement; he need not prove breach of both.

6.31   As with satisfactory quality, the reasonable fitness rule depends on certain qualifying factors. The section says that the sale must be in the course of a business, as mentioned above, and requires that the buyer has expressly or impliedly told the seller of his intended use of the goods. Since the purpose of most goods is self-evident – clothes for wearing, cars for driving about in, and so on – it is only necessary for the buyer to state his needs expressly when they are more specialised or demanding than usual. The case of *Teheran-Europe* v. *Belton*, 1968, however, observes that what might be called the seller's 'incidental' awareness of the buyer's plans – here, to export the goods to Iran – does not of itself oblige him to ensure their fitness for that purpose.

6.32   The buyer's claim depends also on his reliance on the seller's skill and judgment in selecting his goods. Reliance is normally presumed and does not have to be proved. 'A buyer goes to the shops in the confidence that the tradesman has selected his stock with skill and judgment': *Grant* v. *A.K.M.*, 1936. But this presumption may be displaced if the buyer undertakes his own expert examination of the goods, or if, for example, the goods are made to the buyer's own design – in which event the seller might be answerable only for the quality of his materials and workmanship and not for the success of the design: *Cammell Laird* v. *Manganese Bronze*, 1934; *Dixon Kerby* v. *Robinson*, 1965. In the very unsatisfactory case of *McDonald* v. *Empire Garage*, 1975, the fact that the buyer had the goods examined beforehand by an expert enabled the seller to escape liability even though the examination could not have revealed the fault which caused the accident. We note that any provision in the contract of sale which falsely states that the buyer examined the goods or did not rely on the seller's skill and judgment is void at common law: para. 7.9.

6.33   Subject to these qualifications and to the acceptance rule, above, sellers must ensure their goods are reasonably fit, or, if not, take them back and return the price. The standard of fitness is again not one of perfection, but depends on the complexity, price and age of the goods, the way they are described and packaged, instructions as to use – *Wormell* v. *RHM*, 1987 – and normal expectation and usage.

6.34   We can perhaps best illustrate the law's requirements by further reference to cases on new and used motor vehicles. At one end of the spectrum is *Farnworth Finance* v. *Attryde*, 1970 (a hire-purchase case, but raising the same issue as under the SGA). This concerned a new British motor cycle which within the first few months of use developed a series of lethal defects, including headlight failure, a broken chain and faulty lubrication system. The Court of Appeal agreed that this was 'not really a workable machine' and allowed repudiation of the contract. Because of the inconvenience he had suffered the hire-purchaser was not obliged to make any allowance for the 4,000 miles he had in fact driven. The importance of the case is that it clearly identifies *danger* as a breach of condition; not, of course, *any* danger, however trivial or remote, but a real, unusual and unnecessary risk of significant injury.

6.35   In contrast is the Scottish case of *Millar* v. *Turpie*, 1976. The day after taking delivery of a new Ford Granada the buyer noticed an oil leak from the power-assisted steering box. He took it back to the dealer, who failed to mend it properly. The next day the buyer found another leak from the same source, and at that point sought to return the car and recover his money. On the evidence the judge held that the oil leaks did not represent any imminent danger. They were only a minor defect which could and should have been easily and cheaply repaired. That being so, said the judge, the car was still reasonably fit for its purpose – which meant that the buyer had no redress at all. It is questionable whether the reference to 'freedom from minor defects' in the new Section 14(2B) would even today justify repudiation on these facts.

6.36   This case raises in passing the question whether a buyer has any duty to take defective goods back to the seller and give him the opportunity to remedy the fault before exercising any right he may have to repudiate the contract. In the absence of any express contractual obligation, the answer should be 'no', since the goods should be reasonably fit at the time of the sale: *Friskin* v. *Holliday*, 1977 (Canada).

6.37   On the other hand it may be that except as regards immediate and serious dangers, some goods, such as cars, are sold 'subject to service', i.e. on the basis that they must be repaired or adjusted after the sale. The buyer then has no real alternative but to return the goods to the dealer to find out exactly what is wrong with them. Unless he does that it may be impossible to say whether the fault is serious or trivial, or repairable or not. In practice then the buyer must behave reasonably and the seller will often get another chance to put things right. Commercial buyers are in any case discouraged from rejecting goods by the new Section 15A, above. This is the position also under the Convention on International Sale of Goods.

6.38   We come now to what is probably the commonest problem area, that of goods whose faults put them somewhere in the middle of this range of possible liabilities. There may be little or no element of danger, but failures in operation from time to time, or a number of minor faults or blemishes.

6.39   *Rogers* v. *Parish*, 1987, is a leading case which from the consumer's point of view suggested a marked improvement in the generally dismal standards previously set by English law. It concerned a new Range Rover costing some £16,000. Six months after delivery the engine was still misfiring at all speeds and there was excessive noise from the gearbox and transfer box. The vehicle had 'substantial' bodywork defects. Its condition reflected 'great discredit' upon factory inspection procedures. Attempts were made to rectify faults, and in the meantime the plaintiff was able to drive the vehicle for 5,500 miles, 'albeit', said the judge, 'in a manner which gave him no satisfaction'.

6.40   At the trial, the plaintiff's claim for his money back was rejected. In accordance with previous decisions, the High Court judge said it was sufficient that most of the faults were cured and the remainder capable of cure. On appeal Lord Justice Mustill made it clear that that was not the point. The purpose for which this car was required was not merely that of driving from one place to another, but of doing so 'with the appropriate degree of comfort, ease of handling and reliability, and . . . of pride in the vehicle's outward and interior appearance . . . Deficiencies which might be accepted in a second hand vehicle are not to be expected in one purchased as new . . . The factor of price is also significant . . . The buyer is entitled to value for his money . . . These defects lie well outside the range of expectation'. On this basis the buyer's claim was upheld.

6.41   Reasonable fitness is inevitably all a matter of degree. Teething troubles must be expected in many different kinds of products, and as we have noted many contracts expressly provide for them and seek to limit buyers' rights accordingly. But the Court of Appeal's decision in *Rogers* was clearly right, and is confirmed by the more consumer-oriented terms of the 1994 amendments to the SGA.

viii. Used goods

6.42   Section 14 applies equally to both new and used goods. Contrasting cases on second-hand goods include *Bartlett* v. *Marcus*, 1965, and *Crowther* v. *Shannon*, 1975. Both concerned Jaguar cars. In *Bartlett* the dealer sold the car for £950, at that time a substantial price, warning the buyer that minor clutch repairs might be needed. They became necessary almost immediately and cost a further £50. The buyer's claim for damages failed because the car was usable, though not perfect. 'It was fit to be driven along the road in safety.' Second-hand cars are likely to need repairs, and expensive cars need expensive repairs, as the buyer should have known.

6.43   In *Crowther* the car was sold for £390 after doing 80,000 miles. Shortly afterwards the engine seized up completely and had to be renewed for another £400 or so. The Court of Appeal distinguished these facts from those in *Bartlett*. This car was not fit for the road at all, and on the basis of evidence that Jaguar cars were supposed to last for at least 100,000 miles, the buyer had got very much less than he was reasonably entitled to expect. His claim succeeded accordingly. 'The matter is one of fact and degree', as was pointed out in *B.A.S.* v. *Nationwide Credit*, 1988. The plaintiff here had paid £14,850 for a two and a half year old Mercedes which had done about 35,000 miles. After he had driven it for a further 750 miles it suffered loss of compression and power because the valves and valve guides were worn or burned out. The Court of Appeal refused to allow rescission on these grounds.

6.44   *Feast* v. *Vincent*, 1974 (N.Z.), is another instructive case. The buyer bought a reconditioned engine for his road building machinery from a wayside dealer. It cost several thousand dollars. He bought it without testing it, and knowing that it was not exactly the kind of engine he needed. After he had installed the engine it ran for a day and then broke down completely. His purchase was clearly speculative, based on his own expertise and without reliance on the seller's skill or judgment, and so his claim was rejected. The case thus makes again the salutary point that one may spend a great deal and get little or nothing in return, but still not necessarily have any claim for compensation against anybody.

ix. Durability

6.45   Until the 1994 amendment, the Sale of Goods Act was silent as to the relationship between the fitness of goods and their durability, although no doubt at common law they would be expected to remain fit for a reasonable time after purchase. Durability is now, however, specified in Section 14(2B) as an element of satisfactory quality. What that might mean would depend entirely on the normal life expectancy, age, price and quality of the particular product, as illustrated in *Crowther*, above. A similar issue is whether goods should be regarded as unfit if no adequate repair service is provided, as when a new model is introduced and spare parts for the old immediately become unobtainable. Many so-called durables are made virtually worthless in this way. New Zealand's Consumer Guarantees Act 1993 obliges manufacturers to ensure facilities for repair and spare parts for a reasonable period, but there are no comparable statutory requirements in England and no common law rulings to provide guidance. With the support of various codes of commercial practice approved by the Office of Fair Trading, we might suggest that goods could properly be regarded as defective if the absence of spare parts means that they cannot be repaired within their normal life span.

x. Sale by sample

6.46   We note briefly Section 15 of the SGA. It lays down in contracts of sale by sample implied conditions that the bulk of the goods will conform with the sample in quality, that the buyer will have reasonable opportunity of comparing bulk with sample, and that the goods will be free of any defect which would make them unsatisfactory but which would not be seen on inspection. The only significant point is that to make a sale by sample there must be an express or implied term of the contract to that effect, as where off-cuts of cloth, carpet, etc. are provided to 'speak for themselves': *Drummond* v. *Van Ingen*, 1887. Merely using a product for the purposes of demonstration or illustration does not bring the sale within the section.

xi. Strict liability

6.47   In the rules examined above we find one of the most important principles of English sales law. Section 14 of the SGA says that goods sold in the course of a business *must be reasonably fit.* How or why they fall short of that standard is immaterial so far as the law is concerned. The seller may well offer goods designed, made, packed and distributed by other parties over whom he has no control, but he must still in effect guarantee the suitability and safety of those goods. He remains liable, in other words, whether the defect is known or unknown, and whether or not he tries or is able to remedy it. So in *Frost* v. *Aylesbury Dairy*, 1905, the defendants were liable for selling milk with typhus germs though at the time quite unable to detect the presence of the germs. Similarly in *Spencer* v. *Rye*, 1972, a car dealer was liable for a car whose radiator boiled over every hundred miles, even though this was a manufacturing fault which the dealer was unable even to trace, let alone cure.

6.48   *Contract law thus imposes the primary liability for the fitness of goods upon the seller, not the manufacturer.* The rule has many advantages for the buyer when the seller is in the High Street and likely to be responsive to threats of legal proceedings and bad publicity. From the seller's point of view it might seem unfair to be held liable for someone else's fault, but the law's answer is that the seller should then recover his losses by suing the wholesaler or manufacturer, as the case may be, under the same section of the same Act. The extent to which any such claims by consumers or business buyers may be affected by sellers' exclusion clauses is discussed in Chapter 7.

6.49   Liability without fault is called *strict liability*. But strict liability is not absolute liability. Business sellers are liable only for losses or injuries caused by goods which are not reasonably fit. If the goods reach this standard but nonetheless cause loss or injury the seller is not liable. So if a buyer is injured through failing to carry out his own responsibilities properly, e.g. by not having his car serviced or not connecting electrical equipment safely, he cannot sue the seller. When plastic containers melted, ruining their contents, because the buyer exposed them to extreme heat, the sellers were not to blame: *Aswan* v. *Lupdine*, 1986. The buyer had no claim for the losses caused by continuing to use equipment he knew was unsafe: *Lambert* v. *Lewis*, 1981. In *Board* v. *Hedley*, 1951, and *Griffiths* v. *Conway*, 1939, detergents and clothing safe for everyone else caused dermatitis in one or two individuals because of their wholly abnormal and undisclosed susceptibilities. Again the sellers were not liable.

6.50   We cannot say in advance how many people have to be harmed before goods will be regarded as unsafe, nor how serious the injury must be. The more serious the harm, the fewer people should suffer it before the product is condemned. So in *Kendal* v. *Lillico*, 1966, the judge said: 'I should certainly not expect food to be held reasonably fit if even on very rare occasions it killed the consumer.' But as before, if the food is harmful only because the buyer does not prepare it properly, he or she may have no claim against the seller. In *Heil* v. *Hedges*, 1951, the buyer bought raw pork meat which was infected by worms. She did not cook the meat sufficiently, and suffered trichinosis. She lost her claim because this was said to be a normal condition of raw pork, and the onus was on her to ensure safe preparation.

xii. Credit transactions

6.51   Certain forms of credit transactions affecting goods are treated differently from sale. English law distinguishes between credit sales, conditional sales and hire-purchase. In a credit sale the buyer becomes owner of the goods immediately even though payment is postponed. In a conditional sale, there is an agreement to sell, but ownership does not pass until the last payment is made. In a hire-purchase contract there is no agreement to sell; only an agreement to hire under which the hirer becomes owner on payment of a certain number of instalments.

6.52   The same conditions as to title, description and fitness implied by the Sale of Goods Act apply also in hire-purchase transactions under Sections 8–11 of the Supply of Goods (Implied Terms) Act 1973, but they bind the owner of the goods, not the dealer as such. Since credit is usually provided by a finance company to which the dealer sells his goods, it is the company which is responsible for passing a good title and ensuring the quality of the goods. The dealer is only an intermediary. He displays the goods and acts as credit broker, and that means that his responsibility usually ends when he has enabled the consumer to make a contract with the

141

finance company: *Drury* v. *Buckland*, 1941. It follows that although in theory the hire-purchaser has the same legal rights as a buyer, the fact that he has them against a finance company and not against the dealer may leave him at a disadvantage. The company will probably be less accessible and less responsive to threats of legal action and bad publicity.

6.53   The legal position of hire-purchasers was well described by Lord Justice Harman in *Yeoman Credit* v. *Apps*, 1961: 'The difficulty and the artificiality about hire-purchase cases arises from the fact that the member of the public involved imagines himself to be buying the article by instalments from the dealer, whereas he is in law the hirer of the article from a finance company with whom he has been brought willy-nilly into contact, of whom he knows nothing, and which, in its part, has never seen the goods which are the subject-matter of the hire.' We might then wonder whether the substantial practical differences in the parties' rights and duties can be justified by reference to the technicalities of this everyday transaction.

6.54   We should note, however, certain qualifications to the general rule. Exceptionally the dealer could be held liable if he were to make an express promise as to the quality or fitness of the goods. In *Andrews* v. *Hopkinson*, 1956, the dealer told the customer that a particular car was 'a good little bus' and would be trouble-free. The customer was persuaded thereby to take the car on hire-purchase from a finance company. It was in fact dangerous, and the injured customer sued the dealer. The court held that by contracting with the finance company the customer had given the necessary consideration (Chapter 3) for the dealer's promise, and could therefore enforce it against him. It is not certain whether a dealer might alternatively be liable for breach of an *implied* promise as to the fitness of the goods. The judge in *Andrews* suggested that he should be, on the ground that the transaction was so like a sale that the common law should imply the same sort of obligations as are imposed on business sellers by the Sale of Goods Act. This view was followed by the County Court in *Robotics* v. *First Co-operative Finance*, 1983. But while the liability of the dealer may still be doubtful, English law tries at least to ensure that a dissatisfied consumer will have a claim against the finance house. The necessary protection is given by Sections 56 and 75 of the Consumer Credit Act, 1974, whose effect is noted under the heading of Privity of Contract in para. 3.62.

6.55   If a supplier accepts payment by credit card or charge card the buyer thereby fulfils his contract with the supplier. Should the finance company then fail to pay the supplier, he has no claim against the buyer: *Re Charge Card Services*, 1988.

xiii. Hire and service contracts

6.56 We have discussed above the relevant terms of the Acts governing sales and hire-purchase transactions. Other kinds of contracts transferring ownership or possession of goods are dealt with by the Supply of Goods and Services Act 1982, as amended in 1994. The Act does not apply in Scotland. Sections 1 to 5 of the 1982 Act concern goods supplied under contracts for services, e.g. installation or repair contracts, and Sections 6 to 10 those supplied on hire or loan. The obligations as to title, description and fitness imposed on the supplier in both cases are essentially the same as those under Sections 12–15 of the Sale of Goods Act and Sections 8–11 of the Supply of Goods (Implied Terms) Act, above. Standards of quality and fitness are therefore strict, as illustrated in *Myers* v. *Brent Cross Service,* 1934 – garage liable for accident caused by fitting a component with a hidden defect in the course of a car repair – and in *Stewart* v. *Reavell's Garage,* 1952 – repairer liable for sub-contractor's negligence.

6.57 But strict liability is not a guarantee of complete safety or security. A burglar alarm, for example, might still be reasonably fit for its purpose even though it can be wrenched off the wall and silenced: *Davis* v. *Afa Minerva,* 1974. In any event, liability is strict only in relation to the buyer, e.g. to the car owner and not to his passengers or other road users. Their only claim against the garage for supplying defective parts which caused an accident would be in negligence, below, which in a case like *Myers* they would be unable to prove: *Sigurdson* v. *Hillcrest Service,* 1977 (Canada).

6.58 Liability can be avoided if the consumer does not – or in the circumstances should not – rely on the supplier's skill and judgment. This might happen where the consumer specifies exactly the type of material or product he wants. The supplier then warrants only the quality of the goods, not their fitness for purpose: *Young* v. *McManus Childs,* 1969, *Hunter* v. *Syncrude,* 1989 (Canada).

6.59 The 1982 Act also covers contracts for services, whether or not they involve transfer of goods. Section 13 says that *in contracts for the supply of business services there is an implied term that the services will be carried out with reasonable care and skill.* An important distinction thus appears between contracts for services and contracts affecting goods. A supplier of goods must ensure they are reasonably fit, whereas a supplier of services undertakes only to comply with the normal standards of his trade or profession. The argument is that since the success of a service cannot be guaranteed – e.g. that a doctor will cure his patient or a lawyer win his case – the standard required by law is necessarily lower. It is essentially the same as in a negligence action, below. If the supplier reaches the normal standard but his work is not successful he is not liable (unless the contract expressly lays down some higher standard). It is significant also that the obligation

143

stated in Section 13 is described as a 'term', not, as in the 1973 and 1979 Acts, as a condition or warranty. The law thereby recognises that different breaches of contract may not all be equally important, that damages may be more appropriate than repudiation, and that it is generally of the nature of services that they cannot be repudiated, i.e. returned to the supplier.

6.60 Examples of successful claims for damages for faulty services in general include *Taylor* v. *Kiddey*, 1968, where a car repairer was held liable for failing to check the safety of a wheel under the terms of a contract specifying only attention to the steering, and *Bell* v. *A.S.M.*, 1969 – liability of driving school for failing to instruct properly. There are also, of course, many cases on the liabilities of doctors, lawyers, architects and other professionals, which are beyond the scope of this present work, but which endorse the standard of reasonable care in the particular professional context.

6.61 The liability of the service provider may differ according to whether the fault in question was caused by his employee or by an independent contractor. Under the common law rule of vicarious liability *an employer is liable to persons suffering injury or loss through the wrongful acts of his employees committed in the course of their employment.* The rule is discussed again below, with regard to injuries caused by negligent workmanship, but is mentioned here as regards unsatisfactory services provided by independent contractors. The problem is that with few exceptions the rule of vicarious liability extends only to one's own employees, not to independent contractors. The main contractor's liability in this situation turns largely on the terms of his contract with the customer. The supplier may make himself responsible thereby not only for his own negligence but also for that of his sub-contractors. In *Wong* v. *Kwan Kin Travel Services*, 1995, the Privy Council held that a Hong Kong tour operator's contract with a holiday-maker made him liable for a Chinese ferry company's negligence which caused the holiday-maker's death. But much more commonly, suppliers' contracts expressly permit use of sub-contractors' services, and so enable suppliers to disclaim responsibility for their negligence. Where, for example, a tour operator reserves hotel rooms for his clients he can usually be liable at common law only for his own personal failure to select and inspect the hotel with reasonable skill and care. This is because the rule of vicarious liability applies only as between employers and employees, and does not extend to independent contractors. So in *Wall* v. *Silver Wing*, 1981, the tour operator was not liable for injuries suffered by holiday-makers unable to escape from a hotel fire because a hotel employee had locked the fire escape. The operator had taken reasonable care in selecting and inspecting the hotel, but was not then responsible for the acts of its employees, who were all independent contractors so far as he was concerned.

6.62 This unsatisfactory situation was partially resolved by the 1990 European Directive on Package Holidays, transposed into English law by the

Package Travel, Package Holidays and Package Tour Regulations 1993. The Regulations cover pre-arranged holidays lasting more than 24 hours or including overnight accommodation, and providing at least two of the three components of transport, accommodation, and 'other significant tourist services' at an inclusive cost. Regulation 15 makes business organisers and/or travel agents liable to consumers (including both the principal contractor and his or her family or group) for the proper performance of the contract, whether or not performance is undertaken by the organisers or agents themselves. They thus become liable for any injury or loss except that which is the fault of the consumer, or is due to unforeseeable or unavoidable acts of third parties unconnected with the supply of services under the contract, or to *force majeure* – i.e., other unusual or unforeseeable circumstances beyond the organiser's or agent's control, and unavoidable even with all due care. *Wall's* case would therefore be differently decided today. In contrast, however, is *Wilson* v. *Best*, 1993. The hotel guest here injured himself by walking through a glass door. The door was made in accordance with local (Greek) legal requirements. Since there was therefore no fault on the part of the tour operator or any of his independent contractors, the guest lost his claim – a decision which would not be affected by the 1993 Regulations.

6.63   Apart from package holidays, liability for defective services still depends on proof of negligence, and there is still no general principle of vicarious liability for the acts of independent contractors. In the absence of any more rational system of compensation, it might then seem desirable to impose much the same kind of strict liability for defective services as applies to defective goods, above, but the 1991 draft Directive on liability for defective services went no further than to reverse the burden of proof of fault. This proposal was not well received, and did not become law.

6.64   Reverting to the 1982 Act, we note finally the rule in Section 14, endorsing the common law, that *if no time is fixed for the performance of a contract for services it must be fulfilled within a reasonable time.* Everything depends on the type and scale of the work involved. Cases include *Charnock* v. *Liverpool Corporation*, 1968, where a service garage was held liable for taking eight weeks over repairs which should have taken five, and thus had to pay for three weeks' car hire; and *Stanners* v. *High Wycombe Borough Council*, 1968, where the Council was held responsible for delay in building work which enabled thieves to break into an adjoining warehouse.

xiv. Manufacturers' guarantees

6.65   Our concern so far in this chapter has been with obligations arising under contract, and in particular those arising under contracts of sale. Sellers' duties under the Sale of Goods Act are commonly reinforced by

145

manufacturers' guarantees – but as we said in Chapter 3, English law is still very uncertain as to what if any legal effect such guarantees may have because of the difficulty of deciding whether the buyer has given any consideration for the manufacturer's promise. On general principle most manufacturers' guarantees are at present probably unenforceable, but offered and fulfilled voluntarily and in the interests of the manufacturer's good name. Guarantees must in any case expressly state that they do not in any way limit the buyer's primary contractual rights against his seller: Consumer Transactions (Restrictions on Statements) Order 1978.

B. Negligence

6.66   Contractual liabilities are strict, but by definition narrow. If a product injures someone other than the buyer or hire-purchaser, e.g. his employee or wife or child, that injured person has no rights under the Sale of Goods Act or any of the other Acts mentioned above (but *see* para. 6.79 as to US practice). At common law, a non-contractual (i.e. tortious or delictual) claim can succeed only on proof of another party's negligence. Negligence – or fault, or failure to take reasonable care – is a complex legal concept and the burden of proof on the plaintiff a heavy one.

6.67   The arbitrary consequences of the different rules may be shortly illustrated. Mr. A buys an item of domestic electrical equipment. He suffers a severe electrical shock when using it in the proper fashion. His claim is against the seller in the High Street, and insofar as he can prove the fact of his injury in these circumstances he thereby establishes that the goods are not reasonably fit for their purpose. But if it is his wife who is injured in exactly the same way she has no claim against anyone unless she can prove negligence. It is unlikely that the seller has been negligent since he is merely a conduit for pre-packed goods. If anybody has been negligent, it is probably the manufacturer. The manufacturer may not be local or as responsive to pressure as the seller would be, and indeed may well be based in a different country. Mrs. A's claim is therefore against a different defendant and her burden of proof is quite different from that which her husband would have had – and much more difficult to discharge. The mere fact of the accident does not of itself prove that the manufacturer was negligent. Injury might be caused despite his having taken all due care; perhaps, for example, through the fault of a component supplier. If it seems that a particular accident can only have been caused by the defendant's negligence, the effect of applying the *res ipsa loquitur* rule of evidence is to reverse the burden of proof and require the defendant to disprove fault, but such cases are rare.

6.68   The possibility of holding manufacturers liable in negligence for injury to the ultimate users or consumers of their products was established in the UK in the crucial case of *Donoghue* v. *Stevenson*, 1932. The House of Lords awarded damages here to a consumer made ill by drinking ginger beer from a bottle containing a decomposed snail. The bottle, which had been bought by someone else, was opaque and sealed, and so could not have been inspected or tampered with after leaving the manufacturer. On these facts, the manufacturer was in breach of his duty to take reasonable care for the safety of the ultimate consumers of his products. Following that decision, liability for negligence developed rapidly. The law in this area is concerned primarily to compensate for physical injury or damage to property. If the loss or damage is purely economic – e.g., loss of business profit, normally recoverable only in a breach of contract action – it may exceptionally be recoverable in tort if caused by incorrect or misleading information given negligently within a 'special (not necessarily contractual) relationship'; that is, to someone who is known to rely on the information being given carefully: *Hedley Byrne* v. *Heller*, 1964; *Smith* v. *Bush*, 1989. It is doubtful whether pure economic loss caused by other forms of negligent service such as bad workmanship may also give rise to liability. In *Muirhead* v. *Industrial Tank*, 1985, for example, a manufacturer escaped liability for pure economic loss caused to the ultimate buyer of his defective goods. At the present time it is difficult if not impossible to state any general principle of liability for negligence under English law. We can only say that in the leading case of *Murphy* v. *Brentwood D.C.*, 1991, the House of Lords held that liability depended essentially on the claim coming within the terms of either *Donoghue* or *Hedley Byrne*. The resulting exclusion of non-contractual liability for pure economic loss caused by defective workmanship has been disapproved in certain Commonwealth countries, e.g. New Zealand – *Chase* v. *de Groot*, 1994 – and Australia: *Bryan* v. *Maloney*, 1995. The courts in these countries have not yet decided whether such liability applies only to land and buildings or extends also to goods – though there seems no difference in principle.

6.69   *Donoghue* v. *Stevenson* and later cases say that a supplier's duty to anyone likely to be injured by his goods, but with whom he has no contract, is to take *reasonable care* to see that the goods are reasonably safe. In effect he has a duty to *try* to reach the approved standard of safety – to 'do his best' – as contrasted with the seller's contractual duty to *succeed* in reaching that standard. We have emphasised before that the issue of negligence does not usually arise in contracts between buyers and sellers, where the general rule is one of strict liability. Exceptions arise in contracts which require 'reasonable care' or 'best endeavours', or other such qualified commitments.

6.70   Cases on negligence suggest there are at least five main factors to be considered and balanced against each other in order to decide whether reasonable care has been taken in any given situation. These are the *likelihood* of accident, its potential *seriousness*, the *obviousness* of the risk, the *cost* of taking precautions, and the *inherent risks* of the goods or activities

147

in question. It is virtually impossible to predict how a judge will assess or balance these factors one against the other in any particular case. The following examples illustrate the main problem areas.

i. Materials

6.71   Many essential materials create serious dangers for those who have to extract or use them in their natural or processed forms. The risks are irreducible beyond a certain point, and injuries inevitable: *Pearson* v. *N.W. Gas Board*, 1968 – no liability for unforeseen risk of gas explosion. The law only prohibits use of such materials on proof of the gravest dangers, as for example with white or yellow phosphorus and blue asbestos. On medical advice or under threat of legal action manufacturers may also feel obliged to stop using certain materials even without any statutory prohibition. In less immediately serious cases the precautions usually required affect storage, issue and use of protective equipment, warnings and the like.

ii. Design

6.72   The law requires the manufacturer to do his best to reduce so far as is reasonably practicable the dangers associated with his products, of which as an informed and prudent businessman he knows or ought to know. He cannot plead ignorance of technical information regarding the design or constituents of his products which is available to others in the same line of business, as distinct, say, from information in medical journals: *Wallhead* v. *Rushton*, 1973. He may be liable for inadequate research at the outset – *Vacwell* v. *B.D.H.*, 1971 (new chemical compound) – or failure to warn of subsequently discovered dangers – *Wright* v. *Dunlop*, 1972 (carcinogenic compound); *Walton* v. *B.L.*, 1978 (liability for failing to recall dangerously defective cars). He must take precautions against predictable *misuse* of his products. Cars, for example, must be designed to minimise injury in the event of a crash. *Spruill* v. *Boyle-Midway*, 1962, was an American case which would have been decided in the same way by an English court, concerning a child injured by eating floor polish. The manufacturers were held negligent in giving no warning that the polish was poisonous, which would have advised the parents to keep it out of the child's reach.

6.73   We have presumed so far that risk of injury is or ought to be known to the manufacturer but is unknown to the user. If the risk is or should be equally obvious to the user, careless or foolish use may amount to contributory negligence or consent to injury, and liability partly or wholly reduced accordingly. So in *Crow* v. *Barford*, 1963, the user lost his claim for damages for injury caused when he put his foot in a large 'grass ejection aperture' in the engine casing of a garden mower. But the proper question in these cases should not be whether the danger was obvious; it should be whether it was *necessary* – i.e. inherent and unavoidable. Any other conclusion must simply encourage bad design, as recognised in comparable American cases such as *Wright* v. *Massey Harris*, 1969, and *Martinez* v. *Atlas Bolt*, 1982.

6.74   While most product liability cases are brought against manufacturers, there is still the possibility of holding the distributor or seller liable for negligence if he likewise knows or should know the design is defective. In *Fisher* v. *Harrods*, 1966, Mrs Fisher had been given a bottle of jewellery cleaner which a friend had bought from Harrods. As she opened the bottle it exploded and temporarily blinded her. Since she had no contract with Harrods her claim could only be in negligence. She was unable to sue the manufacturer, as she might have wished, because by that time he was insolvent. She therefore had the more difficult task of proving negligence against Harrods, the retailer. Harrods established that they sold the cleaning fluid only after testing it to see it was effective – which was all a retailer might normally be expected to do with a new product. It was Mrs Fisher's task to show that further and more stringent precautions should have been taken in relation to this particular product. She succeeded, on the basis that Harrods should have appreciated that the cleaner contained chemicals, and so should have asked about the manufacturer's qualifications (which were non-existent), and checked the volatility of the contents and the safety of the bottle. Retailers might be required to take such precautions with other potentially dangerous new products, e.g. electrical equipment. Being able to hold a retailer liable for negligence in circumstances like these might well be preferable to a claim against a probably less accessible or responsive manufacturer.

6.75   *Goodchild* v. *Vaclight*, 1965, illustrates the possibility of making a UK distributor liable for an overseas manufacturer's dangerous design and inadequate warnings. Liability was imposed here because the distributor was more than a mere conduit. He had imported the goods in bulk over many years, put his own brand name on them and issued his own instruction booklet. By so doing, he became responsible for their safety. *Devillez* v. *Boots*, 1962, concerned a supplier's liability for inadequate labelling and bottling of corn solvent, which he knew contained acid, and so that it might be dangerous to softer skin on which it might accidentally fall. The case is of particular interest in illustrating that an unblemished sales record does not necessarily disprove negligence. Other intermediaries such as independent inspectors or certifiers of fitness, possibly even government departments, may also be liable for negligence: *Rutherford* v. *A-G.*, 1976 (N.Z.); *Willis* v. *F.M.C.*, 1976 (Canada); *Swanson Estate* v. *Canada*, 1991 (Canada).

iii. Advice and warnings

6.76   Manufacturers may sometimes escape liability for injury by showing they have given warnings or instructions which would have prevented injury had they been followed, though such information should not be regarded as a substitute for safe design. Warnings which are intended simply to exclude liability will fall within the terms of the Unfair Contract Terms Act, Chapter 7, and may therefore be of no effect. Instructions and warnings will probably be effective only if in writing and referring clearly and concisely to the particular hidden or inherent hazards the manufacturer should have in mind, as illustrated in *Fisher*, *Goodchild* and *Devillez*, above. If a particular product is bound to be used under the control of an expert, it may be sufficient to warn him alone and leave him to warn those who use the product under his direction: *Holmes* v. *Ashford*, 1950. On the other hand there may be no need to warn the expert; only the amateur. Again all depends on the likely use – or misuse – of the product, and the obviousness or otherwise of the risks. American courts have held, for example, that suppliers are not obliged to warn users of trampolines against the unsound judgment of bouncing on the equipment on their heads, nor to warn users of chest expanders of the danger of prematurely releasing one end.

iv. Workmanship

6.77   Where physical injuries or damage to property are caused by negligent handling, processing, packaging or distribution of goods creating unnecessary risks, the principle of English law most likely to apply is that of *vicarious liability*: para. 6.62. We have seen that at common law *employers are liable to persons injured by their employees' wrongful acts committed in the course of their employment*. The plaintiff must prove fault on the part of the employee, for which the employer is blamed. Often enough the plaintiff can only show that he or she has been injured by the product, and is unable to say which employee at which stage of production or distribution was at fault. If nonetheless it is clear that the basic design is sound and that there must have been negligence somewhere within the employer's enterprise, the injured party is not required to 'lay his finger on the exact person in all the chain who was responsible': *Grant* v. *A.K.M.*, 1936. An employee acts in the course of his employment only if what he does is *a way* of doing his job, even if it is a disobedient or stupid or dishonest way. So in *Iqbal* v. *London Transport*, 1973, a bus conductor's employer was not liable for an accident caused when the conductor drove a bus, because driving was no part at all of his work. In cases where an employer is held to blame he may seek an indemnity from the negligent employee, or more probably will have good grounds for dismissal.

6.78   We emphasise once more the general rule of common law that the doctrine of vicarious liability applies only to the relationship of employers and their employees. Where injury is caused by a defective part supplied by a sub-contractor, the employer who incorporated that part in his finished product is not vicariously liable for the sub-contractor's negligence, though he may be liable for any personal failure to select the sub-contractor with care, or to provide appropriate specifications or test his work: *Taylor* v. *Rover Car*, 1966. But *see* para. 6.82 below.

C. Strict liability

6.79   The position we have reached so far is that a seller's contractual liability under the Sale of Goods Act is strict, but benefits only the buyer. If there is no contract between the parties, liability under English law has depended on proof of negligence. To a greater or lesser extent Continental legal systems have likewise recognised differences between contractual and non-contractual rights. (American law, on the other hand, has extended express and implied contractual warranties to the buyer's family and guests – Section 2–318 of the Uniform Commercial Code – and imposed liability without fault on sellers in other non-contractual relationships: Section 402A of the Second Restatement of Torts.) The resulting difficulties and inadequacies of English law have been widely criticised for many years, particularly in the light of numerous drug tragedies.

6.80   In 1985 the Member States of the Common Market, seeking both to reform the law and ensure comparable conditions of trade, agreed on the terms of a product liability Directive. The short effect of the Directive was to make manufacturers liable for injuries without proof of fault. Britain purported to give effect to the Directive by the Consumer Protection Act 1987. Part I of the Act changes the rules of civil liability; Part II extends the criminal law, subject now to the General Product Safety Regulations 1994, below.

6.81   The main provisions of Part I are as follows. Section 1 defines the terms used in the Act. A 'producer' is the manufacturer of a product, or a person who 'won or abstracted' it (by harvesting, fishing, etc.) or carried out the industrial or other process providing its essential characteristics. A 'product' includes any goods, component parts, electricity, or gas, but not game (wild animals) or agricultural products or fish which have not undergone industrial processes: Section 2(4). Injuries caused by the use of pesticides or fertilisers on crops are thus apparently excluded. Supply of a product containing component parts is not in itself supply of the components, a provision affecting Section 2(3), below.

6.82   Section 2 states the new basic rule of civil liability. *The producer, or a person holding himself out as such by putting his name on the product or using a trade mark or other distinguishing mark, or one who has imported the product into the Common Market for commercial purposes, is liable for any damage wholly or partly caused by a defect in the product.* 'Defect' is defined in Section 3 and 'damage' in Section 5, below. By Section 2(3), any other supplier may be liable unless at the injured party's

151

request he can identify the producer. This latter rule might make retailers of generic goods such as chemists liable for defective products unless they keep records enabling them to identify their suppliers. Section 2 also declares that where two or more persons are liable under the Act each may be wholly liable. It seems then that when a product causes injury because of a defective component supplied by an independent contractor, either the 'head' producer or the independent contractor or both could be liable for the injury, thus overcoming the *Taylor* v. *Rover Car* problem mentioned above. Other existing contractual or tortious liabilities are not affected.

6.83   The full significance of the new rule is made clear by the definition of 'defect' in Section 3. There is no guarantee of safety. *'A product is defective if it is not as safe as persons generally are entitled to expect'*, as indicated by its marketing, 'get-up' or appearance, instructions, likely use and time of supply. Later developments do not of themselves prove earlier products unsafe. Subject to Section 4, below, it follows that the vital question now is whether or not the product is *reasonably safe*, not whether someone has been negligent in designing or producing or marketing it. The new standard of liability upon the producer is thus essentially the same as that long since imposed on the seller by the Sale of Goods Act, above. It may still be extremely difficult to say what standard of safety 'persons generally are entitled to expect'. Can one reasonably expect that drugs will never have side effects, or that car components will never fail?

6.84   Compensation may be claimed for 'damage', as defined in Section 5. This includes death or personal injury and loss of or damage to property including land. Damage to the product itself, or to any product supplied with the defective product in it (e.g. damage to a tyre, or to a car damaged because of the tyre), is excluded, as is damage to non-domestic property, or to domestic property if it costs less than £275 to remedy. This seemingly arbitrary figure derives from the Directive's 500 ecu limit. It can be altered by statutory order.

6.85   The immediate result of the Act is that the injured party need only show he was injured because of some unnecessary or exceptional danger in the goods. The burden of *disproving* liability is then upon the producer. He may do this by means of various defences provided by Section 4. These include compliance with statutory or Common Market duties, proof that he was not the supplier, or did not supply in the course of business, or that the defect did not exist in the goods when he supplied them, or, if he is a component supplier, by showing that the defect was caused by the design of the finished product or compliance with the producer's requirements.

6.86   The most controversial and important defence, however, is that of the 'state of the art' or 'development risk', as provided by Section 4(1)e. The producer – unlike the seller under the Sale of Goods Act – escapes liability if he can show that *'the state of scientific or technical knowledge at the relevant time* [i.e. when the producer or supplier first supplied the goods to another person] *was not such that a producer of products of the same description as the product in question might be expected to have discovered the defect if it had existed in his products while they were under his control'*. There is clearly much room for argument over the effect of this wording – as to what was in fact known, and where and by whom, about any particular hazard, and whether this particular supplier 'might be expected' to know about it. 'Expected' presumably means 'reasonably expected', so that the test seems to be whether the supplier had reasonable grounds for believing he had taken all proper precautions – which is still a test of negligence. The European Community Commission understandably argues that the test is not in accordance with the EC Directive, which says that the defence applies only where the state of knowledge *'was not such as to enable the existence of a defect to be discovered'* – clearly a very much more demanding standard.

6.87 The Directive on product liability and the Consumer Protection Act which followed it were the results of many years' discussions. What did they actually achieve? Very shortly, it seems that the main effect of the Act may be to help plaintiffs in relatively minor cases by means of the reversed burden of proof, para. 6.85. On the other hand, it will not necessarily avoid extremely expensive and speculative litigation for those seeking compensation for major injuries caused, for example, by new drugs. In so far as that is the position, the Act has failed in its objective. We might note in passing here the apparent superiority in this and other personal injury contexts of the reform introduced in New Zealand in 1974; now the Accident Rehabilitation and Compensation Insurance Act 1992. The Act abolishes all claims for damages for personal injury caused by accident and instead entitles accident victims to insurance payments up to 80 per cent of lost earning capacity, within a statutory ceiling currently of some £450 per week. Provision is also made for payment of medical expenses and dependents' allowances.

6.88 Other provisions in Part I of the Consumer Protection Act preserve existing rights to sue in contract and tort, as set out at length above. An injured person must therefore consider very carefully which of the three 'regimes' of compensation would be most helpful. As a buyer, he or she might still find it easier to sue the seller in the High Street, or, in the absence of a contractual relationship, a plaintiff might prefer to rely on proof of negligence against a domestic distributor rather than make a claim against a Continental producer. Part I of the Act also retains the rules of contributory negligence, reducing the victim's claim according to his own degree of fault, and invalidates any contract term or notice limiting or excluding liability under the Act: Sections 6 and 7. Claims must be brought within three years of the plaintiff knowing he has a right to sue, and in any case within ten years of supply. It should be noted that the Act does not impose

153

any financial limits on liability, nor does it compel producers to insure themselves.

D. Criminal law

6.89   Producers' and suppliers' civil liabilities are reinforced by a range of criminal liabilities. Under the General Product Safety Regulations 1994, based on a European Union Directive, it is a criminal offence for a manufacturer or an importer into the EU to put on the market consumer goods which are not safe. Distributors also may be liable if their activities affect the safety of a product. A safe product is defined as one which under normal or reasonably foreseeable conditions does not present any risk or only the minimum risks compatible with its use. Producers must take appropriate steps to ensure safety, in particular by warning consumers against hidden dangers, and, e.g., sample testing, investigation of complaints and informing distributors of any safety problems. The Regulations do not apply to second-hand goods which are antiques, nor to products expressly supplied for repair or reconditioning before use.

6.90   There are many other more specific rules of criminal law on the safe composition or construction of products ranging from food to furniture and from cars to prams. Many of the rules are in the form of regulations made under powers now contained in the Consumer Protection Act. Prosecution does not affect the validity of the contract of sale. Apart from prosecution, local authority enforcement agencies can require display of warning notices or withdrawal of dangerous goods.

6.91   We note also that Section 6 of the Health and Safety at Work Act 1974 makes it an offence for designers, manufacturers, importers, suppliers, and installers of articles and substances for use at work, and of fairground equipment, to supply such goods without ensuring so far as reasonably practicable that they will be safe in all reasonably foreseeable circumstances. The rule represents an important means of reducing industrial accidents and reinforcing civil liabilities.

Danish law

6.92   The Danish Sale of Goods Act of 1979 says that a seller is liable for supplying defective goods if:
  i.   the goods are of a different or inferior kind from that indicated by the agreement or surrounding circumstances;
  ii. the goods do not conform with their description;

iii.   the seller or a previous supplier in the sales chain has given incorrect or misleading information affecting the buyer's expectations; or

iv.   the seller negligently failed to give information affecting the buyer's expectations.

These rules apply also in sales of used goods by private individuals. Even where goods are sold 'as is' they must still not be significantly poorer than the buyer could reasonably expect.

6.93   A buyer cannot complain of a defect unless he notifies the seller within a reasonable time after he has or should have discovered it. In contrast with the English rule on acceptance, however, it is clear that the duty to notify does not arise until the fault has or ought to have been discovered. On the other hand again, all complaints must be made within one year of delivery, or within five years in the case of building materials, unless the seller has expressly warranted the article for a longer period or has acted in bad faith. Under the Product Safety Act 1994 limitation rules do not apply if a recall or destruction of a product is ordered. Manufacturers' guarantees are separately enforceable.

6.94   The buyer's remedies are reduction in price, supply of the article contracted for, damages, or cancellation of the contract, as appropriate. Claims for damages for personal injury or damage to property are outside the Sale of Goods Act. They are regulated by Danish common law as now supplemented by the 1989 Product Liability Act. The courts have held that any supplier in the chain of production and distribution is liable if the goods or services are not as safe as might reasonably be expected and this is due to a fault of the supplier in question or any previous supplier. Suppliers are thus vicariously liable for the fault of any previous link in the chain. The burden of disproving liability is upon the supplier. The new Act extends these rules by making producers strictly liable, subject to a 'state of the art' defence, and holding subsequent suppliers vicariously liable on the same basis.

6.95   Danish product liability law thus differs from English law in two important respects. First, the supplier's liability to the buyer is the same as to any other injured party; second, the injured party may claim damages from the link in the chain closest to him.

Dutch law

6.96   In the absence of more specific requirements set by the parties themselves, the basic standard of fitness of goods is that laid down in Article 7.17 of the Code; that the goods must conform to the contract. They do not conform if they do not have the qualities for normal and/or specified use which the buyer is entitled to expect according to the contract, or if they are of a different kind or deviate in number, size or weight from what was agreed. An innovation in Article 7.18 is that conformity in a consumer contract may be determined by reference to advertisements and other such information provided by or on behalf of the seller. Articles 6.185–193 transpose the EC Product Liability Directive into Dutch law. The rules are therefore essentially the same as under English law – paras. 6.81–8 – except that the Dutch wording of the development risk defence follows the Directive more closely. The producer is liable 'unless it was impossible to discover the existence of the defect on the basis of the state of scientific and technical knowledge at the time when he put the product into circulation'. In the most important recent judgment on the question, *Van Ballegooyen* v. *Bayer Nederland*, NJ 1994, 535, the Hoge Raad held for the first time that all the manufacturers of a dangerous drug ('DES') could be held jointly liable for injuries caused by the drug.

French law

6.97   Article 1603 of the Civil Code provides that the vendor has two main obligations: 'to deliver and to warrant the thing which is sold'. Under Article 1604 *et seq.* relating to delivery obligations, the courts have laid down the principle that the vendor must deliver a thing whose characteristics correspond to the request of the purchaser: Civ. 1 December 1987. In the case of 'default in conformity' the sale can be rescinded. Article 1641, on the other hand, provides 'the seller is bound to guarantee the goods against hidden defects (*vices cachés*) which make them unfit for the use for which they are intended or which so impair such use that the purchaser would not have bought them, or would have bought them at a lower price, if he had known of such hidden defects'.

6.98   The distinction between actions arising from hidden defects and actions for non-conformity has become of major importance in the French law of sales because of the different procedures they involve. An action based on hidden defects in the goods can be started at any time after delivery, provided that it is started within a short period of time (*bref délai*) after the disclosure of the hidden defects: Article 1648. An action in conformity, however, is not subject to the *bref délai* requirement; but cannot be started if the goods were accepted without reserve at the time of delivery. In addition, a purchaser starting an action on grounds of hidden defects can take such action either against his seller or by the *action directe* against any previous seller, up to the manufacturer, despite the absence of a contractual relationship between them. This is because Article 1641 creates a warranty obligation, the benefit of which is transferred by subrogation to each successive buyer: Com. 4 November 1982. Although the grounds for the two actions are different, they may well overlap, and both are usually started together by dissatisfied purchasers. The distinction between the actions is much criticised because of the practical difficulty of distinguishing between hidden defects and faults in conformity.

6.99 Another aspect of the distinction relates to exclusion clauses. A seller cannot limit his duty to deliver a thing which conforms to the requirement of the purchaser, since this is the subject-matter of the contract, but he may to some extent limit his liability for hidden defects. Such limitations of warranties are, however, enforceable subject to certain conditions. In particular, a professional seller can exclude liability only against a professional buyer. As against a consumer, a professional seller is deemed to have acted in bad faith and to have known of the hidden defect at the time of the sale.

6.100 The obligations of suppliers of goods and services have been steadily extended in the field of contract throughout the century, in order to make available to contracting parties remedies which were not practicable under tort law because of the requirement of fault – *faute* – under Article 1382. A landmark decision (Civ. 21 November 1911) held that 'the carrying out of the contract of carriage implies . . . for the carrier an obligation to carry the passengers safely to their destination' – thus permitting the passengers to start their action on the basis of the contract simply by showing that this obligation of safety had not been complied with, and without needing to show distinct 'fault' as required by Article 1382. A variety of decisions and a number of statutory or regulatory provisions followed, creating obligations for suppliers of goods or services equivalent in effect to strict liability.

6.101 As regards product liability, the implementation of the EEC Directive is not generally seen as significantly affecting either the rights of consumers or the duties of distributors and manufacturers. Numerous decisions have already evidenced or created obligations on the part of distributors and manufacturers to ensure the safety of the users of goods. This type of responsibility is of a contractual nature: it is tantamount to strict liability in that any failure to abide by such safety obligations makes the supplier liable. In addition, where damage is caused by a hidden defect in the goods, the *action directe*, above, enables the manufacturer and all those involved in the chain of distribution to be held liable. The Directive will supplement French law in cases where because of the absence of a contractual relationship with the manufacturer, and in the absence of rights of subrogation, the remedy is in tort under Article 1382. This has, however, already partly been effected by an Act of 31 July 1983 on consumers' safety, and in any case the courts tend to presume fault under Article 1382 merely on proof of delivery of goods which are not reasonably safe. We note also the imposition of vicarious liability under Article 1384. But a point in discussion in France is the right the Directive gives a manufacturer to escape liability on the grounds of ignorance of the danger of the product in the state of science and knowledge at the time of manufacture. French case law has always rejected this type of excuse and held manufacturers liable regardless of the general state of knowledge. This difficulty explains why a Bill to adapt French law to the Directive which was proposed in 1991 has not yet become law.

German law

6.102 In German law the differences between contractual and tortious rights are even more important than in English law. The BGB imposes strict liability in contract upon retailers if their goods or services are not reasonably fit. But this implied warranty of fitness applies only to the goods or services themselves and not to any injury or damage caused to the buyer or his property. Claims for injury or damage require proof of negligence. This may be established in a breach of contract action against the dealer or in a tort action against someone else such as the manufacturer.

6.103 Sales warranties are regulated by Article 459 *et seq.* of the BGB. The rules apply to both consumer and business transactions and to used goods as well as new ones, but their application may be limited or excluded, as mentioned below. Article 462 entitles a buyer of defective goods to cancel the contract or pay a lower price, or under Article 480 to demand a replacement. Much the same definition of 'defect' applies as in English law (but we note that a German court might find the seller in *Phillips* – para. 6.15 – in breach of contract: (1993) NJW RR 57 – car made 8 months earlier was not 'factory new'). Warranty actions must be begun within six months of purchase. Under the Commercial Code, any complaint by a business buyer must be made immediately after delivery. The application of the warranty rules to new goods cannot be completely excluded. If the seller's attempts to repair or improve defective goods are unsuccessful, the buyer cannot be deprived of his right to end the contract or pay a reduced price. All the implied warranties may be excluded in sales of used goods, but even here the courts may insist on minimum standards. As in *Bartlett*, para. 6.42, for example, a car must be 'fit to be driven along the road in safety'.

6.104 Claims for damages for negligence may be based on Article 823 – the basic tort law provision of the BGB. They may be brought against the seller or the manufacturer. There is no *non cumul* rule like that in French law (para. 1.45). Article 823 declares: 'A person who, wilfully or negligently, unlawfully injures the life, body, health, freedom, property or other right of another must compensate him for any damage arising therefrom'. Since this provision does not cover pure economic loss, there is no rule of German tort law equivalent to that of *Hedley Byrne* (para. 6.68). It may sometimes be possible to overcome this unsatisfactory position by the application of principles of contract law, notably *positive Vertragsverletzung* (para. 5.70), which may have protective effects for third parties, or *culpa in contrahendo*: para. 5.71.

6.105   Product liability law in particular is case law based on Article 823, supplemented by the Product Liability Act of 1990. The leading case on Article 823 is the fowl-pest case of 1968 (BGHZ 51,91), where a chicken farmer sued the manufacturer of a defective serum which killed thousands of his chickens. The *Bundesgerichtshof* – the Federal Supreme Court – held in this case that the burden of proof should be reversed and that it was for the manufacturer to disprove fault. In cases in the 1980s the Court developed a duty upon producers to 'observe' their products after sale and to warn consumers if they proved dangerous. In the most recent *Milupa* cases, the manufacturer of a sweet tea for babies was held liable for injury to the babies' teeth. Case law generally gives better remedies in products' cases than the Product Liability Act, but there is no liability for development risks under either the BGB or the new Act. Claims for pain and suffering can only be made under Article 823.

6.106   Article 831 makes employers liable in tort for injuries caused by failure to supervise their employees, but does not directly provide for a doctrine of vicarious liability. The courts have, however, interpreted Article 831 very strictly, and hold employers and suppliers personally liable for the negligence of employees or independent contractors unless they can disprove personal fault. In a contract action, the employer is strictly liable for the faults of employees or other assistants, and cannot escape such liability: Article 278. To overcome the problems of Article 831, the courts have developed so-called *Verkehrssicherungspflichten* (duties of care). So a case somewhat similar to *Wall*, para. 6.63, was differently decided. In the German case a tour operator was held liable for the injuries of a holiday maker who fell from a hotel balcony because the railing was loose. The tour operator was not liable for the hotelier's fault, but for breach of his own obligation to ensure the safety of the railing.

Italian law

6.107   As under English law, the nature of a supplier's liability under Italian law for the fitness of his goods or services depends on whether he is sued in contract or in tort. In contract, he must supply goods without defects which affect their normal use or appreciably reduce their value, and which have the qualities normally found in such goods or promised by the seller:

159

Articles 1490–7 of the Civil Code. The same rules apply to credit transactions. The buyer must notify the seller of any complaint within eight days of delivery or of the time he discovered or should have discovered the fault. He cannot complain of faults he should have seen when he made the contract, unless the seller promised a higher quality.

6.108   Italian standards of fitness of goods are essentially the same as those in the UK Sale of Goods Act. The seller must in effect guarantee the reasonable fitness of his goods for their normal or specified purposes. But he is not liable for failure to comply with the buyer's special requirements unless he expressly or impliedly contracts on that basis. The overall standard is that of 'average quality': Article 1178. Price or other circumstances may justify a different standard.

6.109   These liabilities arise whether or not the seller sells in the course of business – and equally the buyer's professional knowledge or the lack of it will be taken into account in deciding whether his reasonable expectations have been met.

6.110   The buyer's remedies in contract are the right to pay a lower price, or to end the contract if the faults are fundamental: Articles 1455, 1492. Use of the goods does not of itself prevent rescission. He can claim damages against the seller only if the seller knew or should have known the goods were defective: Article 1494. The buyer has no right as such to repair or replacement of the goods. In practice many goods are sold with a warranty of fitness – *garanzia di buon funzionmento* – which entitles the seller to repair or replace within a fixed period: Article 1512.

6.111   Injury to the buyer or his goods may give rise to a claim in tort against the seller or manufacturer or other party against whom negligence or wilful fault can be proved. Following a Court of Cassation case in 1980 concerning a soft drink bottle which exploded, the burden of proof, still theoretically upon the plaintiff, is much reduced. As in this particular case, the judge may infer fault from the nature of the process and the event. The supplier is vicariously liable for the faults of his employees – Article 2049 – and, in contrast with English common law, the faults of other parties whose services he uses to fulfil his obligations: Article 1228. Such liability could until recently be excluded by agreement, but this is not now possible: Trib. Milano, 14 September 1990.

6.112   In 1988 a product liability law was passed to give effect to the European Directive of 1985. Its terms are very similar to those of the UK Consumer Protection Act, and have been likewise criticised by the EU Commission with regard to the wording of the state of the art defence.

Spanish law

6.113   Sellers' contractual duties under Spanish law vary to some extent according to whether or not they are acting in the course of business. Under the Civil Code, sellers are responsible for hidden defects in goods sold which make them unsuitable for intended use or reduce their value: Article 1484. The seller is liable for hidden faults even though unaware of them, unless otherwise agreed: Article 1485. He is not liable for obvious faults. His responsibility under ordinary 'civil' contracts ends six months after handing over the goods: Article 1490. But in commercial contracts, i.e. where goods are bought by businesses for resale, complaints must be made within thirty days: Article 342 of the Commercial Code. No claim can be made if the buyer agrees on receipt that the goods are satisfactory: Article 336.

6.114   The Supreme Court has distinguished between delivery of goods with hidden defects and failure to deliver or delivery of different goods. In the latter situation of 'full non-compliance', the six month limitation period above is replaced by a fifteen year period. An example of non-compliance was a case of 15 July 1987, concerning garage spaces which were not adequate for their intended use because of defects in construction.

6.115   The Law of 19 July 1984 on the protection of consumers and users sought to give effect to European Community standards, though its precise effect is not yet clear. Goods and services must be reasonably fit for their purpose: Article 8. Total exclusions of liability are contrary to good faith and therefore void, as are limitations relating to the 'utility or essential purpose' of the product or service: Article 10. Article 11 entitles the consumer to recover the whole or appropriate part of the cost of the goods in case of 'error, defect or deterioration' constituting a breach of contract by the seller. The consumer or user can claim damages for injuries caused by the goods, unless attributable to his own fault: Article 25.

6.116   The Law of 6 July 1994 implements the 1985 European Directive on product liability. The new law is considerably wider than that of 1984, above, e.g. in protecting all injured persons and not only 'consumers'. Producers of goods are now strictly liable for defects in their products, subject to the injured party proving a causal connection between the defect and his or her injury.

Swedish law

6.117   As regards sale of goods, Swedish law is no longer so close to Danish law. Sweden enacted a new Sale of Goods Act in 1990. This Act was intended largely to conform with the 1980 Convention on Contracts for the International Sale of Goods. The basic standards as to fitness of goods

161

and services are set by this new Act, and also by the Consumer Sale of Goods Act 1990 and the Consumer Services Act 1858. There are rules in '*jordabalken*' (an Act concerning land) Chapter 7–14, concerning leases of land and apartments. There is no Act regulating hire of goods. Instead general principles and analogies from the Sale of Goods Act and the rules in '*jordabalken*' are applied. There is no statutory regulation of contracts for services between businesses. General principles of law and trade usage are applied. Trade usage has developed by well established and agreed documents, such as AB 92 concerning building contracts. We note that the Sale of Goods Act applies also to sale of shares, patents and other intangibles. Non-contractual product liability rules are the same as in Denmark, and as provided by the 1985 European Directive on product liability.

6.118   As mentioned in Chapter 5, Swedish law has no rule like that of English law, dividing contract terms into conditions and warranties. The consequences of the breach are considered, and if sufficiently fundamental the buyer is allowed to repudiate the contract. In other cases the buyer is entitled to demand that the seller delivers new goods free from fault, or that the seller repairs the goods (cure), or that he reduces the price. The seller is almost always liable to pay damages for direct costs. For other losses the seller is only liable if he has given a guarantee of conformity or if he has acted against good faith. The seller has a legal right to try to repair the goods if he can do so without too much inconvenience for the buyer.

6.119   According to the Sale of Goods Act the buyer loses his right to repudiate the contract, and his other rights, if he accepts the goods. Acceptance may be express or implied. If the buyer does not give the seller notice ('*reklamation*') within a reasonable time after delivery, he is deemed to have accepted the goods. The buyer has an obligation to examine the goods after delivery in accordance with good trade usage. If he fails to do this, and if he fails to give notice, he cannot claim that there has been a breach of contract. Similar rules are found in the other Acts mentioned above.

6.120   As under English law, the seller is strictly liable for any failure to give a good title to the goods. Article 17 of the Sale of Goods Act says that goods sold must be in conformity with the contract and fit for normal use. The obligation as to fitness extends also to the packaging of the goods. Article 17 states a further general obligation as to fitness; the goods must conform with the reasonable expectations of the buyer. The seller's liability is strict. Goods must also conform with manufacturers' advertisements which may have influenced the buyer, if the seller is aware of the advertisement: Article 18 of the Sale of Goods Act.

6.121   A claim for non-conformity must be made within two years after delivery. After that time the buyer may only make a claim if the seller has given a guarantee for a longer period, or has acted against good faith.

Chapter 7

Exclusion clauses and other unfair contract terms

A. Exclusion clauses

7.1　We have looked at length now at the nature of sellers' liabilities under English law for the fitness of their goods. But while the basic rules may be reasonably clear and even-handed, we must remember that each party is seeking to ensure as far as possible that he is not bound too tightly by his contract and that his liability will be limited if things go wrong. In theory at least each party is free to decide for himself the extent of his commitment and his liability, and to frame his offer or acceptance accordingly. In practice the weaker party – the smaller business or the consumer – may be unable to negotiate effectively or at all, and so find himself exploited and without a remedy because and insofar as he seems to have accepted the terms of the other's standard form. Our concern in this chapter is with the rules of law controlling the use and content of such forms.

7.2　An impressive introductory example of the kind of clause under discussion is the following, until not so long ago in use on a cross-Channel service: 'Normandy Ferries shall not be liable for the death of or any injury, damage, or loss, delay or accident to passengers, their apparel or baggage, whensoever, wheresoever and howsoever caused and whether by negligence of their servants or agents or by unseaworthiness of the vessel (whether existing at the time of embarkation or sailing or at any other time) or otherwise. Normandy Ferries may in its absolute discretion and without any liability whatsoever alter the ports of embarkation or disembarkation and time of sailing and arrival, change the route, call at any port whatsoever without previous notice to the passengers. A passenger accepts that Normandy Ferries give no condition or warranty express or implied that the vessel used for the carriage is fit for the carriage of passengers, their baggage or accompanied vehicles.' Airline tickets typically seek to avoid the consequences of what might be unavoidable problems by saying: 'Times shown in timetables or elsewhere are not guaranteed and form no part of this contract. Carrier may without notice substitute alternate carriers or aircraft, and may alter or omit stopping places shown on the ticket in case of necessity. Schedules are subject to change without notice. Carrier assumes no responsibility for making connections.' Railway timetables routinely deny any necessary connection between the printed and the actual times of arrival and departure of trains.

i. Common law

7.3   English law has been slow to respond to the risk of abuse inherent in exclusions or limitations of liability. The common law in particular, with its basic attitudes to life embedded in nineteenth century *laissez-faire* attitudes, confirmed by the doctrine of obligatory precedent, failed to provide any very effective challenge. It was left to Parliament to tackle the problem in the Unfair Contract Terms Act of 1977, recently reinforced by the Unfair Terms in Consumer Contracts Regulations 1994. But that is not to say that the common law could not recognise an evil, nor that it made no attempt at all to control it. It is still necessary to look at the rules of common law before considering the Act and the Regulations.

7.4   The key to an understanding of the common law rules is that they are all concerned with the application, construction or interpretation of *particular clauses in particular contracts.* They are variations on two basic questions: *did the weaker party – the buyer or consumer – know, or could he have known, of the existence of the clause, and, if so, did the wording of the clause clearly cover the events which occurred?* Professor Atiyah describes these as questions of procedural fairness. With one short-lived exception, below, the common law has made no attempt to control the terms themselves – to say, for example, that certain kinds of clauses are forbidden, or that they must all be fair and reasonable, or anything of that kind. We shall see shortly that the statutory provisions do not affect the validity of these rules of interpretation, limited though they are. Their effect may be summarised and illustrated as follows.

7.5   The first rule of interpretation is that the consumer must have reasonable notice of the existence of the exclusion clause. The clause will be ineffective unless the supplier can show he took reasonable steps to bring it to the consumer's attention, though not of course to ensure that he reads or understands it. The nature of the necessary reasonable steps has never been altogether clear, but modern cases certainly suggest that the responsibilities are greater today than in the past. In *Thompson* v. *L.M.S. Railway*, 1930, for example, a passenger was held to have had sufficient notice of the existence of an exclusion clause, and therefore to be bound by it, by the fact that the ticket stated it was 'issued subject to the company's rules and regulations' – even though the details could have been found only by purchase of a timetable. A point of incidental interest was that the plaintiff could not read – but as the judge so aptly remarked: 'Illiteracy is a misfortune, not a privilege'. In contrast with *Thompson*, a clause in a folded programme was invalidated in *White* v. *Blackmore*, 1972, because it was not immediately apparent.

7.6   *White* v. *Blackmore* illustrates the recent trend to require the supplier to do his best to ensure that the consumer knows the clause is in fact an exclusion clause. So in *Spurling* v. *Bradshaw*, 1956, Lord Denning said: 'Some clauses which I have seen would need to be printed in red ink on the face of the document with a red hand pointing to it before the notice could be held to be sufficient.' This argument was developed in *Interfoto* v. *Stiletto*, 1987, an important case on the supplier's duty to warn of onerous clauses in general, discussed in more detail at the end of this chapter. The modern view is further developed in *Baltic Shipping* v. *Dillon*, 1993, an Australian case arising out of the loss of the cruise ship 'Mikhail Lermontov' off the coast of New Zealand. The court said that a consumer could properly suppose there would be no unusual provisions in his ticket of which he was not 'on notice', and specifically none which limited or excluded the supplier's liability. On this basis the consumer had to have a reasonable opportunity to see and agree to the terms on his ticket. His agreement was not to be presumed simply from his beginning upon his holiday.

7.7   The second rule – a variation on the first – is that the document or notice containing the clause must appear as a contractual document. If it appears merely as a receipt or note which the consumer might properly think he need not read, it is not binding. So in *Chapelton* v. *Barry U.D.C.*, 1940, a clause on a deckchair ticket was held ineffective, as was a set of conditions printed in a cheque book in *Burnett* v. *Westminster Bank*, 1965. But in *Parker* v. *S.E. Railway*, 1877, terms on a 'left luggage' ticket were binding because the consumer knew he could only recover his luggage on production of and in accordance with the ticket. In *Sprigg* v. *Sotheby*, 1986, an auctioneer's standard form instructions for sale were likewise held to be part of the contract.

7.8   Another way of looking at the same issue is that the exclusion clause must not be added after the contract has been made. So in *Thornton* v. *Shoe Lane Parking*, 1971, it was held that a notice inside a car park where entry was controlled automatically was of no effect, and in *Olley* v. *Marlborough Court Hotel*, 1949, a notice in a hotel bedroom did not relieve the hotel of liability for theft because the contract had already been made at the hotel desk. But it is not always easy to say when the contract was in fact concluded, nor what its terms are. As we saw in Chapter 1, both parties may contract on the understanding that detailed particulars – which might contain an exclusion clause – will be provided at a later date, which could then still be regarded as part of the contract. This is more likely to be so as between businesses, as illustrated in *British Crane Hire* v. *Ipswich Plant Hire*, 1976, para. 1.22, than in consumer transactions: *Hollier* v. *Rambler Motors*, 1972; *Hollingworth* v. *Southern Ferries*, 1977. In either kind of contract there is always the possibility that previous dealings between the parties should have alerted one side to the other's use of exclusion clauses – very much a question of fact in each case: *McCutcheon* v. *McBrayne*, 1964. In *Hollier*, for instance, the Court of Appeal refused to accept that a clause was included in a contract on the basis of three or four transactions between the parties over a period of five years.

7.9   Another rule is that fraud or misrepresentation as to the effect of an exclusion clause will invalidate it: *Curtis* v. *Chemical Cleaning*, 1951. Clauses will not be enforced if they tell a lie, e.g. by saying falsely that the customer has examined the goods and found them in good condition: *Lowe* v. *Lombank*, 1960. Similarly, if the supplier gives an express oral promise on or before making the contract, that will probably override any standard form provision to the contrary: *Evans* v. *Merzario*, 1976 – oral promise to ship goods between decks – goods carried on deck and lost overboard – written exclusion clause nullified by previous oral promise.

7.10   Next is the rule that ambiguous or obscure clauses will be interpreted by the judges in the way least favourable to the party relying on them – the supplier. This is the *'contra proferentem'* rule. If for example a contract clause purports to deprive a buyer of his right to reject defective goods, he may still be able to claim damages: *Ashington Piggeries* v. *Hill*, 1972. It will be presumed that a contract clause refers only to contractual liability and not to liability in tort for negligence, unless the wording clearly covers negligence or could have no other meaning, e.g. excluding liability for loss or damage 'howsoever caused': *White* v. *Blackmore*, 1972. The very common formula 'E & OE' – errors and omissions excepted – seems to protect the supplier only against minor miscalculations and certainly does not license him generally to give inaccurate information: *Van Berg* v. *Landauer*, 1925. A contract which makes the supplier 'sole judge' of satisfactory performance of the contract does not exclude the operation of the law: *West of England Insurance* v. *Cristal*, 1995. Exclusion clauses normally protect only the supplier, but if he contracts expressly on behalf of his servants or agents they also may escape liability: *Adler* v. *Dickson*, 1954; *N.Z. Shipping* v. *Satterthwaite*, 1974: para. 3.9.

7.11   If a buyer signs a contract containing an exclusion clause, then at common law he is bound by his signature: *L'Estrange* v. *Graucob*, 1934. But this proposition is subject to the rules just mentioned as to fraud and misrepresentation, and the clarity or otherwise of the clause in question. It is also expressly limited by the Unfair Contract Terms Act, below.

7.12   We have now summarised current common law responses to exclusion clause problems. Until relatively recently we would have had to discuss also the so-called 'doctrine of fundamental breach', but since this rule now seems of no substantial effect in English law we shall mention it only briefly. It should be noted, however, that the doctrine still plays a part in certain Commonwealth jurisdictions. The basic principle or presumption was that since no-one would wish to make a contract which allowed one side to break his promise in some fundamental respect without incurring any liability whatever, any clause which appeared to have this effect would be declared void. The difficulty which then arose was in deciding how serious a breach had to be to go 'beyond the limit'. A line had to be drawn between supplying goods which were completely useless (which would nullify the clause) and those which were merely very faulty, which would leave the clause in operation – a fine and eventually impossible distinction. When the issue came before the House of Lords in *Suisse Atlantique* v. *NV Rotter-damsche Kolen Centrale* in 1967 their Lordships rejected the doctrine altogether, a ruling they confirmed in *Photo Productions* v. *Securicor*, 1980, and *Mitchell* v. *Finney Lock*, 1983, below. Apart from its inherent difficulty, their Lordships thought that while the doctrine might help consumers it was unnecessary as between businessmen negotiating on more equal terms. They objected to it also because by making certain types of clauses void it appeared as a rule of substantive law, and as such irreconcilable with the overall approach of the common law to this problem – that of reliance on rules of construction only.

7.13   The effect of the ruling is well illustrated in *Photo Productions*. The defendants contracted to provide security services at the plaintiffs' factory. They supplied a watchman who, anxious to make a good impression, started a small fire which he then intended to extinguish and to report accordingly on his own good work. Unfortunately the fire went out of control and destroyed the factory. The plaintiffs sued the defendants for their whole loss. Their claim was rejected because the contract excluded the defendants' liability for damage done by employees unless such damage was due to the defendants' negligence – which was not so here because they had no reason to suspect the watchman's integrity – and limited their liability in any event to £25,000. Since the plaintiffs had adequate notice of the clause it was held binding upon them. Any other decision would in effect have made Securicor insurers of the factory, which was not what they undertook or charged for.

7.14   This case and the others mentioned thus reduce the doctrine of fundamental breach from a rule of law to a rule of construction. Its effect then seems much like that of the *contra proferentem* rule, above. When faced with a contractual term whose meaning or scope is uncertain the judge will try to interpret it in a way which upholds rather than destroys the contract. He will presume on the parties' behalf that they would not intend both to make and at the same time to nullify a contract by enabling one side completely to disregard his obligations. A less strict approach may therefore be taken if the clause reduces liability without excluding it altogether, although liability may be limited to so small a sum as effectively to nullify the contract. In *Ailsa Craig* v. *Malvern Fishing*, 1983, a ship worth £55,000 sank because of Securicor's negligence or breach of contract. The House of Lords upheld a term in Securicor's contract limiting their liability to £1,000. In *Darlington* v. *Delco*, 1986, the High Court of Australia refused to follow *Ailsa Craig*.

7.15   But we emphasise that the presumption in favour of contractual utility applies only where the clause is not clear. A sufficiently clear and comprehensive clause may indeed defeat the whole object of the contract and yet be upheld by the courts – unless, perhaps, as suggested by Lord Diplock in *Photo Productions*, there is then no contract at all, in which case the clause would become meaningless and unenforceable: *Firestone* v. *Vokins*, 1951. Conversely, of course, as Professor Brian Coote, the New Zealand academic, has pointed out, there is always the possibility that what might look like an exclusion clause is actually only a limited commitment by the supplier. If he promises, for example, only to take reasonable care, he cannot then be criticised for not ensuring perfection.

ii. Unfair Contract Terms Act

7.16   For more substantial protection we must turn to statute law. The position here is unfortunately complicated by the existence of two completely separate and unrelated sets of rules. The original UK legislation, the Unfair Contract Terms Act 1977, was overlaid in 1994 by the Unfair Terms in Consumer Contracts Regulations. The Regulations were intended to give effect word-for-word to a European Union Directive, and so made no mention of the 1977 Act. Although the two provisions substantially overlap, they are still quite distinct, and theoretically at least could give different answers to the same problem.

7.17   We examine first the details of the Unfair Contract Terms Act – noting immediately that the title of the Act is a little misleading. The Act does not concern all unfair terms; only exclusion clauses – although, unlike the 1994 Regulations, it regulates such clauses in contracts between businesses as well as in consumer contracts. And despite its title, the Act is not limited to terms in contracts. It extends also to non-contractual notices, such as those excluding liability for loss or damage in public buildings or parks. The Act divides exclusion clauses into two categories; those which are void in all circumstances – the black list – and those which may be valid if found to be reasonable in the circumstances – the grey list. The 1994 Regulations, as we shall see, have only a grey list, making all consumer contract terms subject to a test of fairness.

7.18   Section 1 of the 1977 Act defines some of the terms used in the Act and explains its objectives. For the purposes of Sections 2 and 3, negligence is defined as breach of any contractual or legal duty to take reasonable care. It is immaterial whether the fault is deliberate or accidental, personal or vicarious (defined in Chapter 6). The Act applies only to exclusions of business liability (*see* Section 14, below). Section 2(1) says that *contract terms or non-contractual notices excluding or limiting liability for death or personal injury caused by negligence are void* (though their use is not illegal). *But liability for purely economic loss or damage to property caused by negligence can be excluded if the clause is reasonable in the circumstances*: Section 2(2). A person's knowledge or apparent acceptance, e.g. by signature, of a term excluding liability for negligence does not prove he has agreed to run the risk: Section 2(3). To this extent therefore the Act overrides *L'Estrange* v. *Graucob*, above.

7.19   By way of comment on Section 2, we stress that it applies only to injury or loss caused by negligence. Liability for injuries or losses caused, e.g., by natural or unavoidable dangers may still properly be avoided. We observe also that liability for negligence can always be excluded if there is no duty of care in the first place. A person using a car park, for example, usually pays only for space, not care. Negligence is not likely to be an issue unless there is a bailment, i.e. a temporary entrusting of possession of one's property to another, as where a car owner leaves his car key with an attendant: *Ashby* v. *Tolhurst*, 1937; *Mendelssohn* v. *Normand*, 1970.

7.20   As to what is reasonable in any given case, each case must, of course, turn on its own facts. But two recent House of Lords' decisions on surveyors' duties are encouraging from the consumer's point of view. In *Smith* v. *Bush*, 1989, a building society asked an independent surveyor to value a house at the lower end of the property market which the plaintiff wished to buy. The plaintiff received a copy of the valuer's report and was charged for his services. The survey was negligent and the plaintiff suffered loss when he tried to resell his house. The surveyor's report said it was made without acceptance of any responsibility by the surveyor or the society, gave no warranty that statements or opinions in it were accurate or valid, and advised the purchaser to obtain independent advice. The House of Lords held that in view of the plaintiff's likely reliance and indeed dependence on the report this general disclaimer was unreasonable and invalid.

7.21   When deciding *Smith*, above, their Lordships decided also the case of *Harris* v. *Wyre Forest District Council*. This was another negligent valuation problem, coupled with an exclusion clause which the Court of Appeal had upheld as reasonable. The purchasers here applied to the council on a standard application form for a mortgage, and paid a fee for an inspection of the property which the council was obliged by law to carry out. The mortgage application form said that the valuation was confidential and solely for the council's own benefit, that the council accepted no liability for the value or condition of the house, and that purchasers should obtain independent valuations. The purchasers did not see the valuer's report, but the council told them about it and offered them a mortgage, which they accepted. When subsequently they tried to resell the house, faults were found which should have been seen originally and which made it uninhabitable and unsaleable. The House of Lords held that even though the council had a statutory duty to value property, it still owed a duty of care to purchasers. The council knew that most house buyers relied entirely on the valuers' expertise, particularly in the case of buyers of cheaper houses, and had every reason and incentive to do so. In these circumstances it was unreasonable to exclude all liability to them.

7.22   Section 3 gives substantial protection against abuse of bargaining power not only to consumers contracting with retailers but also to retailers or other businessmen contracting with bigger businesses. A person deals as a consumer for the purposes of this section if he makes a contract, written or spoken, which is not in the course of his business nor at auction or by tender, but which is in the course of the other's business, and any goods involved are ordinarily bought for private use or consumption: Section 12. Retailers and other businesses are within Section 3 if they contract on another business's written standard terms. The section says that *contract terms limiting or excluding the stronger party's liability for breach of contract, or enabling him to carry out his contract in a different way, or not to perform at all, are valid only if reasonable in all the circumstances.* If liability is not excluded altogether but limited to a specified sum of money, it is necessary to consider the supplier's resources and whether he could have insured against claims for breach of contract: Section 11; *St. Albans D.C.* v. *I.C.L.*, below.

7.23   It is therefore still perfectly possible for business people to protect themselves against liability to consumers or to other businesses for breach of contract, but the terms on which they do so are subject to 'policing' by the courts in the light of what is fair and reasonable. A tour operator, for example, might properly disclaim liability for the economic consequences of bad weather or strike action or other such circumstances beyond his control, e.g. by a *force majeure* clause, below. He might also lawfully reject complaints unless made within a specified short time after return from holiday: *Sargant* v. *Citalia*, 1994.

7.24   One might suppose – though one can never be sure – that standard form exclusions of liability for all possible consequences of delay or other breach such as the following are far too wide to be reasonable – though still in current commercial use. 'Any time or date quoted by the company for delivery or performance is given and intended as an estimate only and the company shall not be liable in any manner whatsoever or for any loss or damage whatsoever for failure to deliver or perform within such time. No delay, failure or other default in respect of any delivery, performance, part delivery, part performance or instalment shall entitle the customer to treat the contract as repudiated'.

7.25 Suppliers of goods and services very commonly use *'force majeure'* or *'vis major'* clauses as a means of excusing long delays or possibly even complete failure to fulfil their contracts. The clause might say, for example: 'The seller shall not be responsible for any failure or delay on his part or on the part of his sub-contractors to perform the contract or any part thereof due to, or principally due to, acts of God, embargo, governmental act, fire, accident, war, riot, inclement weather, strikes, lockouts, trade disputes or labour troubles, breakdown of plant or machinery, interruptions to supplies or any other cause whatsoever (whether of the like nature to those specified above or not) beyond the control of the seller'. The effect might be to end the contract or suspend or vary it, depending on the wording of the clause. We note in passing that the expression 'Act of God' does not mean simply 'an accident'. English law defines it as an event which, if not wholly unpredictable, is at least beyond normal expectation and power of prevention, and generally disastrous in its consequences – a possibly somewhat unflattering view of Divine intervention in man's affairs.

7.26 It is not strictly necessary to specify wars, riots, embargoes (still sometimes picturesquely known as 'restraints of princes') etc. in *force majeure* clauses. This form is common: 'Without prejudice to the generality of any previous or subsequent exclusion or limitation of liability the company shall not be liable for any failure to fulfil any term of any transaction governed by these conditions if fulfilment has been delayed, hindered or prevented by any circumstances whatsoever which are not directly within the company's control and if the company is able to fulfil some but not all of the demands for any of its products it may allocate its available supplies amongst its customers, including its parent, subsidiary or associated companies in such manner as it in its absolute discretion considers fair'. But such a clause would still apply only to circumstances of the same degree of gravity as those listed in more traditionally worded clauses, and not to mere inconvenience or unprofitable alteration in the terms of trade. It has been held insufficient simply to refer to *'force majeure* conditions', because *force majeure* has no precise meaning in English law and needs at least some explanation in the contract: *British Electrical Industries* v. *Patley*, 1953. *Force majeure* clauses cannot in any case be invoked unless the problems are indeed beyond the supplier's control. So in *B & S Contracts* v. *Green*, 1984, the contractors were unable to rely on such a clause to protect themselves from liability for breach of contract caused by a strike, because they had not tried hard enough to resolve the strike. The related question of frustration of contracts is discussed in Chapter 12.

7.27 Tested under Section 3 of the Unfair Contract Terms Act, one might suppose that *force majeure* clauses meeting the above requirements would usually be found valid as between businessmen. Depending still more on a rigorous interpretation of their coverage and clarity, they would probably also be upheld as reasonable in consumer transactions – though much less often used in that context.

7.28   A more difficult question arising under Section 3 might be as to the efficacy of a typical clause like this: 'Since the company's policy is one of continuing improvement in the design, specification and manufacture of its products, and since all goods are agreed to be supplied subject to reasonable availability to the company of suitable material, the right is reserved without notice to substitute materials, components and units other than those mentioned in the contract.' Clearly a line has to be drawn somewhere. Minor discrepancies should be acceptable, particularly if they are in fact improvements, but the range of permissible variations could not reasonably extend to the provision of goods significantly different in quality, quantity or price.

7.29   Another common device is the use of 'anti-technicality' clauses to limit buyers' rights to repudiate or claim damages for breach of contract on what might be regarded as 'technical' or 'letter-of-the-law' grounds. Sellers might insist thereby on having an opportunity to try to repair or replace defective goods, which English law does not otherwise give them. A straightforward example is: 'After delivery the purchaser may only apply for cancellation of the contract if the vendor does not within a reasonable time take steps to eliminate or otherwise repair defects covered by the guarantee'. Where no personal danger or serious economic loss is involved, such clauses seem eminently reasonable on condition that the seller takes the necessary steps quickly and competently.

7.30   Section 4 says that *contract terms which require a consumer to indemnify another person against any liability incurred by that other for breach of contract or negligence are unenforceable unless reasonable in the circumstances.* Terms of this kind are widely used. When hiring out domestic electrical equipment, for example, the owner would usually be liable to anyone injured by defects in the equipment, but by such a clause might try to make the hirer reimburse him. Similarly in a vehicle hire contract we might find a term such as this: 'The hirer will indemnify the company against all fines, charges and other penalties incurred during the contract of hire and imposed upon the company by virtue of any statute.' Typical wording in a vehicle repair contract is: 'The customer hereby authorises any person duly authorised by the company to drive any such vehicle on the customer's behalf and at the customer's risk and responsibility'. It seems most unlikely that clauses of this kind could ever be regarded as reasonable in the consumer context, least of all those requiring indemnification against criminal liability. They might possibly be reasonable for the purposes of Sections 2 and 3 if it is merely a matter of deciding which of two businesses should be liable to the injured party, rather than denying all liability: *Thompson* v. *Lohan*, 1987.

7.31   Section 5 affects guarantees of consumer goods. A guarantee is defined as anything in writing which promises that defects will be made good. The section says that *guarantees are of no effect in so far as they exclude or restrict liability for loss or damage caused by the manufacturer's or supplier's negligence.* For these purposes therefore manufacturers cannot invoke the test of reasonableness in Section 2(2), above, which would otherwise apply. The section does not affect purchasers or hire-purchasers buying directly from manufacturers. Their rights as buyers are dealt with under Section 6.

iii. Defective goods

7.32   Section 6 is of fundamental importance. So far as consumers are concerned it brings to an end the previously almost unchallenged rights of sellers to exclude liability for defective goods, and for small businesses also it may provide a significant measure of protection. It deals with contract clauses or notices excluding the operation of Sections 12–15 of the Sale of Goods Act or equivalent sections of the Supply of Goods (Implied Terms) Act 1973 relating to hire-purchase transactions, as described in Chapter 6. The section says first that *no seller or owner can escape liability for failing to give a good title* to the goods sold or hire-purchased. Then as regards the other vital duties, the section draws a distinction between consumer and non-consumer transactions. *In a consumer transaction (see para. 7.22 above) any clause or notice excluding the requirements as to description, sample, satisfactory quality and reasonable fitness is void,* and moreover it is a criminal offence to use such a clause: Consumer Transactions (Restrictions on Statements) Order 1978. A blatant example of an illegal clause in current use is: 'The products are guaranteed in accordance with the Sale of Goods Act, but such guarantee will be void if the full price is not paid on the due date'. Another rule we should note here is that consumers' rights to examine goods before being held to have accepted them cannot be excluded: Section 35, Sale of Goods Act.

7.33   *In non-consumer contracts* – i.e. contracts between businesses – *duties as to description, sample, merchantability and fitness can be excluded, but only if the clause satisfies the test of reasonableness.* The consumer, in other words, is given more protection against the retailer than the retailer has against his wholesaler, or the wholesaler against the manufacturer. As between businesses, the effectiveness of any particular exclusion clause thus determines which party – retailer, wholesaler or manufacturer – should carry the burden of insurance against his customers' claims – or perhaps face ruin if he cannot meet them.

173

7.34   Section 7 makes the same provision as Section 6 as to exclusions of liability under the Supply of Goods and Services Act 1982 in relation to goods which are not bought or hire-purchased but hired or provided under contracts for services, e.g. repairs.

7.35   The key questions under Sections 6 and 7, therefore, are first as to whether the contract is a consumer or business transaction, and second as to the reasonableness or otherwise of exclusion clauses in business contracts. Section 12 says that a person 'deals as consumer' when he buys for private use, and not in the course of his own business, from a business seller. *Symmons* v. *Cook*, 1982, and *R & B* v. *U.D.T.* 1987, are instructive cases. Both involved purchases of cars by companies for the use of their directors, and both were held to be consumer contracts because they were 'occasional' purchases and car buying was not an integral part of either company's business. These decisions suggest a generally very liberal interpretation of the phrase – but in the end it is all a matter of the facts of the particular case, as with the corresponding question of whether a sale is 'in the course of a business' (as to which, *see* Chapter 6).

iv. The test of reasonableness

7.36   As to what is involved in the test of reasonableness in the foregoing Sections, Schedule 2 requires the court to consider in particular the parties' relative bargaining power, availability of other sources of supply, inducements such as a lower price in return for a higher risk, whether other suppliers used such exclusion clauses, whether the buyer had adequate notice of the clause, practicability of compliance with the clause (e.g. notification of complaint within seven days), and whether the goods were made to the buyer's own specifications. The burden of proving that the clause is reasonable is upon the seller or supplier who relies on it.

7.37   A leading case on the reasonableness of exclusion clauses in contracts between businesses is *Mitchell* v. *Finney Lock*, 1983. Merchants sold cabbage seed to a farmer. The crop was worthless because the seeds were not as described nor of merchantable quality. The conditions of sale excluded all express or implied conditions or warranties as to fitness and limited the seed merchants' liability for defective seeds to their original purchase price. The House of Lords held the clause valid at common law, as noted in para. 7.12, but unreasonable under the Act. In deciding that the clause was unreasonable, the judges took into account that a similar limitation of liability had been included in the terms of trade between seedsmen and farmers for many years, and although it had not been negotiated with the farmers, neither had their union objected to it. This evidence was 'equivocal', said their Lordships. More significant was the fact that when anything went wrong the seedsmen usually made payment above the strict contractual limits, apparently recognising that the clause was not fair. It was also found that the supply of the wrong seed was due to negligence, in that the seedsmen knew the kind they delivered could not be grown in the buyer's area, and that seedsmen could insure against crop failure without greatly increasing prices. The court thus decided 'without hesitation' that it would not be fair or reasonable to allow them to rely on the clause.

7.38 *Green* v. *Cade*, 1978, was another dispute over seeds. Under terms of sale agreed between seedsmen and farmers' representatives all complaints had to be made within three days of purchase and damages were limited to the contract price. The time limit was rejected as plainly unreasonable, but the court upheld the damage limitation clause because it had been collectively agreed and because the farmers had the choice of buying at a higher price seeds guaranteed free of disease.

7.39 If the kind of two-tier price system discussed in *Green* exists, a buyer of the cheaper range of goods or services may be said to buy at his own risk and to be bound by any exclusion clause. The basis of the supplier's liability in *Woodman* v. *Photo Trade*, 1981, was his failure to provide an optional alternative service, as recommended by his own trade association, which would have been more expensive but more reliable. One might nonetheless question the wisdom of encouraging differentials in prices and levels of service for the same commodity. But if the choice is offered it must be a real and conspicuous one, not just a minor detail on the contract form: *Woodman*.

7.40 In *St. Albans D.C.* v. *I.C.L.*, 1995, the local authority bought a computer and related software from I.C.L. to work out local tax liabilities. A fault in the system led to the computer overestimating the numbers of taxpayers, which left the authority with a shortfall of £1.3 million. In defending itself against the authority's claim for this sum, I.C.L. relied on a clause in the contract limiting its liability to £100,000 – although it was insured for losses up to £50 million. Mr. Justice Scott Baker said the parties' bargaining positions had been unequal. The authority was 'over a barrel' in negotiating with I.C.L. because of government pressures. In the circumstances I.C.L.'s clause was not fair or reasonable. 'On whom is it better that a loss of this size should fall – a local authority or an international computer company?' the judge asked. 'The latter is well able to insure, and in this case was insured, and pass on the premium cost to the customers. If the loss is to fall the other way it will ultimately be borne by the local population, either by increased taxation or reduced services. I do not think it unreasonable that he who stands to make a profit should carry the risk'.

7.41 *White Cross Equipment* v. *Farrell*, 1983, on the other hand, is a good illustration of the grounds on which a court might uphold an exclusion clause. The plaintiffs sold a machine called a waste compactor to the defendant salvage disposal operator. They gave a six month guarantee, but

175

excluded all liability thereafter. The machine began giving trouble a little beyond the guarantee period and so the defendant refused to make any further payments. His argument that the exclusion clause was invalid was rejected by the judge for the following reasons:

7.42   'These parties were very much at arms' length. I have no doubt that the defendant could have bargained away the plaintiff's terms had he so wished. If the plaintiffs had not been willing to give up [this] condition the defendant could undoubtedly have gone elsewhere. It is to be noted, secondly, that the plaintiffs do undertake to replace parts or the entire machine if necessary and, apart from that, to repair or replace parts which are defective, due to workmanship or design, subject to certain safeguards. That undertaking is good for six months which should, in the ordinary course of events, be ample time for any major deficiency to emerge. Thirdly, once a compactor is in use, it can be subjected to an almost infinite variety of conditions of use and abuse, both as to the waste which is fed into it, the operators who are using it and the conditions under which it is being used. These considerations, in my view, amply justify the plaintiffs saying to a purchaser: "After six months you are on your own as far as defects of design or workmanship are concerned." I have borne in mind carefully that this is not a case where the parties could easily insure and, indeed, insurance against breaches of the implied condition of suitability or a representation as to performance would not be a practical proposition at all. So I have viewed this matter simply as a question of allocating risks between two commercial parties of equal bargaining power; and having taken into consideration all the circumstances, I find that the requirements of reasonableness are in fact satisfied.'

7.43   We move on now to Section 8. This section says that *contract terms excluding or restricting liability for pre-contractual statements or representations will be upheld only if they are reasonable.* There is a similar provision in the Unfair Terms in Consumer Contracts Regulations, below. Such clauses are often used to exclude liability for things said in advertisements and sales literature, or by over-enthusiastic salesmen. Examples range from optimistic assertions as to the company's policy of continuing improvement and resultant changes in specifications to terse rejections of all previous commitments: 'All specifications, drawings and particulars of weights and dimensions submitted with our tender are approximate only, and the descriptions and illustrations contained in our catalogues, price lists and other advertisement matter are intended merely to present a general idea of the goods described therein, and none of these shall form part of the contract.' Another possibility is to say in the contract form that no representation shall be of any effect unless written and signed.

7.44   In *McGrath* v. *Shah*, 1989, the device of an 'entire agreement' or 'integration' clause was used to exclude all previous representations. The written contract stated that all the terms agreed between the parties were contained in that one document. The court held that this provision effectively prevented any reference to or reliance on anything previously said or written, and accordingly that there was no scope for arguing whether or not the clause itself was reasonable under Section 8. The decision seems to go a long way to defeat the purpose of the section. Cases to the contrary include *Alman* v. *Associated Newspapers*, 1980, and *Witter* v. *T.B.P. Industries*, 1994. Where Section 8 applies, its effect will probably be to uphold such exclusion clauses in business contracts since professional parties should know of their existence and intention. Consumers may be less aware of their significance, and correspondingly more effort might be needed to bring the point to their attention – as indicated above in relation to common law rules on notice. In either case the court will have to guard against the possibility of fraud or misrepresentation (Chapter 11). We have seen that express oral promises will override written standard forms – *Evans*, above – and that clauses which assert falsehoods are unenforceable – *Lowe*, above. We note also that a seller or supplier may not be allowed to deny that he has made any representation in the first place. In *Cremdean* v. *Nash*, 1977, for instance, a buyer was able to claim for a pre-contractual misrepresentation as to the size of the property despite an accompanying clause that 'accuracy is not guaranteed and the purchaser must satisfy himself' as to the particulars of the property.

7.45 The remaining sections of the Act can be dealt with more shortly. Section 9 says that if an exclusion clause is subject to the test of reasonableness it remains so whether or not the contract as a whole has been broken or repudiated. Section 10 stops suppliers from evading liability by collateral or secondary contracts (and so, for example, a creditor cannot escape his liability under Section 75 of the Consumer Credit Act – *see* para. 3.62 – by reference to a term in the contract between debtor and dealer). *Tudor Grange* v. *Citibank*, 1991, is an important case on Section 10 and the scope of the Act generally. The plaintiffs had agreed to release the defendants from 'all claims, demands and causes of action prior to this date', but now said the Act made their agreement invalid. The High Court held that the Act affected only clauses modifying future liabilities, not past claims or settlements such as this. Sections 11 and 12, already noted, refer respectively to liability to insure and the meaning of 'dealing as consumer'.

7.46 Section 13 explains that terms admitting liability but only on onerous or restrictive conditions, or restricting any right or remedy or penalise a person for exercising his rights, are still within the Act. *Stewart Gill* v. *Myer*, 1992, is a notable case on the operation of this section. The seller's contract included a term which stopped the buyer from withholding payment 'for any reason whatsoever'. The Court of Appeal said that the term fell within the scope of Section 13, and that it was therefore subject to the test of reasonableness laid down in Section 3. This particular term was held to be self-evidently unreasonable. Clauses limiting amounts of compensation, charging for repairs, requiring complaints to be made within very short periods, or making the supplier's decision final, would also come within this section, which, however, upholds written agreements to submit to independent arbitration. Section 14 defines various terms used in the Act, including 'business', which includes a profession and the activities of any government department or local or public authority. A 'notice' is an announcement, written or spoken, and any other communication or pretended communication. Sections 15–25 repeat all the foregoing provisions in terms appropriate to the law of Scotland.

7.47   The remaining sections apply to the UK as a whole. Section 26 says that the Act does not affect international contracts, i.e. contracts for the sale of goods made by parties in different States, under which goods are to be carried from one State to another, or offer and acceptance take place in different States, or the goods are to be delivered to a State other than that where the contract was made. By Section 27 the Act does not apply either where parties who would not otherwise be bound by English law have voluntarily adopted that system – but the Act does apply where another country's law has been chosen simply in order to evade English law (*see also* para. 5.39). Section 28 permits exclusion of liability in contracts of carriage by sea where neither the port of departure or arrival are in the UK. Section 29 says that the Act does not affect terms required or approved by statute or treaty. A contract term or notice approved by a 'competent authority' – a court, arbitrator, government department or public authority – is presumed to satisfy the test of reasonableness. Code of practice adopted by certain trades and industries and approved by the Office of Fair Trading might therefore confer a degree of immunity which could otherwise be forbidden.

7.48   Schedule 1 of the Act is of considerable importance in making further exceptions to the scope of the Act. The Schedule provides that Sections 2 to 4 do not apply to contracts of insurance (in contrast with the Unfair Terms in Consumer Contracts Regulations, below), contracts relating to the creation, transfer or ending of interests in land, patent rights, copyrights or other intellectual property rights, formation or dissolution of companies or partnerships or their constitutions or the rights and duties of their members. Contracts of marine salvage or towage, charter parties (hirings) of ships or hovercraft and contracts for the carriage of goods therein are covered by Section 2(1) (annulling terms which exclude liability for death or injury caused by negligence), but otherwise Sections 2, 3, 4 and 7 only apply to these particular contracts in favour of consumers. Section 2(1) and (2) does not extend to contracts of employment except in favour of employees. Schedule 2 lays down guidelines on reasonableness, as discussed earlier.

v. Unfair Terms in Consumer Contracts Regulations

7.49   We turn now to consider more fully the Unfair Terms in Consumer Contracts Regulations 1994: *see* Appendix 1. As we noted earlier, the Regulations are both wider and narrower than the 1977 Act. They seek to cover unfair consumer contract terms in general, and not merely exclusion clauses, but unlike the Act they do not affect non-contractual clauses. The two sets of rules seem to conflict with each other, in that clauses declared void by the Act are still subject to a test of fairness under the Regulations – but presumably this general rule would give way to the specific prohibitions in the Act.

7.50   The Regulations apply to 'pre-formulated standard terms' – i.e., terms which have not been individually negotiated – in contracts between individual consumers and sellers of goods or suppliers of goods or services. 'Services' appears to include contracts affecting land, such as those made with estate agents. Terms clearly and intelligibly defining the nature of the goods or services in question are excluded, as is the issue of the fairness or otherwise of the price: Regulations 2 and 3. Schedule 1 of the Regulations excludes also contracts relating to employment, succession rights under family law, company and partnership incorporation and organisation, and terms required by law.

7.51   When is a contract term 'unfair'? Regulation 4 answers this basic question in language more familiar to Continental lawyers than their English counterparts. A term is unfair if 'contrary to the requirement of good faith [it] causes a significant imbalance in the parties' rights and obligations . . . to the detriment of the consumer'. Fairness in general depends on the nature of the goods or services and the circumstances at the time the contract was made, and on the more detailed guidance given by Schedules 2 and 3, below.

7.52   Schedule 2 of the Regulations says that a decision as to good faith turns on the bargaining power of the parties, whether the goods or services were supplied to the consumer's special order, and any inducements given to the consumer. Schedule 3 gives many examples of terms which may be held unfair, which show very clearly that the Regulations are much more far-reaching than the Unfair Contract Terms Act. As well as exclusion clauses of the kind already covered by the Act, the list, which is not exhaustive, includes terms entitling sellers or suppliers to keep consumers' pre-payments in certain circumstances; sellers' or suppliers' rights unilaterally to interpret or end the contract; rights to end contracts of indefinite duration without reasonable notice; terms binding consumers although they have had no real opportunity to understand them; limits on consumers' rights to take legal action or terms obliging them to go to arbitration, and the like. The rights of suppliers of financial services to end or vary certain contracts on due notice are not affected.

7.53 The remaining rules are shortly as follows. Regulation 6 requires written contracts with consumers to be in plain and intelligible language. It should follow that 'gobbledegook' – trade or legal jargon – could of itself invalidate a contract. Regulation 7 says that where contracts have close connections with European Union States, the Regulations will apply despite terms invoking the laws of non-member States. Regulation 8 obliges the UK Director of Fair Trading to consider complaints about consumer contract terms in general use. If he finds them unfair, he may then seek undertakings from the users, or an injunction from the High Court forbidding further use of such terms. We note here that the original Directive enabled organisations officially recognised as representing consumer interests to take action as under Regulation 8. This provision could and surely should have been used to enhance the work of the Consumers' Association, as well as giving new powers to the Director General.

7.54 It will be seen that the Regulations pose several interesting questions of interpretation and application, not least as regards the good faith rule. In particular, what would be the effect of the good faith rule on exclusion clauses already subject to a test of reasonableness under the Unfair Contract Terms Act? The two tests are evidently not exactly the same – since good faith involves a wider inquiry as to honesty and openness – but one might hope that the courts would interpret them to give the same result where both apply. In the long term, the Regulations must greatly influence the acceptance of good faith as a general principle of English contract law.

vi. Common law and statute

7.55 These then are the main statutory controls of exclusion clauses and other unfair terms in commercial and consumer contracts. Between them they provide much more effective protection than the rules of common law. But the common law may still be relevant and useful. A consumer might argue, for example, that he did not have reasonable notice of the existence of an exclusion clause and that on that common law ground alone he should not be bound by it. If his argument was successful it would not then be necessary to look at the Unfair Contract Terms Act or the new Regulations at all. The questions posed by the legislation, as to whether this particular kind of clause is void, or valid only if fair or reasonable – and, if so, whether it is indeed fair or reasonable in the circumstances, would not arise for decision.

B. Other unfair contract terms

7.56 As we have said in Chapter 5 on the question of implied terms, there is not yet any overall requirement of fair dealing in English contract law. The law's basic attitude is that it is for the parties themselves to decide on the advantages or disadvantages of their bargain. In *Brodie Marshall* v.

Sharer, 1988, for instance, the court upheld an estate agent's contract entitling him to commission even though the purchaser of the property was found by the seller himself. In recent years, however, the law has come to recognise more clearly that certain kinds of contracts are so obviously unfair and exploitive as to be unacceptable. The Unfair Contract Terms Act and the 1994 Regulations, above, are the main examples of interventionism, but as we have seen they are largely concerned with exclusion clauses. Another statutory development is in Section 139 of the Consumer Credit Act 1974, which enables the court to set aside 'extortionate' credit transactions, though the courts' apparently very limited understanding of what is extortionate means that the power has been very little used. We should mention also the Consumer Arbitration Agreements Act 1988; a measure intended to stop arbitration clauses in consumer contracts from taking away consumers' rights to go to court. A major Act from Australia, the Contracts Review Act 1980, is noted below.

7.57   Equally interesting are the potentially far-reaching developments slowly taking place in the common law. We note first *Lloyd's Bank* v. *Bundy*, 1975, a leading case on abuse of bargaining power. The facts were that an old man anxious to help his son's business mortgaged all his own land – a farm – to his bank in return for a loan to his son. When the son's business failed the bank sought to foreclose, i.e. to take over the farm. The Court of Appeal rejected the bank's claim. Although the terms of the loan were clear, the contract was unenforceable because of the relationship of trust which existed between the bank and its elderly customer, under which the bank should have ensured that he had independent advice before risking the loss of all his assets.

7.58   Lord Denning derived this novel principle from various common law rules protecting weaker parties such as children and patients against 'undue influence' by parents, doctors, etc. The principle was that of 'inequality of bargaining power', under which English law gave relief to a person who without independent advice entered into a 'very unfair' contract because of his own needs and the pressures of the other party. The rule did not presuppose any wrongdoing by the stronger party, nor necessarily his domination of the weaker. 'One who is in extreme need may knowingly consent to a most improvident bargain, solely to relieve the straits in which he finds himself. Again, I do not mean to suggest that every transaction is saved by independent advice. But the absence of it may prove fatal'. Mere inequality of bargaining power, then, is not a sufficient ground for invoking this rule; it is necessary to show exploitation or manipulation of another person's ignorance or inability to protect his own interests. It follows that the duty found in *Bundy* will apply only rarely: *Barclays* v. *Khaira*, 1991; *National Westminster Bank* v. *Morgan*, 1985.

7.59   An illustration is *Schroder* v. *Macauley*, 1974, where the House of Lords recognised the principle of 'protection of those whose bargaining power is weak against being forced by those whose bargaining power is stronger to enter into bargains that are unconscionable'. In *Davis* v. *W.E.A. Records*, 1975, Lord Denning likewise criticised the manager of a 'pop group' who had taken the copyright of the group's music (if that is the appropriate word) for a consideration of a few pennies for each work, and had undertaken no obligation in return. He said it was unconscionable that the group should have agreed to such terms because of their economic dependence and without legal advice. To the contrary was the case of *Panayiotou* v. *Sony Entertainment*, 1994, where a pop singer failed in his attempt to set aside a recording contract because, as the High Court found, he had been property advised as to the terms and their effects.

7.60   There is clearly a possibility of abuse of power in the employment context in particular. Many conditions of employment are regulated by Act of Parliament, but by no means all. There are, for example, no general rules laying down minimum rates of pay or maximum hours of work. The common law has made no significant contribution here. It will not enforce 'conditions of servitude', but we cannot say with any certainty how that rule might apply today. The common law's 'rule of reason' approach to contracts in restraint of trade is noted in Chapter 11.

7.61   The second important case-law development in contract law in general is in *Interfoto* v. *Stiletto Programmes*, 1987 – a case with immediate effects on the drafting of business contracts. It concerned a two week contract of hire of certain photographic transparencies. The delivery note sent with the transparencies said, under the heading 'Conditions', printed prominently in capital letters, that if the transparencies were not returned on the due day the hirers would be charged a 'holding fee' of £5 per day for each transparency. It was very important for the owners that the transparencies should be returned on time, since they were their stock in trade. The hirers did not read the delivery note, and were two weeks late in returning the goods. They then received from the owners a bill for holding fees of nearly £4,000, which they rejected as unreasonable (though there is no rule of English law requiring prices to be reasonable).

7.62   The Court of Appeal said it had to be recognised that most people did not trouble to read printed contract forms. For this reason the Court held, following *Spurling*, above, that *if one condition in a set of printed conditions is particularly onerous or unusual the party relying on it must show he has fairly brought that condition to the other side's attention.* In the present case, said the Court, the owners had done nothing of the kind, and so the holding fee requirement never became part of the contract. The Court granted the owners a much reduced award for the hirers' breach of contract, based on other agencies' holding fees of £3.50 per transparency per week.

7.63   One would accept that as between business and consumer there could well be a duty to give specific notice of onerous terms – though even that is something of a novelty in English law – but it is more than a little surprising to find this duty imposed as between businesses dealing with each other on equal terms, familiar with the use of standard forms and presumably expected to read them. Can a businessman now say he did not trouble to read another's terms and so should not be bound by them? What sorts of terms or charges are so onerous that they should be especially emphasised on the contract form? (*See Brodie*, para. 7.56, where *Interfoto* was considered but not applied.) There is no immediate answer to these questions, but it will be seen that the case suggests further possibilities of judicial intervention on grounds of procedural fairness.

7.64   *Interfoto* is a case of interest to the comparative lawyer also, since one of the judges, Lord Justice Bingham, invoked Continental principles in support of his decision – a rare event in English practice – but perhaps a foretaste? His judgment included the following instructive comparison of methods and attitudes: 'In many civil law systems, and perhaps in most legal systems outside the common law world, the law of obligations recognises and enforces an overriding principle that in making and carrying out contracts parties should act in good faith. This does not simply mean that they should not deceive each other, a principle which any legal system must recognise; its effect is perhaps most aptly conveyed by such metaphorical colloquialisms as "playing fair", "coming clean" or "putting one's cards face upwards on the table". It is in essence a principle of fair and open dealing. In such a forum it might, I think, be held on the facts of this case that the plaintiffs were under a duty in all fairness to draw the defendants' attention specifically to the high price payable if the transparencies were not returned in time and, when the 14 days had expired, to point out to the defendants the high cost of continued failure to return them. English law has, characteristically, committed itself to no such overriding principle but has developed piecemeal solutions in response to demonstrated problems of unfairness.'

7.65   The absence of any such 'overriding principle' to inform litigants and guide judges is, as mentioned earlier, a ground of criticism of the common law. It is encouraging then to see developments within the Commonwealth seeking to remedy this deficiency. Of particular interest here is the Contracts Review Act of 1980 in New South Wales. The Act enables the courts to invalidate or vary 'unjust' contracts – defined as those which were 'unconscionable, harsh or oppressive' at the time they were made. In making its order a court must take into account the public interest in the observance of contracts, and factors such as inequality of bargaining power. A party who makes a contract in the course of his business cannot claim the protection of the Act. The fundamental importance of the Act was acknowledged in the judgment in *West* v. *AGC Ltd*, 1986: 'It is revolutionary legislation whose evident purpose is to overcome the common law's failure to provide a comprehensive doctrinal framework to deal with "unjust" contracts. Very likely its provisions signal the end of much of classical contract theory in New South Wales'. The Act was applied by the N.S.W. Supreme Court in *Baltic Shipping* v. *Dillon*, 1993, so as to annul a middle-aged widow's settlement for less than $5,000 of a claim for injury, shock and breach of contract worth more than $50,000.

7.66   In America, Section 2–302 of the Uniform Commercial Code gives the courts the power to annul contracts in whole or part if they find 'the contract or any clause of the contract to have been unconscionable at the time it was made'. The concept of unconscionability was discussed at length by the Court of Appeal for the District of Columbia in *Williams* v. *Walker-Thomas Furniture Co.*, 1965 (where a contract for instalment sales of household goods, with each item subject to repossession until all items were paid for, was held void). Unconscionability was said to turn on the absence of meaningful choice for one party and terms unreasonably favourable to the other, and not merely on inequality of bargaining power. 'Did each party to the contract, considering his obvious education or lack of it, have a reasonable opportunity to understand the terms of the contract, or were the important terms hidden in a maze of fine print and minimised by deceptive sales practices? Ordinarily, one who signs an agreement without full knowledge of its terms might be held to assume the risk that he has entered into a one-sided bargain. But when a party of little bargaining power, and hence little real choice, signs a commercially unreasonable contract with little or no knowledge of its terms, it is hardly likely that his consent, or even an objective manifestation of his consent, was ever given to all the terms. In such a case the usual rule that the terms of the agreement are not to be questioned, should be abandoned, and the court should consider whether the terms of the agreement are so unfair that enforcement should be withheld.'

Danish law

7.67   English common law methods of controlling exclusion clauses and the like are also used by Danish courts as an indirect way of controlling the content of agreements to secure fair and reasonable outcomes. The more burdensome the contract term the more severe the requirements for reasonable notice and the more restrictive the judicial interpretation.

7.68   Furthermore, under Article 36 of the Contracts Act any agreement may be directly and openly set aside, in whole or in part, if it is unreasonable (though the courts tend to prefer the more traditional, covert approach, above). What is reasonable depends on 'the circumstances at the time of the conclusion of the agreement, the content of the agreement, and later developments'. More specific statutory provision has been made in a number of areas where one-sided contract terms have been particularly misused, e.g. as regards the rules on consumer sales in the Sale of Goods Act. Such legislation contains detailed rules maintaining standards of performance and remedies in case of breach which cannot be excluded. The Contracts Act was amended in 1995 to implement the EU Directive on Unfair Terms in Consumer Contracts – though existing Danish law gives consumers significantly better protection.

Dutch law

7.69 Articles 6.231–47 of the Dutch Civil Code regulate the use of general conditions in contracts, i.e., suppliers' standard written terms. These conditions will be void if a supplier does not give the other party reasonable notice of them, which he may do by giving him a copy of them or by telling him they are available and will be sent on request. General conditions will be annulled if unreasonably onerous. Articles 6.236–7 contain two black lists of the types of clauses seen as unreasonably onerous for consumers. They include clauses enabling the seller to compel acceptance of a price increase within three months of making the contract, and clauses 'materially limiting' his obligations or entitling him to perform the contract in a materially different way. Terms limiting or excluding rights to compensation are likewise voidable. In practice the lists may be important also in purely commercial contracts. These rules have not been amended to take account of the EU Directive on Unfair Consumer Contract Terms, but the courts will apply Dutch law in conformity with it.

7.70 A further important way of controlling contractual abuses is provided by Articles 6.240–3 of the Code. These rules enable both consumer and business organisations to seek injunctions against unreasonable clauses, whether or not of a kind specified in the Code. They cannot, however, claim damages.

7.71 Before the new rules were introduced, the courts had developed various ways of trying to solve the problem posed by unfair terms. At first they applied doctrines similar to the English rules of interpretation – as in the ticket cases, the requirement that the document appears as a contractual document, fraud or misrepresentation invalidating the clause – and the like. From the case of *Saladin* v. *Hollandsche Bank-Unie NV*, NJ 1967, 261, the courts took the more significant step of applying the good faith rule in the old Code, and so were able to exert more open and direct control over the terms themselves.

French law

7.72   As in England, exclusion clauses and other unfair or 'abusive' terms are regulated in France both by the efforts of judges and by the legislature. The judges will intervene if the weaker party was apparently unaware of the existence of an exclusion clause in a standard form contract. Even if a contract is signed an exclusion clause will be ineffective unless clearly readable: Cass. Civ., May 1943. The *Cour de Cassation* has held that an exclusion clause mentioned in the body of the contract but stated in full below, the parties' signatures or on the back of the agreement is unenforceable: Civ. 3 May 1979.

7.73   Provisions in separate or supplementary documents are not necessarily void, but the supplier must show the weaker party knew about them before contracting. On occasion, clauses in documents which he received subsequently – flight tickets, invoices, etc. – have been invalidated: Civ. 15 November 1982. A notice exempting a hotel from liability for theft on the premises which was exhibited in the reception area was held ineffective by the court in Lyons, 12 June 1950. Previous dealings between the parties are relevant in all such cases.

7.74   To enforce a clause, the supplier must show not only that the other party should reasonably have been aware of it, but that it was expressed in clear and unambiguous terms: Article 1162 of the Civil Code. If these requirements are fulfilled any agreement signed by the parties will then generally be enforceable subject to the following rules, despite possible unfairness in its terms.

7.75   More specific provision has been made by statute to deal with particular types of agreement, e.g. insurance (Act of 30 July 1930); leases (1 September 1948); building (4 January 1978; Articles 1792–5); carriage of passengers by sea (18 June 1966). This latter measure would make terms like the Normandy Ferries' conditions cited in para. 7.2 unenforceable. The Act of 10 January 1978 – the *Loi Scrivener* – gives the government very wide powers to issue decrees controlling unfair clauses. A decree of 24 March 1978 forbids clauses excluding or limiting consumers' rights against sellers who are in breach of contract, and also clauses entitling sellers unilaterally to change the characteristics of the goods or services contracted for. Subsequent case law has extended the application of this decree to abusive clauses in general. The second decree, of 22 December 1987, establishes a model standard form for contracts of guarantee and after-sales service relating to domestic electrical equipment.

7.76   A Commission (*Commission des clauses abusives*) was created by the Act of 1978 to make recommendations on the contents of consumer contracts. It has issued some 30 sets of recommendations which, while not obligatory, are usually followed by traders and trade associations.

7.77 The Act of 5 January 1988 enables approved consumer organisations to ask the court to forbid the use of particular forms of words in traders' standard form contracts with consumers. Such organisations may intervene in a case after it has been begun privately, and even though no specific decree has been issued under the *Loi Scrivener*. All these measures have now been incorporated in the Consumer Code of 1994.

7.78 In 1995 the EU Directive on Unfair Terms in Consumer Contracts was transposed into French law: Act no. 95–96. The text of the Directive has been modified in the interests of consumers. It is not necessary to prove that an unfair term is contrary to good faith, nor is any distinction drawn in the new Act between standard forms and terms individually negotiated.

German law

7.79 German courts have intervened to control unfair contract terms since about 1900, basing their jurisdiction on the general clauses of the BGB – e.g., Article 138, which makes a contract void if one person exploits another's needs or weakness to gain an 'obviously disproportionate' pecuniary advantage, or the good faith requirement of Article 242. In 1976 the Standard Contract Terms Act (AGBG) was introduced, again containing a general clause on the requirement of fairness which has been the basis of further case law development on the merits of particular clauses. As well as the general clause are two lists, a 'black' one and a 'grey' one on terms in consumer contracts either prohibited or only allowed on certain conditions. Consumer associations can take cases to court if they think particular clauses are unfair. In effect the test is one of reasonableness, which includes considerations of notice and the like as under the common law. Any lack of clarity as to the supplier's obligations is also important. So, for example, deceptive statements of interest rates have been declared void.

7.80 The German Act has a broader scope than the 1977 UK legislation, since it is not limited to exclusion clauses. It does not make the same distinction as in Section 2 of the Unfair Contract Terms Act between death or injury and economic loss caused by negligence; para. 7.18. Under the German Act liability cannot be excluded in either case for damage caused intentionally or by gross negligence. A Bill is currently (1995) before Parliament to give effect to the EU Directive on Unfair Terms. The Directive is wider than the AGBG in affecting clauses used in only one contract.

187

7.81   *Force majeure* clauses will protect a seller against failure to deliver, unless he has himself already been supplied with the goods in question. Changes in the method of performance of the contract or in the price are not totally forbidden, but regulated by the court. A seller cannot exclude a buyer's right to repudiate the contract or pay a lower price if the goods are defective and not repaired, but under the contract may require the buyer to submit the goods for repair before he can reject them.

7.82   The German court would decide cases like *Green*, para. 7.39, in a different way. The argument that a lower price could justify a limitation of liability has been discussed but rejected. Pre-contractual statements are outside the Standard Contract Terms Act unless they become part of the contract. Contrary to Section 26 of the Unfair Contract Terms Act, para. 7.46, the German Act may apply to international contracts. The courts can thereby control choice of law clauses in business contracts.

7.83   Cases where abuse of bargaining power has led to a contract becoming unenforceable, such as in *Lloyd's Bank* and *Schroder*, paras. 7.50, 7.52, are paralleled in German law by an important case decided by the Constitutional Court in 1994, NJW 36. The Court annulled a DM 100,000 guarantee given to a bank by the debtor's 21 year old daughter, a factory worker. It was held that she had not been adequately advised, and that freedom of contract had to be regulated where there was unequal bargaining power. It is of particular interest that this case was brought by a consumer association. As regards consumer credit contracts, the courts have said that interest rates must not be more than double the bank rate at the time the contract was made.

Italian law

7.84   Subject to the familiar difficulty of distinguishing between clauses limiting obligations and those limiting liability for breach of such obligations, Article 1229 of the Italian Civil Code declares void all clauses excluding or limiting liability for deliberate breach of contract or gross negligence – *culpa gravis*. Ordinary negligence or other breach of contract – *culpa levis* – may, however, be excused, unless the obligation affects some basic question of public policy and in particular public health. The 1988 Product Liability Act forbids exclusion clauses in that area: Article 12.

7.85   Apart from these measures the protection afforded to consumers by the law's general conditions of contract has been limited and unsatisfactory. The supplier has needed only to ensure that his standard terms are clearly stated and known by or accessible to the buyer: Article 1341. This Article specifies a number of unfair clauses – *clausole vessatorie* – including exclusion clauses, which are effective only if signed by the buyer – but that is no protection for a buyer without bargaining power. Ambiguous or uncertain clauses are interpreted *contra proferentem*: Article 1370. Consumers are now much more effectively protected by the EU Directive on Unfair Terms in Consumer Contracts. The Directive has been accepted as Italian law without the need for further legislation.

Spanish law

7.86   The Spanish Civil Code does not expressly regulate exclusion clauses, but several of its general provisions are applicable. Thus, Article 1105 excludes liability for the consequences of *force majeure*. 'No-one is liable for events which could not have been foreseen or which, though foreseen, were unavoidable'. Another general rule affecting exclusion clauses is in Article 1288, which says that the interpretation of obscure clauses should not favour the party responsible for the obscurity. We note also the principle in Article 1256 that the validity and execution of contracts should not depend on the decision of one contracting party.

7.87   The Law of 19 July 1984 for the protection of consumers and users regulates the use of 'general contract clauses' or standard forms by businesses. Under Article 10 such clauses must conform with good faith and fairness as between the parties – *justo equilibrio de las contraprestaciones*. Unacceptable or 'abusive' clauses include those imposing disproportionate losses on consumers. Article 10 stops suppliers from excluding all liability to consumers and in particular from avoiding liability 'relating to the usefulness or essential purpose of the product or service'. Clauses forbidden by the Act are null and void, and may invalidate the whole contract. The full effect of the Act has not yet been tested. It has in any case been modified by the Law of 6 July 1994, giving effect to the European Directive on product liability. Exclusions or limitations of liability under this Act are void.

7.88   As regards contracts of insurance, the Law of 8 October 1980 says that the general conditions must not have a 'character unfair or harmful to those insured', and the terms must be 'clear and precise'. Exclusion clauses must be specially emphasised and accepted in writing.

Swedish law

7.89   Article 36 of the Swedish Contract Act 1915 enables the courts to alter or annul contracts containing unfair terms, whether exclusion clauses or other types of clause. Under the Consumer Contract Terms Act 1994 and the Business Contract Terms Act 1994 the court may decide that a certain type of condition is unfair and prohibit a business from using it in the future. Cases under the Consumer Contract Terms Act 1994 are normally brought to court by a *'konsumentombudsman'*(consumer ombudsman) who is employed by the State. A prohibition does not affect the relationship between the businessman and other contracting party, but the decisions form a catalogue of terms which are *per se* unfair and a basis for judgment when a party to a contract wants the contract to be adjusted or put aside under Article 36 of the Contract Act. On principle, in contracts between businesses it is not unfair to exclude liability for consequential loss: NJA 1979 s.483.

7.90   Examples of terms which have been considered unfair are those which are not in conformity with mandatory legislation, and terms which give misleading information about consumers' legal rights. In a consumer contract the seller may not exclude his liability for new goods by an exclusion clause that the goods are sold 'as is'. Even in contracts between businesses, a person who sells goods 'as is' must disclose known defects, and the goods must not be substantially inferior in quality to that reasonably expected by the buyer: Article 19, Sale of Goods Act. Compulsory arbitration clauses in consumer contracts have been considered unfair. Clauses in consumer contracts entitling the seller to alter the price are generally not accepted unless the seller himself has no control over price increases. In contracts between businessmen, price alteration clauses are acceptable if the index or cause of price alteration does in fact reflect a higher cost for the seller.

Chapter 8

Risk

Ownership

8.1   The problem before us in this chapter is to find the precise moment in time at which according to English law the risk of accidental loss or damage, or of the consequences of insolvency on one side or the other, passes from seller to buyer. A simple and generally agreeable answer would be the principle that risk depends on possession of the goods, and therefore passes to the buyer when he takes delivery of them, or on tender of delivery. This is the American view, as expressed in Chapter 2 of the Uniform Commercial Code, and that of Article 69 of the Vienna Convention on the International Sale of Goods, but unfortunately not that of English law. The basic principle of English law, stated in Section 20 of the Sale of Goods Act 1979, amended by the Sale of Goods (Amendment) Act 1995, is that whoever is the *owner* of the goods at any given time must bear the risk of things going wrong – and of course ownership does not depend on physical possession. In order to discuss problems of risk, therefore, we must also consider the question of ownership.

8.2   The rules as to transfer of ownership are set out in a commendably clear sequence of ideas in Sections 16–20 of the UK Sale of Goods Act. We should say a word first, however, about the language used in these sections. They refer to 'the transfer of property as between seller and buyer'. In ordinary English usage the word 'property' refers to something tangible – these goods, or this piece of land – but in the Act the expression signifies rights of ownership, as in 'the property in the goods'. We note also that the rights in question are those arising between seller and buyer, which are not necessarily equally valid against the world at large. The possible difficulties over third parties' rights to goods, as where A, the owner, sells to B but before delivering the goods to him sells them again to C, are dealt with in Sections 21–26 of the Act, but are not relevant to the present inquiry.

8.3   It is very important to observe that the law sees problems of risk and ownership as quite separate from those of alleged breach of contract. The fact that the buyer has become owner does not of itself affect his right to repudiate the contract or claim damages for goods which are not in conformity with the contract, as explained in Chapter 5. If he is entitled to repudiate, ownership then reverts to the seller (though the contract might make the buyer responsible for returning the goods at his own risk). In contrast, Article 2–510 of the American Uniform Commercial Code seeks to ensure that a buyer in these circumstances will not be at risk even temporarily. It provides that risk of loss remains on the seller until the defect is cured or the goods are accepted.

8.4   Section 16 of the Sale of Goods Act, amended in 1995, begins the inquiry as to the transfer of ownership of goods by saying that *ownership cannot pass unless and until the goods in question are 'ascertained'*. With one exception, below, goods are ascertained when one particular article or collection of articles can be identified or earmarked as the unique subject-matter of the contract. So, for example, a buyer who orders a new Model X car, as one of a type or species of goods, cannot become owner at least until he and the seller have expressly or impliedly agreed upon the one specific car which is to be his (*see* rule 5, Section 18, below). The exception to the rule, introduced in 1995, is that goods may also be ascertained or specific if they form a specified fraction or percentage of a larger bulk of identified and agreed upon goods from which they have not yet been separated. Thus an order for 50 tons out of a specific cargo of 100 tons could result in a passing of ownership of 50 tons, in the circumstances and with the consequences discussed below.

8.5   The effects of making risk depend on ownership are largely a matter of chance. Sometimes the buyer benefits; sometimes the seller – or his creditors. In *Healy* v. *Howlett*, 1917, for instance, a buyer in England ordered 20 boxes of fish from a seller in Ireland. The seller shipped 190 boxes, instructing the carrier to take out 20 boxes at a certain railway station for this particular buyer. By the time the boxes were taken out for him the whole consignment had gone bad. Since the fish had gone bad before the boxes were earmarked for the buyer, it followed that they still belonged to the seller and that he had to run that risk of their deterioration. The buyer was therefore not obliged to accept or pay for the fish. In *Re Wait*, 1927, a buyer contracted to buy half of a ship's cargo. Before delivery the seller became insolvent. Because it was not then possible to say which half of the cargo belonged to the buyer, the result was that the whole of it remained the property of the seller. It could then be sold for the benefit of all his creditors.

8.6   Similarly, in *Re London Wine Co.*, 1986, buyers bought certain quantities and descriptions of wine which remained stored in the seller's warehouse. The seller subsequently went into liquidation and his other creditors claimed all the wine in the warehouse. It was held that although there were in fact wines in the warehouse corresponding with the quantities and descriptions ordered by the buyers, they had not been picked out for them individually, and so still belonged to the sellers. Again, therefore, the buyers were left with empty claims for damages. Other similar but contrasting cases include *Re Goldcorp* and *Re Stapylton Fletcher*, both reported in 1994, and both emphasising that each case turns on its own facts and the intentions of the parties. It will be seen that the new and enlarged definition of specific or ascertained goods which we noted in para. 8.4, affecting rights of ownership over undivided parts of a larger bulk, could lead to different solutions to some of these problems: Section 20A, below.

8.7   Assuming that we are dealing with specific or ascertained goods, Section 17 says *it is for parties themselves to decide when ownership shall pass*. They may agree on the point expressly or by implication. The most common practice is to say that ownership shall pass on delivery, or when payment is made after delivery. Typical contract terms of the latter kind are: 'The vehicle and accessories shall remain the property of the vendor until actual delivery has been effected and the full purchase price paid' – or again: 'The property in the goods shall remain with the seller until the price together with any other payment due to the seller has been discharged in full'. Delivery may take place when the seller hands the goods to an independent carrier: para. 9.6. If the goods are then damaged in transit, a buyer who is not yet owner has no claim against the carrier: *Leigh and Sillivan* v. *Aliakman Shipping*, 1986.

8.8   We discuss below other possible complications of these 'retention of title' clauses, but note here that while the seller may retain ownership thereby he is nonetheless free to disclaim responsibility for risk and impose liability on the buyer from the moment the latter takes delivery. So for example the contract might say: 'All risk of loss or damage to the goods shall pass to the buyer on delivery to him, notwithstanding that property in the goods may not have passed to the buyer'. Indeed risk might pass even before delivery. A strong seller might require the buyer's agreement to such a clause as this: 'If, for any reason beyond the seller's control, goods remain in seller's works beyond the agreed delivery date, seller may request payment in full at once. Thereafter, goods remaining in seller's works do so at buyer's risk and expense'. The validity of a clause of this kind would seem to depend on the test of reasonableness in Sections 2 and 3 of the Unfair Contract Terms Act: paras. 7.18–29.

8.9   Where there are no such clear provisions in the contract it may still be possible to infer the parties' intentions from other aspects of their agreement, or even from their conduct. A simple requirement of 'cash on delivery', for instance, might indicate that ownership passes thereupon – though conversely allowing the buyer to postpone payment does not necessarily stop him from becoming the owner. If the contract obliges the buyer to insure the goods at a certain time, that might indicate the goods are at his risk from that time, which might in turn also suggest that he has become owner. Ownership of goods shipped under c.i.f. contracts, where the price includes cost, insurance, and freight, is deemed to pass on delivery of the documents of title – the bills of lading. Under f.o.b. contracts ('free on board' signifies that the price covers the seller's responsibility to have the goods loaded on board ship), ownership usually passes when the goods are over the ship's rail. (But as to risk in these cases, *see* para. 8.37.) A seller's retention of documents of title after delivery might well show that he still owns the goods: *Cheetham* v. *Thornham*, 1964. Other possibilities are that ownership might be deemed to pass on shipment of the goods, or on posting the bill of lading: *The Albazero*, 1977. Intentions expressed after the contract is made have no effect, as in *Dennant* v. *Skinner*, 1948, where after the sale the seller unsuccessfully tried to insist on retaining ownership until the buyer's cheque was cleared. It is evidently difficult to say how the court will interpret the parties' dealings, but certainly the objective is to give effect to the parties' intentions so far as they are discoverable.

8.10   But if – and only if – the parties' intentions at the time of contracting cannot by any means be discovered, then the matter must be decided by law. Section 18 lays down the necessary rules. Rule 1 of Section 18 provides that *in unconditional contracts for the sale of specific goods in a deliverable state ownership passes when the contract is made, even though delivery or payment be postponed.*

8.11   On further points of definition in rule 1, an 'unconditional contract' seems to be one which is immediately effective, and 'specific' goods are those identified and agreed upon at the time of sale – apparently the same as 'ascertained' goods, above. In *Kursell* v. *Timber Operators*, 1927, a sale of all the trees in a forest which by a given future date had reached a certain size was held not to be sufficiently specific to pass ownership at the time the contract was made, since it was impossible to say then which trees would qualify. On the other hand, a sale of all the goods on a certain site there and then conforming with contractual requirements could be a contract for specific goods: *Reid* v. *Schultz*, 1949 (Australia); *Eldon* v. *Hedley*, 1935. The fact that there can only be an estimate of the number or quantity of goods involved, e.g. as to the size of a herd, may not prevent the contract from being specific.

8.12   Goods are 'deliverable' for the purposes of rule 1 if nothing more needs to be done to them under the contract (apart from any question of remedying subsequently discovered defects or deficiencies). So if the contract requires the goods to be repaired – *Tiffin* v. *Pitcher*, 1969 – or machinery to be dismantled before delivery – *Underwood* v. *Burgh Castle*, 1922 – it is not immediately deliverable, and if a carpet is to be sold and fitted on the buyer's premises the seller is still owner until it is duly laid, and so must bear the loss if it is stolen from the buyer's premises before then: *Head* v. *Showfronts*, 1969. Again, this rule is subject to agreement to the contrary. The parties may agree that goods are 'deliverable' before everything which needs to be done with them is finished: *Re Blyth*, 1926 – contract to build a ship; payment by instalments as the work progressed; ownership to pass on payment of the first instalment.

8.13 It may seem surprising for the law to make ownership pass at the time the contract is made even when the goods remain in the seller's hands, and the more so in the light of the general rule that it is the owner who bears the risk of accidental loss or damage. The effect is that when a buyer orders, say, a specific item of furniture in a shop he thereupon becomes owner, and so if he leaves it in the shop pending delivery he still has to pay for it even though it is destroyed that night in a fire on the premises. Conversely, the seller has no duty to provide a replacement. Consumers are probably unaware of this extraordinary rule, but businessmen commonly do their best to avoid it by making the kind of express provision mentioned above – e.g., that risk shall not pass until delivery. The judges themselves are reluctant to apply rule 1. If they can find any element of uncertainty or delay in the contract, e.g. as to terms of payment, they will say the contract is not unconditional, and so outside the rule. 'In modern times very little is needed to give rise to the inference that the property in specific goods is to pass only on delivery or payment': *Ward* v. *Bignell*, 1967. This is in any case the position of American law in Article 2–509 of the Uniform Commercial Code which takes due account of the fact that it is usually the seller who is insured against loss until delivery, and not the buyer.

8.14 Another practical result of taking this more modern view is the effect of a buyer's refusal to accept goods on or before delivery. Section 49 of the Sale of Goods Act entitles an unpaid seller to sue for the price only if the buyer has already become owner (and in certain other circumstances not relevant here). If the buyer is not yet owner at the time when he rejects the goods the seller's claim is for damages at large for breach of contract ('unliquidated' damages, as noted in Chapter 13). Anyone claiming damages at large must do his best to reduce his own losses ('mitigation'; Chapter 13), e.g. by selling elsewhere the goods rejected by the buyer. That in turn means that if rule 1 of Section 18 does not apply, the disappointed seller's claim against the buyer will probably be for a much smaller sum than the price originally agreed between them: *Ward*, above.

8.15 The next two rules in Section 18 concern particular terms which make contracts conditional and so prevent ownership passing straightaway. Rule 2 states that where the seller is bound under the contract to do something to the goods to put them in a deliverable state – as in *Underwood*, above – ownership does not pass until he has done that thing and told the buyer. Rule 3 says that where the contract requires the seller (but not, alternatively, the buyer: *Nanka Bruce* v. *Commonwealth Trust*, 1926) to

195

weigh, measure or test goods to establish their price, ownership does not pass until that has been done and the buyer notified (so that he can insure the goods if he wishes).

8.16   Rule 4 deals with the situation where the prospective buyer receives goods 'on approval' or on a 'sale or return' basis. Here the property in the goods passes to the buyer only when he tells the seller he wants them or in some other way confirms or 'adopts' the transaction, e.g. by keeping them for a long time or by selling them to someone else. In these circumstances he can pass a good title, unless the terms of the original contract forbid him, as e.g. by providing that 'goods remain the seller's property until settled for or charged'. Even so the seller may still lose the goods to an innocent third party if he, the seller, holds out his buyer as authorised to sell them in the way of business: Section 21, Sale of Goods Act.

i. Unascertained goods

8.17   Rule 5 of Section 18, amended by the Sale of Goods (Amendment) Act 1995, is a very important provision. It affects goods which are *not* specific at the time of sale – those which are generic, or unidentified parts of a whole in which sole ownership cannot pass under English law, as in *Healy*, *Wait* and *London Wine*, above – and determines the point in time *after* the contract is made at which they become the buyer's. The rule says that *unless the parties otherwise agree, the buyer becomes owner of unascertained or future goods* (those which are not yet in the seller's hands) *as and when goods as described in the contract and in a deliverable state*, above, *are unconditionally appropriated to the contract by seller or buyer with the express or implied approval of the other*.

8.18   The key question here is as to the meaning of unconditional appropriation. The case of *Federspiel* v. *Twigg*, 1957, is helpful in this connection. An overseas buyer ordered bicycles from an English seller, and paid for them in advance. The cycles were packed in crates marked with their ports of destination, registered for consignment and shipping space ordered. Before they could be shipped, however, the seller became insolvent and the cycles were held for his creditors. The buyer did not want an empty claim for damages against an insolvent seller. Instead he argued that the goods had been appropriated to the contract, and so had become his, and that he was entitled to delivery of them. The judge held that the cycles still belonged to the seller, explaining as follows what the rule involves.

8.19   'Rule 5 . . . is one of the Rules for ascertaining the intention of the parties as to the time at which the property in the goods is to pass to the buyer unless a different intention appears. Therefore the element of common intention has always to be borne in mind. A mere setting apart or selection by the seller of the goods which he expects to use in performance of the contract is not enough. If that is all, he can change his mind and use those goods in performance of some other contract and use some other goods in performance of this contract. To constitute an appropriation of the goods to the contract the parties must have had, or be reasonably supposed to have had, an intention to attach the contract irrevocably to those goods, so that those goods and no others are the subject of the sale and become the property of the buyer . . . [U]sually, but not necessarily, the appropriating act is the last act to be performed by the seller. For instance, if delivery is to be taken at the seller's premises and the seller has appropriated the goods when he has made the goods ready and identified them and placed them in position to be taken by the buyer and has so informed the buyer, and if the buyer agrees to come and take them, that is the assent to the appropriation. But if there is a further act, an important and decisive act, to be done by the seller, then there is *prima facie* evidence that probably the property does not pass until the final act is done.'

8.20   Appropriation must therefore be 'conclusive' or 'irretrievable' to be effective. But it may still be hard to say what that means. In contrast with *Federspiel* is the case of *Re Stapylton Fletcher*, 1995. Here wine which was stored in bulk was held to have been appropriated to individual buyers when cases were made up and separately stored and docketed. The 1995 amendment of rule 5 says that goods sold in bulk are appropriated when they are reduced (e.g. by sales to other buyers) to the quantity required by the buyer, or to a smaller quantity, and the buyer is the only person entitled to that quantity. When goods which are not in bulk are sent by sea, appropriation usually occurs when they are loaded across the ship's rail. Delivering identified goods to an *independent* carrier – *Harrison* v. *Lia*, 1951 (Australia) – or sending them by post, is usually regarded as an unconditional appropriation, on the assumption that the buyer expressly or impliedly agrees to this method of delivery. It might be helpful to make express provision to that effect, e.g.: 'Delivery to a carrier or to any person, firm or company operating on the buyer's behalf shall constitute delivery to the buyer. Signature of such delivery note by any agent, employee or representative of the carrier or buyer shall be conclusive proof of the delivery of the goods.' Curiously enough, however, if the buyer becomes insolvent an unpaid seller is still entitled despite his loss of proprietary rights to stop the goods in transit to the buyer and sell them elsewhere: Sections 46 and 48, Sale of Goods Act. And in any case, of course, appropriation is not unconditional for the purposes of this rule if the contract contains a retention of title clause: below.

8.21   A final version of the problem is as to how goods can be appropriated when they are in the hands of a third party bailee or 'holder', typically, a warehouseman. The judges have held that in this situation it is sufficient for the third party to acknowledge or 'attorn' that he holds the goods on the buyer's behalf, e.g. by acceptance of a delivery order from the buyer:

Wardar v. *Norwood*, 1968; *Sterns* v. *Vickers*, 1923. The conclusion is illogical but realistic, since by giving the buyer a delivery order the seller has done all he can to enable the buyer to collect the goods. The American answer in commercial sales is the same: U.C.C., 2–509.

ii. Retention of title

8.22 Section 19 of the Sale of Goods Act is concerned with retention of title clauses. It says that *under an appropriately worded contract a seller may remain owner of his goods until he is paid for them*. The seller's right must be an express term of the contract of sale. Exceptionally, where goods are shipped to the seller's order, Section 19(2) presumes on the seller's behalf that he retains the right of disposal. The inference is that payment in full is required: *Mitsui* v. *Flota*, 1988. The seller's rights apply equally to specific goods or goods subsequently appropriated to the contract under rule 5 above, and notwithstanding delivery to a carrier or to the buyer himself. The seller's object is, of course, to try to give himself the best available security in the event of the buyer's insolvency; in effect to put himself at the front of the queue of creditors. If he was able only to claim the price rather than to recover the goods he would probably find himself at the other end of the line.

8.23 This particular form of security has been recognised by UK sale of goods legislation since 1893 and has long since been adopted as the basis of hire-purchase transactions. But its full commercial implications were not really appreciated until relatively recently. The issues came to light in the case of *Aluminium Industrie Vaasen* v. *Romalpa Aluminium*, 1976 – a case so significant that retention of title clauses are now commonly known as Romalpa clauses. It may be helpful to begin the discussion by setting out the clause in question in the next two paragraphs.

8.24 The vexed clause in this case was a (not very clear) translation from a Dutch contract. For the sake of clarity we shall divide it into two parts, as follows: 'The ownership of the material to be delivered by A.I.V. will only be transferred to purchaser when he has met all that is owing to A.I.V. no matter on what grounds. Until the date of payment, purchaser, if A.I.V. so desires, is required to store this material in such a way that it is clearly the property of A.I.V. A.I.V. and purchaser agree that, if purchaser should make (a) new object(s) from the material, mixes this material with (an)other object(s) or if this material in any way whatsoever becomes a constituent of (an)other object(s), A.I.V. will be given the ownership of this (these) new object(s) as surety of the full payment of what purchaser owes A.I.V. To this end A.I.V. and purchaser now agree that the ownership of the article(s) in question, whether finished or not, are to be transferred to A.I.V. and that this transfer of ownership will be considered to have taken place through and at the moment of the single operation or event by which the material is converted into (a) new object(s), or is mixed with or becomes a constituent of (an)other object(s).'

8.25   'Until the moment of full payment of what purchaser owes A.I.V., purchaser shall keep the object(s) in question for A.I.V. in his capacity of fiduciary owner and if required shall store this (these) object(s) in such a way that it (they) can be recognised as such. Nevertheless, the purchaser will be entitled to sell these objects to a third party within the framework of the normal carrying on of his business and to deliver them on condition that – if A.I.V. so desires – purchaser as long as he has not fully discharged his debt to A.I.V. shall hand over to A.I.V. the claims he has against his buyer emanating from this transaction.'

8.26   In short, then, the clause provided that the buyer, Romalpa, would not become owner of the aluminium foil in question until he had paid A.I.V. all he owed them: that he should store the foil separately; that A.I.V. owned any new or mixed goods made out of the foil by the buyer as soon as they were made; that the buyer would store the new goods separately and on behalf of A.I.V., and, apparently, that the buyer assigned his rights to the proceeds of sale of new goods to A.I.V. The clause did *not* say that the proceeds of sale of the foil itself belonged to A.I.V., nor that any proceeds of sale should be kept by the buyer in a separate bank account, nor did it give A.I.V. any right to enter the buyer's premises to recover the foil in mixed or unmixed form. It did not affect the buyer's right to sell the goods as principal to a sub-purchaser, which was, of course, the ultimate purpose of the sale, but as against A.I.V. the buyer held the goods only as bailee or fiduciary agent.

8.27   The Court of Appeal held that the clause enabled A.I.V. to recover from the insolvent buyer all the unsold foil still on his premises. Secondly the Court decided that since the object of the clause would be defeated unless it impliedly obliged the buyer to hold the proceeds of sale of unmixed foil on trust for A.I.V., A.I.V. therefore had a right to trace or follow such monies into the buyer's bank account and require payment from it. A.I.V. did not in fact claim either mixed goods or the proceeds of sale of mixed goods, and so the validity of this part of the clause was not discussed – but neither was it disapproved.

8.28   In the event this was a most controversial decision, and much of the Court's reasoning has been questioned in subsequent cases. The ruling gave great reassurance to sellers using such clauses, but caused alarm among less well secured or unsecured creditors of companies in Romalpa's position. It meant that the buyer's apparent stock in trade was not available to them, nor the proceeds of sale. Even banks could lose their priority. The fundamental difficulty was and still is that English law (in common with Continental systems, but unlike American law: Article 9, Uniform Commercial Code) does not require retention of title clauses to be publicly registered, nor any other form of notice to be given, so that without the most diligent inquiries it is impossible to discover a company's real creditworthiness.

8.29   Even from the original seller's point of view, however, there is a problem. English company law recognises the concept of the 'floating charge', under which a company (but not an unincorporated body such as a partnership) may give security for its debts by entitling the creditor to claim against the company's stock in trade, as distinct from a fixed charge on specific assets, if and when the company seems unable to repay him. When this happens, the floating charge 'crystallises', i.e. the creditor can claim the particular assets in the company's hands at that time. Sections 395–6 of the Companies Act 1985 say that such charges are void unless recorded by either party within 21 days of creation and available for public inspection in the company registries in Cardiff or Edinburgh. It follows that if the court interprets a contract of sale as giving a floating charge over the *company's* – the buyer's – goods, and not as keeping the *seller's* rights of ownership over them, the whole purpose of the contract may be defeated. By definition, a seller whose contract claims the goods as his own will not have registered it as giving a right over the buyer's goods. Everything therefore depends on the precise wording and purport of the contract, as later cases have shown. We summarise the most important of these decisions, in chronological order.

8.30   In *Borden* v. *Scottish Timber*, 1979, the seller sold resin which the buyer used in making chipboard, which he then sub-sold. The original contract of sale said only that the resin remained the seller's until the buyer paid his debts to the seller. On the buyer's insolvency the seller tried to recover what was owed by claiming the proceeds of sale of the chipboard. He failed because the contract only gave him ownership of unused resin. Once the resin was used or incorporated in the chipboard it ceased to exist and so did the seller's rights over it. The Court of Appeal stressed that the contract did not in as many words make the buyer a fiduciary holder or bailee of the resin, and so gave the seller no right to trace the resin, nor, still less, to claim the proceeds of its sale or sale of the chipboard. If the seller had any interest in the chipboard, said the Court, it would have been by way of an unregistered floating charge, void against other creditors. On the other hand, the Court was prepared to accept that if '[the seller] wishes to acquire rights over the finished product he can . . . do so by express contractual stipulation'.

8.31   In *Re Bond Worth*, 1979, the seller reserved 'equitable and beneficial ownership' of the goods sold and any mixed goods. These words were held insufficient to entitle him as legal owner either to recover the original goods or to the proceeds of sale. The decision is a doubtful one, seeming to defeat the apparent intention of the parties. The seller in *Re Peachdart*,

1983, sold leather to the buyer to make into handbags. The retention clause entitled the seller to ownership of both leather and handbags, and also said that the buyer held all the goods on a fiduciary basis and subject to the seller's right to trace the proceeds of sale of the handbags – thus seeming to fill all the gaps in the previous cases. It was held nonetheless, following *Borden*, that once goods were incorporated into other goods they ceased to exist and so there was no claim to the handbags. The seller's claim to the proceeds of sale of the bags was also rejected, on the grounds that the buyer was not obliged to keep records of sales or to put the proceeds in a separate account, and overall that there was no way of relating the proceeds of sale of the bags to the value of the leather in them. In effect the seller had only a floating charge on these assets which failed for want of registration. The same view was taken in *Re Andrabell*, 1984, because the contract did not oblige the buyer to keep the goods separately until paid for, nor to keep the proceeds of sale separately from other money.

8.32   *Clough Mill* v. *Martin*, 1984, concerned yarn – 'the material' – which the buyer would spin into fabric. The 'Romalpa' clause here said: 'Ownership of the material shall remain with the seller, which reserves the right to dispose of the material until payment in full for all the material has been received by it in accordance with the terms of this contract or until such time as the buyer sells the material to its customers by way of *bona fide* sale at full market value. If such payment is overdue in whole or in part the seller may (without prejudice to any of its other rights) recover or resell the material or any of it and may enter upon the buyer's premises by its servants or agents for that purpose. Such payment shall become due immediately upon the commencement of any act or proceedings in which the buyer's solvency is involved. If any of the material is incorporated in or used as material for other goods before such payment the property in the whole of such goods shall be and remain with the seller until such payment has been made, or the other goods sold as aforesaid, and all the seller's rights hereunder in the material shall extend to those other goods.'

8.33   It will be seen that this was a clear and comprehensive formula seeking once again to assert the seller's ownership of new or mixed goods. Unfortunately the case involved a claim for damages for wrongful use (conversion) of the yarn by the buyer's liquidators, and so was not directly a test of the validity of this controversial clause. But it is still an important decision, in that the Court of Appeal again recognised the possible validity of the seller's claim. Lord Justice Oliver said: 'English law has developed no sophisticated system for determining title in cases where indistinguishable goods are mixed or become combined in a newly manufactured article . . . [but] I am not sure that I see any reason in principle why the original legal title in a newly manufactured article composed of materials belonging to A and B should not lie where A and B have agreed it shall lie.' This view was supported in the Irish case of *Kruppstahl* v. *Quitmann*, 1988, but doubted in

Specialist Plant v. *Braithwaite*, 1987. Any such claim must of course have practical limits, as in *Specialist Plant*, where a seller supplied goods to be used in repairs and unsuccessfully claimed the repaired article under a retention clause. In *Whenuapai Joinery* v. *Trust Bank*, 1994 (N.Z.), it was held that where a seller sells building materials under a retention clause and the buyer uses the materials to build a house, the mortgagee has a prior claim on the house.

8.34　　The seller in *Hendy Lennox* v. *Puttick*, 1984, sold the buyer engines for incorporation in generators, which the buyer then sub-sold as owner. The engines remained identifiable despite incorporation. The contract said the engines were to remain the seller's until the buyer paid the full purchase price. It also gave the buyer two months' credit, the unintended effect of which was to prevent enforcement of the retention clause during that time. When the buyer became insolvent, the seller claimed the engines still on the buyer's premises and proceeds of the sub-sales of several others. The judge allowed his claim in relation only to the one engine which had not yet been unconditionally appropriated to a sub-buyer. He rejected the seller's claim to the proceeds of sub-sales on the seemingly technical grounds that the buyer's right to credit, and the fact that the proceeds were from the sale of generators – not just the engines – made the buyer simply a debtor and not a fiduciary holder of the seller's own money.

8.35　　In *Pfeiffer* v. *Arbuthnott*, 1988, a German exporter supplied wine to an English importer. The contract entitled the exporter to the benefit of all rights the importer might at any time acquire against his own sub-purchasers, and to any proceeds of sale, which had to be kept in a separate account. Mr. Justice Phillips thought the importer's right to sell the wine in his own name was inconsistent with his alleged status as the exporter's agent (though no difficulty was found in this respect in *Romalpa*). He held that the contract gave the exporter only a general claim – a charge – over the importer's assets. Since the charge was not registered, a third party – a credit factor who had 'bought' the importer's claims against his customers, unaware of the retention clause – had a prior claim to the proceeds. Another case to the same effect is *Compaq Computers* v. *Abercorn*, 1993.

8.36　　Currently therefore the extent of a Romalpa clause's enforceability remains in doubt. Most judges evidently do not like them, presumably because of the substantial but 'secret' advantages they give to trade creditors over all other secured and unsecured creditors. Banks, as major lenders protected by fixed or floating charges, also strongly dislike them. We might still tentatively suggest that a suitably worded clause, whose precise form must depend on the subject-matter of the contract, would be upheld to the extent at least that it establishes the following points: (i) The seller remains owner of the original goods until the buyer pays for them. It seems he might also make transfer of ownership depend on payment of any other sums ('all moneys' clauses) the buyer might owe him: *Armour* v. *Thyssen*, 1990 (Scotland); *Chattis* v. *Ross*, 1992 (Australia); *Pongakawa Sawmill* v. *N.Z. Forest Products*, 1992 (N.Z.). (ii) The buyer holds the goods as bailee and must store and insure them separately on the seller's behalf until used. (iii) The buyer's right to possession ends when he cannot pay his debts to the seller. (iv) The seller is entitled to enter the buyer's premises and recover his goods. (v) The buyer can sub-sell the goods as principal, but as between himself and the original seller he does so as the seller's agent. (vi) Proceeds of sale of the goods in unaltered form must be held by the buyer in a separate account on trust for the seller and the buyer's bank advised accordingly. We have seen there are no very clear answers to questions as to sellers' rights to mixed goods or proceeds of sale, although on principle it would seem that such claims should be possible. Doubts remain over claims to book debts and as to priorities between competing retention clauses.

iii. Ownership and risk

8.37   We come finally to Section 20, which explains the practical effects of the transfer of ownership rules we have been examining. The basic rule is that *goods are at the seller's risk until ownership passes,* and thereafter are at the buyer's risk. It is immaterial whether or not the buyer has taken delivery, or paid for the goods. But the rule is one of convenience only. Contracting parties are free to make other arrangements, divorcing risk from ownership. Commercial contracts often say that risk shall not pass to the buyer until he takes delivery. In both c.i.f. and f.o.b. contracts goods are at the buyer's risk from the time they cross the ship's rail, although in c.i.f. contracts ownership usually passes at a later stage: *Inglis* v. *Stock,* 1885. We have seen that risk may sometimes pass even before ascertainment of the goods, as where a third party acknowledges that he holds goods on the buyer's behalf: *Wardar*; *Sterns,* above.

8.38   The scope of the basic rule in Section 20 was much enlarged by the amending Act of 1995. The purpose of Sections 20A and 20B, added by the new Act, is to give a measure of protection to buyers of unascertained goods. Such buyers might otherwise have no protection at all in the event of the seller's bankruptcy, as we saw in paras. 8.5 and 8.6. Section 20A affects buyers of specified quantities of unascertained goods which form part of an identified bulk; for example, half of a cargo of grain in a particular ship. If and when the buyer pays for some or all of those goods, he thereupon becomes owner in common of the appropriate proportion of the bulk – unless the parties agree otherwise. Under Section 20B, he is taken to have the agreement of the other owners in common to deal in that share of the whole. The new rules offer a much more satisfactory solution to cases such as *Re London Wine,* above.

8.39   For the purposes of Section 20, risk of loss or damage refers only to loss or damage caused by accident and ordinary risks of deterioration, and without negligence on one side or the other. If delivery is delayed through the fault of one party the goods are at that party's risk as regards any damage which might not otherwise have occurred. So where a buyer of apple juice was late in taking delivery it was held that he had to stand the loss caused by the juice going bad during the period of delay: *Demby Hamilton* v. *Barden*, 1949. And in any case, whoever has possession of the goods must take reasonable care of them pending fulfilment of the contract.

8.40   By way of postscript we note also the rule in Section 7 of the Sale of Goods Act, that if goods specified in a contract of sale perish without the fault of either side and before risk passes to the buyer the contract is thereby avoided, i.e. frustrated. We have seen that in an unconditional contract for the sale of specific goods in a deliverable state, risk and ownership pass as soon as the contract is made, unless otherwise agreed: Section 18, rule 1; Section 20. We are concerned here accordingly with the exceptional case where the contract says that neither risk nor ownership has passed before the goods perish. 'Perishing' usually signifies the destruction of the goods, but may cover their disappearance, e.g. through theft, and possibly also loss or damage affecting only part of the goods if the contract is 'entire' and not 'severable', i.e. can only be fulfilled by delivery of the whole: *Barrow* v. *Phillips*, 1929. If the buyer takes the remaining part of the goods, he must pay accordingly: *Sainsbury* v. *Street*, 1972.

8.41   If the contract is avoided under Section 7, the effect is that the seller is not liable for failure to deliver the goods and the buyer is not obliged to pay for them. Any payment already made can be recovered if the buyer has received nothing in return. The seller cannot claim payment for expenses incurred under the contract. The rules on frustration of other kinds of contracts are set out in Chapter 12.

Danish law

8.42   Under the Danish Sale of Goods Act the question of risk is quite separate from that of ownership. Problems of protecting the buyer against the seller's creditors, or *vice versa*, or deciding priorities between two buyers of the same goods, are dealt with on their own merits and not by reference to any fixed rule as to the time when ownership passes. Ownership may therefore pass at different stages, depending on the type of conflict involved. So, for example, a buyer of specific goods is protected against the seller's creditors from the time the contract is made. If the goods are generic he is protected as soon as they are identified and set aside for the fulfilment of the contract. On the other hand a seller is protected against the buyer's creditors until the goods or documents of title are actually in the buyer's hands – and even after that if ownership is retained.

8.43   Risk of accidental loss or damage passes at the time specified in the contract, or otherwise on delivery. Delivery takes place when the seller does what is required under the contract to enable the buyer to take possession of the goods, e.g. by having them ready for collection from his premises or transferring them to an independent carrier. If the goods are so defective that the buyer is entitled to cancel the contract, they are not at any stage at the buyer's risk.

8.44   A retention of title clause does not of itself affect the passing of risk. Such clauses are valid without registration, except as regards sales of registered motor vehicles and registered bonds. Buyers of goods subject to retention of title can pass a good title to their sub-buyers. The original seller may claim the proceeds of sub-sales if the buyer is authorised to sub-sell and obliged to keep the proceeds separately, and the seller does his best to ensure compliance with this condition.

Dutch law

8.45   Dutch law distinguishes between questions of risk and of ownership. Questions of risk arise when the goods perish or get lost between the moment of sale and that of delivery. The question of ownership is of interest in cases of insolvency and third-party rights. The Civil Code provides that risk passes on delivery of the goods: Articles 10 and 11 Book 7. Ownership passes on transfer of possession, or, if the goods are not yet in the seller's hands, as agreed by the contract.

8.46   As far as risk is concerned, the effect of the rules before the new Code was introduced was very similar to that of Sections 16–20 of the UK Sale of Goods Act, but under the new law, risk passes at the moment of delivery of the goods: Articles 7.10–11. If, however, the buyer seeks to set the sale aside for breach of contract the goods remain at the seller's risk. The buyer must then take reasonable care of the goods. Under Article 3.90, ownership passes from seller to buyer on transfer of possession, or, if the goods are not yet held by the seller, as agreed by contract: Article 3.95. Retention of title – *eigendomsvoorbehoud* – is permitted by Article 3.92. In such a case payment of the price automatically brings about transfer of the title to the goods to the buyer. To a limited extent, the new Code allows the seller to stipulate that, as a condition of the transfer of title, not only must the price of the goods in question be paid but also all other outstanding debts. If payment is not made the seller may recover possession of the goods. This applies also in the case of the buyer's bankruptcy. The buyer is entitled to process or sell the goods in the ordinary course of business. The unpaid seller loses his ownership rights if the goods are made into a different product or if they are sold and delivered to a *bona fide* purchaser.

French law

8.47   Risk and transfer of ownership are linked under French law in much the same way as in English law. French law differs accordingly from German law, which has kept the Roman rule that ownership and risk pass on delivery. Under Articles 1138 and 1583 of the Civil Code, risk is borne by the owner of the goods at any given time, and passes at the same time as ownership is transferred. In the absence of any provision to the contrary, ownership is transferred when the contract is made. Article 1583 states: '[The sale] is complete between the parties and ownership is automatically transferred to the purchaser in his relationship with the vendor when the parties have agreed the subject matter of the contract and the price, even if the goods have not yet been delivered nor the price paid'.

8.48   Transfer of ownership and transfer of risk are therefore entirely disconnected from transfer of possession and delivery. Because most national laws on the Continent, drawing from German law or complying with the 1964 Hague Convention on International Sales of Goods, differ from the French rules, most commercial contracts provide in practice that ownership and risk pass only upon effective delivery to the purchaser. The rules set out in the Civil Code are not mandatory but apply in the absence of contractual provisions to the contrary.

8.49   The above rules apply to the extent that the goods in question have been identified (*individualisés*). Sales of generic goods are made only when the goods have been duly weighed or measured (Article 1585), unless the goods are sold *en bloc* (Article 1586; e.g., crops). The transfer of goods still to be manufactured takes place when the goods are ready for delivery even if actual delivery has not yet taken place. Since the rule is not mandatory, one can also provide that the purchaser shall acquire ownership of the equipment as and when it is built or upon effective delivery.

8.50   The statute of 12 May 1980 and Article 115 *et seq.* of the Act of 25 January 1985 on bankruptcy, modified by the Act of 10 June 1994 and by case law, have set out the basic rules regarding the validity and enforceability *vis-à-vis* third parties of reservation of title clauses. The basic requirement is that for evidentiary purposes the clause should be inserted in a document agreed by both vendor and purchaser before the actual delivery of the goods. A reservation clause mentioned for the first time on the invoices of the vendor is not enforceable *vis-à-vis* the purchaser, since invoices are usually issued on or after delivery: Nancy, 12 July 1983. Even in the context of an on-going business relationship between vendor and purchaser, with a succession of similar sales, receivers or liquidators are usually successful in setting aside clauses mentioned only in invoices: (Com. 3 January 1989; *contra*: Com. 5 November 1985). A clause inserted in a master agreement is in theory sufficient, but it is prudent to remind the purchaser of the reservation upon each delivery: Nancy, 12 July 1983. The clause must be apparent, i.e., in bold letters, and it must have been clearly agreed by the purchaser. Where the conditions of the purchaser nullifying in advance any reservation clause contradict the conditions of the vendor including such clause, the courts have held that there is no agreement and the clause is not enforceable: Com. 22 June 1983.

8.51   Although no formality of registration, publication, affixing of a plaque, etc., is required for a retention clause to be enforceable *vis-à-vis* third parties, such precautions are useful whenever possible. When goods sold under a reservation clause are sold on to a *bona fide* third party, they cannot be claimed from him. The owner can only claim (*revendiquer*) the price payable by the second purchaser to the first purchaser. In the absence of contrary contractual provisions, risk of accidental loss or damage remains with the owner. The purchaser under a reservation of title clause has an obligation to use his best endeavours to safeguard the goods (Com. 19 October 1982), unless the contract provided for the transfer of risks upon delivery notwithstanding the retention of ownership by the vendor.

8.52   In connection with ownership and bankruptcy, special attention should be given to Article 115 of the Bankruptcy Law of 25 January 1985. This imposes upon an owner of goods an obligation to claim back from the receiver or liquidator of an insolvent company any of his goods in the possession of the company. Although this obligation was initially devised for goods under reservation of title clauses, it has been extended by case law to any circumstance in which an insolvent company possesses goods or equipment belonging to a third party, even when the right of ownership of the latter is not challengeable, e.g., when the equipment is rented under a lease contract. Failure to claim back the goods or equipment within 3 months of the judgment declaring the company under receivership or liquidation results automatically in the unenforceability (*inopposabilité*) of the owner's right of ownership. The goods or equipment are deemed to be owned by the insolvent company and for the benefit of its creditors.

German law

8.53   The basic principle of German law is that risk passes on delivery. Ownership may pass at the same time, but need not do so – as where there is a retention of title clause in the contract. *Re Wait* and *Re London Wine*, para. 8.5, would be decided in the same way under German law, but for a different reason. In German law the reason would be that the goods had not been delivered, and not that they were still unascertained. Similarly the furniture example, para. 8.13, would not be a question of passing of risk, but of the seller's liability for failure to fulfil his contract. If unascertained goods are destroyed by fire the seller is liable for the buyer's loss only in cases of negligence. If the seller is not negligent he does not have to perform the contract and the buyer does not have to pay.

8.54 German law has no provision like that in rule 5 of Section 18 of the Sale of Goods Act, because only risk passes and not necessarily ownership when goods are 'unconditionally appropriated' to the contract. The idea of unconditional appropriation is nonetheless important in German law because the limitation period for breach of warranty claims runs from that time and the buyer may be liable for failure to accept the goods. *Federspiel*, para. 8.18, would be decided in the same way, but on different grounds, as above.

8.55 As a rule, ownership passes to the buyer only if he obtains actual possession. So when the seller entrusts goods to an independent carrier, risk passes but not ownership – unless the contract provides otherwise. In such a case the seller's contractual rights against the carrier may be transferred to the buyer under the judge-made rule of *Drittenschadensliquidation* or 'transferred loss'. This principle enables German law to give a different answer from that given by English law in cases such as *Leigh*; para. 8.7.

8.56 Retention of title clauses are declared valid by Article 455 BGB though this deals only with 'simple' clauses – *einfacher Eigentumsvorbehalt* – and not with extended claims to mixed goods or other debts. The problems involved are regulated by case law. Theoretically the courts could control such clauses in the same way as other standard form provisions, but in practice this power is not often used. *Romalpa* clauses are widely used and rarely challenged. The main difference between English and German law here seems to be in the company's right to make a floating charge over its assets. Contrary to English law such clauses are valid in Germany without registration. It is not then possible to limit retention clauses by regarding them as invalid charges over stock in trade. As regards securities taken by banks in particular, the courts require banks to ensure that the level of their securities does not exceed their customers' indebtedness.

8.57 In a case like *Re Peachdart*, para. 8.32, a seller of materials or components under German law could include a term in the contract of sale dividing ownership between himself and the manufacturer of the finished product in accordance with the value of the materials. A clause making the seller of the materials the sole owner of the finished product would be void.

Italian law

8.58 The Italian rules on risk of accidental loss or damage to goods are effectively the same as the English. Ownership passes when the contract is made, or on subsequent ascertainment of the goods: Articles 1376–8 of the Civil Code. Ascertainment needs the agreement of the parties, which may be implied, and it must be conclusive. If the goods then remain in the seller's possession they must be clearly identified and, probably, cannot be substituted. The Code makes no mention of the goods being in a 'deliverable state' before ownership can pass. But if the goods are defective the buyer can still return them. Property and risk pass when the goods are delivered to an independent carrier: Article 1378.

8.59 The contracting parties are free to make other arrangements as to ownership and risk. In particular, under Article 1523 they may agree that the risk shall fall on the buyer immediately but that the seller remains owner until the goods are paid for. As in England the seller needs to establish written evidence of the retention of title clause, bearing a date before the date on which he seeks to enforce it: Article 1524. A notarised or registered agreement is advisable to support a claim against third parties: Article 2704. The seller loses his rights to recover the goods when the buyer uses them in his production process, or when he resells them.

Spanish law

8.60 In theory Spanish law upholds the principle of *res perit emptori*, i.e. that goods are at the buyer's risk. But in practice there are many exceptions. The parties may expressly agree that risk passes only with possession, which usually coincides with acquisition of ownership: Articles 609 and 1462 of the Civil Code. In commercial contracts risk passes to the purchaser only when the goods are handed over: Article 333 of the Commercial Code.

8.61 If the goods are not specific at the time of sale, but are, for example, unidentified parts of a whole, or have yet to be weighed or measured, Spanish law provides – much as in English law – that risk passes when the goods are identified or weighed or measured: Article 334, Commercial Code: Article 1452 of the Civil Code.

8.62 Spanish law allows sellers expressly to keep their title to goods until paid in full. Title to goods in bulk (wheat, oil, etc.) cannot be retained unless the seller's goods are kept separately from other goods of the same kind, and are not used. But the contract of sale may entitle the seller to claim the same quantity and quality of such goods: Articles 1753–4 and 1768 of the Civil Code; Article 309 of the Commercial Code.

Swedish law

8.63   In Swedish law, as in Danish, risk is not connected with ownership of the goods. Unless otherwise agreed, risk passes at the time of delivery: Article 13, Sale of Goods Act. If delivery is delayed because of the buyer's fault, he is responsible for any resulting loss or damage not attributable to the seller. When goods are sold in transit, risk passes at the time of sale: Article 15. In any event, risk cannot pass until goods are identified as intended for the buyer, e.g. by a transportation document or by marking: Article 14.

8.64   By a retention of title clause the seller may remain owner of the goods until he is paid for them, despite delivery to the buyer. These clauses are, however, invalid where the buyer has the right to resell the goods before he can pay for them, or if he intends to mix the goods with other property: NJA 1974 s.660. In NJA 1960 s.221, for example, there was a retention of title clause in a contract for the sale of doors, which the buyer intended to install in a building. Even though the doors had not been installed at the time when the buyer went into liquidation, the retention of title clause was rejected. Sellers' rights to secure their interest when delivering goods in advance of payment are in practice limited to sales of goods such as machinery and other capital equipment which is not intended for resale.

Chapter 9

Delivery, price and payment

A. Delivery

9.1   Terms of delivery of goods and services are for the parties themselves to decide upon. In commercial contracts it is particularly important to specify when and how delivery takes place, since, as we saw in Chapter 8, risk and/or ownership of goods may pass at the same time as delivery, and the seller's compliance with conditions of delivery is a pre-requisite of liability upon the buyer. Delivery to an independent carrier is often expressly stated to be delivery to the buyer, as is in any case presumed by the Sale of Goods Act, below, and signature of the carrier or any agent or employee of the buyer is said to constitute proof of delivery. In appropriate cases buyers might be well-advised to insist upon terms in the contract entitling them to inspect or test goods before delivery. They might then find it helpful to add a clause such as this: 'Any inspection, checking, approval or acceptance given by or on behalf of the buyer shall not relieve the seller or his sub-contractors from any obligations under the contract.'

9.2   Section 28 of the Sale of Goods Act 1979 says that unless otherwise agreed, delivery of the goods and payment for them are 'concurrent conditions'. That means that the obligation of each is dependent upon the other's willingness and ability to perform his side of the agreement. Conversely, if the seller is ready and willing to deliver the goods or documents of title but the buyer refuses to take them, his refusal usually (though not inevitably: *see* Chapter 13) entitles the seller to treat the contract as repudiated. Whether the seller delivers or the buyer collects is for the parties to decide; otherwise the law presumes that delivery will be made at the seller's place of business: Section 29(2). Acceptance of delivery does not affect the right to reject the goods at a later date if they are defective, but the right to reject is itself a short-lived right, as we noted in Chapter 6.

9.3   If the contract is for the sale and delivery of specific goods, but without any definite delivery date, delivery must take place within a reasonable time: Section 29(3), SGA. If a date is fixed, *prima facie* time is then of the essence – *Hartley* v. *Hymans*, 1920 – or it may subsequently be made so: *Rickards* v. *Oppenheim*, 1950. We discussed in Chapter 5 the attitude of English courts towards times and dates in shipping contracts in particular, noting that such terms were assumed to be crucial in that one special context, but otherwise very uncertain in their effect. Demand for, or tender of, delivery must be at a reasonable hour. Unless otherwise agreed, the seller must bear the cost of putting the goods into a deliverable state: Section 29(6); Chapter 8.

9.4   Again subject to agreement to the contrary, Section 30 says that if the seller delivers a smaller quantity of goods than the buyer ordered, the buyer can reject them all. This remains so even after the buyer has accepted part of the goods in the course of delivery by instalments: *Gill* v. *Berger*, 1984. But if the buyer accepts the whole of the smaller delivery he must pay *pro rata*. If a greater quantity is delivered than was ordered, the buyer may take only what he ordered – or reject everything, or accept everything, again paying *pro rata*. These rights will of course be limited if the contract itself allows for variations in the amount, or where the variations are of no importance – the *de minimis* rule. In *Shipston* v. *Weil*, 1912, the excess delivery was at the rate of one pound in every 100 tons (approximately 500 g in 112,000 kg). This was held to be too trivial to justify repudiation. The right to reject given by Section 30 is in any case more likely to benefit consumers than business people. A buyer in the course of business cannot reject if the shortfall or excess is so small as to make it unreasonable for him to do so.

9.5   The buyer need not accept delivery by instalments unless the contract so provides. Section 31 says that it depends on all the circumstances of the case whether failure to deliver – or, as the case may be, to pay – under an instalment contract justifies repudiation or only a claim for damages (as to which *see also* Chapter 5). The effect of this rule is that breach of an instalment contract may have less drastic consequences for the seller than breach of an ordinary 'entire' contract under Section 30: *Maple Flock* v. *Universal Furniture*, 1934. The case of *Regent* v. *Francesco*, 1981, is noteworthy because it indicates a judicial preference for interpreting contracts as instalment contracts if possible. Here the contract was held to be for delivery by instalments even though there was no agreement on the number or scale of such deliveries, which were left to the seller's discretion. The seller's failure to deliver one suit out of a consignment of suits therefore did not entitle the buyer to repudiate as he might possibly have been able to do under an entire contract. Each accepted delivery must be paid for, regardless of other breaches of contract by the seller.

9.6   Under Section 32 the seller's delivery of goods to an independent carrier is deemed to be delivery to the buyer. The seller must make reasonable provision for carriage. If he does not do so and the goods are lost or damaged in transit the buyer may repudiate the contract and/or sue for damages. It is not reasonable to send goods at the buyer's risk if no proper provision for safe carriage is made: *Young* v. *Hobson*, 1949. When sending goods by sea the seller should normally give enough notice to enable the buyer to insure them. If the seller does not give notice, the goods are at his risk while in transit. The contract might expressly entitle the buyer to reject goods damaged in transit, whether or not the carrier is at fault.

9.7   Section 34 allows the buyer a reasonable time after delivery in which to inspect the goods before any question of acceptance (*see* Chapter 5) arises. He must tell the seller if he rejects the goods, but is not obliged to return them himself. He can recover storage costs if the seller does not collect the goods promptly after receiving notice of rejection: *Kolfor* v. *Tilbury Plant*, 1977.

B. Price and payment

9.8   Prices for goods and services are essentially matters for negotiation. It is most important then that the sums due and the circumstances in which they become due should if possible be clearly stated in the contract. A seller is not usually under any duty to draw the buyer's attention to the price before making the contract, although *Interfoto* v. *Stiletto*, para. 7.61, suggests that that might be good practice if the price is unusually high. We saw in Chapter 1 that parties relying on 'reasonable price' or 'price to be agreed' clauses might well find there was no enforceable agreement between them, though they might still have to pay a price fixed by the judge for goods actually delivered. We also saw that even where a firm price is stated, e.g. in a price list or in answer to an inquiry, that of itself may possibly be no more than an invitation to treat and as such of no contractual significance.

9.9   The Price Marking Order 1991, intended to give effect to EEC Directives of 1979 and 1988, requires the prices of certain food and non-food products offered or advertised for sale by retail to be stated in writing, though not necessarily in a form immediately visible to the passer-by: *Allen* v. *Redbridge L.B.C.*, 1994. The Price Indications (Method of Payment) Regulations 1991 says that where goods or services supplied in the course of business are available at prices which vary according to the method of payment (notably, by cash or on credit), the supplier must inform the consumer accordingly. Written statements of the differing prices must be displayed at the point of payment and at other conspicuous points on the premises. Various other statutory orders regulate display of certain credit advertisements, prices of food and drink in cafes and restaurants, hotel prices, petrol prices and estate agents' services. Many trade associations, including those for car suppliers and repairers, travel agencies, laundries and suppliers of photographic material and services, have agreed codes of practice with the Office of Fair Trading, under which prior display of prices is required. Failure to comply with the statutory provisions or a code of practice would not, however, affect the validity of a contract.

9.10   As and when the seller gives details of his charges he should make clear what they cover, e.g. whether they include packing, posting and insurance. In particular he must say whether value added tax or any service charge is included. It is a criminal offence under Section 20 of the Consumer Protection Act 1987 to state a price which is less than that actually charged, as also to advertise manufacturers' recommended prices which the advertiser knows are not generally followed by retailers: Section 24. Again, offences under the Act do not affect the contract of sale.

9.11   We noted problems of giving 'estimates' and 'quotations' in Chapter 1, together with the possibility of charging for such services. If the seller chooses to give an estimate or quotation it should be clear beyond doubt which exactly he is offering. In theory an estimate is only an informed guess as to the likely cost, and as such not binding. A quotation, on the other hand, may be regarded as a definite statement of the price. It may then be seen not as an invitation to treat but as the offer accepted by the buyer when he makes the contract, and so binding upon the seller. He cannot then demand more money if the contract proves unprofitable, nor can the buyer seek a reduction if he finds the goods or services overvalued. It may nonetheless be difficult to distinguish an estimate from a quotation. No particular magic attaches to the words themselves. It is more a matter of the intention and understanding of the parties. An 'estimate', described as such, may still be binding: *Croshaw* v. *Pritchard*, 1899.

9.12   Even where a statement of price is clearly only an approximation, that does not mean it can have no legal effect. Goods are often bought and tenders granted on the basis of low and competitive estimates. The buyer should be entitled to protection if the estimate proves to have been misleading or completely inaccurate, for whatever reason. In *Kidd* v. *Mississauga Commission*, 1979 (Canada), the plaintiff estimated his charges at $5,000 but finally the bill was for $14,500. It was held on the facts of the case that the defendant was entitled to rely on the plaintiff's expertise and care in making the estimate and was not therefore required to pay more than $5,000. Similarly in *Nye* v. *Bristow*, 1987, the Court of Appeal held an architect negligent in failing to mention the likely effect of inflation when giving an estimate of building costs, and so not entitled to any fee when the project was abandoned because of the extra cost.

9.13   Prices in individual contracts may be agreed expressly or by implication. Written statements of prices must be given to buyers only in consumer credit transactions, where individuals are given credit up to £15,000. If the seller's charges are available on request but the buyer chooses not to inquire what they are, he is still deemed to have agreed to them when he orders the goods or services in question (but *see Interfoto*, above). Once the price is settled the seller cannot charge more unless the contract contains a price variation or revision clause. The fact that his goods or services become more difficult or expensive for him to supply does not in itself enable him to charge more – nor, as we see in Chapter 12, can he give up the contract on the ground that it is thereby frustrated. If without a price variation clause he does in fact charge more and makes the buyer promise to pay the increase or actually pay it, the combined effect of the rules of consideration and economic duress (Chapters 3 and 11) is likely to be that the promise is unenforceable. Any payment made in these circumstances will then be recoverable, if the buyer acts promptly.

9.14   Price variations may be stated to depend upon certain specified *indicia* such as the cost of living index, or other more indeterminate factors. Examples are: 'In the event of any increase in the cost to the company of overheads, labour, goods, materials, insurance or transport after the date of quotation or agreement, or in the case of any error by the company in quotation, the company reserves the right to change its prices correspondingly', and 'prices are based on present day costs of manufacture and design, and having regard to the delivery quoted and uncertainty as to the cost of labour, materials etc., during the period of manufacture we regret that we have no alternative but to make it a condition of acceptance of order that goods will be charged at prices ruling upon date of delivery'. Building contracts and the like commonly provide that if more work is necessary than was originally agreed it shall be charged *pro rata* or on a *quantum meruit* basis (para. 1.25) – but that, of course, does not enable the contractor to do whatever extra work he thinks fit and charge accordingly: *Foreman* v. *The Liddesdale*, 1900. Price variation clauses generally can be a fertile source of disputes, particularly if, as in the examples above, the basis on which they operate is not completely clarified.

9.15   The contract may ask for a deposit or down payment. A deposit is intended as a form of guarantee or security and is usually forfeited if the buyer is in breach of contract (unless it is regarded as a penalty: Chapter 13). A part-payment, if described as such, is not automatically lost if the contract is not fulfilled. The buyer may be able to recover it, subject to the seller's claim for damages.

9.16   Remaining questions affect when and how payment must be made. These are again essentially matters for the parties themselves to decide upon. Very often the terms are simply 'C.O.D.' – cash (or cheque: *see* below) on delivery. Other standard formulae are 'unless otherwise agreed, payment in full shall be due for goods on notification by us that they are ready for dispatch', and 'the price shall become due for payment by the buyer in full within thirty days of date of invoice'. Late payment does not necessarily entitle the seller to interest on the debt: para. 13.16. In view of the widely recognised difficulties facing small firms in particular in securing payment, incentives and penalties may be added, as e.g.: 'All invoices are subject to 5 per cent discount only for prompt cash paid by the end of the month following the month during which the goods are invoiced. The seller reserves the right to charge interest at 2 per cent above the Bank of England minimum lending rate for the time being in force on all outstanding sums, interest to run from day to day and to accrue after as well as before any judgment'. We note in passing that English law is unusual among legal systems in having no specific limits on interest rates, although 'extortionate' credit agreements may be reopened under the Consumer Credit Act 1974. The courts have used their powers very sparingly.

9.17   Rights to advance payments, or to part-payment in accordance with stages of completion of the contract, or payment by instalment, credit, security for payment (*see* bankers' confirmed credits, below, and retention of title in Chapter 8), 'retention money' (sums withheld by the buyer pending satisfactory completion of the contract), and the like, are not given by law – unlike the right of lien, below – and can only be conferred by the express terms of the contract. Every effort must be made therefore to ensure that such terms are clear and unambiguous, setting out precisely the circumstances in which the rights arise.

9.18   The Sale of Goods Act 1979 lays down rules as to the time of payment which apply in the absence of agreement to the contrary. Section 10 says that as a general rule contractual provisions as to time of payment are not 'of the essence', i.e. late payment does not entitle the seller to repudiate the contract. We noted in Chapter 5 the courts' more rigorous interpretation of such clauses in the shipping context. Section 28, as mentioned above, presumes that the price becomes payable when the goods are delivered or tendered. Payment due on a certain day may be made at any time until midnight on that day: *Afovos* v. *Romano Pagnan*, 1982. The Convention on International Sale of Goods adds in Article 58 that a buyer is not bound to pay unless he has had an opportunity to inspect the goods.

9.19   So far as the form or method of payment is concerned the basic rule is that it be made in 'legal tender' – current coin and banknotes. In practice payment by cheque is acceptable, if the seller agrees. The buyer remains liable for payment even if the cheque is lost or unpaid for reasons beyond his control. If the seller or other creditor authorises payment by cheque through the post, however, the risk of loss falls on him: *Norman* v. *Ricketts*, 1886. We saw in Chapter 3 that where payment is assured by the buyer's bank giving confirmed credit, i.e. promising to pay the seller on receipt of documents of title to the goods, English law enforces the seller's claim against the bank despite the absence of consideration. The bank must pay even if the seller is in some way in breach of the contract of sale. It can only refuse to pay if the documents of title appear to conflict with the terms of credit, or there is evidence of fraud, or payment would be illegal.

9.20   A buyer's failure or inability to pay does not of itself end the contract, nor necessarily excuse the seller from fulfilling his side of the contract. Sellers therefore commonly protect themselves with express provisions of this kind against the buyer's insolvency: 'If the buyer defaults in paying any sum due or if any distress or execution is levied upon the buyer, his property or assets [in Scotland; sequestration], or if the buyer makes or offers to make any composition [agreement to pay less] with creditors or commits any act of bankruptcy, or act which would be an act of bankruptcy if committed by an individual, or if a petition be presented for a receiving order in the case of an individual or liquidation in the case of a company, the seller is entitled at any time thereafter to end any contract without prejudice to the seller's right to recover money due and damages.'

9.21   A final possible remedy against a defaulting buyer is the seller's right to hold back the goods promised to the buyer. This right of 'lien' is given by Section 41 of the Sale of Goods Act (and by the common law in certain other cases where property can be kept until work is paid for). It can be exercised only when the goods are still in the unpaid seller's possession, and no terms as to credit have been agreed, or any terms agreed have expired, or the buyer is insolvent. If the buyer is insolvent the seller has also the right to stop delivery and recover possession of goods already in the hands of an independent carrier and on the way to the buyer. Neither the exercise of the right of lien nor stoppage in transit necessarily bring the contract to an end. But the seller can lawfully end it and resell the goods if they are perishables, or if he warns the buyer he will resell unless paid, or if, as above, the contract expressly enables him to do so: Section 48. His right to claim damages against the buyer is not affected by holding back or reselling the goods.

Danish law

DELIVERY

9.22   As under English law, Danish law regards delivery and payment as concurrent conditions unless the parties have agreed otherwise. A contract may exist even though the parties have not expressly agreed on times or place of delivery or payment. These terms may be filled out by the provisions of the Sale of Goods Act, e.g. by requiring delivery and payment at the seller's place of business (as illustrated in 1919 UfR 938), and payment of a reasonable price if no price has been agreed. When a commercial contract fixes a date for delivery or payment, that implies that time is of the essence.

9.23   If a seller delivers more than is required the buyer cannot reject the whole if without cost or inconvenience he can separate the surplus and let the seller take it back. If he delivers too little, the buyer can cancel the contract only if the shortfall is a significant breach of contract.

PRICE AND PAYMENT

9.24   It is a criminal offence in Denmark for a business to exhibit goods for sale without clearly indicating the tax-inclusive price. A price display is a binding offer.

9.25   A seller cannot cancel a contract because of the buyer's subsequent insolvency unless the buyer has failed on demand to put down an adequate deposit: Article 39, Sale of Goods Act. An unpaid seller has a legal right to interest on the debt.

Dutch law

DELIVERY

9.26   The rights and duties of the parties to a contract of sale under Dutch and English law are not very dissimilar. A time fixed for delivery is considered to be binding: Article 6.83.

PRICE AND PAYMENT

9.27   Price variations at the discretion of the seller are regulated by Articles 6.236 and 7.35 of the Civil Code: *see* para. 7.69. Where a contract of sale does not state the price, the buyer must pay a reasonable price: Article 7.4. The seller must pay any delivery costs: Article 7.12.

French law

DELIVERY

9.28   The seller's duty to deliver the goods sold arises as soon as the contract is made (Article 1138). Delivery takes place when the goods are transferred into the control and possession of the buyer. If the contract does not say where delivery is to be made, it must be at the place where the goods are when the contract is made (Article 1609). When the goods are not delivered at the agreed time, the buyer can seek rescission of the contract under Article 1184, or enforced delivery under Article 1610.

9.29   The seller's basic obligations are to deliver goods in conformity with the contract, free from hidden defects (subject to his limited right to exclude liability: para. 6.99), and to guarantee protection against undisclosed rights of third parties over the goods: Articles 1640–6.

9.30   The obligation to deliver the subject-matter of the contract is suspended if the price is not paid in accordance with the contractual provisions. The vendor can then retain the goods until such time as payment is made or the contract is rescinded in court.

PRICE AND PAYMENT

9.31   The purchaser must pay the price at the time and place provided in the contract of sale (Article 1660), or, failing any indication in the contract, at the time and place of delivery. Interest starts accruing in case of late delivery (i) if provided for in the contract; or (ii) if the goods produce revenues or other 'fruits'; or (iii) in any event, upon a notice to pay, as from the date of the notice: Article 1652.

9.32   Price variation clauses are permitted to the extent that they relate to the goods or services which are the subject-matter of the contract. Clauses providing for indexation based on the cost of living index or on salary increases not related to the subject-matter of the contract are void: Ordinance of 30 December 1958. Except in 'international' contracts (implying, according to case law, transfers of goods or services beyond national borders), all payments made in France must be in French francs: Civ. 11 October 1979. The choice of a foreign currency as 'money of account' is, however, valid: Civ. 25 March 1981.

9.33   A court has discretion to grant a debtor additional time for payment in consideration of his financial position, up to a maximum of 2 years: Article 1244.

German law

DELIVERY

9.34   The equivalent of Section 28 of the Sale of Goods Act, para. 9.2, is Article 273, BGB. This enables either side to give up the contract on the other's unjustifiable failure to perform (*Zurückbehaltungsrecht*). If a party wishes to withdraw because of the other's delay he may make time of the essence under Article 326, or, if delay has made the contract pointless, cancel it and claim damages. Under Article 271, corresponding with Section 29(3), delivery must take place immediately, and not merely within a reasonable time, if no date is fixed. Where a smaller quantity of goods is delivered, the German court would decide as in *Shipston*, para. 9.4.

PRICE AND PAYMENT

9.35 The rules governing the display of prices before contracts are made are in the measure known as the *Preisangabenverordnung*. This requires among other things that the price labels of goods in shops must include VAT and that a credit offer has to include the true annual interest rate. Breach of the statute does not affect the validity of the contract, except that failure to declare the true interest rate leads to a lower rate. As in English law, estimates and quotations are usually given free of charge. Charges must be expressly provided for.

9.36 Price variation clauses are regulated by case law on the basis of the Standard Contract Terms Act. Increases within four months of the making of the contract are void. Otherwise, the circumstances in which the price may be increased must be exactly defined in the contract, which must also expressly state the buyer's right to reject the contract if the increase demanded is higher than the increase in the cost of living index. Questions as to when and how payment may be made are for the parties to decide.

Italian law

DELIVERY

9.37 Article 1476 of the Italian Civil Code specifies delivery as one of the main obligations of the seller. This does not necessarily require a physical transfer of possession. Where goods are held by a third party on behalf of the seller, for example, delivery is effected when the holder acknowledges the buyer's rights to possession. When goods are delivered in accordance with the contract it is then the buyer's duty to accept them. If he refuses, the seller after giving the buyer notice may deposit the goods in a public store or place determined by the judge: Article 1514. The buyer has to pay the resulting expenses, and the goods are at his risk.

9.38 A buyer need not accept partial delivery nor delivery by instalments, unless the contract so provides: Article 1181. If it provides for periodic deliveries of fixed quantities or as required by the buyer, termination of the contract does not affect the buyer's right to keep what has been delivered nor the seller's right to be paid for it: Articles 1458, 1559.

PRICE AND PAYMENT

9.39   As a general proposition, a contract is not binding unless the parties have fixed the price or agreed on a way to fix it – Articles 1346, 1418 – but there are many exceptions.

9.40   A clear intention to agree upon a fair price may enable the court to settle the price, or the court may assume the parties' willingness to be bound by current market prices: Article 1474. If a third party is to fix the price, it should be fair. The validity of a contract which leaves the seller free to fix or vary the price is not certain. The prevailing view is that he should be able to vary the price only with regard to specific elements such as cost of petrol, wage increases, etc.

9.41   Failure to fix the cost of services before they are rendered does not make the contract void. Disputes over prices and fees will be settled by reference to current rates or usages, or by the judge's view of what is reasonable in the circumstances – *ex bono et aequo.*

9.42   The price must be paid at the agreed time and place, or otherwise at the time and place of delivery: Article 1498. In contracts involving carriage of goods, the price is usually payable when the seller hands over documents of title: Article 1528.

Spanish law

DELIVERY

9.43   Spanish law requires a seller to deliver the thing sold at the time and place agreed, putting it 'in the power and possession of the buyer': Article 1462 of the Civil Code. Where a commercial contract does not fix a time for delivery the seller must hold the goods ready for the buyer within 24 hours of making the contract: Article 337 of the Commercial Code.

9.44   A creditor or buyer need not accept something different from what is due under the contract even if it is of equal or greater value: Article 1166. Nor need he accept partial or instalment payment or delivery, unless otherwise agreed: Article 1169.

PRICE AND PAYMENT

9.45   The price must be paid at the time and place fixed by the contract, or, if no such agreement has been reached, at the time and place of delivery: Article 1500.

9.46   Prices may be agreed expressly or by implication. A price may be established by reference to a specific thing or formula or costs, or by the decision of a specified person: Article 1447. Stabilisation clauses, whose purpose is to take account of inflation, are often used in leases and are based an official inflation indices.

Swedish law

9.47   Swedish rules on delivery and payment are essentially the same as under Danish law, above, subject to minor modifications under the Sale of Goods Act 1990. When the contract is for services, payment is normally due after the service is finished, unless the parties have otherwise agreed.

Chapter 10

Mistake

10.1   In this and the next two Chapters we look at various grounds on which apparently valid contracts may nonetheless be held unenforceable. We consider first the effects of mistakes by one or both parties in making their contracts. All legal systems find difficulty in laying down precise rules on this question, since the possibilities and consequences of mistakes are limitless. In England the position is further complicated by the fact that the rules are entirely the product of case law and thus still more fragmentary and less predictable in operation. It was for good reason that Professor Anson, author of one of the leading text books on contract law, wrote in this connection: 'The principles upon which the courts will intervene, and the circumstances in which they will do so, have never been precisely settled, and the decided cases are open to a number of varying interpretations'.

10.2   The first major difficulty is that there are two quite different approaches to the problem – that of common law and that of equity. Both are case law, but as explained in our Introduction they are historically distinct sources of law and may give fundamentally different answers to similar questions. We might say very shortly at this stage that at common law a contract alleged to be affected by a mistake of fact will be either wholly valid despite the mistake or wholly void because of it. There is no half-way house. But if the rules of equity apply the contract may be held voidable at the option of one or both parties, or unenforceable, or enforceable only at the discretion of the court and on the terms which it imposes. It is almost impossible to predict which set of rules will apply in any given case.

A. Common law

10.3   With these forewarnings and forebodings we consider the two sets of rules in more detail. Many writers begin their discussion of the common law by distinguishing between common mistakes (i.e. where both parties are under the same mistake), mutual mistakes (where each is under a different mistake) and unilateral mistakes (where only one is mistaken). In the present writer's understanding this is not a particularly useful approach, first because of the difficulty of deciding which kind of mistake falls into which category, and second because as a general rule the law's answers do not depend upon and are not affected by this classification.

10.4 The primary interest of the common law is in whether the mistake is fundamental. *A fundamental mistake makes a contract void.* No title to the goods can pass; goods or money must be returned to their original owner. If the mistake is trivial, or even though serious is only incidental to the main object of the contract, the contract is valid and must be fulfilled. The problem then of course is in deciding what is fundamental to the contract and what is not. Lord Denning put it this way in *Solle* v. *Butcher*, 1950: *'Once a contract has been made, that is to say, once the parties, whatever their inmost states of mind, have to all outward appearances agreed with sufficient certainty in the same terms on the same subject-matter, then the contract is good unless and until it is set aside for failure of some condition on which the existence of the contract depends, or for fraud, or on some equitable ground'.*

10.5 This dictum explains very clearly the starting point of the common law, which as we said in Chapter 1 is that parties who *look as if* they are agreed will normally be bound as if they had in fact agreed – despite their perhaps very different understandings of the purpose or effect of the contract. The doctrine of estoppel – Chapter 3 – also supports this conclusion, to the extent that it makes statements binding even though made in error. We might then propose a two-part test to help us to decide whether any such mistake in their understanding is indeed so fundamental as to displace the presumption of liability: (i) What did the party alleging mistake appear to want from the contract? (ii) What did he actually get from it? It will be seen that if the answers to the two questions are the same, then, other things being equal, he has no very substantial ground for complaint. But if the answers are different, something has evidently gone seriously wrong and there may well be grounds for legal intervention.

10.6 Let us apply this suggested test to one or two of the leading cases. *Bell* v. *Lever Bros.*, 1932, perhaps the most important – though at the same time somewhat obscure – decision on the subject, concerned a company which made a large redundancy payment which it believed due to a manager on the ending of his overseas contract. The company did not know at the time that the manager was himself in breach of contract and could have been dismissed. When this was discovered the company immediately demanded repayment. The case went to the House of Lords, which rejected the company's claim. The basis of the decision was that the parties seemed to be agreed in the same terms on the same subject-matter. Looked at objectively, the contract was intended to enable the company to get rid of the manager, and that is what they succeeded in doing. Their mistake as to their liability was only incidental to the achievement of this primary purpose. This answer is certainly very unsatisfactory from the company's point of view, and also raises questions as to the manager's responsibility to disclose the true facts. But the House of Lords held that in the absence of any fraudulent intention on his part – and none was found – he had no duty to volunteer information he was not asked for.

10.7   The reasoning behind this particular aspect of the decision was expressed in the following passage by Lord Atkin, which gives a most important insight into the general level of morality still characteristic of English law. 'A buys B's horse; he thinks the horse is sound and he pays the price of a sound horse; he would certainly not have bought the horse if he had known, as the fact is, that the horse is unsound. If B has made no representation as to soundness and has not contracted that the horse is sound, A is bound and cannot recover back the price. A buys a picture from B; both A and B believe it to be the work of an old master, and a high price is paid. It turns out to be a modern copy. A has no remedy in the absence of representation or warranty. A buys from B an unfurnished dwelling-house. The house is in fact uninhabitable. A would never have entered into the bargain if he had known the fact. A has no remedy and the position is the same whether B knew the facts or not, so long as he made no representation or gave no warranty. A buys a roadside garage from B abutting on a public thoroughfare; unknown to A but known to B it has already been decided to construct a bypass road which will divert substantially the whole of the traffic from passing A's garage. Again A has no remedy. All these cases involve hardship on A and benefit to B, as most people would say unjustly. They can be supported on the ground that it is of paramount importance that contracts should be observed, and that if parties honestly comply with the essentials of the formation of contracts – that is, agree in the same terms on the same subject-matter – they are bound, and must rely on the stipulations of the contract for protection from the effect of facts unknown to them'.

10.8   The English lawyer's duty to anticipate the unknown and guard against it, as prescribed here by his Lordship, is no doubt one of the main reasons why contracts subject to English law are usually very much longer and more detailed than those made under civil law systems. Civil lawyers seem generally to rely on the implication of terms normal in the trade or industry concerned, and in particular on underlying obligations of good faith. But while the traditional and dubious moral position stated in *Bell* is still the basis of English law, it is increasingly criticised. A notable development was a Law Commission paper published in 1988 on *'Caveat Emptor* in Sales of Land'. The paper urged reversal of the rule in *Bell* and a duty upon sellers of land to disclose all material faults of which they knew or should have known. *Bell* was roundly condemned, in terms which may seem little short of amazing to anyone familiar with common law ways of thought: 'In other words, certainty was to him [Lord Atkin] better than justice. This may be thought an old-fashioned attitude in our more consumer-orientated days, and circumstances as well as times change. Certainty is no longer, if it ever was, an overriding consideration in the general law of contract'. Adoption of the Commission's proposals would in fact represent a fundamental change in the basic principles and attitudes of English contract law. (Very much in passing, we might note a slightly unusual illustration of a disclosure duty in the American case of *Stambovsky* v. *Ackley*, 1991. The New York Supreme Court held a buyer entitled to the return of his deposit because the vendor did not tell him the house was haunted. The Court said the 'buyer beware' rule could not apply because even the most diligent examination of the house would not have revealed this particular feature of the property.)

10.9   Another important case on mistake is *Amalgamated Investment* v. *Walker*, 1975. The owner of a building contracted to sell it to a property developer, knowing that he intended to convert the building into flats. Neither party knew nor could have known at the time of purchase that the building was about to be listed as having historical interest, and therefore could not be developed. The result was that the developer paid a great deal of money for a property which was almost worthless to him. He tried to recover his money on the ground that the contract was void for mistake (or alternatively that the contract was frustrated: Chapter 12). His claim was rejected. The apparent object of the contract was the purchase of 'this building', not 'this building suitable for development', and that was what he got. Theoretically at least he should have protected himself against the possibility of a preservation order not just by inquiries but by a term in the contract ensuring redevelopment rights. And on the same line of argument, if contracting parties agree to buy 'A', both mistakenly believing it to be 'B', again the contract is binding: *Rose* v. *Pim*, 1953.

10.10   We have suggested that these cases illustrate the basic principle that a contracting party cannot complain if he gets what he seems to want – a principle from which major exceptions must now be made. It will be recalled that Lord Denning said a contract could be set aside for failure of some condition on which its existence depended. So if, for example, the goods which are the subject-matter of the contract are no longer in existence, or it is otherwise impossible to identify or transfer them, the contract must be void: *Associated Japanese Bank* v. *Crédit du Nord*, 1988; *Couturier* v. *Hastie*, 1856. But there may be difficulty here in defining the subject-matter of the contract. Suppose in *Couturier*, where the ship's captain sold the cargo *en route* because it had gone bad, that not all the goods had been 'lost' in this way. It would then be necessary to decide whether the original contract was entire or divisible, i.e. whether it was for exactly the number and quantity of goods specified, no more and no less, or whether an approximation would suffice.

10.11   We should bear in mind also another and entirely different way of looking at this question. It might be possible to interpret a contract as promising that the goods are still in existence, in which case failure to supply them could be seen as a breach of contract. The remedy would then be a claim for damages. This possibility is illustrated by the curious facts of *McRae* v. *Commonwealth Commission*, 1950 (Australia). The Commission invited tenders for salvaging a shipwreck, said to be on a certain reef off the Australian coast. When the plaintiff's tender was accepted he spent large sums of money on a salvage expedition. Unfortunately neither the wreck nor even the reef had ever existed. The plaintiff successfully sued for breach of the implied undertaking that the wreck did in fact exist. For someone in *McRae*'s position, an award of damages for breach of a valid contract would clearly be a much more useful remedy than a declaration that the contract was and always had been void for mistake, which would give him no compensation at all for his losses. If demonstrably untrue or negligent statements have been made, there might alternatively be claims for damages for misrepresentation or negligent advice.

10.12   Another problem of definition arose in *Scott* v. *Coulson*, 1903. The contract was for the sale of a life insurance policy under both parties' mistaken belief that the assured (named Death) was alive. Since he was not, the contract was declared void and the seller thus entitled to the return of the policy and money due under it. It could be argued here that the apparent object of the contract was to sell 'this policy', and that that was what the seller achieved. On this interpretation the contract would have been valid. But properly speaking this was more than a sale of a document; it was of 'this policy on the life of a living person', which was not what the seller achieved.

10.13   Questions of the existence or essential identity of the subject-matter of the contract are to be contrasted with questions as to its value or other less fundamental characteristics. *Bell* and *Amalgamated Investment*, above, make it perfectly clear that one side's mistaken hopes or expectations as to the quality or benefit of his purchase do not affect the validity of the contract. A buyer's mistaken belief that a certain brand of kapok was pure when in fact it contained impurities which made it useless was held not to be a ground for annulling the contract in *Harrison* v. *Bunten*, 1953. Neither did the buyer's mistake as to the identity of the painter entitle him to set aside a contract for the sale of 'this painting' – which he might have been able to do if the contract had been for 'this painting by X': *Leaf* v. *International Galleries*, 1950. Similarly, a £5 million contract for the purchase of building land could not be annulled by discovery of a sewer which reduced the value of the land by £20,000: *Sindall* v. *Cambridgeshire C.C.*, 1994.

10.14   It is also clear from *Bell* that the fact that one side *knows* the other party is mistaken as to the value or utility of his purchase is immaterial –

227

unless, of course, the mistake results from misrepresentation. But when one side knows or should know that the other is under some much more fundamental misapprehension, i.e. as to the actual terms of the contract – the basis of their agreement – he cannot hold the other to his error. So where a buyer offered the seller £2,000 for his land, which the seller refused but agreed instead to accept £1,250, the buyer could not insist on contracting at that price which he knew was a slip of the pen: *Webster* v. *Cecil*, 1861. *Taylor* v. *Johnson*, 1983 (Australia) is a similar case, similarly decided. This conclusion, though obviously the just and necessary one, may seem inconsistent with the test proposed earlier. The seller in *Webster* seemed to want to sell at £1,250. Why should he not then be compelled to do so? The answer must be that the buyer knew appearances were deceptive. He was not in any way misled by the offer. A person cannot rely on the principle of objective appearance of agreement when he knows subjectively there is no such agreement. In contrast is *Centrovincial Estates* v. *Merchant Investors*, 1983, where a landlord was held bound by his mistaken but apparently genuine offer to renew the lease at a slightly reduced rent.

i. Identity

10.15 The same considerations apply where a party knows that his identity is in effect one of the basic terms of the contract – in other words that the other party would not deal with him except on the basis that he is who he says he is. This issue arises in cheque fraud cases, where the law often has to decide who is entitled to goods acquired thereby. Should they be returned to their original owner, or should the third party who has bought them in good faith from the swindler be allowed to keep them? English law says that the answer may depend on the importance of the buyer's identity in the original sale. If the original owner would not have sold to anyone other than the person the swindler claims to be, then the contract between them is void for mistake and so the rogue has no title to the goods. Since he has no title, he can give no title. The true owner is thus entitled to the return of the goods or their value from any purchaser from the swindler: *Ingram* v. *Little*, 1960. But if the original owner was more concerned with the wealth or reliability of the person he was dealing with – his business attributes rather than his identity – there is no basic mistake and the effect of fraud on the contract between them is only to make it voidable in equity, below: *Citibank* v. *Brown Shipley*, 1991. This is the usual situation in practice. As and when the owner discovers his loss, therefore, he can take steps to avoid the contract, e.g. by telling the police: *Car Finance* v. *Caldwell*, 1964 (doubted in the Scottish case of *McLeod* v. *Kerr*, 1965). But if the rogue has already sold the goods to an innocent third party he did so under a contract which was at that time valid, and so the third party can keep the goods: *Lewis* v. *Averay*, 1972. The answer in *Lewis* seems more consistent with the reality of the situation than that given in *Ingram*. Typically, the seller of a car is tricked into allowing the rogue to drive off in it, as if the rogue were now the owner. By so doing he seems to have given the rogue at least a conditional right to use and even to dispose of the car, and must therefore run the risk of losing it. That might not be a very agreeable conclusion from the seller's point of view, but he has to take the blame for his folly in accepting a cheque from a complete stranger.

ii. Mistaken signature

10.16   A similar problem similarly resolved affects documents signed under mistaken beliefs as to their nature or content. Such mistakes are usually brought about by fraud. If the rogue then uses the document as security for credit from an innocent third party, again the law must decide which of two innocent parties – the signatory or the third party – should be protected. On principle, signatures are binding: *L'Estrange* v. *Graucob*, 1934. In *Saunders* v. *Anglia Building Society*, 1971, however, the House of Lords recognised that where the signatory's mistake is basic, in the sense that the effect of the document is fundamentally different from what he believes, he might exceptionally be able to invoke the defence of *'non est factum'* – 'it is not my deed'. If the defence is established, the document is void and no-one can acquire any rights under it. But how different must it be? The signatory in *Saunders*, who was elderly and short sighted, signed a contract of sale of her house to a rogue, believing it to be a deed of gift of the house to her nephew. Their Lordships held her bound by her signature, since in either event the document was a disposition of her property. In any case the defence is open only to a person who has taken every reasonable care before signing. If he is careless, the effect of the fraud is to make the document voidable. It can therefore be avoided, but only until such time as a third party relies upon it in good faith: *U.D.T.* v. *Western*, 1976. It may be very difficult to decide what constitutes carelessness in the case of the elderly or infirm or illiterate; a question discussed at length in *Saunders*.

B. Equity

10.17   Thus far we have considered the stark choice at common law of having a contract declared either valid or void. But the many different kinds of mistake, the gravity of their possible consequences and the degrees of blameworthiness or otherwise which may be involved, all suggest that this is both too simple and too drastic a remedy. We turn accordingly to the rules of equity in search of more just solutions.

10.18   The need for some solution or solutions different from that of the common law is apparent from the case we began with: *Solle* v. *Butcher*. The problem here concerned a lease which both parties mistakenly believed was not controlled by the Rent Acts. When the tenant found he had been paying a higher rent than was allowed by the Acts he sued to recover his overpayments. The landlord counter-claimed that the lease should be immediately declared void for mistake. In these circumstances it would be equally unsatisfactory to say either that the contract was valid, because that would mean overriding Acts of Parliament which made it illegal, or that it was void – because the result of that would be that for no good reason the tenant would both recover all his rent and at the same time be evicted. Some middle way was needed. Lord Denning held the lease voidable in equity and gave the tenant the first option on a new lease at a lawful rent – a very acceptable solution on the facts, albeit obscure as to the law. We note that *Solle* is also important in drawing a subtle distinction between mistakes as to private rights, which are regarded as matters of fact, and mistakes of law. Ignorance of the law is said not to be a ground for invalidating a contract in England. So in *Gee* v. *News Group*, 1990, an agreement made on the basis of mistaken legal advice as to liability to pay interest on legal costs was held binding. The rule has been strongly criticised. In *Morgan Guarantee Trust* v. *Lothian R.C.*, 1995 (Scotland), and *Air Canada* v. *British Columbia*, 1989 (Canada), it was held that the distinction between mistakes of law and mistakes of fact should play no part in questions of restitution of money mistakenly paid. The same view has been taken in Australia: *David Securities* v. *Commonwealth Bank*, 1992.

10.19   It remains true to say that the circumstances in which an equitable remedy will be given, and the precise nature of that remedy, are largely unpredictable. The interrelationship of equitable and common law rules is also uncertain, though it appears that equitable remedies may be available for mistakes which are not quite so fundamental as to make contracts void at common law. We have to rely on some very broad though generally agreeable sentiments such as those in *Burrow* v. *Scammell*, 1881: 'Courts of equity have at all times relieved against honest mistakes in contracts where the literal effect and specific performance of them would be to impose a burden not contemplated and which it would be against all reason and justice to fix upon a person who, without the imputation of fraud, has inadvertently committed an accidental mistake; and also where not to correct the mistake would be to give an unconscionable advantage to either party'. Lord Denning said in *Solle* that 'A contract is also liable in equity to be set aside if the mistake of one party has been induced by a material misrepresentation of the other, *even if it was not fraudulent or fundamental*' (author's emphasis). But he has also said, no doubt to encourage a more flexible approach to the whole question, that 'A common mistake *even on a most fundamental matter* does not make the contract void at law but . . . voidable in equity' (*Magee* v. *Pennine Insurance*, 1969), which seems flatly to contradict the generally accepted view described above. In *Sindall*, above, Lord Justice Evans contributed some equally baffling observations. He thought there was 'a category of mistake which is "fundamental", so as to permit the equitable remedy of rescission [below], which is wider than the kind of "serious and radical" mistake which means that the agreement is void and of no effect in law . . . The difference may be that the common law rule is limited to mistakes with regard to the subject matter of the contract, whilst equity can have regard to a wider and perhaps unlimited category of "fundamental" mistake.'

10.20 In the absence of anything resembling a clear statement of principle, we can only give examples of the use of equitable remedies in individual mistake cases. We note that very few of the cases have involved ordinary commercial contracts. In his *'Sale of Goods'*, Professor Atiyah considers it would be undesirable to apply equitable remedies in this area, where 'the law . . . is on the whole both well-known and reasonably definite. It might create considerable uncertainty in business relations if a vague and discretionary doctrine of mistake in equity were to be applied to the sale of goods'. In other contexts, perhaps the most important equitable remedy is in the discretionary *granting or withholding of an order for specific performance*. This is an order compelling a party to carry out his contract. As we see in Chapter 13, such orders are usually given only for contracts affecting land. An illustration is the case of *Grist* v. *Bailey*, 1966. There was a contract here to sell a house at a price well below market value, both parties believing it was occupied by a tenant protected from eviction by the Rent Acts. On closer inspection the tenant proved to be dead, and so the seller refused to complete the sale. The contract was undoubtedly valid at common law, but Mr. Justice Goff refused to enforce it. There was a 'material difference' between the situation as it was believed to be and as it was in fact. Enforcement in these circumstances would have given the buyer a wholly unjustifiable benefit. The judge ordered instead that the buyer be given the first right to negotiate a new and fair price if the seller still wished to sell.

10.21 A buyer's bid at an auction for an altogether different piece of land from the one he wanted was not specifically enforced in *Malins* v. *Freeman*, 1837, though damages for breach of contract were awarded against him. In *Tamplin* v. *James*, 1880, on the other hand, an order was made to compel the defendant to buy the land he had bid for, even though he had been mistaken as to its size. These decisions clearly turn on the degree of hardship involved in the particular case. It is nonetheless generally true that a mistake by one party which is not known to or induced by the other is not a ground for invalidating a contract either at common law or in equity: *Riverlate* v. *Paul*, 1974. So in *Centrovincial Estates* v. *Merchant Investors*, above, the landlord who claimed a lower rent than intended was estopped from demanding more when he discovered his mistake.

10.22 Another equitable remedy is that of *rescission* – by which the contract is declared ended, but not necessarily void from the start. As illustrated above in the cases of *Solle* and *Grist*, the contract may be rescinded on terms laid down by the court enabling the parties to renegotiate their agreement, or possibly apportioning the loss caused by mistake, even where the contract is void at common law: *Cooper* v. *Phibbs*, 1867; *Taylor*, above. In *Huddersfield Banking* v. *Lister*, 1895, a bank agreed to the sale of an insolvent company's goods under the mistaken belief that it had no claim to them. It later appeared that the bank's agreement was induced by wrongful interference with the goods by a third party, and on this basis its agreement was rescinded.

10.23 A further possibility is an order for *rectification* of a contract. The court here orders the amendment of a written agreement to make it express more accurately (and thereby to allow enforcement of) the terms of a previous oral agreement. It must be clear that the previous oral agreement expresses the common intention of the parties. Mere confusion over what has been agreed is not a ground for rectification: *Cambro* v. *Kennelly*, 1994. But in *Commission for the New Towns* v. *Cooper*, 1995, the Court of Appeal recognised that other circumstances might arise which would make it unjust or inequitable to refuse rectification. In this case, A misled B as to the effect of their contract. The Court allowed rectification to enable B to enforce the contract as he had understood it. Conversely, rectification will not be granted to a party who knows of or has induced the other's mistake. Nor will it be granted merely because the original oral agreement was itself mistaken, as in *Rose* v. *Pim*, above, nor where there has been an unreasonable lapse of time in seeking such order, nor where third parties would be prejudiced.

C. Commonwealth and American rules

10.24 The same basic principles of common law and equity – such as they are – apply in most Commonwealth countries, explained and illustrated in those countries' own contributions to the common law. A major exception is New Zealand, which has attempted to reform and codify the law in its Contractual Mistakes Act 1977. This interesting and important venture in effect adopts the classification of common, mutual and unilateral mistake which we mentioned at the beginning of this chapter, but differs from the common law in the way it defines the grounds for intervention and in giving more comprehensive relief. The question for the court is whether the mistake resulted in a 'substantially unequal exchange of values' or a benefit or burden 'substantially disproportionate to the consideration therefor'. In such cases the court can make whatever order seems just, including a declaration of entire or partial validity of the contract, cancellation or variation of the contract, restitution or compensation.

10.25 These considerations indicate the influence of American contract law, as expressed in the second Restatement. While the Restatement adopts the language and classifications of English common law it also seeks a more flexible approach. The overall test of enforcement is whether the result would be 'unconscionable', nearer the Continental model, which in many cases depends more on the extent of the loss involved on one side or the other, assuming that neither is at fault, rather than on the precise form of the mistake: comment (a) of Section 153 of the Restatement. *Aluminium Co. of America* v. *Essex Group*, 1980, is an interesting example. Both parties contracted in ignorance of very large increases in the costs involved. If the contract had been enforced the plaintiff would have lost $60 million. The court held that there was a mutual mistake on a matter of fundamental importance, and that the contract should therefore be set aside. The reasoning is similar to that used in frustration cases: Chapter 12.

Danish law

10.26   Under Danish law the overall test of enforcement of a contract is whether the result would be reasonable: Article 36, Contracts Act 1975. Even if the result would be unreasonable the contract is not necessarily void, but may be set aside in part to give a reasonable outcome. Danish law thus provides much more flexible solutions to cases of mistake than English law. There is no need for classification of the type of mistake, and various different kinds of relief may be granted.

10.27   Article 32 of the Contracts Act concerns promises whose effect is different from that intended by the promisor because of his mistake. It says that where the promisee knows or ought to know of the mistake, the promisor is not bound. The contract is not necessarily void, but may be binding in the terms originally intended. It is thus not a question of all or nothing as under English law, but of finding a reasonable solution.

10.28   It follows that in the circumstances of non-disclosure discussed by Lord Atkin in *Bell*, para. 10.7, the buyer there would certainly have a remedy for breach of contract if the seller knew the facts; as also in the case he cites of the uninhabitable house – even if in that case the seller did not know there was anything wrong. The Danish solution to a case such as *Solle*, para. 10.18, would be that the tenant would remain in possession at the lawful rent and could recover his overpayment.

10.29   Rights of third parties are again determined by what is fair and reasonable in the circumstances, and do not depend, as in English law, upon the precise importance the original seller attaches to the identity or attributes of his buyer.

Dutch law

10.30 Dutch law provides, subject to some exceptions, that in case of mistake a contract may be annulled or its effect modified to avoid hardship. Articles 6.228–30 of the Civil Code give these remedies when there is an error without which the contract would not have been made, provided (a) the mistake was caused by reliance on information given by the other party, or (b) the other party should have informed the mistaken party, or (c) there has been a significant mutual mistake. No remedy will be given for a mistake solely as to a future fact or one for which according to 'common opinion or the circumstances of the case' the mistaken party must take responsibility. Dutch case law requires a prospective seller, far more often than does English law, to disclose relevant information he may have regarding the property to be sold. So in *Van Lanschot Bankiers* v. *Bink*, NJ 1991, 759, a debtor's mother escaped liability under a suretyship agreement with the bank, because the bank had not warned her of the risks involved. In *Gerards* v. *Vijverberg*, NJ 1994, 291, a car seller told the buyer the car had been driven 45,000 km when in fact it had been driven over 90,000 km. The contract was held invalid, despite an exclusion clause.

10.31 A case such as *Solle*, para. 10.18, under Dutch law would not be treated as one of mistake but rather as a problem of an illegal contract.

French law

10.32 Article 1109 provides that 'there is no valid consent, if the consent has been given only by mistake, or if it has been extorted by duress or by fraud'. Article 1110 provides that 'mistake is a cause of nullity of the contract only if it relates to the very substance of the subject-matter. It is not a cause of nullity if it relates only to the person with whom one intends to contract, unless this person is the main reason for the contract'.

10.33 Of the numerous distinctions flowing from contradictory case law, one flows from Roman law (Carbonnier, '*Les obligations*'; Cabrillac, *op. cit.*, paras. 56 *et seq.*) which distinguishes between three categories of mistakes: *erreur-obstacle*, which prevents any agreement; *erreur-nullité*, which vitiates the consent of one of the parties; and *erreur-indifférente*, which covers all the other sorts of mistakes and does not permit avoidance of the contract.

10.34 The *erreur-obstacle* can be a mistake as to the very nature of the contract. Where, for example, one party believes he is making a contract of sale and a loan agreement for financing it, while the other party intends to provide the equipment under a hire-purchase agreement, there is in fact no agreement at all: Req. 9 December 1913. Another example was where the vendor intended to sell shares in a property company, while the purchaser believed he was buying an apartment owned by the company: Paris, 8 July 1966. No contract was made when a party waived his rights under a lease because of the inaccurate statement of a notary that the lease was invalid: Req. 13 December 1927. This latter example overlaps with nullity for 'false cause' provided for in Article 1131.

10.35   The *erreur-nullité* is that which is referred to in Article 1110 as vitiating the consent of the parties either because of a mistake as to the substance or 'substantial qualities' of the subject-matter of the contract, or in contracts made because of a mistake as to the identity of the other party. Error on the substance is that which 'relates to those essential and substantial qualities and characteristics of the subject-matter' of the contract which have been the very reasons for making the contract. The Poussin case (last decision: Versailles, 7th January 1987) is a classic example. A seller sold a painting in the style of Poussin at the fair market value of paintings of the Poussin School, and discovered only afterwards that the painting had been authenticated as a genuine Poussin by the Louvre. On appeal, the sale was nullified. The court held that 'in public sales of works of art with certifications by experts, the identity of the artist is both for the seller and for the purchaser a substantial quality of the subject-matter of the contract'. It is questionable whether an English court would have decided the case in the same way (*see* para. 10.7). A mistake as to the identity of the other contracting party can annul the contract only if it concerns the essential qualities of that person, whether physical, intellectual, moral or legal, which have been the basis for the contract – e.g., where a person thought he was contracting with an experienced corporate commercial agent, not with an individual: *Saint-Denis de la Réunion*, 16 October 1989.

10.36   *Erreurs indifférentes*, i.e., mistakes which do not nullify a contract, are all other sorts of mistakes – notably mistakes on qualities or characteristics of the subject-matter of the contract which are not essential, mistaken motives (unless so important that they can be characterised as the cause of the contract), and mistakes as the economic terms of the contract (value of the goods, profit to be drawn from the operation, etc.). From the Poussin case, among others, it will be seen that it may be very difficult to distinguish between the value and the actual substance of the subject-matter of the contract, and that French courts do not always draw the distinction as rigidly as they might.

10.37   In any case, a mistake will invalidate a contract only if it is 'excusable'. In deciding this question, the courts take account of the professional qualification or abilities of the party alleging mistake and of whether the parties performed their obligations in good faith, in particular in giving the other party all the required information prior to contracting: Article 1134.

10.38   Claims for nullity under Article 1110 must be lodged within five years of the discovery of the mistake. If the mistake resulted from negligent or deliberately misleading behaviour by the other party, such party can be held liable in damages.

German law

10.39   German contract law does not regulate mistakes in the same complicated way as in England. The basic rule is in Article 119, BGB, which says that only in certain limited circumstances is a party free to avoid his contract because of mistake. These circumstances include slips of the pen, as in *Webster*, para. 10.13, and the use of terms or expressions whose meaning or effect the party has not understood. Mistaken motives do not make a contract void. So for example a German court would make the same decision on the facts of *Amalgamated Investment*, para. 10.9, as in England. If avoidance is allowed, the contract is void *ab initio*.

10.40   In German law a contract is either valid or void. Compromise solutions such as those provided by the rules of equity are not available. *Solle*, para. 10.18, would not have been decided by reference to the law of mistake, but in accordance with statute. In *Grist*, para. 10.20, a German court would have held the original contract valid. Cases like *Lewis*, para. 10.15, would be decided the same way, but for a different reason – the strict separation between the law of obligations and the law of property in the BGB. When a person buys goods from a seller who is not owner, he becomes the owner if he buys in good faith (e.g. without knowledge of a retention of title clause). But this rule does not apply to lost or stolen goods: Articles 932–5. The remedies of rescission, making a contract void retrospectively, and rectification, are not known in the context of mistake.

Italian law

10.41   A mistake which a reasonable man would recognise as fundamental makes a contract voidable under Italian law: Articles 1429–31 of the Civil Code. This might be such a mistake as would lead a party to make a contract he would not otherwise make – an *errore vizio* – or it might be an incorrect statement of what has been agreed – an *errore ostativo*.

10.42 According to Article 1429, a mistake is fundamental in any of the following circumstances: when it concerns the nature or purpose of the contract; the identity of the subject-matter or a quality of it which according to common understanding or in the particular circumstances must have been crucial to the party's consent; the identity or other personal and essential qualities of the other contracting party; or a mistake of law which is the main reason for making the contract. Errors in calculation are not usually of this fundamental nature but may justify correction of the contract: Article 1430. Mistakes about the value of goods do not in themselves affect the validity of a contract: Corte di Cassazione, 24 July 1993, n. 8290.

10.43 A mistaken party who has not yet suffered any loss cannot demand annulment of the contract if the other side offers to fulfil the contract in the terms originally intended: Article 1432.

10.44 A claim for annulment can only be brought by the mistaken party. He must claim within five years of discovery of the mistake. Mistaken payments must then be returned and goods and services paid for or returned: Article 2033.

Spanish law

10.45 Articles 1265–6 of the Spanish Civil Code say that a mistake makes a contract voidable if it relates to or alters the substance of the thing which is the object of the contract, or affects those features or conditions of it which were the main reasons for making the contract. Mistake as to identity has the same effect if likewise crucial to the contract. A mistake merely in mathematical calculation will be corrected. A claim to annul a contract because of mistake must be brought within four years after it was made.

10.46 Examples of the 'substance' of the contract include Supreme Court cases annulling the purchase of a car as new when in fact it was second-hand and the buying of property which unknown to the buyer was subject to a compulsory purchase order. The court distinguishes between the common intention of the contracting parties and the objectives or intentions of each individual party. If both parties' intentions are the basis of the contract, but not fulfilled because of a mistake, the contract is voidable. But if only one party fails to fulfil his objectives he has no claim unless they were stated as terms of the contract: Supreme Court decision of 24 November 1978.

10.47 The Supreme Court has also said that mistake will only invalidate a contract if it is excusable, i.e. could not have been avoided by ordinary care. Business responsibility includes a *deber de informarse* – a duty to inform oneself. So in a decision of 21 June 1978 the Court refused for this reason to annul the sale of a building expressly described as old which the buyer found was not fit for his intended business purposes.

Swedish law

10.48 Mistake as to basic assumptions may affect a contract where one party, even though unaware of the mistake, would still accept that if the assumption failed it would be of fundamental importance to the other party. There is a theory in Swedish law, connected with the German *Wegfall von Geschäftsgrundlage,* called *'förutsättningsläran'*; i.e., that mistake in basic assumptions may make a contract void. This principle appears in legislation, notably in the Sale of Goods Act concerning non-conformity and in Article 36 of the Contract Act regarding unfair contract terms. But the application of *'förutsättningsläran'* outside express legislation is uncertain.

Chapter 11

Misrepresentation, duress and illegal contracts

11.1   In the previous chapter we considered how contracts governed by English law might be affected by the mistakes of one or both parties as to their terms or advantages. We discuss now a further and wider range of circumstances in which contracts may be invalidated – because of a party's innocent or deliberate misstatement, abuse of influence, or other action which for one reason or another is held to be against public policy. We should bear in mind the possible overlap of mistake and misrepresentation. Misrepresentations usually cause mistakes – though not necessarily recognised as such by the law – but mistakes may be made without misrepresentations. The differing solutions are described below.

A. Misrepresentation

11.2   The word 'representation' has various possible meanings in everyday usage and in law. In formal contracts, e.g. for the sale of a business, it is sometimes used interchangeably with or in addition to 'warranty' – as in: 'The vendor warrants and represents . . .' In this way the vendor promises the truth or accuracy of statements he has made in the contract, or perhaps confirms contractual prerequisites such as his right to sell, the profitability of the business, its freedom from indebtedness, etc. The contract might then expressly or impliedly entitle the innocent party to repudiate the contract if the promise is broken. But the usual legal meaning of the word, and the one we are concerned with in this Chapter, is more technical and restricted, as follows: *A representation is a statement of fact made by one person to another which influences that other in making a contract with the representor, but which is not necessarily a term of that contract.* The statement may be made at or before the time the contract is made. It may be made by or to an agent of the party in question. Exceptionally, the definition may cover a contract made by a third party if the representor knows the third party is likely to be influenced by his statement. So in *Yianni* v. *Evans*, 1982, a building society valuer was liable for a negligent valuation which led the plaintiff to take a loan from the society in order to buy the house.

11.3   A simple example of a representation would be where a person who wants to sell his car tells an interested inquirer that the car has had only one previous owner, or done only 50,000 miles. Either of these statements might influence a decision to buy the car, but neither of them would usually be regarded as an express term of the contract. If after the sale the statement is proved false, what should be the buyer's remedy? There should be no difficulty in helping him if the falsehood is deliberate, but if the seller made his statement in good faith, e.g. in reliance on what a previous owner had told him, we may see a problem both in penalising the seller and in compensating the buyer on grounds which neither thought important enough to include in the contract. Before considering the rules and remedies under English law, however, we might observe that other legal systems do not seem to have the same difficulties in dealing with this problem. America's Uniform Commercial Code, Section 2–313, abolished the distinction between terms and 'non-terms' by regarding all 'affirmations of fact made by the seller about the goods during a bargain' as part of the description of those goods, and therefore binding. Continental systems likewise do not see misrepresentations as a separate legal wrong, as we note at the end of this Chapter.

11.4   For the purposes of English law, the first requirement of a representation is that it be a statement of *fact* – usually, that is to say, a positive assertion (*see Walters* v. *Morgan*, below) capable of being proved right or wrong. As a general rule therefore things said in advertisements and sales talk cannot be representations because they cannot be tested. They are merely 'puffs', and as such have no legal significance. The same has been true of much 'poetic licence' invoked by estate agents – who are now subject to the Property Misdescriptions Act 1991. The Act makes it an offence for an estate agent or property developer to make false or misleading statements about land, but an offence does not as such affect contractual obligations. As we saw in *Carlill's* case in Chapter 1, claims which *can* be tested may give rise to liability. So the seller was liable in *Goff* v. *Gauthier*, 1991, and *Smith New Court* v. *Scrimgeour Vickers*, 1994, for falsely telling a prospective purchaser he had another buyer willing to pay a higher price, as also in *Atlantic Estates* v. *Ezekiel*, 1991, where premises described as a wine bar bringing in a regular rent had in fact lost their liquor licence and were occupied by a tenant who was in arrears. Border line cases include *Long* v. *Lloyd*, 1958, where the assertion that a lorry was in 'exceptional condition' – which in its own way it was – was held to be a misrepresentation, and *Ecay* v. *Godfrey*, 1947, where the seller said his boat was in good condition – a (false) statement of fact – but advised the buyer to have it surveyed, which was held to nullify the misrepresentation.

11.5   Much the same point is made by contrasting statements of fact with statements of opinion. To say: 'To the best of my knowledge and belief this car has done 50,000 miles' is on the face of it a statement of opinion, and so the buyer has no claim if the estimate is wrong: *Humming Bird Motors* v. *Hobbs*, 1986; *Bisset* v. *Wilkinson*, 1927. On the other hand it is a question of fact whether the representor actually holds that opinion, or at least has some good reason for holding it. If he knows what he says is untrue, or does not care whether it is true or false, he is guilty of a misrepresentation. A landowner's reference to his 'most desirable tenant' was a misstatement of fact when he knew the tenant was in arrears with the rent: *Smith* v. *Land Corp.*, 1884. When an expert gives what might seem only an opinion, he might nonetheless be liable for an implied misstatement of fact if and in so far as he wrongly suggests that he has exercised his special skill and judgment on the question: *Sindall* v. *Cambridgeshire C.C.*, 1994; *Esso* v. *Mardon*, 1976; *Brown* v. *Raphael*, 1958 – solicitor's statement of tax liability deemed to be statement of fact. A car dealer's assessment of a car's age might be seen in this way when a layman's would not be: *Bentley* v. *Smith*, 1965; *Chess* v. *Williams*, 1957. That does not, of course, mean that *everything* an expert says is necessarily a statement of fact: *Gilchester* v. *Gomm*, 1948. So, for example, a solicitor is not necessarily liable for the accuracy of advice given to him by a third party: *Gran Gelato* v. *Richcliff*, 1992 (even though on the facts of this particular case one might have expected the solicitor to check the accuracy of the advice before passing it on).

11.6 Statements of existing fact contrast also with statements or promises as to future events or intentions. A person who gives an assurance as to his intentions which he fails to fulfil is not liable for misrepresentation – unless he deliberately misstates his intentions by saying that he will do something which he has in fact no intention of doing. Surrounding circumstances might provide the necessary evidence of his true frame of mind. In the absence of a deliberate misstatement of intention, a person giving an assurance as to the future could be liable only for breach of promise – which presupposes that a contract has been made which includes that promise and that the other side has thereby given consideration for it (Chapter 3).

11.7 Yet another distinction is between fact and law. A misstatement of the law of the land is not a misrepresentation, unless the representor does not believe in the truth of his statement. A misstatement as to the law's application in particular circumstances, however, may be one of fact. It appears from *Solle* v. *Butcher*, 1951, para. 10.18, for example, that representations as to private rights are regarded as matters of fact. Similarly in *Horry* v. *Tate & Lyle*, 1982, a misstatement as to the effect of a legal settlement was held to be one of fact. Statements of foreign law are regarded in the same way, except as regards EEC law: Section 3, European Communities Act 1972.

i. Silence

11.8   We have said there must be a 'positive assertion' of fact. It follows that keeping quiet cannot usually constitute a representation – particularly because, as we saw in *Bell* v. *Lever Bros.*, para. 10.6, English law imposes no overall duty to volunteer information for which one is not asked. So, for example, a seller is not obliged to advise a buyer as to the wisdom of his purchase, as was said in 1861 in *Walters* v. *Morgan*. The position remains much the same today, though increasingly subject to criticism: para. 10.8. The judgment in *Walters* also tells us that it may still be possible to interpret silence as a positive assertion: *'There being no fiduciary relation between vendor and purchaser in the negotiation*, the purchaser is not bound to disclose any fact exclusively within his knowledge which might reasonably be expected to influence the price of the subject to be sold. *Simple reticence does not amount to legal fraud, however it might be viewed by moralists.* But a single word, or a nod or a wink or a shake of the head, or a smile from the purchaser intended to induce the vendor to believe the existence of a non-existing fact, which might influence the price of the subject to be sold, would be sufficient ground for a Court of Equity to refuse a decree for a specific performance of the agreement' [Author's emphasis].

11.9   An early example of the basic principle is *Ward* v. *Hobbs*, 1878 – a case discreetly omitted from most modern text books as evidently indefensible. The seller here sold his pigs in the market 'with all faults', knowing they were infected with typhoid. He was held to be under no duty to disclose their true condition. No doubt his exclusion clause would fail today under the Unfair Contract Terms Act, but what if he had simply said nothing? In theory he would still not be liable because of the basic rules that one is not obliged to volunteer information and that one cannot make a representation by silence. But by today's standards the conclusion in *Ward* is clearly repugnant, and as we have seen there are signs of the law trying to work its way toward a more morally acceptable position. It could be argued, for example, that simply by putting goods up for sale a seller makes a representation by conduct as to their fitness. In *Hurley* v. *Dyke*, 1979, Lord Hailsham thought that *Ward* should be 'reconsidered' in the light of developments in the law of negligence indicating a duty to warn of danger or loss. Lord Justice Slade agreed that there was such a duty in *Banque Financière* v. *Skandia*, 1988. In *Doherty* v. *Allen*, 1989 (Canada), the failure of the lessor of a petrol station to warn the lessee of a petrol leak was held to be an 'implicit negligent misrepresentation' that no precautions were necessary. Even if the rules were reconsidered, however, there would probably be no change in the view taken in *Turner* v. *Green*, 1895, where the plaintiff's solicitor kept to himself information about a proposed settlement which was against the interests of the defendant. The settlement was nonetheless binding. Similarly in *Percival* v. *Wright*, 1902, a company director buying shares from a shareholder in that company was held under no obligation to disclose his knowledge of their true value.

11.10   Certain limited exceptions to the general requirement of a positive statement are already well recognised. We note briefly the proposition that things left unsaid may distort what has been said. Half-truths, in other words, may amount to falsehoods. Examples may be found particularly in the company law context, as in *R* v. *Kylsant*, 1932, where a director was convicted for saying that his company had paid regular dividends, but failed to mention they were paid out of capital. Another qualification of the silence rule is that the representor must correct his previous statement if before the contract is made he receives new information which makes his earlier statement substantially incorrect – e.g. as to the profits of a business to be sold: *With* v. *O'Flanagan*, 1936. This case may be contrasted with *Wales* v. *Wadham*, 1977 where it was held that a divorce settlement, reached on the basis of a wife's previously stated intention not to remarry, was not affected by the fact that she had changed her mind by the time of the settlement but had not told the husband. The reason for the decision was the rule mentioned earlier that an honest statement of intention is not a statement of fact.

ii. Fiduciary relationships

11.11   More significant commercially is the duty of disclosure which the common law imposes in contracts *uberrimae fidei*. In the limited circumstances in which the rule applies, below, English law recognises a good faith rule and with it an obligation to disclose all relevant information. Failure to disclose makes the contract voidable and obliges the wrongdoer to account for secret profits, but is not in itself a misrepresentation and does not give rise to a claim for damages: *Banque Financière* v. *Skandia*, 1990; *Uphoff* v. *International Energy Trading*, 1989; *Bank of Nova Scotia* v. *Hellenic Mutual*, 1992. Contracts of this kind include family arrangements, insurance contracts, and contracts where one party is in a fiduciary relationship with another. In sales of land, defects in the seller's title must be disclosed. Under current proposals, the seller should reveal also any other faults in the property of which he knows or ought to know: para. 10.8.

11.12   For present purposes probably the most important of these issues is that of insurance. English law here is in an unsatisfactory state. While the main burden of disclosing all material facts is necessarily on the party seeking insurance – though the insurer should tell him of facts which reduce the risk – there have been several controversial decisions as to what constitutes materiality, and what should be the effect of failure to disclose. *Pan Atlantic Insurance* v. *Pine-Top Insurance*, 1994, defines material facts as those which a prudent insurer needs to know – but the problems remain. The insured may be penalised, for example, because he has omitted facts which he has not specifically been asked about but which the insurance company regards as material, or even because he has failed to declare facts of which he was unaware, such as a latent illness. In *Dawsons* v. *Bonnin*, 1922, the House of Lords held that an inadvertent and unimportant misstatement by the insured nullified the whole policy because the proposal form required strictly accurate answers to all questions. The Law Commission has criticised such decisions and the insurance policies they were based on. Complaints about insurance practices may usefully be made to the Insurance Ombudsman, rather than by going to law.

11.13   Fiduciary duties arise also as between partners, principal and agent, shareholders in a company, and other such 'dependency' relationships. In *Armstrong* v. *Jackson*, 1917, it was held that a stockbroker should have told his client that he was selling his – the stockbroker's – own shares to him. But the principle involved is more far-reaching than might appear, and raises questions of the overall duties of banks and other such institutions to their customers. What if any advisory responsibilities for example, might a bank have to a customer before lending him money? This question was examined at length in *Lloyd's Bank* v. *Bundy*, 1975, which we discussed in Chapter 7 and which, it may be recalled, led to the conclusion that in certain exceptional circumstances one party might only be able to enforce his contract if he had first warned the other that he should seek independent advice. In *Barclays Bank* v. *O'Brien*, 1993, the House of Lords held that a bank lending money to a husband should do its best to ensure that his wife has independent advice before she contracts with the bank to act as surety for the loan. This rule is not part of the law of Scotland: *Mumford* v. *Bank of Scotland*, 1995.

iii. Material reason

11.14   English law gives no remedy for misrepresentation unless it led the representee to enter into a contract with the representor. The misrepresentation need not be the main or only reason for making the contract, but it must have been a significant influence. There can be no claim for inaccuracies in a prospectus if they did not influence the judgment of the investor: *Smith* v. *Chadwick*, 1884. In *JEB Fasteners* v. *Marks*, 1983, company A took over company B in order to secure the services of B's directors. Company A knew at the time of the takeover that B's financial position had not been correctly stated by the auditors, but the extent of the inaccuracy was not known. When the true figures were established A tried to avoid the contract. It was held that the contract was binding because the state of B's accounts had not been sufficiently crucial to A's decision. B had been taken over for other reasons, and despite A's knowledge that the accounts were not correct.

11.15   An old but still controversial decision is *Horsfall* v. *Thomas*, 1862. Here the seller hid a defect in a gun which the buyer bought without examining it. The court held that the buyer had therefore not been influenced by the concealment. The correct rule is probably that found in *Redgrave* v. *Hurd*, 1881. In this case a seller of a business provided papers purporting to show the value of the business. The buyer did not read them. On their being proved false he was still able to rescind the contract because, said the court, he had taken the seller's word and was not obliged to check the accuracy of the papers.

iv. Remedies

11.16   The remedies for misrepresentation depend first on whether the misstatement was only an inducement – an element in the representee's decision to make a contract – or whether it was sufficiently important to become an express or implied term of that contract. An example of the latter is *Bannerman* v. *White*, 1861, where the prospective buyer asked for certain assurances about the quality of the goods and made it clear that he would not buy them unless the assurances were correct. Those assurances were therefore held to be implied terms of the contract. An expert car dealer's assessment of the age of a valuable vintage car was held to be a term in *Bentley* v. *Smith*, above. That being so, the buyer's remedies are as for any other kind of breach of contract, namely the remedies described in Chapters 5 and 13. For a breach of warranty – a minor term – he can claim damages; for breach of condition – a fundamental term – damages and/or repudiation of the contract.

11.17   In contrast to these familiar remedies, available for any breach of contract as such, there are others which are available only for misrepresentation, whether or not the statement in question is a term of the contract. The position then becomes more complicated. To find the appropriate remedy we must ask whether the misrepresentation was made fraudulently, negligently or innocently. The remedies for fraud are laid down by the common law; those for negligent and innocent misrepresentation by statute.

v. Fraud

11.18   A statement of fact is fraudulent if the person making it knows it is false, or is reckless or indifferent as to whether it is true or false. A statement based on a mistake or misunderstanding cannot be fraudulent: *Derry* v. *Peek*, 1889. *Fraud gives rise to liability for damages for the tort of deceit and/or the right to rescind the resulting voidable contract* (below), or, as the case may be, the right to refuse to perform it. Damages here are intended to ensure that the victim recovers actual lost expenditure. So if he buys for £1,000 goods fraudulently represented to be worth that sum, but with a current market value of only £250, he can recover £750, together with any direct consequential loss, but excluding the loss of profit he might have expected to make in contract. No additional damages can be claimed if the current market value is itself based on fraud or a hidden defect discovered only after the purchase: *Smith New Court* v. *Scrimgeour Vickers*, 1994 (Court of Appeal).

vi. Negligence

11.19   Statements which are not deliberately false nor made recklessly may nonetheless make the representor liable if he spoke or wrote in good faith, but could and should have known they were incorrect. Liability on these grounds was introduced by the Misrepresentation Act 1967 (an Act unusual and commendable among English statutes for its brevity, yet at the same time worded in such a way as to make it almost entirely incomprehensible). A vexed example of negligent misrepresentation is *Howard Marine* v. *Ogden*, 1978. In answer to a question from a prospective hirer, a barge owner gave the capacity of his boats as 1,600 tonnes, based on his recollection of the Lloyd's Register figure of 1,800 tonnes. The correct figure, which was stated in shipping documents the owner had previously seen, was 1,055. The barges were hired, but without any reference to their capacity in the contract. They proved too small for the work involved. The hirers refused to pay and successfully sued for damages for negligent misrepresentation.

11.20   We should note that the law of tort likewise gives a remedy for negligent misstatements which cause financial loss: *Hedley Byrne* v. *Heller*, 1964. The differences between the tortious and contractual claims are that in tort it is necessary to show a 'special relationship' of trust and dependence between the parties, but not to show that the misstatement resulted in a contract. On the other hand again, in a tort action the onus of proving negligence is on the plaintiff, whereas under Section 2(1) of the Misrepresentation Act it is for the defendant representor to prove that he had reasonable grounds for making his statement. If he fails, as he did in *Howard Marine, the representor is liable in damages and/or the contract may be rescinded*. In *Cemp Properties* v. *Dentsply*, 1991, the Court of Appeal said that damages for innocent and fraudulent misrepresentation alike represented basically the difference between what was paid and the actual market value of what was received. If that sum did not cover the losses sustained, other direct losses should be compensated. Under *Hedley Byrne*, damages are for reasonably foreseeable losses.

vii. Innocent misrepresentation

11.21   A statement made in good faith and on good grounds, but nonetheless incorrectly, may give rise to liability for innocent misrepresentation. English law has always been reluctant to 'punish' for this particular kind of error, particularly where the statement was not subsequently made a term of the contract. Before the Misrepresentation Act no remedy at all was given

246

if the ensuing contract was actually carried out, and if it remained executory – *in futuro* – there was only the right to rescind and the possibility of an indemnity. An indemnity may not be as substantial as an award of damages. It reimburses the representee only for those expenses which he was strictly obliged to meet rather than those which were merely the direct consequences of the representation and the contract. So in *Whittington* v. *Seale Hayne*, 1900, a person who bought a farm on the basis of an innocent misrepresentation as to its sanitary condition recovered the money he was compelled to spend on the drains by local authority order, and also his outgoings on rates, but had no claim for his manager's illness and the loss of poultry, though both were directly caused by health hazards at the farm.

11.22 Under Section 2(2) of the Misrepresentation Act *the remedy for innocent misrepresentation is either an award of damages or, at the discretion of the court, an order for rescission and indemnity.* The court might see damages as preferable to rescission if the loss caused by the misrepresentation is small and rescission appears as too drastic a solution in the circumstances. If so, the damages should do no more than make up the shortfall in the expected value of the subject-matter of the contract.

11.23 Rescission is a somewhat speculative remedy. It will not usually be granted unless it is possible to return the subject-matter in effectively the same state as when originally transferred – *restitutio in integrum.* Any undue delay or unnecessary use may therefore preclude the remedy. Keeping a picture for five years prevented its return for alleged misrepresentation in *Leaf* v. *International Galleries*, 1950. Similarly, the possibility of rescission will be lost if the representee appears to affirm or accept the effects of the misrepresentation, as with the buyer who tried to repair and continued to use the defective lorry in *Long* v. *Lloyd*, above. (But he may still claim damages: *Production Technology* v. *Bartlett*, 1988.) On the other hand merely using the goods or property so far as is necessary to see they conform with the contract, or other normal deterioration, should not prevent rescission. If a third party has acquired rights over the goods or property before the representee tries to avoid the contract, rescission is likewise barred: *Lewis* v. *Averay*, 1972. But if the misrepresentation was such as to lead the representee to make a contract under a basic mistake, e.g., as to the representor's identity, then the contract is not merely voidable but void from the outset – under the rules on mistake discussed in Chapter 10. Goods delivered or money paid must then be returned. In *Ingram* v. *Little*, 1960, for example, a rogue acquired a car from the owner by a false pretence as to his identity. He then sold the car to an innocent third party. Since the owner's mistake was regarded as basic, the rogue could not pass a good title, and so the third party had to return the car.

viii. Misrepresentation and breach of contract

11.24   We may see now that the remedies given for misrepresentation are different from those for breach of contract as such. But what if the misrepresentation is also a breach of contract? If a misrepresentation were at the same time a breach of warranty, that would appear to mean either the possibility of a right to rescind under the Misrepresentation Act, or a definite right to claim damages, but not to rescind, at common law. If the misrepresentation involved also a breach of condition, then as such it would give the representee a right to repudiate the contract which is not limited by the restrictive rules on rescission. It seems to be for the representee to choose whichever remedy he prefers.

ix. Exclusion clauses

11.25   We noted in Chapter 7 the common use of standard form contracts which expressly exclude liability for pre-contractual misrepresentation, and we discussed also the control of such clauses by Section 8 of the Unfair Contract Terms Act. Another way of dealing with the problem, equally commonly used, is by making it clear in the contract that the terms set out there are the sole basis and content of the contract and cannot be altered without specific authority. Typical wording is: 'This written agreement constitutes the entire agreement between the customer and the company and no changes of any kind shall alter this agreement unless in writing signed by an authorised signatory of both parties'. Or again: 'No employee or officer of the company has authority to contract on any other terms or to vary, waive or amend these terms, unless such other terms, variation, waiver or amendment are evidenced in writing signed on behalf of the company'. These are not strictly exclusion clauses, but have the same purpose and so should be subject to the same statutory controls – but *see* para. 7.44.

B. Duress and undue influence

11.26   The common law has long since recognised that contracts made under threat of physical injury or imprisonment can be avoided by the weaker party. More recently – and more importantly for present purposes – the law has accepted also that the same may be true of contracts made under economic duress. Economic duress may occur when one party threatens to do something unlawful, e.g. to break his own contract, unless the other gives in, or exerts such a degree of otherwise lawful pressure as to leave the other party with no alternative but to agree to his demands. This issue arose also in the course of our discussion of valuable consideration in Chapter 3.

11.27   Examples of the meaning and effect of duress include *Atlas* v. *Kafco*, 1989. The plaintiff contracted to carry the defendant's goods for a certain price, and then a few weeks later decided the price he had asked was too low. He demanded a higher price, and refused to carry the defendant's goods, then awaiting delivery, unless he agreed to pay. The plaintiff knew the defendant had promised to supply the goods to a major customer, and knew also that the customer would sue the defendant for breach of contract and stop dealing with him if he failed to deliver. The defendant was 'over a barrel', unable to find another carrier immediately, and so was obliged under protest to agree to pay the higher price. After the plaintiff had delivered the goods the defendant paid only the original price. The plaintiff's claim for the additional sum was rejected, both on grounds of economic duress and his failure to give consideration for the second agreement. Strikes or threats of strikes could have the same effect: *B & S Contracts* v. *Green*, 1984. A trade union's threat to 'black' a ship and prevent it sailing unless money was paid to the union's 'benevolent' fund, in circumstances where there was no legitimate trade dispute, led to recovery of the payment in *Dimskal* v. *I.T.F.*, 1991. In *North Ocean Shipping* v. *Hyundai*, 1978, the defendant shipbuilders refused to complete a ship unless a much larger price was paid than originally agreed. The plaintiff buyers had contracted to supply the ship to a third party and so had no choice but to pay the increased price, though in return they were given increased credit. They had not asked for this benefit, but it was nonetheless held to be new consideration. Eight months after taking delivery of the ship they sued to recover the overpayment. The judge agreed that the defendants' demand was unlawful, but the plaintiffs' claim failed because in the judge's view their failure to protest and their delay in seeking repayment meant they had agreed to the new terms.

11.28   There is a very narrow dividing line between cases such as these where economic duress is proved and others where the judges find only the normal cut and thrust of business. Contracts will not be set aside for duress merely because one business party exploits another's weakness. It is not illegal, for example, to threaten to revoke a loan or to sue for repayment unless new security is given, nor to refuse to supply until a debt is paid: *C.T.N.* v. *Gallagher*, 1994. In *Pao On* v. *Lau Yiu Long*, 1980, one side's threat to break a contract unless it was renegotiated was accepted by the other on legal advice and without protest and after due consideration of the advantages and disadvantages. The Privy Council rejected a subsequent claim that the new agreement was invalidated by duress. Lord Scarman said that duress involved 'coercion of the will which vitiates consent . . . It is material to inquire whether the person alleged to have been coerced did or did not protest; whether, at the time he was allegedly coerced into making the contract, he did or did not have an alternative course open to him such as an adequate legal remedy; whether he was independently advised; and whether after entering into the contract he took steps to avoid it'.

11.29   We mention in passing the subject of undue influence. This is concerned with the possibility of abuse of a personal relationship of confidence and care or, even without such relationship, of the domination of one person's will by another. 'Suspect' relationships include those of legal, medical, financial or spiritual advisers and their clients or advisees. Transactions between the two parties may be vitiated and set aside if the dependent party did not receive all material information from the other and, in appropriate cases, independent legal advice. Ordinary commercial relationships are not as such within these rules, but as we see in *Lloyd's Bank* v. *Bundy*, 1975, Chapter 7, similar issues may very occasionally arise in commercial contexts and contracts may then be invalidated as unconscionable; *Barclays Bank*, above.

C. Illegal contracts

11.30   A contract may be held illegal in English law on many widely differing grounds, with consequences ranging from express prohibition and punishment under Act of Parliament to partial or total unenforceability for breach of common law rules. Apart from the countless specific prohibitions contained in Acts of Parliament the judges have declared many different types of contract against the public interest. These include contracts in restraint of trade, contracts with enemy states, contracts for illegal or immoral purposes (as e.g. in *Lemenda* v. *African Petroleum*, 1987, where the defendant's promise to pay the plaintiff a commission if he used his influence with a foreign government minister to benefit the defendant was held unenforceable), and contracts which purport to be legally binding but prevent access to the courts (Chapter 1). We shall attempt here to state the basic principles of the effects of illegality at common law, and then examine in more detail the one particular commercially significant issue of contracts in restraint of trade.

11.31   The usual result of illegality is to make the contract void. But that tells us very little as to the rights of the parties, since the word 'void' has no uniform meaning or effect in English contract law. It certainly does not mean that no legal rights can ever arise under such a contract.

11.32   The court must first discover the basic purpose of the prohibition. Does it seek directly to forbid a particular kind of contract altogether, or is the contract only incidentally affected by a prohibition intended to achieve some other objective? In the first case, the usual result is that the contract is wholly unenforceable. That may in turn cause hardship to an innocent party. In *Re Mahmoud*, 1921, the facts were that the law forbade all sales of linseed oil unless both parties were licensed. The seller in this case was licensed, the buyer not. The buyer deceived the seller into believing he was licensed, and on this basis the seller entered into the contract. The buyer then refused to take delivery. When the seller sued for damages for breach of contract the court held that since the contract itself was illegal the seller had no claim despite the fact that his loss was brought about by the buyer's deception, and despite the corollary that the buyer could invoke the contract's illegality for his own benefit. A possible remedy in such a case might be a claim for damages for misrepresentation or fraud, but that was not pursued in *Mahmoud*. A modern parallel with a more satisfactory outcome is *Re Cavalier Insurance*, 1989. The company undertook insurances without being licensed to do so, which was a criminal offence. The policies were therefore held invalid and unenforceable, but at least the insured parties were able to recover their premiums.

11.33 If the contract is legal, but the problem is that it has been carried out in an illegal way, then the parties' motives and respective degree of blameworthiness become relevant. One party's illegal intentions, formed after the contract was made, do not affect the contract's validity: *Skilton* v. *Sullivan*, 1994. Contrasting with *Mahmoud*, above, are the cases of *Archbolds* v. *Spanglett*, 1961, and *St. John Shipping* v. *Rank*, 1957. In *Archbolds* the defendant carriers contracted with the plaintiffs to carry certain goods in their vehicle, though it was not licensed for this purpose. The goods were stolen on the journey. The plaintiffs' claim was upheld, because the fundamental concern of the licensing requirement was the safety and efficiency of the transport industry, not to prohibit carriage of these particular goods. Similarly in *St. John* the crime committed by the ship owner in overloading his ship did not affect the innocent cargo owner's rights against him.

11.34 Another case to the same effect is *Euro-Diam* v. *Bathurst*, 1987, where it was held that a contract of insurance was not invalidated by the false valuation given by the insured in order to deceive tax authorities. In *Pavey* v. *Paul*, 1990 (Australia), a builder provided work and materials under an oral contract which was required by law to be in writing. He was held entitled nonetheless to a *quantum meruit* payment, because his client would otherwise have benefited unjustly from the work done for him. In none of these cases was it necessary to rely on the illegality to enforce the contract. These decisions seem more equitable than that in *Mahmoud*, and the lines of argument more likely to be adopted if circumstances permit. But if, of course, the innocent parties in any of these latter cases had known beforehand of the others' illegal intentions they would probably have lost their rights (as in *Ashmore* v. *Dawson*, 1973, where the plaintiff knew the defendant's lorry was overloaded), unless falling within the following rules.

11.35 Even where both parties originally agreed to an illegal contract, or an illegal method of performance, they are not always equally penalised. The common law may be able to distinguish between the parties and assist whichever is less blameworthy – he who is not *in pari delicto* – as with the partial remedy in *Cavalier*, above. It may also support a party who repents and tries to withdraw from the contract before the wrongful act is done: *Ouston* v. *Zurowski*, 1985 (Canada). But we see from *Mahmoud* and *Cavalier* that the possibilities are limited. Certain statutes likewise seek to protect the weaker party against being forced into an illegal contract. So, for example, where a landlord compels a tenant to pay an illegal premium the 1977 Rent Act enables the tenant to get his money back.

11.36 Other Acts again provide that the offences they create shall have no effect at all on contracts arising out of these offences. An important commercial example is the Trade Descriptions Act 1968. The Act outlaws various kinds of deceptive advertising but expressly preserves the validity of contracts resulting from such deception.

Contracts in restraint of trade

11.37 Employees likely to gain confidential information about their employer's businesses are often bound by express restraint of trade terms in their contracts (and may be bound also, but to a lesser extent, by implied duties of loyalty and good faith). These restraint terms are intended to stop employees from abusing the confidences reposed in them, if and when they leave in order to begin business on their own account or in someone else's employment. Typically they prevent the ex-employee from working for competing businesses for so many months or years and within so many miles in any capacity involving the use of confidential information and/or from canvassing his or her former employer's customers. But while the law supports the employer in seeking to protect his own interests, it has to ensure also that he does not overreach himself and try to keep his former employees out of the market altogether. The common law resolves the problem by holding all restraint terms *prima facie* void. The onus is then on the employer to persuade the court to the contrary. If he can prove that the restrictions are *reasonable*, both as between himself and his employee and so far as the larger public interest is concerned, the restriction will be upheld: *Nordenfelt* v. *Maxim Nordenfelt*, 1894.

11.38 The reference to the public interest is one of lip service only, hardly ever relevant in practice. In effect then an employer acts reasonably if he gives himself no more than the minimum necessary degree of protection in terms of time and space, and does not claim protection for more than his own proprietary interests. His proprietary interests are his trade secret and business connections – matters of fact which he has devised or developed or acquired for himself in the course of his work, even though not necessarily wholly confidential, as distinct from the skills and know-how which any diligent person working for him would and should acquire. In contrast with his proprietary interests, in other words, the employer has no legal right to have the business itself protected. He cannot prevent former employees simply from competing against him, nor even, without a restraint term, from soliciting his customers – unless they do so by means of copied or stolen company records: *Faccenda* v. *Fowler*, 1986, *Robb* v. *Green*, 1895. But clauses which seem expressly to forbid competition may still be upheld if in fact concerned with proprietary rights: *Littlewoods* v. *Harris*, 1978.

11.39   The same test of reasonableness will apply to agreements between employers not to employ each other's employees – a practice adopted in order to avoid competition in pay and conditions of employment. The agreement will be void if it does not distinguish between employees who could bring confidential information and those who could not: *Kores* v. *Kolok*, 1958. An employee affected by this kind of agreement can ask the court to test its validity: *Eastham* v. *Newcastle Football Club*, 1963.

11.40   A court upholding a restraint term in a contract of employment will grant an injunction against the ex-employee to stop him from working in breach of that term for the period agreed there – *Bullivant* v. *Ellis*, 1987 – and might also award damages against him. The former employer may seek an injunction against the new employer: *Hivac* v. *Park Royal*, 1946. Where only a part of the restraint is reasonable the court may be willing to sever or cut out the unreasonable part and enforce the remainder, but the circumstances in which it will do so are obscure and unpredictable: *Goldsoll* v. *Goldman*, 1915. Contrasting cases are *Business Seating* v. *Broad*, 1989, and *Hinton* v. *Murphy*, 1989. In *Business Seating* the court upheld a clause prohibiting the ex-employee from soliciting his former employer's customers, but cut out a clause which stopped him from contacting associated employers' customers. In *Hinton* a clause of this latter kind was one of several which the court found objectionable, and so it held the whole agreement void. English courts claim neither the power nor the inclination to rewrite the parties' agreements in order to make them more acceptable; in contrast, for example, to the general Continental practice and the law in New Zealand and certain American jurisdictions. The consequences of this unhelpful English attitude were all-too-well illustrated in *Commercial Plastics* v. *Vincent*, 1964, as follows.

11.41   Rejecting the entire restriction, the judge in this case said: 'The decision is in a way regrettable because the plaintiffs' case has underlying merits. They appear to have important confidential information for which they might reasonably claim protection – by a suitably worded covenant . . . It is unfortunate that a home-made provision, that is to say, not professionally drafted, offered and accepted in good faith between commercial men . . . has to be ruled out . . . It would seem that a good deal of legal "know-how" is required for the successful drafting of a restrictive covenant'.

11.42   Other types of restraint which should be noted are those entered into between sellers and buyers of businesses and 'solus' or sole agency agreements. Since the parties here are on a more equal footing than employer and employee the law is less likely to intervene, and in any case recognises a wider range of interests which may be protected. A buyer of a business usually buys also the goodwill of its customers, and so should be able to stop the seller from beginning or continuing a competing business. A clause in the contract of sale protecting the buyer against such competition will be upheld if reasonable in the circumstances. Restrictions may be local, national or even international – *Nordenfelt*, above – depending on the scale of the business.

11.43 Solus agreements have been examined in a number of cases where oil companies have provided the capital to enable people to set up in business as garage proprietors; the proprietors agreeing in return to sell that company's petrol only and undertaking various other restrictions. The courts have accepted that the oil companies need efficient distribution schemes and that this is an interest which may properly be protected – but only for reasonable periods of time. A twenty-one year commitment has been held excessive, while a four and a half year restraint has been upheld. What is acceptable, however, depends essentially on all the surrounding circumstances of the agreement: *Esso* v. *Harper*, 1967; *Lobb* v. *Total Oil*, 1985. It is not just a matter of unequal bargaining power. As Lord Justice Dillon observed in *Lobb*: 'It is seldom in any negotiation that the bargaining powers of the parties are absolutely equal . . . The courts would only interfere in exceptional cases where as a matter of common fairness it was not right that the strong should be allowed to push the weak to the wall.' These exclusive purchasing or 'tied house' arrangements are not covered by UK restrictive practices legislation, unless they also involve resale price maintenance, but might be held void under Article 85 of the Treaty of Rome if they were to affect trade between Member States.

Danish law

MISREPRESENTATION

11.44 Misrepresentation, duress and undue influence may invalidate a contract in whole or part under Danish law. A misrepresentation as understood by English law gives rise to an action for breach of contract. Danish law also obliges businesses to volunteer information which they know or ought to know is material to the other contracting party. In consumer contracts a clause excluding liability for misrepresentation or failure to disclose is void.

11.45 Article 30 of the Contracts Act invalidates contracts brought about by fraud. Fraud involves bad faith – either by misstatements or knowledge of and failure to correct the other party's ignorance or error.

11.46 The Insurance Contracts Act 1930 protects the insured party more effectively than English law. Insurance companies cannot avoid liability on the ground that the insured gave incorrect information, as long as it was given in good faith. Non-disclosure invalidates a contract only when the insured should have known the importance of the information and was grossly negligent in keeping quiet about it.

ILLEGALITY

11.47 Economic duress makes the weaker party's promise unenforceable. Insisting on a change in the terms of a contract without legitimate commercial reason is contrary to the good faith requirement.

11.48 Restraint of trade terms may be set aside as unreasonable under Article 36 of the Contract Act or by more specific provisions in Article 38. Article 38 says that restraint terms are invalid if they go further as regards time, place or other circumstances than is necessary to protect against competition or otherwise unreasonably limit access to work. Article 18 of the Salaried Employment Act 1964 lays down the general rule that without special payment employers cannot restrict former employees' freedom of action for more than one year. A restriction is void if the employee is unjustifiably dismissed or obliged to resign.

Dutch law

MISREPRESENTATION

11.49 The English doctrine of misrepresentation often arrives at results which under Dutch law would be reached by the doctrine of *dwaling* (error) although the latter, being construed as a 'defect of the will', has a quite different background. One practical consequence of the different backgrounds is that while it may be possible to exclude liability for misrepresentation in English law, that is not possible under Dutch law. Also in contrast with English law, Article 6.228 says that a party's silence may invalidate a contract if in view of what he knew or should have known regarding the error he should have informed the other party of it.

11.50 Under the Code, a contract may be avoided, subject to the rights of innocent third parties, on grounds of threats, fraud or 'abuse of circumstances': Article 3.44. Threats to both persons and property are taken into account, as under the English doctrine of economic duress. 'Abuse of circumstances' may refer to the mental or physical state of the weaker party.

ILLEGALITY

11.51   As far as illegal contracts are concerned, the courts will have to establish what sanctions the legislature had in mind. They may do so by looking into the Parliamentary proceedings. When the legislator only imposes criminal or administrative sanctions, a contract may still be held illegal and void as being contrary to public policy: Article 3.40.

French law

MISREPRESENTATION

11.52   A contract is voidable where one party's *dol* – intentional deceptive conduct – has prompted the other party to enter into the contract: Article 1116. The principle is similar to that of fraudulent misrepresentation in English law, but somewhat wider because French law does not require a false misleading statement of fact. Conduct intended to deceive may suffice: Com. 18 March 1974. Silence may constitute *dol* when one contracting party had a duty of disclosure, express or implicit: Civ. 2 October 1974.

DURESS

11.53   *Violence* is defined by Article 1112 in terms similar to the English concept of duress, and has much the same consequences. The question is whether a reasonable person would feel that his person or possessions were threatened by some real and present harm. The court takes due regard of the age, sex and circumstances of the parties. The pressures exerted may be either physical or 'moral' (e.g., economic), but must be essentially unjust and illegal to fall within the rule. A contract made because of another person's known intention to go to court or to seize goods because of unpaid debts would not normally be affected. Although threats to enforce a legitimate right are not normally punishable, the utmost care should still be taken, e.g., in threatening to apply for bankruptcy proceedings against a party, since they might be characterised as an 'abuse of law': Civ. 17 January 1984. 'Undue influence' as understood in English law is not a familiar concept in French law.

ILLEGAL CONTRACTS

11.54   A contract can be illegal because its cause or reasons are illegal, as when its purpose is to evade a mandatory provision such as the prohibition of preferred payments by an insolvent debtor. A lawful cause being a condition of the formation of the contract, the contract is automatically void (*nullité absolue*). Similarly, under Article 1128, the object (subject-matter)

256

of the contract must be lawful. So a transaction relating to an estate which the contracting party expects to inherit (*pacte sur succession future*) is void because its object is unlawful: Article 1130.

11.55   Illegality may arise also from the context or consequences of the contract; for example, a contract whereby the president of a company transfers corporate assets to another company in which he has personal interests, or a contract made in breach of exchange control regulations. Whether such contracts are voidable is determined either in the relevant statutory provision or by the courts on a case-by-case basis (often taking into account whether the contracting party was acting *bona fide* or not). The general principle is that there is no nullity without specific legal provision (*pas de nullité sans texte*). So the courts usually held that contracts in breach of exchange control regulations, then in force, were valid, subject to the application of the specific penalties provided for in such regulations. In the field of 'economic public policy' and consumer protection, however, there is a tendency to make nullity a specific sanction, e.g., for improper execution of loan agreements to consumers or for the purchase of real property.

German law

MISREPRESENTATION

11.56   There is no term in German law corresponding to 'misrepresentation', nor does the distinction between statements of fact and opinion have any legal importance. Much as in *Walters*, para. 11.3, there is no general duty to volunteer information for which one is not asked, but there are several exceptions. A car dealer, for example, must tell the purchaser if he knows the car has been damaged in an accident. A bank advising on investment must give all relevant information.

11.57   The remedy for fraud is the right to avoid the contract. In negligent misrepresentation the contract cannot be avoided but the innocent party can sue for damages if he suffers loss. This claim is based on the rules of *positive Vertragsverletzung*: para. 5.70. Because of the separation of obligation and property (*Abstraktionsprinzip*: para. 1.50), holding a contract void does not of itself affect the buyer's ownership of the goods or the seller's right to his money. But both parties may have claims against each other for unjust enrichment, which would then require return of the goods or money: Article 812.

11.58   Compensation is given for innocent misrepresentation only if it amounts to an express promise as to the characteristics of the goods sold. This is part of the sales contract provisions of the BGB: Article 463.

General advertising does not usually involve an express promise, but as an exception to the strict interpretation of Article 463 the courts often grant this remedy in used-car sales – e.g., where a window sticker advertises the wrong mileage.

DURESS

11.59   There is no general principle avoiding contracts made under economic duress, but under Article 138, BGB, a contract is void if one party exploits another's poverty, irresponsibility or inexperience. The courts apply this rule in consumer credit contracts if the rate of interest is more than twice as much as or more than 12 per cent higher than the normal market rate.

ILLEGAL CONTRACTS

11.60   Article 134, BGB, declares void contracts which are in breach of the law. The same problem then arises as discussed earlier in this chapter – that of finding the purpose of the prohibition. So buying food outside shop opening hours may violate the Shop Opening Hours Act, but the contract of sale is not affected. As under the UK Trade Descriptions Act, a violation of the German Act against Unfair Competition would not affect the validity of any resulting contract.

11.61   The Commercial Code allows contracts in restraint of trade between employers and employees, but subject to certain restrictions, e.g. that they do not exceed two years. Solus agreements between oil companies and garage proprietors have not been litigated, but the duration of such agreements between breweries and inns has been limited by the courts. An excessively long restraint is a *Knebelung* – tying – which is immoral under Article 138. Restrictive agreements are in any case subject to the competition rules of the Treaty of Rome.

Italian law

MISREPRESENTATION

11.62   A false statement which is not so fundamental to another's intentions as to constitute fraud, but which merely affects the terms on which that other makes a contract – so-called 'incidental fraud' – does not affect the validity of the contract. But if made in bad faith there is a pre-contractual liability for damages: Article 1337.

FRAUD

11.63   Fraud is defined as any form of deception which alters the contractual will of the victim and leads him to make a contract he would not otherwise have made: Article 1439. Even silence and reticence may amount to fraud when intended to deceive. But *dolus bonus* – sales talk or puff without factual content – is not usually regarded as fraud. The effect of fraud is to make the contract voidable.

DURESS

11.64   Contracts made under unfair conditions because of serious personal danger to the contracting party or his family, their persons or property, or because of necessity, are voidable: Articles 1447 *et seq*. A person is deemed to have taken advantage of another's need if he benefits disproportionately by the contract, i.e. by receiving money, goods or services worth more than half as much again as the value received by the other: Article 1448. A contract made under threat to enforce a legal right in order to obtain an unjust benefit is likewise voidable. Rescission can be avoided if the party at fault offers different terms which make the contract fair.

ILLEGALITY

11.65   Contracts contrary to specific legal prohibitions or requirements, or intended to evade the law, or against public policy or conventional morality (*contra bonos mores*), are void: Article 1343. An otherwise lawful contract may also be held void if both parties have unlawful motives: Article 1345. Where both parties intend to make a contract *contra bonos mores*, neither can seek recovery of anything transferred under the contract: Article 2035. Where one party is innocent, he may claim damages. Damages are to compensate for the 'negative interest' – loss of the opportunity to make a similar but lawful contract, plus interest on any money paid to the wrongdoer: Article 1338.

Spanish law

MISREPRESENTATION AND FRAUD

11.66   Spanish law has no doctrine of misrepresentation like that in English law. But similar problems produce similar solutions. Consent is invalid if resulting from fraud or physical or moral duress. Fraud – *dole* – in its widest sense is equivalent to bad faith. A person is defrauded when induced to make a contract he would not otherwise have made by the words or *maquinaciones insidiosas* – deceptive or underhand conduct – of the other contracting party: Article 1269 of the Civil Code. If the fraud or bad faith was only incidental to the contract the contract cannot be avoided, but the innocent party has a claim for damages.

11.67   The Supreme Court held in a decision of 15 July 1987 that 'underhand conduct' included the 'reticence of a party who takes advantage of another by keeping quiet and not drawing his attention'. The fundamental principle of good faith in Spanish law in Articles 7 and 1258 is important here. Article 1258 says that contractual obligations extend beyond those expressly agreed to all aspects requiring the exercise of good faith. An Act of 8 October 1980 makes insurance contracts voidable if information is held back or inexact.

ILLEGALITY

11.68   If a contract is contrary to law it has no valid *causa* or function and has therefore no effect in law: Article 1275. Currently important causes of nullity of commercial contracts are terms restricting competition or abusing dominant positions. These are regulated by the Law of 17 July 1989 and direct application of the Treaty of Rome.

Swedish law

MISREPRESENTATION AND FRAUD

11.69   Statements as to the quality of goods create obligations. If the statement could be defined as a specific promise (*'garanti'*), the buyer is entitled to damages whether the false statement was made innocently or not. There is uncertainty as to the effects of statements that do not directly concern the goods sold but other circumstances; e.g., in a sale of shares, a statement that a famous person has bought shares in the company; or in a sale of soap, that the soap is used by a certain beautiful actress. If the seller realises that the buyer would not have bought the object on the agreed terms if he or she had known that the statement was false, there is a ground for rescission and damages. In other cases the buyer probably has no claim.

11.70   It is often said that the duty to disclose information which may be against one's own interests is less stringent in English law than in Swedish law. But even though Swedish law might give an impression that contracts are not made at arm's length but in good faith, there are many obstacles for a party whose claim is based on the other party's failure to disclose. He has to show that the other party had actual knowledge of the 'negative' fact, that he himself lacked this knowledge, and that the non-disclosing party realised that he lacked this knowledge and realised that this knowledge was of importance. Even then there may be no liability if the plaintiff should not typically expect to be informed about the fact in question. A seller of a food shop was liable for failing to tell the buyer that the shop did not have health authority approval: NJA 1991 s.808. An employee at a social service bureau was bound to disclose that she had been convicted for serious drug-related crime: AD 1979 no. 143. But there was no duty to inform buyers at an auction that a painting was a reproduction, even though the bidding was very high. The painting was never said to be an original: NJA 1975 s.152. Surprisingly, there was no duty on an insured to disclose to the insurance company when insuring his business that he had been convicted and sentenced to psychiatric care in prison: NJA 1971 s.501.

ILLEGALITY

11.71   Contracts contrary to law, e.g., contracts for prostitution or contracts to commit a crime, are not enforceable. According to the principle of *pactum turpe* (illegal contracts) the courts may refuse to try the case. There are problems in connection with this principle since the rule does not make the contract void. In NJA 1990 s.277 the Supreme Court said *obiter* that a contract between two private parties was void when it was made with the intention to reduce tax liability in a receivership. But the effects of the case are unclear.

Chapter 12

Frustration

12.1   We have seen several times the basic 'hard line' approach of English law to contractual commitments. As a general rule, once a contract has been made it must be honoured, come what may. But inevitably there are exceptions; circumstances where the law has had to recognise the injustice which would arise from strict enforcement, as for example in the context of exclusion clauses. In this chapter we discuss what is certainly from the commercial point of view one of the most important of these exceptions, the doctrine of frustration.

12.2   The common law has accepted for more than a century that events occurring after a contract has been made may make the contract impossible or impracticable to fulfil – because, for example, the law now forbids it or its subject-matter has been destroyed, or a party is prevented by illness from performing the promised services. If such events happen, *the contract is accordingly brought to an end by operation of law* and the parties released thereupon from their obligations, subject to the adjustments required by statute law, below. American rules, as stated in Sections 261–5 of the second Restatement of Contracts and Section 2–615 of the Uniform Commercial Code are to the same effect. The Anglo-American approach contrasts with the Continental, where frustrating events may be seen as a defence, or as the case may be, as a *partial* release from a contract. Article 79 of the 1980 Convention on International Sale of Goods regards such events as merely entitling a party to suspend his performance of the contract until the situation is restored. He cannot be sued for damages in the meantime, but the other party may be free to abandon the contract altogether. The Convention also requires the non-performing party to notify the other of the new circumstances and their effect on the contract.

12.3   Many difficulties may arise in applying the English doctrine. What happens if the contract itself seeks to lay down the parties' liabilities in such events? How can we decide on the basic objective or purpose of the contract, which must be established before we can say whether or not it has been frustrated? Above all, what is meant by 'impossibility' or 'impracticability' of performance? We shall try to answer each of these questions in turn.

i. Contractual provision

12.4   In Chapter 7 we discussed the use of *force majeure* clauses and considered their likely effectiveness as exclusion clauses. We look at them again now, from a different point of view – to see how far they help the parties in circumstances which might otherwise frustrate the contract. The point at issue is that if a *force majeure* clause (or other provision such as a 'hardship' clause, seeking renegotiation of the contract when new circumstances make performance 'unreasonably onerous', or words to that effect) is valid and applicable, the contract is not strictly speaking frustrated. Frustration is a legal concept. Only the law can decide whether a contract has been frustrated, and, if so, what the consequences should be. If the contract clause applies, then the consequences are those laid down by the contract, not by the law. The clause may provide for suspension of obligations, or postponement of delivery, requirements as to notice, etc., whereas the rules of English law provide simply for the *ending* of the contract from the moment of frustration.

12.5   The court's first task therefore is to decide whether the terms of the *force majeure* clause apply to the circumstances which have in fact occurred. Were the events within the parties' contemplation, or were they altogether more serious and far-reaching, and thus outside the terms of the contract? A straightforward example is *Jackson* v. *Union Marine*, 1874. A shipping contract made express provision for delays caused by 'dangers and accidents of navigation'. The ship ran aground and sailing was delayed for eight months. It was held that the clause did not apply and that the contract was void for frustration. The court's view was that in making their contract the parties had not contemplated or intended to provide for such a very long delay. *The Penelope*, 1928, was a similar case, concerning a ship hired to carry coal. The contract provided for delays caused by strike action. A national coal strike ensued, lasting eight months. Again the contract was held void; the parties were held to have envisaged only local disputes of limited effect, not a complete national stoppage lasting for so many months. On the other hand, a shipping contract was not frustrated when a ship in Kuwait was forced to unload by the invading Iraqi army, because the contract contained a war-risks clause allowing for unloading under military direction: *Kuwait Supply Co.* v. *Oyster Marine*, 1994. We see that the courts must interpret the parties' expressed intentions in the light of the gravity of subsequent events.

ii. Impossibility and impracticability

12.6 Next, the court must reach a decision as to the basic purpose or objective of the contract in order to see whether it is still possible or practicable to fulfil it. The difficulty is illustrated by two contrasting cases brought about by the sudden postponement of the coronation of King Edward VII because of his illness. In *Krell* v. *Henry*, 1903, a room was hired to see the coronation. The purpose was not expressly stated, probably because it was obvious. The postponement of the event was held to have frustrated the contract, and so, although the room was still available, the parties were released from their obligations. In *Herne Bay Co.* v. *Hutton*, also in 1903, a boat was hired to see the royal review of the fleet. The royal review did not take place, but the fleet could still be seen – and so the contract remained binding. The distinction between the two cases is a very narrow one. *Krell's* case indicates that a just decision as to the essential point and purpose of the contract may require the court to look beyond the words of the contract and take account of what it can discover of the parties' common motives. But this is not by any means to say that it will put right every miscalculation or misfortune, least of all those which should have been foreseen and guarded against by ordinary commercial prudence.

12.7 In *Amalgamated Investment* v. *Walker*, 1976, for example, a person contracted to buy a building. The seller knew the buyer intended to convert the building into flats, and charged accordingly. After the sale the buyer discovered the building had been listed as of historic interest and so could not be redeveloped. He tried to get his money back by arguing that the contract was void for mistake (as noted in Chapter 10), or, alternatively, annulled on grounds of frustration. But on both counts the court held that the sale of the building had been successfully accomplished. What the buyer was going to do with the building after the sale was his own affair, not expressly or even impliedly fundamental to or part of the contract.

12.8 We come now to the crucial issue – that of defining the kind of circumstances English courts will accept as sufficient to frustrate a contract. Basically it is a question of establishing that it is *impossible or impracticable* to fulfil the contract in the way originally envisaged. 'If it should happen in the course of carrying out a contract that a fundamentally different situation arises for which the parties made no provision – so much so that it would not be just in the new situation to hold them bound to its terms, then the contract is at an end', said Lord Denning in *The Eugenia*, 1964. 'There are two essential requirements', said Lord Justice Griffiths in *Paal Wilson* v. *Partenreederei; The Hannah Blumenthal*, 1982, 'The first . . . is that there must be some outside event or extraneous change of situation, not foreseen or provided for by the parties at the time of contracting, which either makes it impossible for the contract to be performed at all, or at least renders its performance something radically different from what the parties contemplated when they entered into it. [Second] the outside event or extraneous change of situation, and the consequences of either in relation to the performance of the contract, must have occurred without the fault or default of either party to the contract'.

12.9   Before we examine the leading cases in the light of these dicta, two preliminary points arising from Lord Justice Griffiths' observation should be briefly noted. His Lordship said that circumstances could frustrate a contract only if they were 'not foreseen'. It is doubtful whether this is so. In *Tatem* v. *Gamboa*, 1939, for example, a ship hired at very high rates for evacuations during the Spanish civil war was seized by opposing forces. The high rates showed that seizure was a foreseeable and foreseen risk. The judge held that what mattered was not whether the event was foreseen but whether there was any provision in the contract to deal with it. Since there was not, and since the ship could not be used, the contract was frustrated. This seems the more realistic approach. Disasters of almost any kind are more or less foreseeable, but that fact alone does not mean that the parties should provide for them, nor lessen their impact when they occur. On the other hand, of course, a contracting party has only himself to blame if he fails to take account of common commercial risks. And where the whole basis of the contract is the chance that a certain event may or may not occur, its occurrence or non-occurrence should not frustrate the contract.

12.10   The second incidental issue is that of 'fault or default' on one side or the other. A contracting party cannot rely on his own breach of contract or negligence or other 'self-induced frustration' to escape his commitments (although the other party might then be able to do so). In *Maritime National Fish* v. *Ocean Trawlers*, 1935, a company which already had four fishing boats hired another – but then found it could obtain only three fishing licences. The company nominated three of its own boats for the licences, and argued accordingly that the contract of hire was avoided. But since the difficulty was the result of the company's own allocation of the licences it was held liable for breach of contract. A modern example is *Lauritzen* v. *Wijsmuller*, 1989. Here tugboat owners contracted to use either of two named tugs for certain work. They allocated one boat to the job and sent the other elsewhere. Before the work began the allocated boat sank in circumstances within the owners' control. They refused to use the second boat, arguing that the contract was frustrated. The High Court found them liable for breach of contract.

12.11   As to the main issue, ultimately the test of impossibility or impracticability of fulfilling a contract is very much a question of degree, depending on the judge's subjective assessment of the facts and merits of the case, the time at which it comes to court, and other variables. Only comparatively rarely could one say that it is literally impossible to fulfil a contract because the subject-matter has been entirely destroyed (since there may well be another source of supply), or obviously impracticable because the whole transaction has subsequently been declared illegal. More probably the problem will be one of delay or greater difficulty in fulfilling the contract. It may be necessary for the court then to make a speculative decision on the parties' behalf: 'If there is a reasonable probability from the nature of the interruption that it will be of indefinite duration, they ought to be free to turn their assets, their plant and equipment and their business operations into activities which are open to them and to be free from commitments which are struck with sterility for an uncertain future period': *Denny* v. *Fraser*, 1944.

12.12   With all these reflections in mind, we consider now some of the leading cases explaining and illustrating the requirements of English law. One such case is *Davis* v. *Fareham U.D.C.*, 1956. This concerned a building firm which contracted to build houses for a local authority at a fixed price of £94,500. Because of unexpected shortage of materials and labour and the effects of inflation the contract took nearly three times longer to complete than expected, and cost the builders £115,000. They claimed that the contract should be set aside as frustrated, which would have enabled them to claim for the extra expense incurred. The House of Lords held that since the only significant change in what had originally been agreed was that the builder would make a loss instead of a profit, the contract was still binding. It was still possible and practicable to fulfil it, and the builder should have protected himself against such likely business risks by an appropriate term in his contract. Similarly, in *Chaucer Estates* v. *Fairclough Homes*, 1991, delays and difficulties caused by a local authority, which prevented a builder from fulfilling his first year's quota in a four year contract, did not frustrate that contract.

12.13   A party's inability to fulfil his contract because he has no money does not of itself excuse him from performance: *Universal Corp.* v. *Five Ways Properties*, 1979. The same is true if his supplier goes out of business, or if for any other such reason goods are no longer available to him from their expected source: *Dixon* v. *Osborne*, 1983; *Blackburn Bobbin* v. *Allen*, 1918. A contract is still enforceable despite a devaluation in the currency: *British Movietonenews* v. *London Cinemas*, 1951. Even a very long term contract would probably not be regarded as frustrated merely because of inflation, despite Lord Denning's decision to the contrary in *Staffordshire Area Health Authority* v. *South Staffordshire Waterworks*, 1978. As his Lordship said in *The Eugenia*, above: 'The fact that it has become more onerous or expensive for one party than he thought is not sufficient to bring about the frustration. It must be more than merely more onerous or expensive. It must be positively unjust to hold the parties bound. It is often difficult to draw the line. But it must be done'. Whether a contract would be frustrated by changes in circumstances so great as to drive one party into actual bankruptcy has not yet been decided, but the difficulty has at least been acknowledged, below. (Special rules apply where individuals do in fact become bankrupt, or companies insolvent. The Insolvency Act 1986 enables an individual's trustee or company liquidator to disclaim 'onerous' contracts, and thus end liability under them. The other contracting party may then claim compensation.)

12.14   Several important cases arose out of the closure of the Suez Canal by the Anglo-French invasion in 1956. *Tsakiroglou* v. *Noblee Thorl*, 1962, is a particularly instructive decision. A contract was made to ship groundnuts from Sudan to Hamburg, to arrive in November or December 1956. Both parties assumed shipment through the Canal, and calculated their costs accordingly, but made no express provision to that effect in the contract. The Canal was closed for five months from the beginning of November. The sellers claimed the contract had been frustrated and refused to ship the goods. They said availability of the Canal was a fundamental assumption of the contract and that the 'long haul round the Cape' was an entirely different adventure. The distance via Suez was nearly 4,400 miles, but round the Cape was over 11,100 miles. But the buyers were reluctant to give up their purchase and sued the sellers for breach of contract. The case went to the House of Lords.

12.15   In their Lordships' view there were two basic questions, one the corollary of the other. Was passage through the Canal a fundamental term of the contract? Could the contract be carried out by other means? The parties had not stipulated passage through the Canal in the contract, but they had certainly presupposed its use. The judges rejected the consequences which would flow from the sellers' argument. There were many fundamental assumptions in every contract. If the sellers were right, then in effect any extraneous change in the express or tacitly understood conditions on which the contract was to be fulfilled would enable one side or the other to repudiate his obligations. There was no evidence that the buyers would have agreed to the suggestion that the goods should either be shipped through Suez or not at all.

12.16   Given then that failure of a fundamental assumption does not necessarily frustrate a contract, the sellers in *Tsakiroglou* had to show that the alternative route was not practicable. Their profit might indeed be reduced or even eliminated, but, as we have seen, increase of expenses is not a ground of frustration. It was, however, accepted that 'astronomical' increases in costs might create other problems altogether and so, by implication, might possibly justify a finding of frustration. Apart from the cost, the longer duration of the voyage had to be considered, but in the absence of any definite date for delivery or seasonal market to be met, or of evidence of deterioration of the goods, the sellers were again unable to prove that the delay struck at the root of the contract. Their Lordships also held that the usual clause in the contract relieving the parties of their obligations in the event of *force majeure* was of no effect, since the war zone could reasonably have been avoided, and so held the sellers liable for breach of contract.

12.17   The war between Iran and Iraq resulted in many similar commercial difficulties and in a crop of cases examining further the nature and effect of frustration. In *Finelvet* v. *Vinava; The Chrysalis*, 1983, the question was whether the contract was frustrated by the declaration of war or on the later date when shipping circles accepted that this particular ship's escape from the war zone was impossible. The High Court decided that a declaration of war did not itself prevent performance of a contract unless it made the contract illegal because it involved trading with an enemy. Only the physical acts of war determined when the contract had to be abandoned. The curious corollary of that decision, as expressed in *International Sea Tankers* v. *Hemisphere Shipping; The Wenjiang*, 1982, was that on the same facts different arbitrators or judges might find frustration had occurred on different dates. In *Kissavos* v. *Empressa Cubana; The Agathon*, 1982, the charterer continued to unload the ship despite the fighting. On grounds of frustration he then refused to pay the hire charges due. It was held that even though he had not initially regarded the contract as frustrated, retrospectively it might properly be so regarded. *Kodros* v. *Empressa Cubana*, 1982, draws the necessary distinction between frustration and breach of contract. The charterer had warranted that the ship would enter only 'safe ports', but it also had been trapped by the war. The owner then claimed damages for breach of contract. The court held there had been no breach because the warranty was not a guarantee of continuing safety. It required only that the port be safe at the time the charterer ordered the ship to go there, which it was in this case. Again the contract was subsequently ended by frustration.

12.18   *Codelfa* v. *State Rail Authority*, 1983 (Australia), is a good example of the effect of subsequent illegality. The parties entered into a major public works contract, which involved 24 hour-day and 7 day-week building operations. Residents affected by the noise and disturbance won an injunction preventing the builders from working at night and on Sundays. This made the contract much less profitable for the builders. They therefore argued that there were implied terms in the contract that they would be paid more in the event of such difficulties, or that they would be given more time to do the work, or alternatively that the whole contract was frustrated. The court did not find any such implied terms intended or necessary (*see* paras. 5.49–54), but accepted that the effect of the injunction was to make the basis of the contract illegal and impossible to fulfil. It was therefore held to be frustrated. Another example of frustration by operation of law may of course be that of a lengthy imprisonment of one of the parties: *Shepherd* v. *Jerrom*, 1986.

12.19   A further possible cause of frustration is illness or injury. Much depends here on whether the service in question was to be provided by the contracting party personally or could equally well be given by someone else, as also on the length and effect and likely recurrence of the disability. It seems that employees' illnesses are unlikely to be accepted as having frustrated their contracts. The industrial tribunals which decide dismissal rights prefer the employer to tackle the problem by dismissing the absent employee, if he so wishes, and then to justify the dismissal on grounds of incapacity. If the employer argues instead that the employee was away for so long that the contract was frustrated, and dismissal therefore unnecessary, he may well have difficulty in explaining exactly when and why it was frustrated, and what action he took as a result. In *Williams* v. *Watson*, 1990, the Employment Appeal Tribunal held that even an absence of 18 months was insufficient to frustrate the contract.

12.20 In *National Carriers* v. *Panalpina*, 1981, the House of Lords finally accepted that the doctrine of frustration could apply to leases and sales of land – a point previously much doubted and disputed, largely because in the first reported case on the subject, that of *Paradine* v. *Jane* in 1647, a court refused to release a tenant, evicted from his land in the course of the Civil War, from his obligation to pay the rent. *National Carriers* concerned a ten year lease of a warehouse. After some five and a half years the local authority closed the only access road for 20 months. This substantial but temporary difficulty was held not to frustrate the contract.

12.21 If a contract is partly frustrated, e.g. by destruction of some of the goods in question, so that the seller cannot fulfil all his buyers' orders, it seems that so far as the law is concerned the seller is free to do whatever is reasonable in the circumstances with the remainder of the goods. He could supply his buyers *pro rata* – if they agreed – or might supply the first to the exclusion of the others: *Intertradex* v. *Lesieur*, 1978.

iii. Effects of frustration

12.22 With certain significant exceptions, below, and subject to the court's discretion, the legal consequences of frustration are those laid down by the Law Reform (Frustrated Contracts) Act 1943. Section 1 says that *money already paid under the contract is recoverable, while money due ceases to be. Expenses incurred can be retained or recovered, as the case may be, from sums already paid by or already due from the other party. 'Valuable benefits' obtained under the contract before the frustrating event must be paid for.*

12.23 In these various ways, then, the law attempts to adjust the losses unavoidably caused by frustration. The Act's limitations should be noted. In general, its application depends on the court's view on the merits of the case: *Gamerco* v. *I.C.M.*, 1995. More particularly, a party's expenditure, e.g. in putting up a building destroyed by fire before completion, can only be recouped out of sums already due from the other contracting party. If the contract says that payment is not to be made until the work is completed, no money is due to the builder at the time of the fire and so he has no claim under this heading. He might argue alternatively that before the fire he conferred a valuable benefit on the buyer, namely a partially completed building, for which the buyer must pay. But at what point in time is this alleged benefit to be valued? Before the fire, or afterwards? If afterwards, then clearly it has no value at all. The position is not certain, but the latter view of a similarly worded Act was taken by a Canadian court in *Parsons* v. *Shea*, 1965, so ruling out any claim for compensation by the builder. The reasoning of the High Court in *B.P.* v. *Hunt*, 1982 (concerning expropriation of property by the Libyan government), affirmed on other grounds by the House of Lords, is to the same effect. Other Commonwealth statutes, notably those of New South Wales and South Australia, give the courts greater powers to equalise the parties' inevitable losses.

12.24   The Act can be excluded by express agreement between the parties, as where they contract on the basis of a *force majeure* clause which covers the events in question. It does not in any case apply to contracts for the carriage of goods by sea, charter-parties, contracts of insurance, or, in accordance with Section 7 of the Sale of Goods Act 1979, to contracts for the sale of specific goods which have perished without the fault of either party. The reason for this last exclusion in particular is obscure, but at all events these exceptional circumstances are regulated only by the rules of common law. The common law's approach is even more rigorous than that of the Act. 'Each party must fulfil his contractual obligations so far as they have fallen due before the frustrating event, but he is excused from performing those that fall due later': *Fibrosa* v. *Fairbairn*, 1943. In theory therefore money already paid under contract is irrecoverable unless there has been a total failure of consideration, and no claim can be made for valuable benefits conferred before the frustrating event. Apart from these exceptions, we should bear in mind also that there may be obligations unaffected by the frustrating event, such as liability for a previous breach of the contract, which remain enforceable.

Danish law

12.25   Events occurring after a contract has been made may have various different effects in Danish law. If they affect the quality of goods, for example, the seller may be liable for breach of contract. Or the contract may become unreasonable and thus unenforceable under Article 36 of the Contracts Act 1975. The Danish courts have also developed a doctrine of 'failed assumptions'.

12.26   Under this latter doctrine a contract will be declared void if the promisee knows that the other's promise depended on a fundamental assumption, express or implied, which can no longer be fulfilled, and if it is then just and reasonable to put the risk of failure of that assumption upon the promisee. This will depend on factors such as the foreseeability of the risk, possibility of insurance, etc. But generally speaking a seller will be wholly or partly relieved of his obligations only if the subsequent events are of a quite extraordinary nature and beyond normal commercial calculation. The limit is reached when it would be unreasonable to take a particular risk into consideration and charge accordingly for it. Under Danish law, therefore, the test of frustration is not that of impossibility or impracticability, as it is in England, even though the kind of facts involved seem very similar.

12.27   The remedies for frustration are more flexible under Danish law than English. A contract may be declared void, but not necessarily wholly so. The issue may be dealt with not as one of invalidity but breach of contract, in which case the frustrating events can be raised as a defence.

12.28   Overall it is easier to get relief from contractual obligations under Danish law than under English law. While both systems have rules on mistake, misrepresentation, frustration and so on, the basic distinction between them is in the requirements of good faith and fair dealing and the test of reasonableness in the Danish system which have no comprehensive counterpart in England. It has been suggested (Slater: *Journal of Business Law*, 1982) that on these grounds Danish law is not suitable for adoption in international contracts – but it could equally well be argued that Danish law is in fact more in conformity with international trends than English law.

Dutch law

12.29   Under Article 258 Book 6 of the Civil Code, a court may alter or rescind any contract in whole or part in the case of unforeseen circumstances (*imprévision*). 'Unforeseen' is understood as meaning 'not provided for in the contract'. In the previous decade, Dutch courts have anticipated this new principle in a number of important cases, such as *Re Algemeen Ziekenfonds*, NJ 1978, 156, and *Nationale Volksbank* v. *Helder*, NJ 1984, 679. They based their decisions largely on the good faith principle; that it would be unfair and unreasonable to compel performance in new and completely different circumstances. It should be emphasised, however, that the principle is used sparingly and as a matter of last resort. It was not applied, for example, to release parties from long-term commitments despite the inflation which followed the first World War.

French law

12.30   The general principle is that private contracts forming 'the law of the parties' (Article 1134) cannot be amended unilaterally by a party nor amended or revised by the judges, even if performance of a party's obligations has become unprofitable or does not correspond to the party's expectations: Cass. 3 March 1876. Only *force majeure* can suspend one's obligations and permit termination of the contract without fault.

12.31   This general rule is, however, subject to the doctrine of *imprévision* (unforeseen circumstances), which applies to administrative contracts made in the interests of public service. The courts hold that the public interest and in particular the need for continuity of the public service must prevail over the interests of a private party who contracts with the administration. Following on a decision of the Conseil d'État of 20 March 1916, *Compagnie du Gaz de Bordeaux*, they have allowed the French administration to amend unilaterally the terms of performance of an administrative contract, on condition of payment of indemnity to the private contractor.

12.32   *Force majeure*, unless given a more specific definition in the contract, is an event which is external to the parties (including their employees or agents) and which is unforeseeable, irresistible and insuperable. It must fully prevent the fulfilment by a party of his contractual obligations, as opposed to making them more onerous or difficult. The test is one of impossibility, as opposed to impracticability: Cass. 4 August 1915. The occurrence of the *force majeure* event suspends the obligations of the affected party, which in turn suspends the obligations of the other party. If the *force majeure* event is not merely temporary, it results in the termination of the contract without compensation for the affected party: Article 1148.

12.33   A judgment ordering the judicial receivership (*redressement judiciaire*) of a contracting party cannot, taken in isolation, be a reason for termination. Article 37 of the Bankruptcy Act of 25 January 1985, as amended, provides that notwithstanding any legal provision or contract clause, 'no indivisibility, termination or retroactive termination of the contract can result only from the opening of judicial receivership proceedings'. Clauses to the contrary, whatever the governing law of the contract, are deemed void in France. Only the judicial administrator of the bankrupt company can decide to end or continue the contract. If he elects to continue the contract, his decision is binding on the other party irrespective of defaults occurring before the judgment. If he elects to terminate the contract, termination gives rise only to a right to damages.

German law

12.34   The English doctrine of frustration does not exist as such in German law. But where there is a fundamental change in the circumstances underlying the contract – *Wegfall der Geschäftsgrundlage* – German courts deal with the problem in a different way, basing their jurisdiction on the good faith rule in Article 242 of the BGB. After the first World War this doctrine of fundamental change was created by the courts to resolve problems of inflation. Today the doctrine is much discussed in legal literature, but in practice is not very important – even with regard to the economic problems arising out of German reunification. If it applies, its effect is not necessarily to end the contract, as in England, but to adapt it to the new situation.

12.35   The prerequisites of the German doctrine are broadly as described by Lord Justice Griffiths in *Paal Wilson*, para. 12.8. It might possibly apply to a long-running contract if the sum now due seems quite inadequate compared with its value at the time the contract was made. But in a recent decision the German High Court said that there was no *Wegfall der Geschäftsgrundlage* where a contract had run for 25 years and the inflation rate during that time was 133 per cent. The doctrine is not, of course, limited to long-term contracts. It could apply to a fundamental change in the jointly agreed or understood nature or purpose of a single transaction.

12.36   Cases like *Tsakiroglou*, para. 12.14, have not been brought before the German courts, which are not very often concerned with shipping cases, and it is very difficult to say how they might be decided.

Italian law

12.37   Articles 1463–8 of the Italian Civil Code provide for the ending of contracts which have become impossible or too expensive to fulfil. In the case of impossibility of performance the obligations are extinguished by law. When the problem is one of excessive cost the parties may apply to the judge for variation of the contract: Article 1468.

12.38   Impossibility is defined in terms of objective or external forces which prevent execution of the contract, in whole or in part: Articles 1256–8. If it is the debtor's fault the contract cannot be carried out, he remains liable for breach of contract. It may be impossible to fulfil a contract because of a particular event such as destruction of the subject-matter, or circumstances arising over a period of time causing such difficulties or delays as to release one side or the other from his obligation. Goods supplied or money paid must then be returned. Destruction of the specific goods which were the subject of the contract does not necessarily end the contract if others of the same kind are obtainable, at least without such excessive cost and difficulty as to make it 'relatively' impossible to supply them. The rules as to risk should be borne in mind here. They are the same as under Section 18 of the UK Sale of Goods Act. So, for example, specific goods are at the buyer's risk as soon as the contract is made, and he still has to pay for them even though they are accidentally destroyed before delivery.

12.39   The right to ask the court to end a contract because of the excessive cost of performance arises in long-term bilateral contracts affected by exceptional and unforeseen events such as wars, revolutions and collapses of the market. The *Corte di Cassazione* has held that an exceptional rate of inflation might justify termination of the contract. Alternatively the court might order a re-writing of the contract to accommodate changed economic circumstances, possibly in accordance with express 'hardship' or price escalation clauses. Contract clauses of this kind do not of themselves preclude the court from declaring a contract ended: Article 1467.

Spanish law

12.40   Spanish law has no general principle of frustration of contract. In a breach of contract action, however, it is a complete defence under Article 1105 of the Civil Code to prove that unforeseeable or inevitable events have occurred which as *caso fortuito* or *fuerza mayor* make it impossible to carry out the contract. If the obligation is to hand over a specific thing which is lost through no fault of the supplier, or to do something which becomes legally or physically impossible, the obligation is then extinguished: Articles 1156, 1182–4.

12.41   Alternatively, circumstances may arise which are not such as to make it impossible to carry out the contract, but which make it exceptionally onerous to do so. A Supreme Court decision of 6 October 1987 ruled that a person could only be excused performance of a contract in its original terms if: (i) there was an extraordinary alteration of circumstances as between the time the contract was to be fulfilled and the time it was made; (ii) the result would be an exorbitant disproportion or imbalance between the contributions to be made by each party; (iii) the new circumstances were fundamentally unpredictable or unavoidable; (iv) there is no other way of avoiding the loss or damage.

12.42   These conditions are unlikely to be fulfilled. In fact, they have applied only in cases of grave changes in the value of money – as in a case where an option to purchase a luxury hotel for 5 million pesetas was drawn up in 1921 but not to be exercised until 1951.

Swedish law

12.43   Despite the fact that the approach of Danish and Swedish law to questions of frustration differs from that of English law, the outcomes in the end are often similar. For example, according to Swedish law the contractor who has offered a fixed price normally bears the risk of inflation and shortage of materials.

Chapter 13

Remedies for breach of contract

A. Damages

13.1   The usual remedy under English law for breach of contract is an award of damages. The standard Continental remedies of reduction in price, or replacement or repair of defective goods, do not currently exist in English law, apart from the buyer's right to withhold payment of an appropriate part of the price in the event of short delivery: Section 30, Sale of Goods Act. The Convention on International Sale of Goods broadly endorses the Continental remedies, while accepting the possibility of claims for damages. We begin our discussion of the English rules with some definitions. Damages may be nominal or substantial, contemptuous or exemplary or punitive, general or special, liquidated or unliquidated. Nominal damages are token awards, given for a breach of contract which has caused no loss, or only a notional one. So a seller would receive nominal damages if the buyer rejected the contract before the date of delivery, but it could be shown that the seller would not in fact have been able to deliver the goods on that date: *The Mihalis Angelos*, 1970. But even an award of nominal damages usually entitles the plaintiff to have the costs of his claim paid by the defendant, which may be a much more severe penalty. Substantial damages cover the plaintiff's actual losses, assessed in the light of the rules we discuss below, and bearing in mind that if the loss is only small the 'substantial' damages will also be small.

13.2   Contemptuous or derisory damages are likely to be nominal in effect, signifying both the court's acknowledgment and vindication of a technical right but its disapproval of the circumstances in which, or reasons for which, a claim is made. Exemplary or punitive damages are those increased beyond the plaintiff's actual loss in order to mark the court's disapproval of the defendant's conduct in deliberately or recklessly aggravating the plaintiff's loss. They are not available under English law in contract cases.

13.3   General damages are those claimed by the plaintiff as the natural and probable consequences of the breach. The precise amount is fixed by the

277

judge in accordance with the rules considered below. Special damages on the other hand are those precisely quantifiable before the trial – expenses, loss of earnings, repair bills and the like. Unlike claims for general damages, these sums have to be itemised in the plaintiff's statement of claim. Damages are liquidated if and insofar as they are fixed or determined – as where the parties agree in the contract on the amount to be paid in the event of breach. This practice is discussed below. Unliquidated damages are 'at large', to be fixed by the judge.

13.4   The purpose of an award of damages is that 'where a party sustains a loss by reason of a breach of contract he is, so far as money can do it, to be placed in the same situation . . . as if the contract had been performed': *Robinson* v. *Harman*, 1848. The law's concern therefore is to calculate the loss suffered by the innocent party, not to determine the degree of fault of the party in breach. As we have said before, contractual liability is usually strict, and blameworthiness or otherwise therefore irrelevant. But we have to recognise immediately that a successful plaintiff is most unlikely to get back all he has lost. He may be left well out of pocket for a wide variety of reasons; not only because of the possible difficulty of quantifying his losses or the duty to mitigate or limit them (below), or the likelihood of having to pay some part of his costs despite his victory, or the difficulty of extracting money from defendants who refuse to pay or who have no money, but very probably because of the rules of remoteness of damage which we now describe.

i. Remoteness of damage

13.5   The starting point is that proof of cause and effect alone is not enough to entitle a plaintiff to compensation for his loss. He must prove also that the loss he suffered because of the breach was *likely*, not merely foreseeable. It must not be too indirect or remote. Four leading cases must be consulted in any attempt to explain the necessary degree of predictability. The first is *Hadley* v. *Baxendale*, 1854 – the beginning of all discussion in English law as to the assessment of damages. The case concerned a mill shaft which had to be repaired and then returned to the mill. The carriers broke their contract by delaying the return of the shaft. Since this was the only shaft the mill had, it was necessary to keep the mill closed, which caused large production losses. Should the carriers have been liable for all these losses? The judge said that '*a defendant should be liable for those consequences of his breach which were either 'such as may fairly and reasonably be expected to arise naturally, that is, according to the usual course of things from such breach of contract, or such as may reasonably be supposed to have been in contemplation of both parties at the time they made the contract, as the probable result of it*'. This wording has been accepted also in the United States as the basis of assessment of damages in contract: Section 351 of the second Restatement of Contracts.

13.6   Liability is thus imposed first for the kind of losses which might *usually* be expected to occur in a particular situation, and/or, second, for those abnormal or *exceptional* consequences of which the defendant had special knowledge and for which in the circumstances he should be liable. The first inquiry is an objective one; the second, subjective. Applying these rules to the facts of *Hadley*, it followed that the carriers were liable only for a 'conventional' sum and not for the mill's unusually large losses. They had no means of knowing that their carelessness would lead to closure of this large business. We should note that even if they had been told this was the only shaft, that of itself would not necessarily mean they had agreed to run the risk of additional liability. It would be a question whether in all the circumstances, including in particular the price charged for their services, they could reasonably be regarded as having contracted on that basis: *Satef-Huttenes* v. *Paloma*, 1981; *Balfour-Beatty* v. *Scottish Power*, 1994 – electricity supplier not liable for total stoppage of work caused by interruption in supply. If possible, the difficulty should be dealt with expressly in the contract. Such a term might say: 'For the avoidance of doubt the sellers hereby acknowledge that it is within their contemplation that [late delivery, etc.] is likely to cause the buyers exceptional expense arising out of [loss of profits; future trading losses; loss of goodwill; interest charges, etc.]' – preferably with some precise indication of the nature of such expense. Where the seller is the stronger party he may try expressly to reject such extended liability, as illustrated in para. 13.13, below.

13.7   Our second leading case is *Victoria Laundry* v. *Newman*, 1949. The defendants' failure to supply a laundry with a new boiler at the agreed time resulted in the laundry suffering general loss of profits and also loss of a particularly lucrative government contract, which it could not take up because of the lack of extra capacity which the new boiler would have provided. Following *Hadley*, the Court of Appeal held the defendants liable for the laundry's loss of normal profits during the period of delay, but not for the exceptional or 'windfall' loss of the government contract which neither side had known of at the time the contract was made, and which was not, as it was said, 'on the cards' or 'liable to result' from the breach.

13.8   Next is the case of *Czarnikow* v. *Koufos: The Heron II*, 1969, which established that where a supplier knows or ought to know he is supplying goods for resale but is nonetheless late in delivering them, he should be liable for loss of resale profit caused by a drop in market prices in the meantime. This would be a 'usual consequence' of such delay. Normally, however, a supplier does not know that resale is the whole point and purpose of the contract, and so is not liable for loss of resale profit: *Williams* v. *Agius*, 1914; *Hall* v. *Pim*, 1928. Even if the supplier does know of the buyer's intention to resell, he is not necessarily bound to make good any exceptionally large or unreasonable profit lost to the buyer: *Coastal Trading* v. *Maroil*, 1988.

13.9   The most important aspect of *Czarnikow* is in the House of Lords' attempt to correct the Court of Appeal's ruling in *Victoria Laundry* as to the proper standard of foreseeability of loss, and to confirm and explain the test in *Hadley*. Lord Reid said that damages could be recovered for losses which were 'not unlikely', or 'quite likely' – involving 'a degree of probability considerably less than an even chance but nevertheless not very unusual and easily foreseeable'. Lord Hodson favoured 'a real danger' or 'serious possibility'. All deplored Lord Justice Asquith's view in *Victoria Laundry* that losses could be compensated if and insofar as they were reasonably foreseeable or 'on the cards'. Reasonable foreseeability of loss is the test in tort (as laid down in *Overseas Tankship* v. *Morts Dock; The Wagon Mound*, 1961), but in *Czarnikow* their Lordships declared that in contract a higher standard of probability was required. It is perhaps a question of the difference between 'quite possible' and 'quite probable', with the former as the yardstick in tort and the latter in contract.

13.10   Several possible reasons might be advanced for trying to make this very fine distinction: the desire of nineteenth century judges to protect merchants against excessive awards of damages by juries (not now used in such cases), or the ability of contracting parties – unlike that of tort victims – to limit their liability, or perhaps the need to temper strict liability by limiting the awards. Whatever the reason, the distinction is evidently all but impossible to explain or maintain. It seems most undesirable also to complicate the law by laying down different standards of predictability in similar or overlapping areas of law. It is interesting to see that the Canadian Supreme Court has formally abandoned the distinction, and now applies the test of reasonable foreseeability of loss in both contract and tort, subject to any special provision made by contracting parties: *Asamera Corp.* v. *Sea Oil Corp.*, 1979; *B.G. Checo* v. *B.C. Hydro*, 1993. New Zealand courts have taken the same view – *McElroy* v. *Commercial Electronics*, 1993 – as did the Scottish Court of Session in *Ogilvie* v. *Glasgow C.C.*, 1994. The Convention on Contracts for the International Sale of Goods imposes liability for losses which a defendant should have foreseen as a 'possible consequence' of his breach of contract. This seems a remarkably vague test, but it might perhaps be interpreted more strictly. We observe in passing that if reasonable foresight had in fact been the test in *Hadley* the carriers might still have escaped liability on the ground that it was not reasonably foreseeable that such a large enterprise would have only the one shaft and would have to close down without it.

13.11   The fourth major case is *Parsons* v. *Uttley Ingham*, 1978. This concerned a contract to build a hopper – a container – for pig food. The hopper was built without proper ventilation for the food, which then went bad. The mouldy food was fed to the pigs, many of which died because of a very rare disease caused by the food. The Court of Appeal held that the natural and foreseeable consequences of the defective installation were that the food would go bad and the pigs would suffer accordingly. Since some kind of harm was likely it did not matter that the actual damage was more serious than might have been expected or that it was of a very unusual nature. *Parsons* is important because the builder's failure to take reasonable care in his work was both a breach of contract and a tort. The Court therefore had to consider the effect of the ruling in *Czarnikow*. The judges were understandably reluctant to accept that different sums might be awarded for the same wrong, depending on whether damages were assessed in contract or in tort. Lord Denning protested strongly: 'I find it difficult . . . to draw a distinction between what a man "contemplates" and what he "foresees". I soon begin to get out of my depth. I cannot swim in this sea of semantic exercises – to say nothing of the different degrees of probability – especially when the cause of action can be laid either in contract or in tort. I am swept under by the conflicting currents.' The outcome was that their Lordships agreed unanimously, though for different reasons, that the measure of damages was the same in both contract and tort, and that the test was that of reasonable foreseeability of loss. The Court took the same view in *Banque Bruxelles* v. *Eagle Star*, 1995. This conclusion conflicts with that of the House of Lords in *Czarnikow*, and the whole issue remains to be resolved. In the end, of course, whatever the rules may say, the real question in all these cases is whether the judge thinks the plaintiff should win. If he does, he will say his losses were likely. If not, he will say they were too remote.

13.12   We can see from *Parsons* in particular that apparently minor breaches of contract, or breaches which seem minor because of the small cost of the goods or services supplied, may have disproportionately expensive results. The seller of a fire extinguisher, for example, could theoretically be liable for the destruction of a complete building and resulting injuries if the extinguisher failed to work at the vital moment. A car or aircraft component seller could be liable to his buyer for the total cost of a disastrous accident caused by a faulty component. Some legal systems attempt to balance the defendant's resources against the plaintiff's losses, and so limit the defendant's liability to what might appear reasonable in the circumstances. The UK has no comparable rule (although the question of reasonableness was crucial in *Ruxley* v. *Forsyth*, below) but such extensive and possibly ruinous liability might be avoided or reduced by insurance or by exclusion clauses in the contract of sale.

13.13   Many contracts purport to deal with these problems by dividing the losses which might arise from breach of contract into 'direct' and 'consequential', sometimes accepting liability for direct loss but rejecting it for consequential loss. A car warranty, for example, might undertake to supply new parts to replace those found defective but refuse liability for injuries caused thereby. Other contracts again contain more comprehensive denials of liability, as for example: 'In no case will the company be liable in contract, tort (including breach of statutory duty) or otherwise for loss (whether direct or indirect) of profits, business or anticipated savings, or for any indirect or consequential damage whatsoever.' Another such clause seeks expressly to reject liability under rule 2 of *Hadley* v. *Baxendale*: 'The seller shall not be liable for any indirect or consequential loss (including loss of profit) howsoever arising either from breach or non-performance of any of its obligations under the contract, even if the seller has been specifically put on notice of the possibility of such indirect or consequential loss'. It will be seen that these attempts to distinguish between direct and indirect or consequential loss are not in accordance with the *Hadley* test of probability (unless 'direct' is interpreted as 'probable', as it was in *Ogilvie*, above). All such provisions would in any case be subject to the controls over exclusion clauses discussed in Chapter 7.

13.14   The general principles above are more specifically stated for the purposes of sales of goods. Sections 49 and 50 of the Sale of Goods Act 1979 define sellers' rights against defaulting buyers. A buyer who wrongfully refuses to pay for goods after he has become owner is liable for the agreed price, as also if he breaks a promise to pay for them on the due day. But where the buyer has wrongfully refused to accept delivery of the goods in the first place, the seller's claim is for unliquidated damages. The difference is important. In the first situation the amount claimed – the price – is fixed and irreducible; in the second it is at large and affected by the seller's duty to reduce his own losses, below. The measure of damages here is 'the estimated loss directly and naturally resulting in the ordinary course of events from the buyer's breach of contract': Section 50(2). Since the seller should try to sell his goods elsewhere as soon as reasonably practicable after the buyer rejects them, his loss would usually be the difference between the agreed price and the market price, if there is one: Section 50(3).

13.15   Buyers' remedies against sellers are similarly defined in Sections 51–3. Where the seller fails to deliver the goods, the buyer should buy some elsewhere. His damages are then '*prima facie* to be ascertained by the difference between the contract price and the market or current price of the goods at the time or times when they ought to have been delivered': Section 51(3). Section 52 says that an order for specific performance may be made against the seller, but as indicated below this is most unlikely in practice. By Section 53(2), where a seller is in breach of warranty the damages are again those 'directly and naturally resulting', and if the warranty concerns quality the amount is usually assessed as the difference between the actual value of the goods at the time of delivery and the value they should have had at that time. If interest payments or special damages are recoverable they may be claimed by either side under Section 54.

13.16   We observe in passing with regard to Section 54 that a creditor is not entitled to more than the sum owed and so cannot usually claim interest on unpaid debts without express provision to that effect in the contract. Since small business creditors are often kept waiting by larger company debtors, this rule is therefore a common cause of hardship, bearing in mind also the incidental losses caused by inflation. But its effect has been reduced by the decision in *President of India* v. *La Pintada*, 1984, where the House of Lords held that if the debtor knows that delay will stop the creditor from using his money profitably or increase his overdraft charges he should be liable for those additional losses under the second rule in *Hadley* v. *Baxendale*. Delay of itself does not give rise to a claim for interest: *Holbeach* v. *Anglian Water Authority*, 1990. In *President of India* v. *Lips*, 1987, their Lordships said that a late payment of damages could not give rise to another claim for damages, but only a claim for interest on the original sum.

13.17   Reverting to sales of goods, we have seen that the current market price is the yardstick by which damages are usually assessed – but that may beg the question. Market prices are not always a realistic guide, and sometimes there may not even be such a price. The different approaches which may then be needed are illustrated in the following three cases on car sales. In *Thompson* v. *Robinson*, 1955, the buyer wrongfully refused to take delivery of the car he had ordered. The dealers then persuaded their own supplier to take the car back, so that strictly speaking they suffered no loss. But because the supply of this type of car exceeded demand, making this sale a 'lucky break' for the dealers, the judge held that they should be compensated in full by reference to the car's notional market value for their loss of profit on the deal. The answer would be the same even if by chance the dealers found another customer. In *Charter* v. *Sullivan*, 1957, on the other hand, where demand for a certain model exceeded supply, the dealer was awarded only nominal damages against the defaulting buyer. The question in *Lazenby* v. *Wright*, 1976, was how damages should be assessed for a second-hand car. The dealer paid £1,325 for the car and contracted to sell it to the buyer for £1,670. The buyer then changed his mind and refused to take the car. A few weeks later the dealer sold it to someone else for £1,770. From *Thompson* one might infer that the dealer should have been able to claim his original loss of profit, *viz*. £345. But the court held that since every used car is unique it has no generally accepted market value, and so the dealer could be compensated only for what he had actually lost. Since he had in fact made a profit he recovered only nominal damages.

13.18   The 'difference in value' test gives satisfactory answers in simple sale of goods cases, but may not otherwise be helpful. If a builder contracts to do £1,000 worth of work, does half the work and then leaves it, what sum of money would put the householder where he would have been if the contract had been completed? Should he get the difference in value between what was done and what should have been done (£500), or the cost of performance, i.e., of employing another builder to complete the job (which might involve demolition and reconstruction; say £1,500), or the reduction in value of his property brought about by the half-completed work (which might be little or nothing)? And if £1,500 was the right amount, would the householder then be obliged to spend that sum completing the work? In *Ruxley* v. *Forsyth*, 1995, the leading case, a builder contracted to build an indoor swimming pool for some £70,000. The contract required the pool to be 7 ft. 6 in. deep, but the builder made it only 6 ft. deep – though it was still safe for diving. The Court of Appeal held that an award representing the negligible difference in value between a 6 ft. deep pool and a 7 ft. 6 in. deep pool would not give the plaintiff what he had asked for, and awarded him approximately £20,000 to enable him to rebuild the pool. The House of Lords reversed the decision on the ground that damages for reinstatement would be awarded only where it was reasonable to do so. Such damages here would give the plaintiff what was regarded as an altogether excessive and unnecessary benefit – i.e., a usable pool plus £20,000. Applying the difference in value test, however, plaintiff would receive little or nothing. But their Lordships accepted that he had a claim for loss of amenity and enjoyment, and awarded him £2,500. In theory at least it would seem to follow from this controversial judgment that a person in flagrant and perhaps even deliberate breach of contract could buy his way out of liability with little more than a token payment. A comparable American case of interest is *Peevyhouse* v. *Garland*, 1963. Although decided by the Oklahoma Supreme Court in the same way as in *Ruxley*, the case is noteworthy for the objections raised in the strong dissenting judgment of Justice Irwin: 'In my opinion, the plaintiffs were entitled to specific performance of the contract and since defendant has failed to perform, the proper measure of damages should be the cost of performance. Any other measure of damage would be holding for naught the express provisions of the contract; would be taking from the plaintiffs the benefits of the contract and placing those benefits in defendant which has failed to perform its obligations; would be granting benefits to defendant without a resulting obligation; and would be completely rescinding the solemn obligation of the contract for the benefit of the defendant to the detriment of the plaintiffs by making an entirely new contract for the parties.'

13.19   Subject to these problems of quantification, damages can be claimed for a very wide range of other 'direct and natural' consequential losses and expenses, such as repairs and loss of use of goods, storage, innocent party's costs in defending himself against claims brought by sub-purchasers, and so on: *Kolfor* v. *Tilbury Plant*, 1977; *H.L. Motorworks* v. *Alwahbi*, 1977; *Danecroft* v. *Criegee*, 1988. Damages may be awarded for physical injury caused by defective goods or services – *Godley* v. *Perry*, 1960 – and possibly also for disappointment and distress. The general rule is that damages are given on these grounds only if they arise from the physical consequences of the breach; for instance, illness and distress resulting from living in an insanitary house: *Perry* v. *Phillips*, 1982. So a claim for damages for humiliation and stress caused by wrongful dismissal, which of itself has no physical consequences, was rejected by the House of Lords in *Addis* v. *Gramophone Co.*, 1909 – a decision strongly disapproved in *Whelan* v. *Waitiki Meats*, 1991, and *Rowlands* v. *Collow*, 1992 (N.Z.), and *Brown* v. *Waterloo Regional Board*, 1984 (Canada). Anxiety and depression brought about simply by being involved in claiming damages for breach of contract is not compensated: *Hayes* v. *James*, 1990. But where the purpose of a contract is specifically to provide peace of mind, damages will be awarded for breach – as, for example, for the disappointment suffered when promises in a holiday brochure are not fulfilled: *Jackson* v. *Horizon Holidays*, 1975. There are some difficult borderline cases. Damages were awarded for loss of amenity and personal satisfaction in *Ruxley*, above; for 'vexation' when a new car broke down – *Bernstein* v. *Pamsons Motors*, 1987 – but not when a Rolls Royce needed repeated repairs, nor when a new house proved unsatisfactory: *Alexander* v. *Rolls Royce*, 1995; *Knott* v. *Bolton*, 1995. Expenses incurred before the contract was made, but in preparation for it, are recoverable in so far as the party in breach should have foreseen such losses: *Anglia T.V.* v. *Reed*, 1971. Such a claim may be preferable to a speculative claim for loss of profits: *Diamond* v. *Campbell Jones*, 1960. Damages may be awarded in a foreign currency if that is the basis of the contract: *Miliangos* v. *Frank*, 1976. Choice of the appropriate currency may be affected by events such as devaluation: *The Texaco Melbourne*, 1991.

13.20   The mere fact that a loss may be very difficult to quantify does not preclude a claim: *Chaplin* v. *Hicks*, 1911 – damages awarded for loss of opportunity to attend a selection interview. The plaintiff in a case like *Chaplin* has to prove a reasonable prospect of success; otherwise he or she will be awarded only nominal damages: *Obagi* v. *Stanborough*, 1993; *Eastwalsh* v. *Anatal*, 1993 (Canada). No claim can be made for loss of speculative benefits such as discretionary bonus payments. Where the contract gives one party a choice as to the method of performance, it cannot be assumed that he will exercise that choice in a way most favourable to the other side. In *Lee* v. *Zehil*, 1983, the defendant had broken his contract to buy a certain large quantity of clothing from a range of five different grades. The contract did not specify how many items of each grade should be bought. The court rejected the defendant's argument that he could have bought the whole consignment in the cheaper range. The defendant had to make his choice in a reasonable way, consistent with the commercial purpose of the contract. Conversely, a plaintiff cannot claim for difficulties brought about more by his own financial difficulties or unnecessary expenditure than by the breach of contract – *Trans Trust* v. *Danubian Trading*, 1952 – unless, again, the likelihood of such exceptional difficulty is the basis of the contract. In *Pilkington* v. *Wood*, 1953 a solicitor was in breach of contract in failing to ensure that his client, the plaintiff, got a good title to a house he bought in Hampshire. The plaintiff later took employment in Lancashire, but had difficulty in selling his house. He had to stay in a hotel during the week, from which he telephoned his wife every night, and went home at week-ends. The judge refused to award damages for any of these expenses. He pointed out that it was the plaintiff's decision to move, and that he could equally well have got a job in another country – but could scarcely have made his solicitor pay for all the expenses he would then have incurred. His nightly calls to his wife were dismissed as 'exemplary but uxorious'.

ii. Mitigation

13.21   As we have just seen, the plaintiff is not allowed wilfully to make matters worse for the defendant. On the contrary, the common law requires him to try to make the best of a bad job. This duty to lessen or mitigate the effect of the breach underlies the Sale of Goods Act rules on assessment of damages mentioned earlier, and with the exception noted below is of general application in contract law. So, for example, an employee alleging wrongful or unfair dismissal must seek suitable alternative employment: *Lavarack* v. *Woods*, 1966. If a seller breaks his contract by refusing credit, but is willing to take cash on delivery, it may well be that the buyer should agree to the new terms since they may still represent the cheapest way of getting the goods he wants: *Payzu* v. *Saunders*, 1919; *Sotiros* v. *Shmeiet Solholt: The Solholt*, 1983.

13.22   At the same time the law does not expect the plaintiff to do more than is immediately necessary to protect himself. He is not obliged to take more serious commercial risks, or accept an inferior product, or, for example, to recoup his losses by taking legal action against others in the chain of supply. He need not build a wooden fence if the other party contracted to build a brick wall: *Radford* v. *De Frobeville*, 1979. 'The law is satisfied if the party placed in a difficult situation by reason of the breach of duty owed to him has acted reasonably in the adoption of remedial measures, and he will not be held disentitled to recover the cost of such measures merely because the party in breach can suggest that other measures less burdensome to him might have been taken': *Banco de Portugal* v. *Waterlow*, 1932. It is hard to say how soon a plaintiff should act in mitigation. If he delays, he may seem to be speculating in the market at the defendant's expense, and so may recover only nominal damages: *Kaine* v. *Osterreichische W.A.G.*, 1993. But if he acts too quickly, he may make things worse for himself. In *Asamera*, para. 13.10, above, the Canadian Supreme Court accepted that a plaintiff does not always have to take action in mitigation *immediately*. The case arose out of a failure to redeliver certain shares. The Court accepted that the plaintiff might properly delay while seeking a court order against the defendant, and even after that might take several years in buying other shares of comparable value. And if a plaintiff takes what seem at the time to be reasonable steps to reduce his losses, which in the event prove unsuccessful or more expensive than originally supposed, he will not be penalised on those grounds. On the other hand, if the action taken in mitigation is so successful as to avoid any loss at all, then the plaintiff cannot claim any damages. In *British Westinghouse* v. *Underground Electric Railway Co.*, 1912, the plaintiff bought new and more profitable machinery to replace defective machinery supplied by the defendant. He therefore had no claim for damages for breach of contract beyond the time of replacement.

13.23 That brings us to the interesting question of 'betterment'. In seeking to restore the position to what it would have been if the contract had been carried out correctly, e.g. by rebuilding property damaged by the defendant's negligence, the plaintiff may end up with something of greater value than he had before. Sometimes the cost of restoration may far outweigh the value of the property. The courts are very reluctant to allow claims involving either disproportionate expenditure for the defendant or actual benefit to the plaintiff – *Bacon* v. *Cooper*, 1982; *Ruxley*, above – but may occasionally accept that renewal is the only reasonable course open to the plaintiff. In *Harbutt's Plasticine* v. *Wayne Tank*, 1970, for instance, the plaintiffs claimed damages for the cost of rebuilding their factory after it had been destroyed by fire through the defendants' negligence. The defendants argued that they should pay no more than the value of the old one. Lord Justice Widgery allowed the plaintiffs' claim, saying: 'It was reasonable for the plaintiffs to rebuild their factory, because there was no other way they could carry on their business and retain their labour force. The plaintiffs rebuilt their factory to a substantially different design, and if this had involved expenditure beyond the cost of replacing the old, the difference might not have been recoverable, but there is no suggestion of this here. Nor do I accept that the plaintiffs must give credit under the heading of "betterment" for the fact that their new factory is modern in design and materials. To do so would be the equivalent of forcing the plaintiffs to invest their money in the modernisation of their plant, which might be highly inconvenient for them.' Similar Commonwealth cases include *Evans* v. *Balog*, 1976 (Australia) and *Nan* v. *Black Pine Manufacturing*, 1991 (Canada). Even where the plaintiff buys new and larger premises and more profitable machinery he may still succeed in his claim if and insofar as that is still the only reasonable course open to him: *Dominion Mosaics* v. *Trafalgar Trucking*, 1989; *Hussey* v. *Eels*, 1989. The question overall is whether the steps taken by the plaintiff arise directly out of the original broken contract, in which case he has no claim if by chance he makes a profit, or are independent of it: *Famosa Shipping* v. *Armada Carriers*, 1994. It is a distinction equally hard either to apply or to justify. Insurance benefits are not in any case deducted.

13.24 If a plaintiff's loss is caused partly by his own fault as well as by the defendant's breach of contract, one might think the effect would be to reduce the defendant's liability accordingly. The principle of contributory negligence would achieve this result in a tort case. In contract, however, liability is usually strict and not dependent on fault, so this principle rarely applies: *Barclays Bank* v. *Fairclough*, 1994. A seller of defective goods might therefore be held wholly liable for injury caused in part by the buyer's careless use of the goods. But if it is the buyer's own carelessness which is the real cause of his injury, the seller is no longer to blame: *Lambert* v. *Lewis*, 1981 – buyer solely liable for accident caused by his continued use of a defective caravan towing-hitch, knowing of the defect. In 1990 the Law Commission recommended acceptance of the defence of contributory negligence in contract cases. The principle is accepted by the Convention on International Sale of Goods.

iii. Anticipatory breach

13.25   When a contracting party's words or deeds before the time agreed for performance show that he cannot or will not fulfil his obligations, he commits an anticipatory breach of contract. This does not of itself bring the contract to an end or relieve either side of its duties. The breach will only be regarded as repudiatory if clearly such as to make it purposeless to continue, e.g. because the wrongdoer's intention is obviously to damage the innocent party, or he makes excessive and premature demands on him: *Federal Commerce* v. *Molena*, 1979; *Weeks* v. *Bradshaw*, 1993. But if the breach is caused, say, by a misunderstanding on the wrongdoer's part, or is in some way conditional or qualified, for instance by reference to the effect of legal advice, repudiation by the innocent party will probably not be justified: *Toepfer* v. *Itex*, 1993. Repudiation in these circumstances could make the innocent party liable in his turn to the wrongdoer, as in *Woodar* v. *Wimpey*, 1980. The innocent party undoubtedly faces a very difficult choice in these situations.

13.26   Assuming, however, that the breach can properly be regarded as repudiatory, the common law gives the innocent party a choice of remedies. On the one hand, he may expressly or by word of deed – but not merely by silence: *Vitol* v. *Norelf*, 1995 – 'accept' the repudiation, i.e. accept that the agreement is ended, and sue immediately for damages. The sum awarded will represent what he should have received under the contract, minus whatever he did or should have done to mitigate the loss.

13.27   On the other hand he may refuse to accept the repudiation. The contract is then still in being, and so he may carry out his own obligations under it as and when due, or remain ready to carry them out: *Fercometal* v. *Mediterranean Shipping: The Simona*, 1988. Having done that, and run the risk of any downturn in the market, he can then demand full payment or performance from the other side. It will be seen that if he takes this course he is not obliged to mitigate his losses, but on the contrary is free to make them worse.

13.28   The consequences of this curious – sometimes even alarming – rule are well illustrated in *White and Carter* v. *McGregor*, 1962. A company made a contract with a client to produce advertising materials. The client changed his mind and cancelled the contract within hours of making it. The company ignored the breach, produced all the materials, knowing they were not wanted, and then demanded payment. The House of Lords upheld the claim, which was no doubt much more lucrative to the plaintiffs than if they had had to mitigate their loss. It should follow, as indeed their Lordships recognised, that if A agrees with B to attend a meeting in Hong Kong, and then B tells him not to go, A can still go and enjoy himself, and send the bill to B!

13.29   Attempts have been made to modify the rule. In the case itself it was said that the innocent party could not insist on fulfilling the contract if he had no 'legitimate interest' in doing so. This seems a meaningless proviso insofar as he has always had the motive of making his expected profit on the deal, an apparently legitimate objective. In *Hounslow L.B.C.* v. *Twickenham Garden Developments*, 1970, the High Court emphasised that the rule could not apply where the innocent party needed the wrongdoer's co-operation, e.g. where the object of the contract was that the innocent party should do some work on the wrongdoer's land but the latter then changed his mind and refused entry. Clearly the innocent party could not then force his way in and do the work regardless.

13.30   The Court took an important step further in *Clea* v. *Bulk Oil*, 1984, holding that the question was simply whether continued performance of the contract by one side against the wishes of the other was reasonable in the circumstances. In this case a ship chartered for two years needed major repairs after the first year. The charterers rejected the ship, but the owners insisted on repairing it, which took six months, and then kept it fully crewed awaiting the charterers' instructions. The owners' conduct was rightly held to be unreasonable and their claim for hire-charges during the second year was rejected accordingly. On the face of it a requirement of reasonableness would have much the same effect on the assessment of damages as that of mitigation, and should greatly reduce the hazard of the *White and Carter* rule. A Canadian court disapproved the rule in *Finelli* v. *Dee*, 1968, and American courts have in any case rejected this 'harsh and unreasonable doctrine': *Fowler* v. *A. & A. Co.*, 1970; Section 338, Restatement of the Law of Contracts.

iv. Liquidated damages and penalty clauses

13.31   To avoid the expense and uncertainty of litigation, many commercial contracts include clauses specifying in advance the amount or *quantum* of damages payable in the event of breach. Such provisions often appear in major building contracts and also in charter-parties – contracts for the hire of ships – where they are known as demurrage (delay) clauses. The damages are then said to be liquidated, i.e. clarified or settled. The sum might be stated as £X per day or week of delay, or as a deduction of X per cent per day or week from the total price payable. It is in both parties' interests to specify precisely the circumstances in which the clause applies. The buyer may want to ensure that it does not affect his right to claim damages at large for losses caused by the seller's negligence or other blameworthy conduct – e.g., in particular, his having secured the contract in the first place by giving over-optimistic and unattainable delivery dates. On the other hand, the buyer might seek to protect himself by a liquidated damages clause against losses which would otherwise be very difficult to quantify, such as damage to his commercial reputation. For his part the seller will try to make sure the clause does not make him liable for delays caused by *force majeure* (Chapter 7) or other circumstances entirely beyond his control.

13.32 Unlike many other legal systems, *English law will enforce liquidated damages clauses only if they are 'genuine pre-estimates' of the likely losses*. Section 2–718 of the American Uniform Commercial Code is to the same effect. Clauses such as the following seek to emphasise that point: 'The seller acknowledges that time is of the essence under this contract. After a full and frank discussion the buyer and seller together have made a genuine pre-estimate of the likely losses the buyer will suffer in respect of any breach of the seller's time or other obligations under this contract. Accordingly, and in full and final settlement of any claim which the buyer might otherwise have against the seller in respect of such time or other defaults, the price will be reduced by 1 per cent for every week of delay past the delivery date, to a maximum of 5 per cent. But where the seller continues in delay for more than 5 weeks, the buyer shall nevertheless be entitled to claim that the contract is in breach . . .'

13.33 Liquidated damages clauses are often loosely called 'penalty clauses', but if they are in fact penalties or punishments for one side's breach of contract, rather than pre-estimates of the other side's loss, they are *void and unenforceable*. The question is not resolved simply by the wording of the contract, nor, in particular, by use of the word 'penalty'. Guidance was given in the leading case of *Dunlop* v. *New Garage*, 1915. The House of Lords said here that a sum payable on breach is a penalty if 'extravagant and unconscionable' in comparison to the greatest loss the plaintiff could suffer from the breach. Requiring a larger sum to be paid on failure to pay a small sum is penal – but it is, of course, still legal to require a debtor to repay the whole sum lent if he does not comply with the terms of the loan: *The Angelic Star*, 1988. Making the same sum payable on a variety of different grounds, some weighty and others trivial, suggests that the sum is penal – but against that may be the difficulty of settling a suitable figure for each and every different kind of loss. In hire-purchase contracts, clauses making the larger sums payable for breach at the outset, when the goods are still nearly new, are probably penal: *Bridge* v. *Campbell Discount*, 1962 – although one could equally well argue that the greatest depreciation occurs as soon as the goods are used.

13.34   It is still very difficult to say which clauses will be upheld and which rejected, and what exactly are the consequences of such decision. But if a liquidated damages clause is upheld, the plaintiff has only to prove the defendant's breach and he is thereupon entitled to the specified sum without needing to prove he has suffered any particular loss, or indeed any loss at all. He is relieved also of the duty to mitigate, because his claim is for a debt – a fixed sum to which he is entitled by contract: *Abrahams* v. *Performing Rights Society*, 1995. On the other hand it seems he cannot then claim more than his genuine pre-estimate, however great his actual loss: *Cellulose Acetate* v. *Widnes Foundry*, 1933 (House of Lords). But he may – and should – be able to evade this rule if the contract expressly reserves his right to claim further compensation for further provable loss. In *Raymer* v. *Stratton Woods*, 1988 (Canada), for example, a building contract said that if the buyer withdrew from the contract he would lose his deposit, 'in addition to and without prejudice to any other remedy available to the vendor'. The court held that loss of the deposit was not a penalty, and that the clause in question entitled the seller also to claim general damages. The onus of proving that a fixed sum is a penalty is upon the party liable to pay it, but strangely enough it is not always in his interests to do so. If a defendant proves that the sum claimed from him is a penalty, the plaintiff is thereupon freed from the constraints of the clause and can sue the defendant for all his provable losses – up to and beyond the penalty figure: *Wall* v. *Rederiaktiebolaget Luggude*, 1915. This point was expressly left open by the House of Lords in *Cellulose Acetate*, above, though doubted in *Elsley* v. *Collins*, 1977 (Canadian Supreme Court). The position as regards other kinds of penalties, not purely monetary, is likewise obscure. But it seems that where the defendant stands to lose rights of ownership or possession of property because of his breach of contract, the court may at least grant him more time to pay: *Scandinavian Tanker* v. *Flota*, 1983; *BICC* v. *Burndy*, 1985.

13.35   The penalty rules have defied rationalisation, as Lord Justice Diplock remarked in *Robophone* v. *Blank*, 1966, and have indeed been strongly criticised. In his *Remedies for Breach of Contract*, Professor Treitel observes: 'The common law rules for distinguishing between penalties and liquidated damages manage to get the worst of both worlds. They achieve neither the certainty of the principle of literal enforcement, since there is always some doubt as to the category into which the clause will fall, nor the flexibility of the [civil law] principle of enforcement subject to reduction, since there is no judicial power of reduction. On the other hand, they place an undue premium on draftsmanship . . . The chief danger is to "home-made" clauses which may be invalidated even though they are not intrinsically unfair.'

13.36 Contract terms requiring deposits, advance payments or performance bonds, and expressly stating that such sums shall be forfeited on breach, could in theory be seen as liquidated damages clauses. But the rules about deposits and bonds have developed differently, and the penalty provisions do not apply. As we saw in Chapter 9, deposits may be made for different purposes. A deposit may be meant as an assurance that a contract will be fulfilled. The result is then that the depositor loses his money if he is in breach of contract (except possibly in sales of land, where Section 49 of the Law of Property Act 1925 empowers the court to order return of deposits). Alternatively a deposit may be an advance or part-payment, in which case the buyer can recover his money if the contract fails, regardless of fault, but subject to any claim for damages by the seller: *Dies* v. *British Finance*, 1939.

13.37 Another problem is that of drawing the line between a penalty clause and one which simply states the normal legal consequences of a breach of condition. As we saw above in Chapter 5, the long-standing rule is that breach of condition is a repudiation of the contract which usually entitles the innocent party to end the contract and to claim by way of damages all the benefits and profits he would have received under it, subject to his duty to mitigate. A clause to that effect in a contract may seem to produce a claim quite disproportionate to any actual loss, but is still not regarded as a penalty clause: *The Angelic Star*, above. In *Lombard* v. *Butterworth*, 1986, for example, a contract for the hire of a computer made time of the essence in relation to rental payments, and in the event of late payment entitled the owner to end the contract, claim damages, and recover all sums then or subsequently due under the contract. The Court of Appeal held that late payments thus became repudiatory breaches, which on principle entitled the owner to the sums claimed, and that the clause in question was not a penalty clause. Lord Justice Mustill threw a little light on the distinction: 'A clause expressly assigning a particular obligation to the category of condition is not a clause which purports to fix the damages for breach of the obligation, and is not subject to the law governing penalty clauses. I acknowledge, of course, that by promoting a term into the category where all breaches are ranked as breaches of condition, the parties indirectly bring about a situation where, for breaches which are relatively small, the injured party is enabled to recover damages as on the loss of the bargain, whereas without the stipulation his measure of recovery would be different. But I am unable to accept that this permits the court to strike down as a penalty the clause which brings about this promotion. To do so would be to reverse the current of more than 100 years' doctrine, which permits the parties to treat as a condition something which would not otherwise be so. I am not prepared to take this step.'

13.38   We should note again that sellers are as likely as buyers to insist upon liquidated damages clauses, in order to try to protect themselves against the consequences of their own breaches of contract. The clause may then serve as a limitation of liability, and as such its validity would be tested by the Unfair Contract Terms Act: Chapter 7. As a matter of principle a party at fault should not be able to rely on his own liquidated damages clause: *Peak* v. *McKinney*, 1971.

13.39   A final reflection is that the penalty rules apply only on *breach* of contract. They do not apply to contract terms requiring sums of money to be paid or forfeited for reasons other than breach, e.g. the generous awards which company directors negotiate for themselves in the event of their retirement, or a payment due where a party exercises a contractual right to bring the contract to an end, or where an insurance company is justified in avoiding a policy and keeping the premium, or where payment is due under a guarantee, or a repayment must be made: *Export Credits* v. *Universal Oil*, 1983; *Alder* v. *Moore*, 1961. An aspect of hire-purchase law is of interest here. Hire-purchase contracts entitle hirers at any time to end their contracts and return the goods, but only if they pay whatever is required by the contract to compensate the owner for depreciation. Since the penalty rules do not apply to the exercise of these contractual rights, hirers have sometimes had to pay sums much greater than the owner's losses. Possibilities of abuse are now much reduced by the Consumer Credit Act 1974, which limits the amounts payable in these circumstances to instalments already due and/or half the total price, whichever is the greater. The Act applies where credit up to £15,000 is given to individuals.

B. Repudiation

13.40   The extent of an innocent party's rights to treat his own obligations under a contract as ended by the other's breach was considered earlier in this Chapter and at length in Chapter 5. We discussed there the classifications of conditions, warranties and innominate terms and the remedies for breach of these obligations. Our conclusions may be summarised as follows. The innocent party cannot abandon the contract unless the other's conduct amounts to a repudiation of it. That is a difficult question of degree, as illustrated in para. 13.25 with regard to anticipatory breach, and in our discussion in Chapter 5 of cases such as *Schuler* and *Golby*. Another instructive case is *Standard Precast* v. *Dywidag*, 1989 (Canada). The first nine of 133 precast panels ordered by the buyer here were found on delivery to be unsuitable. The seller promised to remedy all the faults. In those circumstances, said the court, the seller's poor performance was not quite so bad as to entitle the buyer at that point in time to bring the contract to an end.

13.41   To establish the parties' rights in these cases, one might ask whether the breach does in fact strike at the root of the contract, or alternatively whether the law or the parties have expressly classified the term in question as a condition. But these inquiries may simply beg the question. It is not always necessary for the innocent party to show he has been deprived of 'substantially the whole benefit of the contract' as Lord Diplock put it in *Hong Kong Shipping* v. *Kawasaki Kisen Kaisha*, 1962. He may not even have to show he has suffered or will suffer any loss at all, as in the shipping cases mentioned in Chapter 5, where the judges have required the strictest compliance with times and dates. In the absence of any legal predetermination of the question it is all a matter of the judge's interpretation of the parties' intentions. From Chapter 5 it will be recalled also that any right the buyer may have to reject goods for breach of condition must be exercised promptly. If his delay suggests acceptance of the goods, he has only a claim for damages.

13.42   If the innocent party is entitled to, or has no alternative but to, treat the contract as ended, that does *not* mean that the contract is now or has always been void. A broken contract is not a void contract. The party in breach remains liable for the consequences of his breach – i.e. for damages – and one side or both sides may remain bound by certain kinds of continuing obligations in the contract, e.g. to submit their dispute to arbitration, or not to compete with the other's business. Depending on the terms of any guarantee given, a debtor's guarantor may also remain liable despite the ending of the contract. We should emphasise also that the right to repudiate for breach of contract is not governed by the same rules as the right to rescind for mistake or misrepresentation. The circumstances in which this latter right may be exercised are considered in Chapters 10 and 11.

C. Specific performance

13.43   A decree or order for specific performance is a court order to the defendant to fulfil his contract. This is an equitable remedy (as to which, *see* the Introduction and paras. 10.20–3), granted at the discretion of the court. In practice such orders are rare, and most unlikely to be given in relation to commercial contracts. English courts have always preferred to enforce contracts negatively or indirectly, i.e. by awards of damages for breach, and do not generally see themselves as competent to compel a party to carry out properly a contract he has repudiated – least of all where personal services are involved. The question then is whether damages are an adequate substitute for performance. In commercial contracts they normally are, since a disappointed buyer can probably find other similar or identical goods on the market and charge the seller for the difference in price and consequential inconvenience, and conversely a disappointed seller can usually sell to someone else. We note that a refusal to order specific performance may itself be a form of remedy, as in the mistake cases in paras. 10.20–1. A claim for damages may be made at the same time as a claim for specific performance, or possibly after the latter claim has been rejected: *N.Z. Land Development* v. *Porter*, 1992 (New Zealand).

13.44 Effectively then it is only when the subject-matter of the contract is unique or irreplaceable, or damages impossible to calculate, that specific performance is likely to be ordered. These conditions apply almost exclusively to contracts for the sale or lease of land. Section 52 of the Sale of Goods Act 1979 enables the court to make such an order in relation to specific goods, but the circumstances will have to be exceptional – e.g. to compel a buyer to take goods made to his personal requirements and without general market value: *Behnke* v. *Bede*, 1927. Ships will probably be treated as unique goods. Exceptional hardship to the innocent party is another possible ground for such an order, as in *Perry* v. *British Railways*, 1980, and *Sky Petroleum* v. *VIP Petroleum*, 1974. In *Sky Petroleum* the court ordered specific performance of a contract for the supply of petrol, as being the only way to avoid the particularly serious consequences which the buyer would otherwise have suffered in a current petrol shortage. Another unusual case is *Beswick* v. *Beswick*, 1967 (Chapter 3), where specific performance of a contract for periodic payments was ordered because of the difficulty of suing for damages for each non-payment. The most controversial decision of recent years is *Co-operative Insurance Society* v. *Argyll Stores*, 1995. The defendants, a supermarket chain, had a 35 year lease as 'anchor tenants' in a shopping centre. Because of trading losses they repudiated the lease after 15 years, and left the premises empty. The Court of Appeal said that unless the defendants could find another tenant acceptable to the landlord they would have to stay open for the duration of the lease, as they had expressly agreed. Lord Justice Millett, dissenting, thought the order oppressive and unrealistic. In America, under Sections 2–709 and 2–716 of the Uniform Commercial Code the courts can order specific performance whenever commercial needs make it equitable to do so – much as in Continental Europe.

D. Injunctions

13.45 An injunction is another equitable remedy; in a sense the converse of an order for specific performance. It is usually in negative form, ordering the defendant not to act in breach of contract, or to prevent an anticipated breach (known then as a *quia timet* – 'because it is feared' – injunction). If in his contract the defendant has promised not to do a certain thing, an injunction given to stop him from doing that thing is called a prohibitory injunction. If on the other hand he has promised positively to do something which he now refuses to do, a mandatory injunction may be granted. By ordering him to stop acting in breach of contract a mandatory injunction may require the defendant to take positive action, e.g. to build a wall, or to deliver goods. This order will depend very much on the 'balance of convenience' between the parties: *American Cyanamid* v. *Ethicon*, 1975. In the light of what we said above, it will be appreciated also that an injunction will not be given if its effect would be that of an order for specific performance, and least of all where damages would be an adequate alternative. Injunctions are accordingly rare in ordinary commercial dealings. In particular they will not be given directly to compel performance of contracts of personal service, although they may be given to prevent breach of such a contract by working for a competitor: *Warner* v. *Nelson*, 1937.

13.46   One particular type of injunction should be noted as an important procedural precaution rather than a remedy in itself. This is the *Mareva* injunction, from the case of *Mareva* v. *International Bulkcarriers*, 1975. It will be given in appropriate cases to stop a defendant from using up assets in Britain or transferring them abroad in order to defeat the plaintiff's claim. A *Mareva* injunction may be coupled with an *Anton Piller* order, enabling the plaintiff to enter and search the defendant's property and seize documentary and other evidence: *Anton Piller* v. *Manufacturing Processes*, 1976. English courts will not make orders freezing assets already abroad and out of the courts' jurisdiction, but they can make personal orders binding on defendants in relation to such assets, which may have substantially the same effect: *Babanaft* v. *Bassatne*, 1988. As with other injunctions, the granting of a *Mareva* injunction depends on the balance of convenience between the parties. A plaintiff who asks for a *Mareva* injunction may have to give security for the defendant's costs in complying with the order, to cover the possibility of the defendant winning the case. An injunction does not determine the outcome of a claim, nor does it give the plaintiff any priority over other creditors.

E. Time limits

13.47   The Limitation Act 1980 lays down time limits within which claims for breach of contract or tort must be brought. In contract the basic rule is that a claim must be begun within six years of the breach − 'the date on which the cause of action accrued': Section 5. There is a danger here, which should be noted. A contracting party may not know immediately that the contract has been broken, and so may run the risk of losing his right to sue before he knows he has a grievance. But if the breach has been concealed from him by the defendant's fraud he has six years from the time when he discovered or should have discovered the fraud. Claims in tort must likewise be initiated within six years of the cause of action accruing. In tort, however, that is not necessarily when the tort is committed but only when actual loss or damage is suffered, which may well be at a very much later date. A plaintiff who has a claim both in contract and in tort, as in *Parsons*, para. 13.11, may take advantage of whichever cause of action gives the longer limitation period: *Arbuthnott* v. *Feltrim*, 1994. In claims for damages for physical injury, whether in contract or tort, the time limit is three years from the date of injury or the time when the plaintiff knew or should have known he had a cause of action. Claims arising from breach of a promise in a deed must be brought within 12 years thereafter.

Danish law

13.48   On principle the basic remedy in Denmark for breach of contract (other than a contract of employment) is an order for fulfilment of the contract. In practice what English law would call orders for specific performance are relatively rare and awarded in much the same circumstances as in England. Generally available remedies are cancellation, reduction of prices, cure of defect, and damages. The appropriate remedy depends on the circumstances – materiality of the defect, possibility of repair, the duty to mitigate and the like. There is no rule equivalent to that in *White & Carter*: para. 13.28.

13.49   Awards of damages usually depend on proof of fault, contrary to English law. But a seller of generic goods is strictly liable for failure to supply, except in cases of frustration, and for defects and breach of an express guarantee. Awards are reduced by contributory negligence and may even lapse altogether in exceptional circumstances: Article 24, Damages Act 1984. Compensation will not be given for losses which are too remote.

13.50   Penalty clauses are subject to the test of reasonableness laid down by Article 36 of the Contracts Act. It is a question of interpretation whether damages will be limited to the sum specified if in fact a greater loss is suffered. If the innocent party could have taken reasonable steps to avoid any loss, the clause will probably be held unreasonable and unenforceable.

Dutch law

13.51   In general liability for breach of contract under Dutch law depends on proof of fault, but there are major qualifications, e.g. a strict rule of vicarious liability, and requirements as to fitness of goods: Articles 6.75–6 of the new Code. There are many differences between the Dutch and English systems, but in both the purpose of an award of damages is to arrive at the same situation as if the contract had been performed. On the question of remoteness, Article 6.98 says only that compensation must be paid for loss or damage, which is 'related to' the breach of contract and which can be 'imputed to' the wrongdoer. The judges have very wide power to decide the precise amount due. They may reduce the award if it would otherwise lead to 'clearly unacceptable results' – Article 6.109 – e.g., because of the plaintiff's share of the blame: Article 6.101. Or they may increase it to take account of the profit the wrongdoer made from his breach of contract. In most commercial cases full damages are awarded even where the plaintiff has been able to shift his loss onto another party, for example, by relying on an exclusion clause as against the person to whom he has sold the goods in question. Awards may be made payable in the light of possible future developments: Article 6.105. Contrary to English law, Article 6.119 entitles creditors to interest on unpaid debts. A duty to mitigate loss is imposed by Article 6.101.

13.52   As regards penalty clauses, Articles 6.91–4 are equally flexible. Any sum specified in the contract as payable on breach is defined as a penalty, whether intended to compensate or to compel performance. A penalty clause is unenforceable if the breach was due to circumstances beyond the defendant's control. The judge may reduce or increase the penalty 'as equity requires'.

13.53   The plaintiff has several other remedies apart from damages. Where a seller of goods breaks his contract, the buyer may demand delivery, or, as appropriate, repair or replacement. An order to repair depends on the seller's ability to comply, and an order for replacement will not be made if the fault is insignificant: Article 7.22. We observe finally that orders for specific performance are not considered as exceptional under Dutch law as they are under English law. They are in fact seen as the most common remedy.

French law

13.54   Article 1184 provides that 'the party *vis-à-vis* whom an obligation has not been performed has the option either of obtaining specific performance when possible or of requesting the termination of the contract with an award of damages'. Specific performance or termination with damages are exclusive of each other.

13.55   Despite this apparent choice the remedy of specific performance is not available whenever the enforcement of the contract requires personal performance by the defendant: Article 1142. In such cases the law can only apply pressure by way of *astreintes* – a penalty sum payable initially to the court and ultimately to the plaintiff for every day of default. If, despite an order for *astreintes*, the defendant does not fulfil his obligations, the only remedy is termination of the contract, with an award of damages. In certain

fields (e.g. construction) it is also customary for the courts to order performance of the contract by a third party at the expense of the defendant. And
in a few very specific areas such as sales of property or sales of shares,
where all the terms of the sale are agreed and only a formality, for instance,
signature of a deed of sale before a notary, is missing, a court judgment can
effect the sale.

13.56   Damages can be awarded only in relation to the actual loss
suffered by the contracting party. Much as under English law, the loss must
be a direct consequence of the breach of contract, and must have been
foreseeable at the time the contract was made: Article 1150. Subject to this
test of remoteness, the damages must cover all the losses, including loss of
income, suffered by the contracting party by virtue of the non-performance
or termination.

13.57   There is no rule as to mitigation, as such, but the same results are
achieved by the courts' refusal to compensate losses caused by the 'reckless
attitude' of the innocent party. Punitive damages are not awarded, although
in many circumstances the judges will take into account the negligence,
reckless attitude or bad faith of the defaulting party in assessing the loss to
be compensated.

13.58   Penalty clauses (*clauses pénales*; Article 1226) often have a dual
nature. They may be either a pre-estimate of the likely loss in case of
default or a real contractual penalty aiming not at compensating a loss but
at forcing the defaulting party to fulfil the contract. They are not illegal
generally, even when they have the nature of a contractual penalty, but the
courts can reduce or increase the agreed amount if it is grossly excessive or
inadequate: Article 1152.

German law

13.59   The scope of awards of damages under German law is quite
different from that under English law. Damages are the usual remedy in tort
law, but only one of the possible remedies for breach of contract. If goods
or services cannot be supplied under the contract, or are not supplied in
time, the supplier is liable for damages only if he has been negligent. After
delivery, the buyer's primary right is to cancel the contract if the goods or
services are defective, or to pay a lower price. He can claim damages if the
seller has broken an express promise as to the characteristics of the goods
(Article 463), or is negligent – e.g., in not giving any necessary information
as to the safe use of the goods. Negligence is a prerequisite of liability for
breach of the subsidiary contractual obligations developed by the courts
under the doctrine of *positive Vertragsverletzung*: para. 5.70.

13.60   The purpose of an award of damages for breach of contract in German law is the same as in *Robinson*, para. 13.4. There are similar attempts to define the kinds of injuries or losses which are too remote to justify compensation. German law requires 'adequate causation', but one cannot say exactly what that means. It is not just a test of foreseeability. It is not clear how *Hadley*, para. 13.6, would have been decided in a German court. On the other hand there are certainly important differences between English and German law. The German law of damages is characterised by an 'all or nothing' principle – mitigated only by a rule of contributory fault or *Mitverschulden*: Article 254 BGB. The plaintiff would therefore always recover his loss of resale profit (contrasting with *Williams* and *Hall*, para. 13.9). It follows also that there is no distinction between direct and consequential losses, though sometimes different limitation periods may apply under the contract.

13.61   Interest is awarded in most claims for damages. Where payment is delayed the plaintiff may claim interest at the rate of four per cent. If he can prove he has had to borrow from a bank because of non-payment, he may recover the interest paid to the bank.

13.62   German contract law does not generally allow claims for disturbance or distress. The only exception concerns package holidays. So a case like *Jackson*, para. 13.18, would be decided in the same way, but only because it concerns a tour operator. On the other hand, tort law allows for damages for pain, suffering and distress – *Schmerzensgeld* – under Article 847. A plaintiff could therefore claim for such losses if the prerequisites of tort law are fulfilled: Article 823 *et seq.*

13.63   In cases of anticipatory breach, the innocent party may as in English law accept the repudiation and sue for damages. But there is no equivalent in German law of the *White and Carter* rule, para. 13.28. Indeed it sounds curious to Continental ears!

13.64   Liquidated damages and penalty clauses are regulated by the Standard Contract Terms Act 1976. There are fewer restrictions on their use than in English law. The sum specified in the contract must represent the average loss in such cases. The party in breach is entitled to show that the loss or damage he has caused is less than the specified sum, and have his liability reduced accordingly.

Italian law

13.65   Where a breach of contract is caused deliberately or negligently, and whether the fault is personal or vicarious, an Italian court may permit repudiation of the contract, if the breach is fundamental, and/or award damages: Articles 1223–5, 1453–5 and 1681 of the Civil Code. Otherwise generally the basic principle is that of restitution, e.g. a debtor is obliged only to repay that which he has borrowed, plus interest. To the extent that negligence may determine the extent of a defendant's liability, it follows that liability for breach of contract is not as strict as is usually the position under English law. Breach and termination of one contract in a number of interrelated contracts (*collegati*) may justify termination of the other contracts: Corte di Cassazione, 30 October 1991, no. 11638.

13.66   Damages may be classified as *damno emergente* or *lucro cessante* – referring first to the damage actually suffered by the plaintiff, and second to his 'expectation' loss, or loss of profit. Awards may be made for 'moral damage', i.e. non-economic loss: Article 2059. Generally, awards are based on the foreseeable, immediate and direct consequences of the breach, but extend to unusual or exceptional losses where the breach is deliberate: Articles 1223, 1225. If a loss cannot be precisely established, damages are subject to 'equitable liquidation' by the judge: Article 1226.

13.67   If a plaintiff is partly to blame for the defendant's breach of contract, his damages will be reduced accordingly (a rule not found in English law). Plaintiffs cannot claim damages for breaches of contract brought about by their own fault, or for losses which they could and should have avoided: Article 1227. The duty to mitigate loss is seen as an expression of the good faith principle. But it does not require a plaintiff to undertake risky or expensive action to limit the effect of the breach of contract: Corte di Cassazione, 21 April 1993, no. 4672.

13.68   A contracting party may limit his liability by a term in the contract, but only to the extent of protecting himself against the consequences of simple negligence and in any case only in accordance with public policy, i.e. customary commercial practice: Article 1229. A limitation in a standard form contract is only effective if signed by the other party.

13.69   Contract clauses stating the amount payable in the event of breach will be upheld unless the sums seem excessive – *'penale'*. If found to be penal the sums may be reduced by the court to whatever seems fair in the circumstances: Article 1384. If a clause is upheld, it will relieve the innocent party of having to prove his losses. It will also prevent him from proving losses over and above the agreed sum, unless the contract so provides: Article 1382.

13.70   The remedy of injunction or *inibitoria* may be granted where damages would be inadequate and fundamental personal rights would otherwise be endangered: Article 700 of the Civil Procedure Code.

Spanish law

13.71   A party in breach of contract is liable to indemnify the other against his losses: Articles 1101 and 1124 of the Spanish Civil Code. On principle he must compensate the innocent party not only for the losses he has suffered but also for the profits he has been deprived of.

13.72   The precise extent of a defendant's liability depends on whether or not he acted in good faith. Article 1107 says that if he acted in good faith he is liable only for those losses which were or might have been foreseen when the contract was made. But if his breach of contract was due to bad faith or fraud he is responsible for all losses known to have been caused by his breach – *que conocidamente se derivan de la falta de cumplimiento*. Article 1103 indicates that the extent of liability for negligence, as distinct from bad faith, may be limited by the courts.

13.73   Spanish law does not recognise a duty to mitigate, as such. But if the loss or damage suffered by the innocent party was his own fault, he has no claim for compensation. If both parties are to blame, liability may be reduced accordingly.

13.74   'Penalty clauses' in contracts are not void under Spanish law even where they contain a punitive element. But the Supreme Court has said – in a judgment of 10 November 1983, among others – that such clauses should be interpreted restrictively. In particular their effect should be moderated by the court where the defendant has at least partially fulfilled his contract: Article 1154.

13.75   If a penalty clause is enforced, the plaintiff cannot also insist on specific performance of the contract: Article 1153 of the Civil Code and Article 5 of the Commercial Code. The clause cannot in any case be enforced if the plaintiff is himself in breach of contract, according to Supreme Court decisions of 6 April and 4 July 1988.

13.76   The basic rules as to breach of contract are laid down in Article 1124 of the Civil Code. The innocent party is entitled thereby to demand either specific performance of the contract or its termination, with payment of damages and interest in either case.

Swedish law

13.77   Under Article 27 of the Sale of Goods Act 1990 a seller is liable to pay damages for direct loss if the cause of late delivery or non-conformity of goods was within his control, which may well involve questions of fault. If the seller has acted against good faith (or given a promise as to specific quality) he is liable to pay damages for every loss, indirect as well as direct. Indirect loss includes loss of production because of faulty or late goods, and loss of reasonable profit. In other contexts the distinction between direct and indirect loss may not be clear, as is true also of the circumstances which may be considered within the seller's control. More generally, the question of fault is normally relevant in assessing damages for breach of contract – unlike the position in English law.

13.78 Article 70 of the Sale of Goods Act is a new rule permitting adjustment of damages which would otherwise be unfair because the loss was not foreseeable or could not be prevented by the liable party – but unfortunately the application of the rule is unclear. The normal considerations concerning remoteness of damage, foreseeability and mitigation should be decided first and then the question as to whether adjustment is appropriate. It is possible that adjustment according to Article 70 might be made in a situation similar to *Harbutt's Plasticine* (para. 13.23) regarding the problem of 'betterment'.

13.79 If a payment is late the debtor must pay interest according to the Interest Act 1975. The annual rate is the bank rate plus 8 per cent (currently ca. 18 per cent). The parties are free to agree on another rate as long as it is not unfair. If a contract is void the effects differ. Interest must be paid from the time the price was paid until it is repaid, at the bank rate plus 2 per cent (Article 2 Interest Act 1975). Profits made after the buyer became aware that the contract was voidable should be returned to the seller. If the buyer has made improvements, and the contract is thereafter voided, he is normally entitled to recover only necessary costs. Unnecessary improvements are normally only recoverable if the seller has acted against good faith.

13.80 Injunctions (both positive and negative) are possible procedural actions according to Swedish law.

13.81 The Limitation Act 1981 gives a general time limit of ten years from the establishment of the right to the declaration of the claim. As against consumers, the time limit is three years. Many special Acts have shorter time limits than ten years. According to the Sale of Goods Act 1990 a claim must be made within two years after delivery. As mentioned above, there is also an obligation to give notice to the party in breach as soon as the breach becomes or ought to have become known to the innocent party.

Appendices

Statutory materials reproduced by kind permission of Her Majesty's Stationery Office.

CONSUMER PROTECTION

The Unfair Terms in Consumer Contracts Regulations 1994

(1994 No. 3159)

Citation and commencement

1. These Regulations may be cited as the Unfair Terms in Consumer Contracts Regulations 1994 and shall come into force on 1st July 1995.

Interpretation

2.—(1) In these Regulations –
'business' includes a trade or profession and the activities of any government department or local or public authority;
'the Community' means the European Economic Community and the other States in the European Economic Area;
'consumer' means a natural person who, in making a contract to which these Regulations apply, is acting for purposes which are outside his business;
'court' in relation to England and Wales and Northern Ireland means the High Court, and in relation to Scotland, the Court of Session;
'Director' means the Director General of Fair Trading;
'EEA Agreement' means the Agreement on the European Economic Area signed at Oporto on 2 May 1992 as adjusted by the protocol signed at Brussels on 17 March 1993[(a)];
'member State' shall mean a State which is a contracting party to the EEA Agreement but until the EEA Agreement comes into force in relation to Liechtenstein does not include the State of Liechtenstein;

(a) Protocol 47 and certain Annexes to the EEA Agreement were amended by Decision No. 7/94 of the EEA Joint Committee which came into force on 1 July 1994 (O.J. No. L160, 28.6.1994, p. 1). Council Directive 93/13/EEC was added to Annex XIX to the Agreement by Annex 17 of the said Decision No. 7/94.

'seller' means a person who sells goods and who, in making a contract to which these Regulations apply, is acting for purposes relating to his business; and

'supplier' means a person who supplies goods or services and who, in making a contract to which these Regulations apply, is acting for purposes relating to his business.

(2) In the application of these Regulations to Scotland for references to an 'injunction' or an 'interlocutory injunction' there shall be substituted references to an 'interdict' or interim interdict' respectively.

Terms to which these Regulations apply

3.—(1) Subject to the provisions of Schedule 1, these Regulations apply to any term in a contract concluded between a seller or supplier and a consumer where the said term has not been individually negotiated.

(2) In so far as it is in plain, intelligible language, no assessment shall be made of the fairness of any term which –
    (a) defines the main subject matter of the contract. or
    (b) concerns the adequacy of the price or remuneration, as against the goods or services sold or supplied.

(3) For the purposes of these Regulations, a term shall always be regarded as not having been individually negotiated where it has been drafted in advance and the consumer has not been able to influence the substance of the term.

(4) Notwithstanding that a specific term or certain aspects of it in a contract has been individually negotiated, these Regulations shall apply to the rest of a contract if an overall assessment of the contract indicates that it is a pre-formulated standard contract.

(5) It shall be for any seller or supplier who claims that a term was individually negotiated to show that it was.

Unfair terms

4.—(1) In these Regulations. subject to paragraphs (2) and (3) below, 'unfair term' means any term which contrary to the requirement of good faith causes a significant imbalance in the parties' rights and obligations under the contract to the detriment of the consumer.

(2) An assessment of the unfair nature of a term shall be made taking into account the nature of the goods or services for which the contract was concluded and referring, as at the time of the conclusion of the contract, to all circumstances attending the conclusion of the contract and to all the other terms of the contract or of another contract on which it is dependent.

(3) In determining whether a term satisfies the requirement of good faith, regard shall be had in particular to the matters specified in Schedule 2 to these Regulations.

(4) Schedule 3 to these Regulations contains an indicative and non-exhaustive list of the terms which may be regarded as unfair.

Consequence of inclusion of unfair terms in contracts

5.—(1) An unfair term in a contract concluded with a consumer by a seller or supplier shall not be binding on the consumer.

(2) The contract shall continue to bind the parties if it is capable of continuing in existence without the unfair term.

Construction of written contracts

6. A seller or supplier shall ensure that any written term of a contract is expressed in plain, intelligible language, and if there is doubt about the meaning of a written term, the interpretation most favourable to the consumer shall prevail.

Choice of law clauses

7. These Regulations shall apply notwithstanding any contract term which applies or purports to apply the law of a non member State, if the contract has a close connection with the territory of the member States.

Prevention of continued use of unfair terms

8.—(1) It shall be the duty of the Director to consider any complaint made to him that any contract term drawn up for general use is unfair, unless the complaint appears to the Director to be frivolous or vexatious.

(2) If having considered a complaint about any contract term pursuant to paragraph (1) above the Director considers that the contract term is unfair he may, if he considers it appropriate to do so, bring proceedings for an injunction (in which proceedings he may also apply for an interlocutory injunction) against any person appearing to him to be using or recommending use of such a term in contracts concluded with consumers.

(3) The Director may, if he considers it appropriate to do so, have regard to any undertakings given to him by or on behalf of any person as to the continued use of such a term in contracts concluded with consumers.

(4) The Director shall give reasons for his decision to apply or not to apply, as the case may be, for an injunction in relation to any complaint which these Regulations require him to consider.

(5) The court on an application by the Director may grant an injunction on such terms as it thinks fit.

(6) An injunction may relate not only to use of a particular contract term drawn up for general use but to any similar term, or a term having like effect, used or recommended for use by any party to the proceedings.

(7) The Director may arrange for the dissemination in such form and manner as he considers appropriate of such information and advice concerning the operation of these Regulations as may appear to him to be expedient to give to the public and to all persons likely to be affected by these Regulations.

SCHEDULE 1   Regulation 3(1)

Contracts and particular terms excluded from the scope of these Regulations

These Regulations do not apply to –
  (a) any contract relating to employment;
  (b) any contract relating to succession rights;
  (c) any contract relating to rights under family law;
  (d) any contract relating to the incorporation and organisation of companies or partnerships; and
  (e) any term incorporated in order to comply with or which reflects –
     (i) statutory or regulatory provisions of the United Kingdom; or
     (ii) the provisions or principles of international conventions to which the member States or the Community are party.

SCHEDULE 2   Regulation 4(3)

Assessment of good faith

In making an assessment of good faith, regard shall be had in particular to –
  (a) the strength of the bargaining positions of the parties;
  (b) whether the consumer had an inducement to agree to the term;
  (c) whether the goods or services were sold or supplied to the special order of the consumer; and
  (d) the extent to which the seller or supplier has dealt fairly and equitably with the consumer.

SCHEDULE 3   Regulation 4(4)

Indicative and illustrative list of terms which may be regarded as unfair

1. Terms which have the object or effect of –
  (a) excluding or limiting the legal liability of a seller or supplier in the event of the death of a consumer or personal injury to the latter resulting from an act or omission of that seller or supplier;
  (b) inappropriately excluding or limiting the legal rights or the consumer vis-à-vis the seller or supplier or another party in the event of total or partial non-performance or inadequate performance by the seller or supplier of any of the contractual obligations, including the option of offsetting a debt owed to the seller or supplier against any claim which the consumer may have against him;
  (c) making an agreement binding on the consumer whereas provision of services by the seller or supplier is subject to a condition whose realisation depends on his own will alone;

(d) permitting the seller or supplier to retain sums paid by the consumer where the latter decides not to conclude or perform the contract, without providing for the consumer to receive compensation of an equivalent amount from the seller or supplier where the latter is the party cancelling the contract;

(e) requiring any consumer who fails to fulfil his obligation to pay a disproportionately high sum in compensation;

(f) authorising the seller or supplier to dissolve the contract on a discretionary basis where the same facility is not granted to the consumer, or permitting the seller or supplier to retain the sums paid for services not yet supplied by him where it is the seller or supplier himself who dissolves the contract;

(g) enabling the seller or supplier to terminate a contract of indeterminate duration without reasonable notice except where there are serious grounds for doing so;

(h) automatically extending a contract of fixed duration where the consumer does not indicate otherwise, when the deadline fixed for the consumer to express this desire not to extend the contract is unreasonably early;

(i) irrevocably binding the consumer to terms with which he had no real opportunity of becoming acquainted before the conclusion of the contract;

(j) enabling the seller or supplier to alter the terms of the contract unilaterally without a valid reason which is specified in the contract;

(k) enabling the seller or supplier to alter unilaterally without a valid reason any characteristics of the product or service to be provided;

(l) providing for the price of goods to be determined at the time of delivery or allowing a seller of goods or supplier of services to increase their price without in both cases giving the consumer the corresponding right to cancel the contract if the final price is too high in relation to the price agreed when the contract was concluded;

(m) giving the seller or supplier the right to determine whether the goods or services supplied are in conformity with the contract, or giving him the exclusive right to interpret any term of the contract;

(n) limiting the seller's or supplier's obligation to respect commitments undertaken by his agents or making his commitments subject to compliance with a particular formality;

(o) obliging the consumer to fulfil all his obligations where the seller or supplier does not perform his;

(p) giving the seller or supplier the possibility of transferring his rights and obligations under the contract, where this may serve to reduce the guarantees for the consumer, without the latter's agreement;

(q) excluding or hindering the consumer's right to take legal action or exercise any other legal remedy, particularly by requiring the consumer to take disputes exclusively to arbitration not covered by legal provisions, unduly restricting the evidence available to him or imposing on him a burden of proof which, according to the applicable law, should lie with another party to the contract.

2. Scope of subparagraphs 1(g), (j) and (l)

(a) Subparagraph 1(g) is without hindrance to terms by which a supplier of financial services reserves the right to terminate unilaterally a contract of indeterminate duration without notice where there is a valid reason, provided that the supplier is required to inform the other contracting party or parties thereof immediately.

(b) Subparagraph 1(j) is without hindrance to terms under which a supplier of financial services reserves the right to alter the rate of interest payable by the consumer or due to the latter, or the amount of other charges for financial services without notice where there is a valid reason, provided that the supplier is required to inform the other contracting party or parties thereof at the earliest opportunity and that the latter are free to dissolve the contract immediately.

Subparagraph 1(j) is also without hindrance to terms under which a seller or supplier reserves the right to alter unilaterally the conditions of a contract of indeterminate duration, provided that he is required to inform the consumer with reasonable notice and that the consumer is free to dissolve the contract.

(c) Subparagraphs 1(g), (j) and (l) do not apply to:
   — transactions in transferable securities, financial instruments and other products or services where the price is linked to fluctuations in a stock exchange quotation or index or a financial market rate that the seller or supplier does not control;
   — contracts for the purchase or sale of foreign currency, traveller's cheques or international money orders denominated in foreign currency.

(d) Subparagraph 1(l) is without hindrance to price indexation clauses, where lawful, provided that the method by which prices vary is explicitly described.

310

United Nations Convention
on Contracts for the International Sale of Goods

PREAMBLE

The States Parties to this Convention,

Bearing in mind the broad objectives in the resolutions adopted by the sixth special session of the General Assembly of the United Nations on the establishment of a New International Economic Order,

Considering that the development of international trade on the basis of equality and mutual benefit is an important element in promoting friendly relations among States,

Being of the opinion that the adoption of uniform rules which govern contracts for the international sale of goods and take into account the different social, economic and legal systems would contribute to the removal of legal barriers in international trade and promote the development of international trade,

Have agreed as follows:

Part I. Sphere of application and general provisions

CHAPTER I. SPHERE OF APPLICATION

Article 1

(1) This Convention applies to contracts of sale of goods between parties whose places of business are in different States:

(a) when the States are Contracting States; or

(b) when the rules of private international law lead to the application of the law of a Contracting State.

(2) The fact that the parties have their places of business in different States is to be disregarded whenever this fact does not appear either from the contract or from any dealings between, or from information disclosed by, the parties at any time before or at the conclusion of the contract.

(3) Neither the nationality of the parties nor the civil or commercial character of the parties or of the contract is to be taken into consideration in determining the application of this Convention.

Article 2

This Convention does not apply to sales:

(a) of goods bought for personal, family or household use, unless the seller, at any time before or at the conclusion of the contract, neither knew nor ought to have known that the goods were bought for any such use;

(b) by auction;

(c) on execution or otherwise by authority of law;

(d) of stocks, shares, investment securities, negotiable instruments or money;

(e) of ships, vessels, hovercraft or aircraft;

(f) of electricity.

Article 3

(1) Contracts for the supply of goods to be manufactured or produced are to be considered sales unless the party who orders the goods undertakes to supply a substantial part of the materials necessary for such manufacture or production.

(2) This Convention does not apply to contracts in which the preponderant part of the obligations of the party who furnishes the goods consists in the supply of labour or other services.

Article 4

This Convention governs only the formation of the contract of sale and the rights and obligations of the seller and the buyer arising from such a contract. In particular, except as otherwise expressly provided in this Convention, it is not concerned with:

(a) the validity of the contract or of any of its provisions or of any usage;

(b) the effect which the contract may have on the property in the goods sold.

Article 5

This Convention does not apply to the liability of the seller for death or personal injury caused by the goods to any person.

Article 6

The parties may exclude the application of this Convention or, subject to article 12, derogate from or vary the effect of any of its provisions.

CHAPTER II. GENERAL PROVISIONS

Article 7

(1) In the interpretation of this Convention, regard is to be had to its international character and to the need to promote uniformity in its application and the observance of good faith in international trade.

(2) Questions concerning matters governed by this Convention which are not expressly settled in it are to be settled in conformity with the general principles on which it is based or, in the absence of such principles, in conformity with the law applicable by virtue of the rules of private international law.

Article 8

(1) For the purposes of this Convention statements made by and other conduct of a party are to be interpreted according to his intent where the other party knew or could not have been unaware what that intent was.

(2) If the preceding paragraph is not applicable, statements made by and other conduct of a party are to be interpreted according to the understanding that a reasonable person of the same kind as the other party would have had in the same circumstances.

(3) In determining the intent of a party or the understanding a reasonable person would have had, due consideration is to be given to all relevant circumstances of the case including the negotiations, any practices which the parties have established between themselves, usages and any subsequent conduct of the parties.

Article 9

(1) The parties are bound by any usage to which they have agreed and by any practices which they have established between themselves.

(2) The parties are considered, unless otherwise agreed, to have impliedly made applicable to their contract or its formation a usage of which the parties knew or ought to have known and which in international trade is widely known to, and regularly observed by, parties to contracts of the type involved in the particular trade concerned.

Article 10

For the purposes of this Convention:

(a) if a party has more than one place of business, the place of business is that which has the closest relationship to the contract and its performance, having regard to the circumstances known to or contemplated by the parties at any time before or at the conclusion of the contract;

(b) if a party does not have a place of business, reference is to be made to his habitual residence.

Article 11

A contract of sale need not be concluded in or evidenced by writing and is not subject to any other requirement as to form. It may be proved by any means, including witnesses.

Article 12

Any provision of article 11, article 29 or Part II of this Convention that allows a contract of sale or its modification or termination by agreement or any offer, acceptance or other indication of intention to be made in any form other than in writing does not apply where any party has his place of business in a Contracting State which has made a declaration under article 96 of this Convention. The parties may not derogate from or vary the effect of this article.

Article 13

For the purposes of this Convention 'writing' includes telegram and telex.

Part II. Formation of the contract

Article 14

(1) A proposal for concluding a contract addressed to one or more specific persons constitutes an offer if it is sufficiently definite and indicates the intention of the offeror to be bound in case of acceptance. A proposal is sufficiently definite if it indicates the goods and expressly or implicitly fixes or makes provision for determining the quantity and the price.

(2) A proposal other than one addressed to one or more specific persons is to be considered merely as an invitation to make offers, unless the contrary is clearly indicated by the person making the proposal.

Article 15

(1) An offer becomes effective when it reaches the offeree.

(2) An offer, even if it is irrevocable, may be withdrawn if the withdrawal reaches the offeree before or at the same time as the offer.

Article 16

(1) Until a contract is concluded an offer may be revoked if the revocation reaches the offeree before he has dispatched an acceptance.

(2) However, an offer cannot be revoked:

(a) if it indicates, whether by stating a fixed time for acceptance or otherwise, that it is irrevocable; or

(b) if it was reasonable for the offeree to rely on the offer as being irrevocable and the offeree has acted in reliance on the offer.

Article 17

An offer, even if it is irrevocable, is terminated when a rejection reaches the offeror.

Article 18

(1) A statement made by or other conduct of the offeree indicating assent to an offer is an acceptance. Silence or inactivity does not in itself amount to acceptance.

(2) An acceptance of an offer becomes effective at the moment the indication of assent reaches the offeror. An acceptance is not effective if the indication of assent does not reach the offeror within the time he has fixed or, if no time is fixed, within a reasonable time, due account being taken of the circumstances of the transaction, including the rapidity of the means of communication employed by the offeror. An oral offer must be accepted immediately unless the circumstances indicate otherwise.

(3) However, if, by virtue of the offer or as a result of practices which the parties have established between themselves or of usage, the offeree may indicate assent by performing an act, such as one relating to the dispatch of the goods or payment of the price, without notice to the offeror, the acceptance is effective at the moment the act is performed, provided that the act is performed within the period of time laid down in the preceding paragraph.

Article 19

(1) A reply to an offer which purports to be an acceptance but contains additions, limitations or other modifications is a rejection of the offer and constitutes a counter-offer.

(2) However, a reply to an offer which purports to be an acceptance but contains additional or different terms which do not materially alter the terms of the offer constitutes an acceptance, unless the offeror, without undue delay, objects orally to the discrepancy or dispatches a notice to that effect. If he does not so object, the terms of the contract are the terms of the offer with the modifications contained in the acceptance.

(3) Additional or different terms relating, among other things, to the price, payment, quality and quantity of the goods, place and time of delivery, extent of one party's liability to the other or the settlement of disputes are considered to alter the terms of the offer materially.

Article 20

(1) A period of time of acceptance fixed by the offeror in a telegram or a letter begins to run from the moment the telegram is handed in for dispatch or from the date shown on the letter or, if no such date is shown, from the date shown on the envelope. A period of time for acceptance fixed by the offeror by telephone, telex or other means of instantaneous communication, begins to run from the moment that the offer reaches the offeree.

(2) Official holidays or non-business days occurring during the period for acceptance are included in calculating the period. However, if a notice of acceptance cannot be delivered at the address of the offeror on the last day of the period because that day falls on an official holiday or a non-business day at the place of business of the offeror, the period is extended until the first business day which follows.

Article 21

(1) A late acceptance is nevertheless effective as an acceptance if without delay the offeror orally so informs the offeree or dispatches a notice to that effect.

(2) If a letter or other writing containing a late acceptance shows that it has been sent in such circumstances that if its transmission had been normal it would have reached the offeror in due time, the late acceptance is effective as an acceptance unless, without delay, the offeror orally informs the offeree that he considers his offer as having lapsed or dispatches a notice to that effect.

Article 22

An acceptance may be withdrawn if the withdrawal reaches the offeror before or at the same time as the acceptance would have become effective.

Article 23

A contract is concluded at the moment when an acceptance of an offer becomes effective in accordance with the provisions of this Convention.

Article 24

For the purposes of this Part of the Convention, an offer, declaration of acceptance or any other indication of intention 'reaches' the addressee when it is made orally to him or delivered by any other means to him personally, to his place of business or mailing address or, if he does not have a place of business or mailing address, to his habitual residence.

Part III. Sale of goods

CHAPTER I. GENERAL PROVISIONS

Article 25

A breach of contract committed by one of the parties is fundamental if it results in such detriment to the other party as substantially to deprive him of what he is entitled to expect under the contract, unless the party in breach did not foresee and a reasonable person of the same kind in the same circumstances would not have foreseen such a result.

Article 26

A declaration of avoidance of the contract is effective only if made by notice to the other party.

Article 27

Unless otherwise expressly provided in this Part of the Convention, if any notice, request or other communication is given or made by a party in accordance with this Part and by means appropriate in the circumstances, a delay or error in the transmission of the communication or its failure to arrive does not deprive that party of the right to rely on the communication.

Article 28

If, in accordance with the provisions of this Convention, one party is entitled to require performance of any obligation by the other party, a court is not bound to enter a judgement for specific performance unless the court would do so under its own law in respect of similar contracts of sale not governed by this Convention.

Article 29

(1) A contract may be modified or terminated by the mere agreement of the parties.

(2) A contract in writing which contains a provision requiring any modification or termination by agreement to be in writing may not be otherwise modified or terminated by agreement. However, a party may be precluded by his conduct from asserting such a provision to the extent that the other party has relied on that conduct.

CHAPTER II. OBLIGATIONS OF THE SELLER

Article 30

The seller must deliver the goods, hand over any documents relating to them and transfer the property in the goods, as required by the contract and this Convention.

Section I. *Delivery of the goods and handing over of documents*

Article 31

If the seller is not bound to deliver the goods at any other particular place, his obligation to deliver consists:

(a) if the contract of sale involves carriage of the goods – in handing the goods over to the first carrier for transmission to the buyer;

(b) if, in cases not within the preceding subparagraph, the contract relates to specific goods, or unidentified goods to be drawn from a specific stock or to be manufactured or produced, and at the time of the conclusion of the contract the parties knew that the goods were at, or were to be manufactured or produced at, a particular place – in placing the goods at the buyer's disposal at that place;

(c) in other cases – in placing the goods at the buyer's disposal at the place where the seller had his place of business at the time of the conclusion of the contract.

Article 32

(1) If the seller, in accordance with the contract or this Convention, hands the goods over to a carrier and if the goods are not clearly identified to the contract by markings on the goods, by shipping documents or otherwise, the seller must give the buyer notice of the consignment specifying the goods.

(2) If the seller is bound to arrange for carriage of the goods, he must make such contracts as are necessary for carriage to the place fixed by means of transportation appropriate in the circumstances and according to the usual terms for such transportation.

(3) If the seller is not bound to effect insurance in respect of the carriage of the goods, he must, at the buyer's request, provide him with all available information necessary to enable him to effect such insurance.

Article 33
The seller must deliver the goods:
- *(a)* if a date is fixed by or determinable from the contract, on that date;
- *(b)* if a period of time is fixed by or determinable from the contract, at any time within that period unless circumstances indicate that the buyer is to choose a date; or
- *(c)* in any other case, within a reasonable time after the conclusion of the contract.

Article 34
If the seller is bound to hand over documents relating to the goods, he must hand them over at the time and place and in the form required by the contract. If the seller has handed over documents before that time, he may, up to that time, cure any lack of conformity in the documents, if the exercise of this right does not cause the buyer unreasonable inconvenience or unreasonable expense. However, the buyer retains any right to claim damages as provided for in this Convention.

Section II. *Conformity of the goods and third party claims*

Article 35
(1) The seller must deliver goods which are of the quantity, quality and description required by the contract and which are contained or packaged in the manner required by the contract.

(2) Except where the parties have agreed otherwise, the goods do not conform with the contract unless they:
- *(a)* are fit for the purposes for which goods of the same description would ordinarily be used;
- *(b)* are fit for any particular purpose expressly or impliedly made known to the seller at the time of the conclusion of the contract, except where the circumstances show that the buyer did not rely, or that it was unreasonable for him to rely, on the seller's skill and judgement;
- *(c)* possess the qualities of goods which the seller has held out to the buyer as a sample or model;
- *(d)* are contained or packaged in the manner usual for such goods or, where there is no such manner, in a manner adequate to preserve and protect the goods.

(3) The seller is not liable under subparagraphs *(a)* to *(d)* of the preceding paragraph for any lack of conformity of the goods if at the time of the conclusion of the contract the buyer knew or could not have been unaware of such lack of conformity.

Article 36
(1) The seller is liable in accordance with the contract and this Convention for any lack of conformity which exists at the time when the risk passes to the buyer, even though the lack of conformity becomes apparent only after that time.

(2) The seller is also liable for any lack of conformity which occurs after the time indicated in the preceding paragraph and which is due to a breach of any of his obligations, including a breach of any guarantee that for a period of time the goods

will remain fit for their ordinary purpose or for some particular purpose or will retain specified qualities or characteristics.

Article 37

If the seller has delivered goods before the date for delivery, he may, up to that date, deliver any missing part or make up any deficiency in the quantity of the goods delivered, or deliver goods in replacement of any non-conforming goods delivered or remedy any lack of conformity in the goods delivered, provided that the exercise of this right does not cause the buyer unreasonable inconvenience or unreasonable expense. However, the buyer retains any right to claim damages as provided for in this Convention.

Article 38

(1) The buyer must examine the goods, or cause them to be examined, within as short a period as is practicable in the circumstances.

(2) If the contract involves carriage of the goods, examination may be deferred until after the goods have arrived at their destination.

(3) If the goods are redirected in transit or redispatched by the buyer without a reasonable opportunity for examination by him and at the time of the conclusion of the contract the seller knew or ought to have known of the possibility of such redirection or redispatch, examination may be deferred until after the goods have arrived at the new destination.

Article 39

(1) The buyer loses the right to rely on a lack of conformity of the goods if he does not give notice to the seller specifying the nature of the lack of conformity within a reasonable time after he has discovered it or ought to have discovered it.

(2) In any event, the buyer loses the right to rely on a lack of conformity of the goods if he does not give the seller notice thereof at the latest within a period of two years from the date on which the goods were actually handed over to the buyer, unless this time-limit is inconsistent with a contractual period of guarantee.

Article 40

The seller is not entitled to rely on the provisions of articles 38 and 39 if the lack of conformity relates to facts of which he knew or could not have been unaware and which he did not disclose to the buyer.

Article 41

The seller must deliver goods which are free from any right or claim of a third party, unless the buyer agreed to take the goods subject to that right or claim. However, if such right or claim is based on industrial property or other intellectual property, the seller's obligation is governed by article 42.

Article 42

(1) The seller must deliver goods which are free from any right or claim of a third party based on industrial property or other intellectual property, of which at the time of the conclusion of the contract the seller knew or could not have been unaware, provided that the right or claim is based on industrial property or other intellectual property:

318

(a) under the law of the State where the goods will be resold or otherwise used, if it was contemplated by the parties at the time of the conclusion of the contract that the goods would be resold or otherwise used in that State; or

(b) in any other case, under the law of the State where the buyer has his place of business.

(2) The obligation of the seller under the preceding paragraph does not extend to cases where:

(a) at the time of the conclusion of the contract the buyer knew or could not have been unaware of the right or claim; or

(b) the right or claim results from the seller's compliance with technical drawings, designs, formulae or other such specifications furnished by the buyer.

Article 43

(1) The buyer loses the right to rely on the provisions of article 41 or article 42 if he does not give notice to the seller specifying the nature of the right or claim of the third party within a reasonable time after he has become aware or ought to have become aware of the right or claim.

(2) The seller is not entitled to rely on the provisions of the preceding paragraph if he knew of the right or claim of the third party and the nature of it.

Article 44

Notwithstanding the provisions of paragraph (1) of article 39 and paragraph (1) of article 43, the buyer may reduce the price in accordance with article 50 or claim damages, except for loss of profit, if he has a reasonable excuse for his failure to give the required notice.

Section III. *Remedies for breach of contract by the seller*

Article 45

(1) If the seller fails to perform any of his obligations under the contract or this Convention, the buyer may:

(a) exercise the rights provided in articles 46 to 52;

(b) claim damages as provided in articles 74 to 77.

(2) The buyer is not deprived of any right he may have to claim damages by exercising his right to other remedies.

(3) No period of grace may be granted to the seller by a court or arbitral tribunal when the buyer resorts to a remedy for breach of contract.

Article 46

(1) The buyer may require performance by the seller of his obligations unless the buyer has resorted to a remedy which is inconsistent with this requirement.

(2) If the goods do not conform with the contract, the buyer may require delivery of substitute goods only if the lack of conformity constitutes a fundamental breach of contract and a request for substitute goods is made either in conjunction with notice given under article 39 or within a reasonable time thereafter.

(3) If the goods do not conform with the contract, the buyer may require the seller to remedy the lack of conformity by repair, unless this is unreasonable having regard to all the circumstances. A request for repair must be made either in conjunction with notice given under article 39 or within a reasonable time thereafter.

Article 47

(1) The buyer may fix an additional period of time of reasonable length for performance by the seller of his obligations.

(2) Unless the buyer has received notice from the seller that he will not perform within the period so fixed, the buyer may not, during that period, resort to any remedy for breach of contract. However, the buyer is not deprived thereby of any right he may have to claim damages for delay in performance.

Article 48

(1) Subject to article 49, the seller may, even after the date for delivery, remedy at his own expense any failure to perform his obligations, if he can do so without unreasonable delay and without causing the buyer unreasonable inconvenience or uncertainty of reimbursement by the seller of expenses advanced by the buyer. However, the buyer retains any right to claim damages as provided for in this Convention.

(2) If the seller requests the buyer to make known whether he will accept performance and the buyer does not comply with the request within a reasonable time, the seller may perform within the time indicated in his request. The buyer may not, during that period of time, resort to any remedy which is inconsistent with performance by the seller.

(3) A notice by the seller that he will perform within a specified period of time is assumed to include a request, under the preceding paragraph, that the buyer make known his decision.

(4) A request or notice by the seller under paragraph (2) or (3) of this article is not effective unless received by the buyer.

Article 49

(1) The buyer may declare the contract avoided:
(a) if the failure by the seller to perform any of his obligations under the contract or this Convention amounts to a fundamental breach of contract; or
(b) in case of non-delivery, if the seller does not deliver the goods within the additional period of time fixed by the buyer in accordance with paragraph (1) of article 47 or declares that he will not deliver within the period so fixed.

(2) However, in cases where the seller has delivered the goods, the buyer loses the right to declare the contract avoided unless he does so:
(a) in respect of late delivery, within a reasonable time after he has become aware that delivery has been made;
(b) in respect of any breach other than late delivery, within a reasonable time:
  (i) after he knew or ought to have known of the breach;
  (ii) after the expiration of any additional period of time fixed by the buyer in accordance with paragraph (1) of article 47, or after the seller has declared that he will not perform his obligations within such an additional period; or
  (iii) after the expiration of any additional period of time indicated by the seller in accordance with paragraph (2) of article 48, or after the buyer has declared that he will not accept performances.

Article 50

If the goods do not conform with the contract and whether or not the price has already been paid, the buyer may reduce the price in the same proportion as the value that the goods actually delivered had at the time of the delivery bears to the value that conforming goods would have had at that time. However, if the seller remedies any failure to perform his obligations in accordance with article 37 or article 48 or if the buyer refuses to accept performance by the seller in accordance with those articles, the buyer may not reduce the price.

Article 51

(1) If the seller delivers only a part of the goods or if only a part of the goods delivered is in conformity with the contract, articles 46 to 50 apply in respect of the part which is missing or which does not conform.

(2) The buyer may declare the contract avoided in its entirety only if the failure to make delivery completely or in conformity with the contract amounts to a fundamental breach of the contract.

Article 52

(1) If the seller delivers the goods before the date fixed, the buyer may take delivery or refuse to take delivery.

(2) If the seller delivers a quantity of goods greater than that provided for in the contract, the buyer may take delivery or refuse to take delivery of the excess quantity. If the buyer takes delivery of all or part of the excess quantity, he must pay for it at the contract rate.

CHAPTER III. OBLIGATIONS OF THE BUYER

Article 53

The buyer must pay the price for the goods and take delivery of them as required by the contract and this Convention.

Section I. *Payment of the price*

Article 54

The buyer's obligation to pay the price includes taking such steps and complying with such formalities as may be required under the contract or any laws and regulations to enable payment to be made.

Article 55

Where a contract has been validly concluded but does not expressly or implicitly fix or make provision for determining the price, the parties are considered, in the absence of any indication to the contrary, to have impliedly made reference to the price generally charged at the time of the conclusion of the contract for such goods sold under comparable circumstances in the trade concerned.

Article 56

If the price is fixed according to the weight of the goods, in case of doubt it is to be determined by the net weight.

Article 57

(1) If the buyer is not bound to pay the price at any other particular place, he must pay it to the seller:

    (a) at the seller's place of business; or

    (b) if the payment is to be made against the handing over of the goods or of documents, at the place where the handing over takes place.

(2) The seller must bear any increase in the expenses incidental to payment which is caused by a change in his place of business subsequent to the conclusion of the contract.

Article 58

(1) If the buyer is not bound to pay the price at any other specific time he must pay it when the seller places either the goods or documents controlling their disposition at the buyer's disposal in accordance with the contract and this Convention. The seller may make such payment a condition for handing over the goods or documents.

(2) If the contract involves carriage of the goods, the seller may dispatch the goods on terms whereby the goods, or documents controlling their disposition, will not be handed over to the buyer except against payment of the price.

(3) The buyer is not bound to pay the price until he has had an opportunity to examine the goods, unless the procedures for delivery or payment agreed upon by the parties are inconsistent with his having such an opportunity.

Article 59

The buyer must pay the price on the date fixed by or determinable from the contract and this Convention without the need for any request or compliance with any formality on the part of the seller.

Section II. *Taking delivery*

Article 60

The buyer's obligation to take delivery consists:

 (a) in doing all the acts which could reasonably be expected of him in order to enable the seller to make delivery; and

 (b) in taking over the goods.

Section III. *Remedies for breach of contract by the buyer*

Article 61

(1) If the buyer fails to perform any of his obligations under the contract or this Convention, the seller may:

 (a) exercise the rights provided in articles 62 to 65;

 (b) claim damages as provided in articles 74 to 77.

(2) The seller is not deprived of any right he may have to claim damages by exercising his right to other remedies.

(3) No period of grace may be granted to the buyer by a court or arbitral tribunal when the seller resorts to a remedy for breach of contract.

Article 62

The seller may require the buyer to pay the price, take delivery or perform his other obligations, unless the seller has resorted to a remedy which is inconsistent with this requirement.

Article 63

(1) The seller may fix an additional period of time of reasonable length for performance by the buyer of his obligations.

(2) Unless the seller has received notice from the buyer that he will not perform within the period so fixed, the seller may not, during that period. resort to any remedy for breach of contract. However, the seller is not deprived thereby of any right he may have to claim damages for delay in performance.

Article 64

(1) The seller may declare the contract avoided:

(a) if the failure by the buyer to perform any of his obligations under the contract or this Convention amounts to a fundamental breach of contract; or

(b) if the buyer does not, within the additional period of time fixed by the seller in accordance with paragraph (1) of article 63, perform his obligation to pay the price or take delivery of the goods, or if he declares that he will not do so within the period so fixed.

(2) However, in cases where the buyer has paid the price, the seller loses the right to declare the contract avoided unless he does so:

(a) in respect of late performance by the buyer, before the seller has become aware that performance has been rendered; or

(b) in respect of any breach other than late performance by the buyer, within a reasonable time:

(i) after the seller knew or ought to have known of the breach; or

(ii) after the expiration of any additional period of time fixed by the seller in accordance with paragraph (1) of article 63, or after the buyer has declared that he will not perform his obligations within such an additional period.

Article 65

(1) If under the contract the buyer is to specify the form, measurement or other features of the goods and he fails to make such specification either on the date agreed upon or within a reasonable time after receipt of a request from the seller, the seller may, without prejudice to any other rights he may have, make the specification himself in accordance with the requirements of the buyer that may be known to him.

(2) If the seller makes the specification himself, he must inform the buyer of the details thereof and must fix a reasonable time within which the buyer may make a different specification. If, after receipt of such a communication, the buyer fails to do so within the time so fixed, the specification made by the seller is binding.

CHAPTER IV. PASSING OF RISK

Article 66

Loss of or damage to the goods after the risk has passed to the buyer does not discharge him from his obligation to pay the price, unless the loss or damage is due to an act or omission of the seller.

Article 67

(1) If the contract of sale involves carriage of the goods and the seller is not bound to hand them over at a particular place, the risk passes to the buyer when the goods are handed over to the first carrier for transmission to the buyer in accordance with the contract of sale. If the seller is bound to hand the goods over to a carrier at a particular place, the risk does not pass to the buyer until the goods are handed over to the carrier at that place. The fact that the seller is authorized to retain documents controlling the disposition of the goods does not affect the passage of the risk.

(2) Nevertheless, the risk does not pass to the buyer until the goods are clearly identified to the contract, whether by markings on the goods, by shipping documents, by notice given to the buyer or otherwise.

Article 68
The risk in respect of goods sold in transit passes to the buyer from the time of the conclusion of the contract. However, if the circumstances so indicate, the risk is assumed by the buyer from the time the goods were handed over to the carrier who issued the documents embodying the contract of carriage. Nevertheless, if at the time of the conclusion of the contract of sale the seller knew or ought to have known that the goods had been lost or damaged and did not disclose this to the buyer, the loss or damage is at the risk of the seller.

Article 69
(1) In cases not within articles 67 and 68, the risk passes to the buyer when he takes over the goods or, if he does not do so in due time, from the time when the goods are placed at his disposal and he commits a breach of contract by failing to take delivery.

(2) However, if the buyer is bound to take over the goods at a place other than a place of business of the seller, the risk passes when delivery is due and the buyer is aware of the fact that the goods are placed at his disposal at that place.

(3) If the contract relates to goods not then identified, the goods are considered not to be placed at the disposal of the buyer until they are clearly identified to the contract.

Article 70
If the seller has committed a fundamental breach of contract, articles 67, 68 and 69 do not impair the remedies available to the buyer on account of the breach.

CHAPTER V. PROVISIONS COMMON TO THE OBLIGATIONS OF THE SELLER AND OF THE BUYER

Section I. *Anticipatory breach and instalment contracts*

Article 71
(1) A party may suspend the performance of his obligations if, after the conclusion of the contract, it becomes apparent that the other party will not perform a substantial part of his obligations as a result of:

(a) a serious deficiency in his ability of perform or in his creditworthiness; or

(b) his conduct in preparing to perform or in performing the contract.

(2) If the seller has already dispatched the goods before the grounds described in the preceding paragraph become evident, he may prevent the handing over of the goods to the buyer even though the buyer holds a document which entitles him to obtain them. The present paragraph relates only to the rights in the goods as between the buyer and the seller.

(3) A party suspending performance, whether before or after dispatch of the goods, must immediately give notice of the suspension to the other party and must continue with performance if the other party provides adequate assurance of his performance.

Article 72

(1) If prior to the date for performance of the contract it is clear that one of the parties will commit a fundamental breach of contract, the other party may declare the contract avoided.

(2) If time allows, the party intending to declare the contract avoided must give reasonable notice to the other party in order to permit him to provide adequate assurance of his performance.

(3) The requirements of the preceding paragraph do not apply if the other party has declared that he will not perform his obligations.

Article 73

(1) In the case of a contract for delivery of goods by instalments, if the failure of one party to perform any of his obligations in respect of any instalment constitutes a fundamental breach of contract with respect to that instalment, the other party may declare the contract avoided with respect to that instalment.

(2) If one party's failure to perform any of his obligations in respect of any instalment gives the other party good grounds to conclude that a fundamental breach of contract will occur with respect to future instalments, he may declare the contract avoided for the future, provided that he does so within a reasonable time.

(3) A buyer who declares the contract avoided in respect of any delivery may, at the same time, declare it avoided in respect of deliveries already made or of future deliveries if, by reason of their interdependence, those deliveries could not be used for the purpose contemplated by the parties at the time of the conclusion of the contract.

Section II. *Damages*

Article 74

Damages for breach of contract by one party consist of a sum equal to the loss, including loss of profit, suffered by the other party as a consequence of the breach. Such damages may not exceed the loss which the party in breach foresaw or ought to have foreseen at the time of the conclusion of the contract, in the light of the facts and matters of which he then knew or ought to have known, as a possible consequence of the breach of contract.

Article 75

If the contract is avoided and if, in a reasonable manner and within a reasonable time after avoidance, the buyer has bought goods in replacement or the seller has resold the goods, the party claiming damages may recover the difference between the contract price and the price in the substitute transaction as well as any further damages recoverable under article 74.

Article 76

(1) If the contract is avoided and there is a current price for the goods, the party claiming damages may, if he has not made a purchase or resale under article 75, recover the difference between the price fixed by the contract and the current price at the time of avoidance as well as any further damages recoverable under article 74. If, however, the party claiming damages has avoided the contract after taking over the goods, the current price at the time of such taking over shall be applied instead of the current price at the time of avoidance.

(2) For the purposes of the preceding paragraph, the current price is the price prevailing at the place where delivery of the goods should have been made or, if there is no current price at that place, the price at such other place as serves as a reasonable substitute, making due allowance for differences in the cost of transporting the goods.

Article 77

A party who relies on a breach of contract must take such measures as are reasonable in the circumstances to mitigate the loss, including loss of profit, resulting from the breach. If he fails to take such measures, the party in breach may claim a reduction in the damages in the amount by which the loss should have been mitigated.

Section III. *Interest*

Article 78

If a party fails to pay the price or any other sum that is in arrears, the other party is entitled to interest on it, without prejudice to any claim for damages recoverable under article 74.

Section IV. *Exemption*

Article 79

(1) A party is not liable for a failure to perform any of his obligations if he proves that the failure was due to an impediment beyond his control and that he could not reasonably be expected to have taken the impediment into account at the time of the conclusion of the contract or to have avoided or overcome it or its consequences.

(2) If the party's failure is due to the failure by a third person whom he has engaged to perform the whole or a part of the contract, that party is exempt from liability only if:

(a) he is exempt under the preceding paragraph; and

(b) the person whom he has so engaged would be so exempt if the provisions of that paragraph were applied to him.

(3) The exemption provided by this article has effect for the period during which the impediment exists.

(4) The party who fails to perform must give notice to the other party of the impediment and its effect on his ability to perform. If the notice is not received by the other party within a reasonable time after the party who fails to perform knew or ought to have known of the impediment, he is liable for damages resulting from such non-receipt.

(5) Nothing in this article prevents either party from exercising any right other than to claim damages under this Convention.

Article 80

A party may not rely on a failure of the other party to perform, to the extent that such failure was caused by the first party's act or omission.

Section V. *Effects of avoidance*

Article 81

(1) Avoidance of the contract releases both parties from their obligations under it, subject to any damages which may be due. Avoidance does not affect any provision of the contract for the settlement of disputes or any other provision of the contract governing the rights and obligations of the parties consequent upon the avoidance of the contract.

(2) A party who has performed the contract either wholly or in part may claim restitution from the other party of whatever the first party has supplied or paid under the contract. If both parties are bound to make restitution, they must do so concurrently.

Article 82

(1) The buyer loses the right to declare the contract avoided or to require the seller to deliver substitute goods if it is impossible for him to make restitution of the goods substantially in the condition in which be received them.

(2) The preceding paragraph does not apply:

(a) if the impossibility of making restitution of the goods or of making restitution of the goods substantially in the condition in which the buyer received them is not due to his act or omission;

(b) if the goods or part of the goods have perished or deteriorated as a result of the examination provided for in article 38; or

(c) if the goods or part of the goods have been sold in the normal course of business or have been consumed or transformed by the buyer in the course of normal use before he discovered or ought to have discovered the lack of conformity.

Article 83

A buyer who has lost the right to declare the contract avoided or to require the seller to deliver substitute goods in accordance with article 82 retains all other remedies under the contract and this Convention.

Article 84

(1) If the seller is bound to refund the price, he must also pay interest on it, from the date on which the price was paid.

(2) The buyer must account to the seller for all benefits which he has derived from the goods or part of them:

(a) if he must make restitution of the goods or part of them; or

(b) if it is impossible for him to make restitution of all or part of the goods or to make restitution of all or part of the goods substantially in the condition in which he received them, but he has nevertheless declared the contract avoided or required the seller to deliver substitute goods.

Section VI. *Preservation of the goods*

Article 85

If the buyer is in delay in taking delivery of the goods or, where payment of the price and delivery of the goods are to be made concurrently, if he fails to pay the price, and the seller is either in possession of the goods or otherwise able to control their disposition, the seller must take such steps as are reasonable in the circumstances to preserve them. He is entitled to retain them until he has been reimbursed his reasonable expenses by the buyer.

Article 86

(1) If the buyer has received the goods and intends to exercise any right under the contract or this Convention to reject them, he must take such steps to preserve them as are reasonable in the circumstances. He is entitled to retain them until he has been reimbursed his reasonable expenses by the seller.

(2) If goods dispatched to the buyer have been placed at his disposal at their destination and he exercises the right to reject them, he must take possession of them on behalf of the seller, provided that this can be done without payment of the price and without unreasonable inconvenience or unreasonable expense. This provision does not apply if the seller or a person authorized to take charge of the goods on his behalf is present at the destination. If the buyer takes possession of the goods under this paragraph, his rights and obligations are governed by the preceding paragraph.

Article 87

A party who is bound to take steps to preserve the goods may deposit them in a warehouse of a third person at the expense of the other party provided that the expense incurred is not unreasonable.

Article 88

(1) A party who is bound to preserve the goods in accordance with article 85 or 86 may sell them by any appropriate means if there has been an unreasonable delay by the other party in taking possession of the goods or in taking them back or in paying the price or the cost of preservation, provided that reasonable notice of the intention to sell has been given to the other party.

(2) If the goods are subject to rapid deterioration or their preservation would involve unreasonable expense, a party who is bound to preserve the goods in accordance with article 85 or 86 must take reasonable measures to sell them. To the extent possible he must give notice to the other party of his intention to sell.

(3) A party selling the goods has the right to retain out of the proceeds of sale an amount equal to the reasonable expenses of preserving the goods and of selling them. He must account to the other party for the balance.

Part IV. Final provisions

Article 89

The Secretary-General of the United Nations is hereby designated as the depositary for this Convention.

Article 90

This Convention does not prevail over any international agreement which has already been or may be entered into and which contains provisions concerning the matters governed by this Convention, provided that the parties have their places of business in States parties to such agreement.

Article 91

(1) This Convention is open for signature at the concluding meeting of the United Nations Conference on Contracts for the International Sale of Goods and will remain

open for signature by all States at the Headquarters of the United Nations, New York until 30 September 1981.

(2) This Convention is subject to ratification, acceptance or approval by the signatory States.

(3) This Convention is open for accession by all States which are not signatory States as from the date it is open for signature.

(4) Instruments of ratification, acceptance, approval and accession are to be deposited with the Secretary-General of the United Nations.

Article 92

(1) A Contracting State may declare at the time of signature, ratification, acceptance, approval or accession that it will not be bound by Part II of this Convention or that it will not be bound by Part III of this Convention.

(2) A Contracting State which makes a declaration in accordance with the preceding paragraph in respect of Part II or Part III of this Convention is not to be considered a Contracting State within paragraph (1) of article 1 of this Convention in respect of matters governed by the Part to which the declaration applies.

Article 93

(1) If a Contracting State has two or more territorial units in which, according to its constitution, different systems of law are applicable in relation to the matters dealt with in this Convention, it may, at the time of signature, ratification, acceptance, approval or accession, declare that this Convention is to extend to all its territorial units or only to one or more of them, and may amend its declaration by submitting another declaration at any time.

(2) These declarations are to be notified to the depositary and are to state expressly the territorial units to which the Convention extends.

(3) If, by virtue of a declaration under this article, this Convention extends to one or more but not all of the territorial units of a Contracting State, and if the place of business of a party is located in that State, this place of business, for the purposes of this Convention, is considered not to be in a Contracting State, unless it is in a territorial unit to which the Convention extends.

(4) If a Contracting State makes no declaration under paragraph (1) of this article, the Convention is to extend to all territorial units of that State.

Article 94

(1) Two or more Contracting States which have the same or closely related legal rules on matters governed by this Convention may at any time declare that the Convention is not to apply to contracts of sale or to their formation where the parties have their places of business in those States. Such declarations may be made jointly or by reciprocal unilateral declarations.

(2) A Contracting State which has the same or closely related legal rules on matters governed by this Convention as one or more non-Contracting States may at any time declare that the Convention is not to apply to contracts of sale or to their formation where the parties have their places of business in those States.

(3) If a State which is the object of a declaration under the preceding paragraph subsequently becomes a Contracting State, the declaration made will, as from the date on which the Convention enters into force in respect of the new Contracting State, have the effect of a declaration made under paragraph (1), provided that the new Contracting State joins in such declaration or makes a reciprocal unilateral declaration.

Article 95
Any State may declare at the time of the deposit of its instrument of ratification, acceptance, approval or accession that it will not be bound by subparagraph (1) *(b)* of article 1 of this Convention.

Article 96
A Contracting State whose legislation requires contracts of sale to be concluded in or evidenced by writing may at any time make a declaration in accordance with article 12 that any provision of article 11, article 29, or Part II of this Convention, that allows a contract of sale or its modification or termination by agreement or any offer, acceptance, or other indication of intention to be made in any form other than in writing, does not apply where any party has his place of business in that State.

Article 97
(1) Declarations made under this Convention at the time of signature are subject to confirmation upon ratification, acceptance or approval.

(2) Declarations and confirmations of declarations are to be in writing and be formally notified to the depositary.

(3) A declaration takes effect simultaneously with the entry into force of this Convention in respect of the State concerned. However, a declaration of which the depositary receives formal notification after such entry into force takes effect on the first day of the month following the expiration of six months after the date of its receipt by the depositary. Reciprocal unilateral declarations under article 94 take effect on the first day of the month following the expiration of six months after the receipt of the latest declaration by the depositary.

(4) Any State which makes a declaration under this Convention may withdraw it at any time by a formal notification in writing addressed to the depositary. Such withdrawal is to take effect on the first day of the month following the expiration of six months after the date of the receipt of the notification by the depositary.

(5) A withdrawal of a declaration made under article 94 renders inoperative, as from the date on which the withdrawal takes effect, any reciprocal declaration made by another State under that article.

Article 98
No reservations are permitted except those expressly authorized in this Convention.

Article 99
(1) This Convention enters into force, subject to the provisions of paragraph (6) of this article, on the first day of the month following the expiration of twelve months after the date of deposit of the tenth instrument of ratification. acceptance, approval or accession,· including an instrument which contains a declaration made under article 92.

(2) When a State ratifies, accepts, approves or accedes to this Convention after the deposit of the tenth instrument of ratification, acceptance, approval or accession, this Convention, with the exception of the Part excluded, enters into force in respect of that State, subject to the provisions of paragraph (6) of this article, on the first day of the month following the expiration of twelve months after the date of the deposit of its instrument of ratification, acceptance, approval or accession.

(3) A State which ratifies, accepts, approves or accedes to this Convention and is a party to either or both the Convention relating to a Uniform Law on the Formation of Contracts for the International Sale of Goods done at The Hague on 1 July 1964

(1964 Hague Formation Convention) and the Convention relating to a Uniform Law on the International Sale of Goods done at The Hague on 1 July 1964 (1964 Hague Sales Convention) shall at the same time denounce, as the case may be, either or both the 1964 Hague Sales Convention and the 1964 Hague Formation Convention by notifying the Government of the Netherlands to that effect.

(4) A State party to the 1964 Hague Sales Convention which ratifies, accepts, approves or accedes to the present Convention and declares or has declared under article 92 that it will not be bound by Part II of this Convention shall at the time of ratification, acceptance, approval or accession denounce the 1964 Hague Sales Convention by notifying the Government of the Netherlands to that effect.

(5) A State party to the 1964 Hague Formation Convention which ratifies, accepts, approves or accedes to the present Convention and declares or has declared under article 92 that it will not be bound by Part III of this Convention shall at the time of ratification, acceptance, approval or accession denounce the 1964 Hague Formation Convention by notifying the Government of the Netherlands to that effect.

(6) For the purpose of this article, ratifications, acceptances, approvals and accessions in respect of this Convention by States parties to the 1964 Hague Formation Convention or to the 1964 Hague Sales Convention shall not be effective until such denunciations as may be required on the part of those States in respect of the latter two Conventions have themselves become effective. The depositary of this Convention shall consult with the Government of the Netherlands, as the depositary of the 1964 Conventions, so as to ensure necessary co-ordination in this respect.

Article 100

(1) This Convention applies to the formation of a contract only when the proposal for concluding the contract is made on or after the date when the Convention enters into force in respect of the Contracting States referred to in subparagraph (1) *(a)* or the Contracting State referred to in subparagraph (1) *(b)* of article 1.

(2) This Convention applies only to contracts concluded on or after the date when the Convention enters into force in respect of the Contracting States referred to in subparagraph (1) *(a)* or the Contracting State referred to in subparagraph (1) *(b)* of article 1.

Article 101

(1) A Contracting State may denounce this Convention, or Part II or Part III of the Convention, by a formal notification in writing addressed to the depositary.

(2) The denunciation takes effect on the first day of the month following the expiration of twelve months after the notification is received by the depositary. Where a longer period for the denunciation to take effect is specified in the notification, the denunciation takes effect upon the expiration of such longer period after the notification is received by the depositary.

DONE at Vienna, this day of eleventh day of April, one thousand nine hundred and eighty, in a single original, of which the Arabic, Chinese, English, French, Russian and Spanish texts are equally authentic.

IN WITNESS WHEREOF the undersigned plenipotentiaries, being duly authorized by their respective Governments, have signed this Convention.

Index